THE PUB QUIZ BOOK

THE PUB QUIZ BOOK

PAUL DREW

Published by Arcturus Publishing Limited
1–7 Shand Street, London SE1 2ES

for Bookmart Limited
Desford Road, Enderby, Leicester LE19 4AD
Registered Number 2372865

This edition published 2002

Printed in Denmark by Norhaven Paperbacks, Viborg

ISBN 1841931381

Written and compiled by Paul Drew

Text: © Central Press Features Limited
Concept and design: © Arcturus Publishing Limited

Cover design by Steve Flight

?

GENERAL KNOWLEDGE

ENTERTAINMENT

SPORT

POP MUSIC

ART & LITERATURE

GEOGRAPHY

HISTORY

WORDS

SCIENCE

PEOPLE

? **GENERAL KNOWLEDGE** ?

1. Who succeeded Richard Nixon in 1974 as U.S. president?

2. Which river was known by the Romans as Rhenus?

3. Which international organisation goes by the acronym COMECON?

4. In the Bible, who was the brother of Martha and Mary?

5. Who was Leader of the House of Commons from 1998-2001?

6. In which play by Shakespeare does the character Sir Andrew Aguecheek appear?

7. Who was president of the European Union Commission from 1981-85?

8. In which year did Monaco join the United Nations?

9. Which American artist painted the 1914 oil Portrait of a German Officer?

10. Which letter in Morse code is indicated by two dots?

11. Who is the Hindu god of desire and lust?

12. Which country's national anthem is entitled Pleng Chart?

13. What is the correct form of spoken address to a baron?

14. Which explorer wrote the 2001 novel The Secret Hunters?

15. What is CBS an abbreviation for?

ENTERTAINMENT

1. Who starred as Miss Jones in the ITV sitcom Miss Jones and Son?

2. Which comedian played Harry Payne in television's Coronation Street in 1978?

3. Who wrote the 1970s television drama The Fishing Party?

4. In which year did Britain's Prince Edward organise the television show The Grand Knockout Tournament?

5. Who directed the film Abba - the Movie?

6. Who plays Satine in the 2001 film Moulin Rouge!?

7. Who was the male lead in the 1971 film The Beguiled?

8. What is Lorraine Bracco's character name in the television series The Sopranos?

9. Who plays gardening expert Georgina Woodhouse in the 2001 film Greenfingers?

10. Who does Geoffrey Rush play in the film Quills?

11. Who directed the 1949 film The Set-Up?

12. Which former pop star was the brains behind The Money Channel, a digital television channel which collapsed in 2001?

13. Who directed the 2000 film The Golden Bowl, which starred Uma Thurman?

14. Who plays Mason Verger in the 2001 film Hannibal?

15. Who directed the 1956 film Invasion of the Body Snatchers?

ANSWERS 1. Paula Wilcox 2. Max Wall 3. Peter Terson 4. 1987 5. Lasse Hallström 6. Nicole Kidman 7. Clint Eastwood 8. Dr. Jennifer Melfi 9. Helen Mirren 10. Marquis de Sade 11. Robert Wise 12. Adam Faith 13. James Ivory 14. Gary Oldman 15. Don Siegel.

SPORT

1. In which car did Gerald Burgess and Sam Croft-Pearson win the 1959 R.A.C. Rally?

2. In which year did French tennis player Max Decugis die?

3. At what Olympic sport have Henry Bailey and Jean-Pierre Amat been champions?

4. In which year was the British Olympic Association founded?

5. At which weight did Leo Randolph win a 1976 Olympic boxing gold?

6. What nationality is rugby union referee Stuart Dickinson?

7. The road known as the Koppenberg is a feature of which cycle race?

8. At what age did cricketer John Blain make his debut for Scotland?

9. How many times did jockey John Osborne win the 2000 Guineas from 1857-88?

10. Who did Wasps play in the quarter-finals of rugby union's Tetley's Bitter Cup in 2000?

11. Who, in 1996, won four TT races on the Isle of Man?

12. What is the nickname of Whitwell-born cricketer C.J. Adams?

13. Which club won the 1973/4 Scottish First Division title?

14. What nationality is rugby league player Yacine Dekkiche?

15. Who won the 1987 Fukuoka men's marathon?

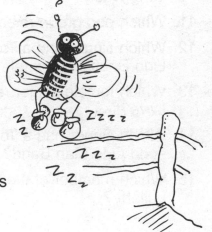

ANSWERS 1. Ford Zephyr 2. 1978 3. Shooting 4. 1905 5. Flyweight. 6. Australian 7. Tour of Flanders 8. 17 years 9. Six 10. Manchester 11. Phillip McCallen 12. Grizzly 13. Celtic 14. French 15. Takeyuki Nakayama.

POP MUSIC

1. Who had a 1979 U.S. No. 1 single with the song Rise?

2. Which rock group released the 2001 single All I Want?

3. In which year did the Animals reach No. 2 in the singles chart with the song We Gotta Get Out Of This Place?

4. Which rock group released the 2001 single Cry For Help?

5. Which pop duo had a 1989 No. 2 single with the song Girl I'm Gonna Miss You?

6. Which legendary songwriter released the 2000 album Live at the Roxy Theatre?

7. Which female singer was once in an all-girl punk band called Spit & Snot?

8. Which group recorded the 1969 album Volunteers?

9. In which year did John Lennon make his final concert appearance?

10. Which female singer had a 1986 Top 20 single with the song Nasty?

11. Which pop group released the 2001 single Karma Hotel?

12. Which singer had a Top 20 single in 1977 with the song Lido Shuffle?

13. Which female singer recorded the 1998 Top 20 single Much Love?

14. Which singer had a Top 10 single in June 1974 with the song One Man Band?

15. Which member of the Spice Girls released the 2001 single Lullaby?

ANSWERS 1. Herb Alpert 2. Reef 3. 1965 4. Shed Seven 5. Milli Vanilli 6. Brian Wilson 7. Björk 8. Jefferson Airplane 9. 1974 10. Janet Jackson 11. Spooks 12. Boz Scaggs 13. Shola Ama 14. Leo Sayer 15. Melanie B.

ART & LITERATURE

1. Which French artist's works include the 1891 painting Poplars on the Epte?

2. Who wrote the 2001 novel Swift as Desire?

3. Which Scottish artist painted a portrait of the philosopher Rousseau in 1766?

4. Who penned the play Another Time?

5. In which century did the painter Pompeo Batoni live?

6. Who wrote the 1951 novel Barbary Shore?

7. Whose paintings include 1913's The Fate of the Animals?

8. Who authored the 1963 novel The Group?

9. In which century did the Scottish painter Robert Herdman live?

10. In which year did the artist Gustave Courbet die?

11. Who wrote the 1920 narrative poem Right Royal?

12. On which Jonathan Tullock novel is the film Purely Belter based?

13. Who authored the 1988 novel Koko?

14. Which movie writer penned the 2000 novel American Rhapsody?

15. Who authored the 1955 novel The Quiet American?

ANSWERS 1. Claude Monet 2. Laura Esquivel 3. Allan Ramsay 4. Ronald Harwood 5. 18th century 6. Norman Mailer 7. Franz Marc 8. Mary McCarthy 9. 19th century 10. 1877 11. John Masefield 12. The Season Ticket 13. Peter Straub 14. Joe Eszterhas 15. Graham Greene.

GENERAL KNOWLEDGE

1. Oxon is an abbreviation for which English county?

2. Which playwright directed and scripted the 1991 film Homicide?

3. In which novel by Thackeray does the character Blanche Amory appear?

4. What is the largest lake in Italy?

5. For which 1993 film was Holly Hunter a Best Actress Oscar nominee?

6. In which year did J. Paul Getty, U.S. millionaire oil executive and art collector, die?

7. What is the name of the Liverpool railway station built in 1867?

8. What type of bird is a nene?

9. Who was a Best Supporting Actress Oscar winner for the film West Side Story?

10. Who were the male and female leads in the 1939 film western Dodge City?

11. What is the standard monetary unit of Iceland?

12. Who was a Best Actor Oscar nominee for the 1954 film A Star is Born?

13. Which Greek hero of the Trojan War killed himself when the armour of Achilles was given to Odysseus?

14. Who was the 1960 Olympic men's 1500m champion?

15. What was the name of the Royal house that ruled in England from 1603-1714?

ANSWERS 1. Oxfordshire 2. David Mamet 3. The History of Pendennis 4. Lake Garda 5. The Piano 6. 1976 7. Lime Street 8. A black-and-grey Hawaiian goose 9. Rita Moreno 10. Errol Flynn and Olivia de Havilland 11. Krona 12. James Mason 13. Ajax 14. Herb Elliott 15. Stuart

ENTERTAINMENT

1. Loft Story was the title of the French version of which Channel Four television programme?

2. What brand of pomade does George Clooney's character favour in the 2000 film O Brother, Where Art Thou??

3. Who directed the 2001 film The Centre of the World?

4. Which actor played the male lead in the 1967 film Bonnie and Clyde?

5. Who took over as presenter of the natural history programme Zoo Time in 1967?

6. Who plays Dr. Brendan McGuire in the drama series Doctors?

7. Who directed the 1987 film Au revoir les enfants?

8. Which actor hosted the Ed Sullivan Show when Elvis Presley first appeared on it in September 1956?

9. What is Al Pacino's character called in the 1983 film Scarface?

10. In which year was the film director Pier Paolo Pasolini murdered?

11. Who played the male lead in the 1988 film Homeboy?

12. Which group appeared on the television show Sunday Night at the London Palladium in January 1967, but didn't take part in the trademark finale on the revolving stage?

13. In which year was the film The Godfather released?

14. Which operetta by Gilbert and Sullivan premiered in London in March 1885?

15. Who played the title role in the 1982 film Hammett?

SPORT

1. How many Olympic gold medals did shooter Otto Olsen win from 1920-4?

2. What nationality is tennis player Marat Safin?

3. With what Olympic sport would you associate Olaf Heukrodt and Larry Cain?

4. Who was captain of the Zimbabwe cricket side during their tour of the West Indies in 2000?

5. Who was the 1925 men's world cross-country champion?

6. Albert Iten was the 1991 men's downhill mountain biking champion. Which country did he represent?

7. What sport do Michelle Rogers and Chloe Cowen compete in?

8. Who was the British Open squash champion in 1938?

9. Who lost the 1979 Scottish F.A. Cup Final on a second replay?

10. What nationality is Formula 1 driver Marc Gené?

11. In which city were the 1985 World Student Games held?

12. In which city were the first figure skating world championships held in 1896?

13. Which boxer was 1985 BBC Sports Personality of the Year?

14. Who were Eastern Division winners of the A.F.C. Conference in American Football in 1970?

15. Sherwood Stewart and Ferdi Taygan won the 1982 French Open men's doubles tennis championship. Which country were they from?

ANSWERS 1. Four 2. Russian 3. Canoe racing 4. Andy Flower 5. Jack Webster. 6. Switzerland 7. Judo 8. James Dear 9. Hibernian 10. Spanish 11. Kobe 12. St. Petersburg 13. Barry McGuigan 14. Baltimore Colts 15. U.S.A.

POP MUSIC

1. Which singer-songwriter recorded the 2001 debut album Small Moments?

2. What is the home town of the U.S. group Calexico?

3. In which year did The Who release the album Tommy?

4. Which group recorded the 2001 album Transmission?

5. Who recorded the 1992 album Magic and Loss?

6. In which year did the group the Pendletones, latterly called the Beach Boys, record their first song, Surfin'?

7. Which band run the record label Emergency Broadcast Systems?

8. Which rock group recorded the 1999 album There is Nothing Left to Lose?

9. Which pop group recorded the 2001 single Don't Stop Movin'?

10. In which year did Lynn Anderson have a U.K. Top 5 single with the song Rose Garden?

11. In which year did The Police release the single Walking on the Moon?

12. In which year was the debut single by The Rolling Stones, Come On, released?

13. Who produced the singles You Really Got Me and All Day and All of the Night by The Kinks?

14. Which group recorded the 1981 album The Visitors?

15. Which group recorded the 2000 album The Menace?

ANSWERS 1. David Kitt 2. Tucson, Arizona 3. 1969 4. Gay Dad 5. Lou Reed 6. 1961 7. Hawkwind 8. Foo Fighters 9. S Club 7 10. 1971 11. 1979 12. 1963 13. Shel Talmy 14. Abba 15. Elastica.

GEOGRAPHY

1. Which country is larger in area - Albania or Belgium?

2. Of which African country is Bangui the capital?

3. Which is the second-largest country in South America?

4. In which city is the Islamic shrine the Kaaba?

5. What is the capital of the Channel Island of Jersey?

6. In which department of France is the village of Azincourt?

7. In which ocean does the country Vanuatu lie?

8. In which African country is the Aberdare National Park?

9. In which African country is the holy city of Kairouan?

10. Which country is larger in area - Panama or Jamaica?

11. In which ocean is the island of Rodrigues, whose capital is Port Mathurin?

12. Foul Bay lies on the coastline of which Caribbean island?

13. In which Asian country is Mount Nebo?

14. In which European country is the ski resort of Courchevel?

15. On which European island is the World Heritage site of Dalt Vila?

GENERAL KNOWLEDGE

1. Which car manufacturer makes the Zafira model?

2. What type of foodstuff is a naga jolokia?

3. How many months are there in the Hindu calendar?

4. In computing, what is an 'orphan page'?

5. In which year did the Chernobyl nuclear power plant close down?

6. Which occurred first in geological time, the Permian period or Cambrian period?

7. Who designed the headquarters for the Hong Kong & Shanghai Bank in Hong Kong?

8. Which seaside town in France has a statue erected to the jazz legend Sidney Bechet?

9. What is Prince Charles's second name of four?

10. In which year did McDonalds first open a restaurant in Greece?

11. In the 1991 census were males or females prevalent on the Isle of Man?

12. How many guns at Edinburgh Castle are fired as a salute to the sovereign on the occasion of their birthday?

13. With which sport would you associate the television commentator Dorian Williams?

14. What is umami?

15. At which sport did Ben Ainslie win gold at the 2000 Olympics?

ANSWERS 1. Vauxhall 2. Chilli pepper 3. Twelve 4. A web page not linked to any other page 5. 2000 6. Cambrian 7. Norman Foster 8. Juan-les-Pins 9. Philip 10. 1991 11. Females 12. 21 13. Equestrianism 14. A supposed fifth basic taste in addition to sweet, sour, bitter and salty 15. Sailing.

ENTERTAINMENT

1. Which two actresses starred as Dorothy and Petula in the 2001 film Beautiful Creatures?

2. What was Frank Sinatra's character's name in the 1960 film Ocean's Eleven?

3. In which year did the National Theatre open in London?

4. Who plays Captain Jonathan Archer in the Star Trek spin-off series Enterprise?

5. What was Walter Matthau's character's name in the 1968 film The Odd Couple?

6. Who starred in the title role of the 2001 Channel 4 television production Shackleton?

7. Which cartoonist produced the television cartoon series 2DTV?

8. Which Oscar-winner plays an American boxing promoter in the 2000 film Shiner?

9. Who composed the 1936 one-act opera Amelia Goes to the Ball?

10. Who wrote the music for the 1923 ballet La Création du Monde?

11. What was the name of the character played by actress Mena Suvari in the 1999 film American Beauty?

12. Which television programme won the Best Soap prize at the 2001 BAFTA TV Awards?

13. Which actor's roles include Milo Hoffman in the 2001 film AntiTrust?

14. Which character was played by Colin Firth in the 2001 film Bridget Jones's Diary?

15. Which opera is often known by the abbreviation 'Cav'?

ANSWERS 1. Susan Lynch and Rachel Weisz 2. Danny Ocean 3. 1976 4. Scott Bakula 5. Oscar Madison 6. Kenneth Branagh 7. Giles Pilbrow 8. Martin Landau 9. Gian Carlo Menotti 10. Darius Milhaud 11. Angela Hayes 12. Emmerdale 13. Ryan Phillippe 14. Mark Darcy 15. Cavalleria rusticana by Mascagni.

SPORT

1. Which football team won the Scottish Premier League in 1999/00?

2. How many dismissals did Australian wicket-keeper Tim Zoehrer make in his career from 1980-94?

3. Which motorcyclist won the Czech 500cc Grand Prix in August 1999?

4. Which woman golfer won the 1990 Nabisco Dinah Shore tournament?

5. With which sport are Brigitte Bécue and Agnes Kovacs associated?

6. Who was the 1992 Olympic women's 5000m speed skating champion?

7. Which sport do you associate with Carlos Sainz and Marcus Gronholm?

8. Who scored Liverpool's winner in the 1978 European Champion Clubs' Cup Final?

9. Who won the 1999 Rally of Finland to take his twenty-third world championship rally?

10. In which year were the World Indoor Athletics Championships first held, in Bercy, France?

11. Who knocked Batley out of the 2000 Silk Cut Challenge Trophy in rugby league?

12. Which jockey rode the Epsom Derby winner from 1921-3?

13. Who beat Yevgeny Kafelnikov in the final of the A.T.P. Legg Mason Classic in August 1999?

14. In which city were the 1952 Winter Olympic Games held?

15. At what weight did Audley Harrison box before becoming a heavyweight?

ANSWERS 1. Rangers 2. 461 3. Tadayuki Okada 4. Betsy King 5. Swimming. 6. Gunda Niemann 7. Rallying 8. Kenny Dalglish 9. Juha Kankkunen 10. 1985 11. Oldham St. Annes 12. Steve Donoghue 13. Andre Agassi 14. Oslo 15. Super-heavyweight.

POP MUSIC

1. Which group had a 1997 No. 1 single with the song Block Rockin' Beats?

2. Which singer was born in Walnut Creek, California in 1959?

3. Which group recorded the 1992 album Stick Around For Joy?

4. Which protégée of Missy Elliott recorded the 2001 album Based on a True Story?

5. Which former member of the Soup Dragons is behind the group The High Fidelity?

6. Which Australian vocalist had a 2000 Top 10 single with the song Absolutely Everybody?

7. Which rock group recorded the 1968 album Tons of Sobs?

8. Which female vocal group had a 1975 Top 20 hit with the song Lady Marmalade?

9. Which member of the Spice Girls released the 2001 album A Girl Like Me?

10. Which rock group released the 2001 single Mr. Writer?

11. In which year did Blur have a Top 5 single with the song Girls and Boys?

12. In which year did the group Gang of Four release the album Entertainment?

13. Which female artist recorded the albums A Maid of Constant Sorrow and Golden Apples of the Sun?

14. Which group recorded the 2001 hit single Last Resort?

15. Which Scottish group recorded the 2000 album The Great Eastern?

ANSWERS 1. The Chemical Brothers 2. Mark Eitzel 3. The Sugarcubes 4. Lil' Mo 5. Sean Dickson 6. Vanessa Amorosi 7. Free 8. LaBelle 9. Emma Bunton 10. Stereophonics 11. 1994 12. 1979 13. Judy Collins 14. Papa Roach 15. The Delgados.

HISTORY

1. In which year was Giuseppe Garibaldi born?

2. Which Kent-born statesman discovered the Babington Plot?

3. Who became mayor of Plymouth in 1581?

4. In which year did Prince Rudolf of Austria die at Mayerling?

5. Which German army officer tried to assassinate Hitler in 1944?

6. In which year was Henry VIII's adviser Thomas Cromwell executed?

7. Who succeeded Antonius Pius as Roman emperor in 161?

8. Who commanded U.S. forces in South Vietnam from 1964-68?

9. In which year did Napoleon I die?

10. What was the sister company of the Dutch East India Company?

11. In which U.S. state was the Battle of Cedar Mountain fought in 1862?

12. In which year was Johann Friedrich Struensee, German-born Danish statesman, executed?

13. In which year was the Vinegar Hill rebellion in Ireland?

14. Who commanded the German 6th Army which advanced into Stalingrad in August 1942?

15. In which year was Eleanor Roosevelt born?

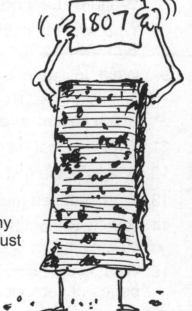

ANSWERS 1. 1807 2. Sir Francis Walsingham 3. Sir Francis Drake 4. 1889 5. Von Stauffenberg 6. 1540 7. Marcus Aurelius 8. General William C. Westmoreland 9. 1821 10. Dutch West India Company 11. Virginia 12. 1772 13. 1798 14. General Von Paulus 15. 1884

GENERAL KNOWLEDGE

1. Who was the Welsh author of the play Night Must Fall?

2. Which German poet authored the novel The Sorrows of Young Werther?

3. Who was a Best Actor Oscar nominee for the film The Prince of Tides?

4. Which river of North Yorkshire flows to the Swale to form the Ouse?

5. What is the longest river in France?

6. What is the name of the tiger in Kipling's The Jungle Book?

7. For which 1947 film were Robert Ryan and Gloria Grahame Best Supporting Actor and Actress nominees?

8. Who wrote the 1951 story collection The Ballad of the Sad Café?

9. What, in Japan, is a kakemono?

10. In which English county is the market town of Pontefract, which houses a racecourse?

11. Who was the 1964 Olympic men's 1500m champion?

12. Who was the first president of the Republic of Indonesia?

13. Who authored the 1929 novel The Near and the Far?

14. Who was the 1993 U.S. Open women's singles tennis champion?

15. What is the name given to the third epoch of the Tertiary period of geological time?

ENTERTAINMENT

1. Who plays Bill Blake in the 1995 film Dead Man?

2. Who plays the father of comedian Chris Rock in the 2000 film Nurse Betty?

3. Who plays Christopher Walken's wife in the 1989 film Communion?

4. Who directed the 2001 film Spy Kids?

5. Who directed the films Scary Movie and Scary Movie 2?

6. Which French revue artist was born Jeanne-Marie Bourgeois?

7. Who did Ray Winstone play in the television series Robin of Sherwood?

8. Who directed the 1985 film Ginger & Fred?

9. The 2001 play Presence by David Harrower is a fiction about which, unnamed, real pop group?

10. Which 2001 film starred Liv Tyler as Jewel Valentine?

11. Who directed the 1999 film The Cider House Rules?

12. Who plays Orson Welles in the 1999 film Cradle Will Rock?

13. Who plays safecracker Gal in the 2000 film Sexy Beast?

14. What is Jack Lemmon's character's name in the 1960 film The Apartment?

15. Who plays musician-turned-boxer Joe Bonaparte in the 1939 film The Golden Boy?

SPORT

1. In which city was the international governing body of fencing, the F.I.E., founded in 1913?

2. Cypheus Bunton is captain of which UK basketball team?

3. Who was the 1988 Olympic women's 400m individual medley swimming champion?

4. Which Spanish golfer won the 1994 U.S. Masters tournament?

5. Who was the manager of Birmingham City F.C. in 1999/00?

6. Which athlete was the 1987 BBC Sports Personality of the Year?

7. Which horse was the leading moneywinner in Britain in 1966?

8. By what score did Argentina beat Scotland at rugby union in August 1999?

9. Who was the women's marathon champion at the 1983 World Athletics Championships?

10. Who partnered Anne Smith to win the 1980 French Open mixed doubles tennis championship?

11. Which New Zealander won the 1960 Argentine Grand Prix in Formula 1?

12. How many gold medals did Spain win at the 1999 World Athletics Championships?

13. Which club have won the rugby league Challenge Cup the most times?

14. Who beat England's men's hockey team in the semi-finals of the 1999 European Cup?

15. Nobuaki Kobayashi was the 1984 world champion at what ball game?

ANSWERS. 1. Paris 2. Derby Storm 3. Janet Evans 4. José-Maria Olazabal 5. Trevor Francis. 6. Fatima Whitbread 7. Charlottetown 8. 31-22 9. Grete Waitz 10. Bill Martin 11. Bruce McLaren 12. Two 13. Wigan 14. Germany 15. Three-Cushion Billiards.

POP MUSIC

1. In which year did Pulp's Common People reach No. 2 in the singles chart?

2. At which Australian university did Robert Forster and Grant McLennan of the group The Go-Betweens study drama?

3. Which group recorded the 1964 single Zoot Suit/I'm the Face?

4. What was the title of New Order's 2001 album release?

5. Which rock group recorded the 1970 album Lizard?

6. Which group had a 1983 Top 10 hit with the single Don't Talk to me about Love?

7. Which chart act recorded the 2001 album Execute?

8. Which pop group recorded the 1975 No. 1 single Can't Give you Anything (But my Love)?

9. Which singer had a Top 20 hit in 1977 with the song What Can I Say?

10. Which boy band released the 2001 single All Rise?

11. In which year did Gary Numan reach No. 1 with the single Cars?

12. In which year did The Rolling Stones release an album entitled Their Satanic Majesties Request?

13. In which year were the group Spiritualized formed?

14. Of which group is Julian Casablanca the lead singer?

15. In which city are the duo Moloko based?

ANSWERS 1. 1995 2. Queensland University in Brisbane 3. The High Numbers 4. Get Ready 5. King Crimson 6. Altered Images 7. Oxide & Neutrino 8. Stylistics 9. Boz Scaggs 10. Blue 11. 1979 12. 1967 13. 1991 14. The Strokes 15. Sheffield.

WORDS

1. What in Australia is a vag?

2. What is the word used to describe the recorded events of one year?

3. On what might you find a vimen?

4. What would be mounted on a pan and tilt head?

5. What in the Caribbean is a duppy?

6. Which musical instrument can be known as a pretzel?

7. To the people of which British colony does the services' slang word scorp apply?

8. If a substance is caseous what is it like?

9. Which British aeroplane was known as a Wimpey?

10. What might you do with a cervelat?

11. What in Australia is known as a jumbuck?

12. What in North American slang is a potsy to a police officer?

13. How many faces does a pebble called a dreikanter usually have?

14. Bags of mystery is a slang term for which food?

15. Of what is ekistics the study?

ANSWERS 1. Vagrant 2. Annal 3. A plant 4. A film camera 5. A spirit or ghost 6. French horn 7. Gibraltarians 8. Cheese 9. Wellington bomber 10. Eat it, it's a smoked sausage 11. Sheep 12. Their badge 13. Three 14. Sausages 15. Human settlements.

GENERAL KNOWLEDGE

1. In which year did Fiji join the United Nations?

2. What does the abbreviation CNN stand for?

3. Which tennis player was awarded the Presidential Medal of Freedom in 1993?

4. Which movie was the 2000 BAFTA Best Film award winner?

5. Who wrote the 1987 novel Close Quarters?

6. Who succeeded Betty Boothroyd as speaker of the House of Commons in 2000?

7. In the Bible, who was the wife of Uriah?

8. Who wrote the 1960s play A Hotel in Amsterdam?

9. What is the colour of the central stripe on the flag of Chad?

10. Which Greece-born painter's works include the 1913 oil Ariadne?

11. What is enteki?

12. Which modern British city was known by the Romans as Magnus Portus?

13. Which 19th-century painter's works include Rent Day in the Wilderness?

14. What is the colour of the beak of an alpine chough?

15. What nationality was the 19th century artist Alexander Munro?

ENTERTAINMENT

1. What is Kevin Kline's profession in the 1990 film I Love You To Death?

2. What is James Stewart's character's name in the film Harvey?

3. What is Elvis Presley's profession in the 1967 film Easy Come, Easy Go?

4. Who directed the 1956 film Tea and Sympathy?

5. Which silent comedy star played a bus driver in the 1944 film San Diego, I Love You?

6. Which city is the setting for Pier Paolo Pasolini's 1961 film Accatone?

7. Which pop star narrated the 1999 animated film Hooves of Fire?

8. Which actor played Mr. Goldberg in the sitcom Are You Being Served??

9. In the 1974 film Earthquake, what relationship is Ava Gardner's character to that of Lorne Greene?

10. Who wrote the score for the 1976 film Taxi Driver?

11. Who was the announcer on the sitcom Soap?

12. The 1988 science-fiction film Nightfall is based on whose classic short story?

13. In which year did Richard Digance become a professional entertainer?

14. Who directed the 1970 Hammer horror film The Vampire Lovers?

15. Who directed the 1972 film The Nightcomers, starring Marlon Brando?

SPORT

1. How many nations were there in the Fédération Internationale de Korfball in 1970?

2. Which country is home to the international governing body of gymnastics, the F.I.G.?

3. In which year did England's football team last win the British Home International Championship?

4. What nationality is weightlifter Li Feng-Ying?

5. Who set a world record of 26:43.53 for the 10,000m on 5th June 1995?

6. Which country did athlete Juliet Cuthbert represent?

7. Which horse won the 1994 Haydock Park Sprint Cup?

8. Which country did athlete Silvio Leonard represent?

9. At what sport was James Dear world champion from 1955-7?

10. In which year did cricketer Rupesh Amin make his county debut for Surrey?

11. With which winter sport is the Worldloppet Cup associated?

12. Who was the winner of the 1999 Australian Grand Prix in Formula 1?

13. In which country was cricketer Mike Procter born?

14. What nationality is runner Kutre Dulecha?

15. Between 15th May and 16th July 1941, in how many consecutive games did baseball player Joe DiMaggio bat safely?

POP MUSIC

1. Who featured on the 1989 single Pump up the Jam by Technotronic?

2. Which studio album by Sting includes the song Russians?

3. Which guitarist recorded the 1978 album Casino?

4. Which song opens the 1974 album Second Helping by Lynyrd Skynyrd?

5. What is rapper Jonathan David better known as?

6. Who played saxophone on Gerry Rafferty's track Baker Street?

7. Which New York group recorded the 1994 album Panic On?

8. Which group had a Top 10 single in 1999 with Drinking in L.A.?

9. Which duo had a 2000 Top 10 hit with A Lttle Bit of Luck?

10. Which band's second album was called Liquid Skin?

11. Which Leeds group recorded the 1994 album Anarchy?

12. Which female singer's albums include Truth From Lies and A Crash Course in Roses?

13. Which member of the group Lush is half-Hungarian and half-Japanese?

14. Tetsu Yamauchi replaced Ronnie Lane in which group in the 1970s?

15. Tabitha Tinsdale and Vinny Cafiso record under what name?

SCIENCE

1. What is the Nobel prize in medicine also known as?

2. Which German-born scientist's published works include Investigations on the Theory of the Brownian   Motion?

3. Physicist Niels Bohr was born and died in which European capital city?

4. Which Nobel prize-winning physicist co-designed the counter-controlled cloud chamber in 1932?

5. Who won the 1999 Nobel prize in chemistry?

6. In which year did Wilhelm Wien begin work on the nature of cathode rays?

7. The first Nobel prize in medicine winner is regarded as the founder of serum therapy. Who was he?

8. In which European country was chemist George A. Olah born?

9. Which Nobel prize-winner wrote the 1938 book Embryonic Development and Induction?

10. Which chemist wrote the 1963 book Boron Hydrides?

11. Of what is toxicology the scientific study?

12. What nationality was the Nobel prize-winning scientist A.H.T. Theorell?

13. Who won the 1949 Nobel prize in chemistry?

14. Which university did Wilhelm Röntgen enter in 1865 to study physics?

15. Of which European country did Nobel prize-winning chemist Ilya Prigogine become a national in 1949?

ANSWERS 1. Nobel prize in physiology 2. Albert Einstein 3. Copenhagen 4. P.M.S. Blackett 5. Ahmed H. Zewail 6. 1897 7. Emil Adolf von Behring 8. Hungary 9. Hans Spemann 10. William N. Lipscomb 11. The nature and effects of poisons 12. Swedish 13. William Francis Giauque 14. University of Utrecht. 15. Belgium.

GENERAL KNOWLEDGE

1. Who wrote the 1820 novel The Abbot?

2. Who wrote the 1880 novel The Duke's Children?

3. On which river is the town of Mold in North Wales?

4. Who was the 1996 Australian Open men's singles tennis champion?

5. Abuja is the capital of which West African republic?

6. Des Moines is the capital of which U.S. state?

7. On which river is the Italian town of Schio, which lies at the foot of the Alps?

8. Who was the 1983 French Open men's singles tennis champion?

9. Which pop singer originally had a No. 1 single with the song When the Going Gets Tough, the Tough Get Going?

10. Who was the 1988 Olympic men's 200m butterfly swimming champion?

11. Who was a Best Actor Oscar winner for the film It Happened One Night?

12. Which play by Shakespeare features the character Ariel?

13. What is the eleventh sign of the zodiac?

14. Who wrote the poem The Jumblies?

15. Which river flows to the North Sea at Sunderland?

ANSWERS 1. Walter Scott 2. Anthony Trollope 3. River Alyn 4. Boris Becker 5. Nigeria 6. Iowa 7. River Leogr 8. Yannick Noah 9. Billy Ocean 10. Michael Gross 11. Clark Gable 12. The Tempest 13. Aquarius 14. Edward Lear 15. Wear.

ENTERTAINMENT

1. Which comedian directed and starred in the 1926 film Battling Butler?

2. Who directed the 1960 film Rocco and His Brothers?

3. Which two actors play criminal partners in the 2001 film Bandits?

4. Which actress plays the title role in the 1999 film Judy Berlin?

5. Who directed the 2000 film Crouching Tiger, Hidden Dragon?

6. Which comedy performer's alter-egos include the chat show host Ali G?

7. What was the name of the central female character in the 1960s children's television drama White Horses?

8. Which 2000 film, written and directed by Sara Sugarman, starred Rachel Griffiths and Jonathan Pryce?

9. What was the registration number of Lady Penelope's pink Rolls-Royce in the television show Thunderbirds?

10. Which actress played Kelly Woods in the 2001 film Get Over It?

11. The magician Drosselmeyer is a character in which ballet?

12. Who directed the 2000 film The House of Mirth?

13. Which British director made the 1953 short film O Dreamland?

14. Who played the male and female leads in the 2000 film Proof of Life?

15. What is Kim Basinger's character's name in the 1997 film L.A. Confidential?

ANSWERS 1. Buster Keaton 2. Luchino Visconti 3. Bruce Willis and Billy Bob Thornton 4. Edie Falco 5. Ang Lee 6. Sacha Baron Cohen 7. Julia 8. Very Annie Mary 9. Fab 1 10. Kirsten Dunst 11. The Nutcracker 12. Terence Davies 13. Lindsay Anderson 14. Russell Crowe and Meg Ryan 15. Lynn Bracken.

SPORT

1. In which year was athlete Koji Ito born?

2. In which month is the Kentucky Derby run in the U.S.A.?

3. In which year was athlete Jeff Laynes born?

4. Who was the 1969 women's individual world archery champion?

5. In which year did L. R. Erskine and Herbert Lawford win the men's doubles tennis title at Wimbledon?

6. Who won the the 1998 Spanish Grand Prix in Formula 1 driving a McLaren?

7. Which country did runner Chidi Imo represent?

8. By what score did rugby union team the British Lions beat Australia at Brisbane in June 1966?

9. What nationality is runner Zahra Ouaziz?

10. Who took over from Joe Walcott in 1906 as undisputed world welterweight boxing champion?

11. In which year did German tennis player Hilde Krahwinkel die?

12. In which year was the Croquet Association founded in England?

13. In which year was athlete Daniel Effiong born?

14. Who was women's overall champion at the 1975 gymnastics World Cup?

15. By what score did Wales beat Scotland in the 2000 Six Nations tournament in rugby union?

ANSWERS 1. 1970 2. May 3. 1970 4. Dorothy Lidstone 5. 1879 6. Mika Hakkinen 7. Nigeria 8. 31-0 9. Moroccan 10. Billy 'Honey' Mellody 11. 1981 12. 1897 13. 1972 14. Lyudmilla Tourischeva 15. 26-18.

POP MUSIC

1. Which group had a 1981 minor hit single with the song We Don't Need This Fascist Groove Thang?

2. Which group did Ian Astbury form following the split of The Cult in 1995?

3. Which group recorded the 2001 studio album Beetroot?

4. Which singer-songwriter recorded the 1969 album Happy Sad?

5. Which female singer fronted the group All About Eve?

6. Which female singer recorded the 2001 single Cowboys & Kisses?

7. Which rock group's 1970s albums included Trilogy and Tarkus?

8. Which rock group recorded the albums Close to the Edge and Relayer?

9. Which boy band released the 2001 album Sooner or Later?

10. Which singer released the 2001 single Heard It All Before?

11. In which year did ABC have a Top 10 single with the song Poison Arrow?

12. Which group recorded the 1966 album A Quick One?

13. Which T.Rex studio album includes the songs Get It On and Jeepster?

14. In which city was guitarist Jimi Hendrix born?

15. Which member of the Wu-Tang Clan recorded the soundtrack for the film Ghost Dog: The Way of the Samurai?

ANSWERS 1. Heaven 17 2. The Holy Barbarians 3. Cast 4. Tim Buckley 5. Julianne Regan 6. Anastacia 7. E.L.P. 8. Yes 9. BBMak 10. Sunshine Anderson 11. 1982 12. The Who 13. Electric Warrior 14. Seattle 15. The RZA.

PEOPLE

1. Who succeeded Oliver Cromwell as Lord Protector in 1658?

2. As what is Katharine Lucy Mary Worsley better known?

3. Actor Arthur White is the brother of which famous television actor?

4. In which year did the artist Jean Baptiste Camille Corot die?

5. Which singer was born Orville Burrell?

6. What nationality is the conductor Susanna Malkki?

7. In which year did the television presenter Jess Yates die?

8. Who penned the play Taking Sides?

9. What is Prince Andrew's second name of four?

10. Which of the five original members of the Beach Boys owns the legal right to the band's name?

11. In which year was the actress Ursula Andress born?

12. What was the name of the wife of King Stephen?

13. Who produced the Tom and Jerry cartoons?

14. In which year did the portrait painter Frans Hals die?

15. Who was Britain's only male high jumper in the 2000 Olympics?

ANSWERS 1. Richard Cromwell 2. The Duchess of Kent 3. David Jason 4. 1875 5. Shaggy 6. Finnish 7. 1993 8. Ronald Harwood 9. Albert 10. Mike Love 11. 1936 12. Matilda 13. Fred Quimby 14. 1666 15. Ben Challenger.a

ENTERTAINMENT

1. Which 1990 film starred Steve Martin as an Italian-American criminal-turned-witness called Vinnie?

2. Who was the father of Sonia Jackson's baby Chloe in EastEnders?

3. Which founder member of the Fugees released his second solo album, The Ecleftic, in 2000?

4. Which Channel 5 newsreader originally fronted the ITV quiz show The People Versus?

5. Which actor played Professor Charles Xavier in the 2000 film version of X-Men?

6. Who played angel Jonathan Smith in the Eighties drama series Highway to Heaven?

7. Which pop legend knocked Spiller from the top of the U.K. charts in 2000 with her single Music?

8. Which 1971 film set on a South American island starred Kirk Douglas and Yul Brynner?

9. Who was the presenter of the BBC1 wildlife series Cousins?

10. Which girl group had a 2002 U.K. number one hit with Freak Like Me?

11. Which group had a 1982 U.K. top five hit with Golden Brown?

12. Which actor played a Marine colonel accused of massacring 83 civilian Yemenis in the 2000 film Rules of Engagement?

13. Which former docusoap star presented the BBC 1 series The Toughest Job in Britain?

14. What was the title of U2's 1991 U.K. number one hit?

15. Which British actress starred in the title role of the 1977 film Julia?

ANSWERS: 1 My Blue Heaven, 2 Martin Fowler, 3 Wyclef Jean, 4 Kirsty Young, 5 Patrick Stewart, 6 Michael Landon, 7 Madonna, 8 The Light at the Edge of the World, 9 Charlotte Uhlenbroek, 10 Sugababes, 11 The Stranglers, 12 Samuel L. Jackson, 13 Jeremy Spake, 14 The Fly, 15 Vanessa Redgrave.

GENERAL KNOWLEDGE

1. In which city is the Eddie Stobart haulage business based?

2. From what did the soprano Helen Armstrong derive the surname for her stage name of Nellie Melba?

3. What is the first year of the Muslim era in the Islamic calendar?

4. In which year did the artist Nicolas Poussin die?

5. What type of foodstuff is a red savina Habanero?

6. Which car manufacturer makes the 307 model?

7. How often is the Maha Kumbh Mela held at Allahabad?

8. Who founded Jersey Zoo in 1959?

9. Which plant is the source of Tequila?

10. What museum does the city of Marikina near Manila in the Philippines famously house?

11. From which port does the ship the Pequod sail in the novel Moby-Dick?

12. On which bridge is the 1928 Tyne Bridge based?

13. Where was Henry IV of England born?

14. In which month of 1986 was the Chernobyl nuclear power plant disaster?

15. Which common vegetable is added to mashed potato to make the dish Champ?

ANSWERS: 1 Carlisle, 2 Her birthplace of Melbourne, Australia, 3 622 A.D., 4 1665, 5 Chilli pepper, 6 Peugeot, 7 12 years, 8 Gerald Durrell, 9 Blue agave, 10 A shoe museum, 11 Nantucket, 12 Sydney Harbour Bridge, 13 Bolingbroke, 14 April, 15 Spring onion.

GENERAL KNOWLEDGE

1. Who was Britain's only male pole vaulter in the 2000 Olympics?

2. On which Caribbean island is the volcano Mount Pelee?

3. Which position is held by the most senior member of the Queen's Household?

4. Which writer is credited with originating the phrase 'better half' meaning spouse?

5. Who was prime minister of South Africa from 1948-54?

6. Of which country was Tomas Masaryk president from 1918-35?

7. Who played bass guitar in the pop group The Beatles?

8. In which 1950's children's puppet series did the character Mrs Scrubbit appear?

9. In which European country is the ski resort of Madonna di Campiglio?

10. What is the name given to the Sunday before Easter in the Christian calendar?

11. In which year did the Nissan Micra first appear in Britain?

12. In which year was the famous 'Lady Chatterley' obscenity trial?

13. How long does a year normally last in the Islamic calendar?

14. Which letter was transmitted in Morse code from Cornwall to Newfoundland in December 1901 to the radio pioneer Marconi?

15. What are sevruga, beluga and ascieta?

ANSWERS: 1 Kevin Hughes, 2 Martinique, 3 The Lord Chamberlain, 4 Sir Philip Sidney, 5 Daniel François Malan, 6 Czechoslovakia, 7 Paul McCartney, 8 The Woodentops, 9 Italy, 10 Palm Sunday, 11 1993, 12 1960, 13 354 days, 14 S, 15 Types of caviar.

GENERAL KNOWLEDGE

1. What organization did Briton Susan Travers uniquely join in the 1940s?

2. The heat of what foodstuff is measured in Scoville units?

3. Which car manufacturer makes the Shogun Pinin?

4. In which U.S city is the infamous Viper Room club?

5. In which year did Britain's Prince Edward quit the Royal Marines?

6. In which county is Fylingdales which famously houses a U.S radar station?

7. In which country is the drink Ovaltine made by the company Novartis?

8. In which European city was the first hotel run by the food chain McDonalds opened?

9. 'The Square' is a magazine for members of which body of people?

10. In which African country was the musical Festival du Desert held in January 2001?

11. On what day of the week did New Year's Day fall in 1805?

12. Which is the longest river in Northern Ireland?

13. Who was Australian prime minister from 1971-2?

14. Who was prima ballerina with the Vic-Wells Ballet from 1933-5?

15. Why do you risk arrest in the USA if you are found with Mary Warner?

ANSWERS: 1 The French Foreign Legion, 2 Chilli pepper, 3 Mitsubishi, 4 Los Angeles, 5 1987, 6 North Yorkshire, 7 Switzerland, 8 Zurich, 9 Freemasons, 10 Mali, 11 Tuesday, 12 Bann, 13 William McMahon, 14 Alicia Markova, 15 It's a slang term for marijuana.

ENTERTAINMENT

1. Which supermodel became Joey's roommate in the comedy series Friends?

2. Which song, a 2000 U.K. number one for A1, was originally a U.K. number two hit for A-Ha in 1985?

3. Who presented the 2000 Britain's Strongest Man competition coverage on BBC1?

4. Which member of the Ally McBeal cast starred alongside Jackie Chan in the 2000 western comedy Shanghai Noon?

5. Who was the original host of the TV quiz show Busman's Holiday?

6. Which Channel 4 show's theme tune hit the U.K. top five in 2000?

7. Which 1988 film starred Timothy Dalton and Anthony Edwards as cancer patients?

8. Which British group had a 1987 U.K. top ten hit with Running in the Family?

9. Which British actor played a school football coach in the 2000 film There's Only One Jimmy Grimble?

10. Which member of Coronation Street's Battersby clan left Weatherfield in 2000 to join Mark Baldwin on his travels?

11. Which 2000 film starred Rachel Griffiths as an investigative journalist who changes places with her alter ego, a housewife?

12. Who presented BBC 2's Edinburgh Review in 2000?

13. Which female vocalist, in collaboration with ELO, had a 1980 U.K. number one hit with Xanadu?

14. Which 1982 film directed by Happy Days' Ron Howard also featured his former co-star Henry Winkler?

15. Who did EastEnders' Melanie surprisingly start dating in 2000 in order to get her own back on Steve Owen?

ANSWERS: 1 Elle MacPherson, 2 Take On Me, 3 John Inverdale, 4 Lucy Liu, 5 Julian Pettifer, 6 Big Brother's, 7 Hawks, 8 Level 42, 9 Robert Carlyle, 10 Leanne, 11 Me Myself I, 12 Mariella Frostrup, 13 Olivia Newton-John, 14 Night Shift, 15 Billy Mitchell.

GENERAL KNOWLEDGE

1. In which country is the Nyamuragira volcano?

2. Which artist did Georgette Berger marry in 1922?

3. To what former denomination of British currency does the slang term O'Goblin refer?

4. Of which country was Imre Nagy the prime minister from 1953-5?

5. At which sport did James Cracknell win gold at the 2000 Olympics?

6. In the Jewish calendar, into how many parts is an hour divided?

7. Which happened first in geological time, the jurassic or silurian period?

8. From which English city would a Brummy come?

9. In which year was the marriage between Princess Margaret and the Earl of Snowden dissolved?

10. Which politician wrote the 1988 book A History of West Indies Cricket?

11. Which 2001 John Boorman film is based on a novel by John Le Carré?

12. In which country is jumbuck a slang term for a sheep?

13. In which year did the actor Sir Ian McKellen first appear with the Royal Shakespeare Company?

14. What was the profession of Benito Mussolini's father?

15. Which tennis player was defeated by Martina Hingis in the Fourth Round of the 2000 Wimbledon women's singles tournament?

GENERAL KNOWLEDGE

1. What was the nickname of Australia Test cricketer N.J.N Hawke, who died in 2000?

2. Who was the Israeli ambassador to the U.N from 1984-8?

3. How many inches were in the old unit of length an English ell?

4. Who authored the 2001 novel Angel?

5. Of which African country is Maseru the capital?

6. Which tennis player penned the 1985 autobiography Being Myself?

7. What car manufacturer makes the Impreza model?

8. Which English city houses the Northcott Theatre?

9. How old was the mountaineer Chris Bonington when he ascended Everest in 1985?

10. Which cathedral houses the tomb of Edward II?

11. In which year did the Jamaica Ocho Rios Jazz Festival start?

12. In which year did the children's television series Vision On begin transmission?

13. Who on average live longer in Iceland - men or women?

14. What is Prince William's second name of four?

15. In which English county was the actor Sir John Mills born?

ANSWERS: 1 Hawkeye, 2 Binyamin Netanyahu, 3 45, 4 Kirstie Speke, 5 Lesotho, 6 Martina Navratilova, 7 Subaru, 8 Exeter, 9 50, 10 Gloucester Cathedral, 11 1991, 12 1964, 13 Women, 14 Arthur, 15 Suffolk.

GENERAL KNOWLEDGE

1. In which Scottish city is Discovery Quay?

2. Which year saw the centenary of the composer Verdi's death?

3. In which English county is the Gaia Energy Centre?

4. For how much did Sheikh Mohammed Bin Rashid Al Maktoum buy the horse Snaafi Dancer in 1983?

5. How old was the actress Marilyn Monroe when she died in 1962?

6. What society did retired journalist John Richards launch in 2001?

7. How many months are there in the Sikh calendar?

8. What nationality was the photographer Lee Miller?

9. In which year in the 1990s was Manchester's Royal Exchange theatre damaged by a bomb blast?

10. Who wrote his Hymn to the Pillory whilst in Newgate prison?

11. Who founded Quebec in 1608?

12. Which country lies between Estonia and Lithuania?

13. Who was appointed the last viceroy of India in 1947?

14. Which film actress did the tennis player John McEnroe marry in 1986?

15. In which year did China adopt the Gregorian calendar for official activities?

ANSWERS: 1 Dundee, 2 2001, 3 Cornwall, 4 $10.2m, 5 36, 6 The Apostrophe Protection Society, 7 12, 8 American, 9 1996, 10 Daniel Defoe, 11 Samuel de Champlain, 12 Latvia, 13 Louis Mountbatten, 14 Tatum O'Neal, 15 1911.

ENTERTAINMENT

1. Which 2000 film saw Arnold Schwarzenegger coming face to face with his clone?
2. With whom did Janet Jackson duet on the 1995 U.K. top five hit Scream?
3. Which actress played the title role in the 1971 film Mary, Queen of Scots?
4. What was the title of George McCrae's 1974 U.K. number one hit?
5. Which former Big Brother contestant presented the game show Trust Me on Channel 4?
6. Which former Beatle had a U.K. top five hit in 1972 with Back Off Boogaloo?
7. Which actor played the title role in the 2000 film version of Hamlet?
8. In the former detective drama series Midnight Caller, what was phone-in host Jack Killian's nickname?
9. Which country singer/songwriter released the album Tomorrow's Sounds Today in 2000?
10. In which city is the 1957 film The Prince and the Showgirl set?
11. Which character's son returned to Weatherfield in the live episode celebrating Coronation Street's 40th birthday in 2000?
12. Which British actor starred as a private-eye hired to find a long-lost daughter in the 1975 film Peeper?
13. Which five-times Olympic gold medallist was named BBC Sports Personality of the Year 2000?
14. Which boy band had a U.K. top five hit with What Makes A Man in 2000?
15. Which actor narrates the audio versions of the Harry Potter books?

GENERAL KNOWLEDGE

1. Which Japanese company created the Hello Kitty brand in 1974?

2. Which actress authored the volume The Olive Farm about her life in France?

3. Is the university town of St Andrews north or south of Edinburgh?

4. Who was chairman of Derby County F.C. from 1987-91?

5. Nippy was a term used for a waitress in which London eating establishment?

6. Which Nobel prize did Walther Hermann Nernst win in 1920?

7. Which jeans brand was founded in 1978 by Renzo Rosso and the Genius Group?

8. Which county is home to the R.A.F Cosford Air Show?

9. With which beverage is the Turkish city of Rize associated?

10. The company Microsoft was founded in Redmond, a suburb of which U.S city?

11. What type of fruit is a tanche?

12. In which year was the Boston Tea Party?

13. In which English seaside town did the actor Peter Cushing buy a house in 1959 and later retire?

14. Which jazz musician wrote the 1971 autobiography Beneath the Underdog?

15. Which author did Syrie Wellcome marry in 1917?

GENERAL KNOWLEDGE

1. Which sports goods manufacturer signed a £100m contract with the Brazil Football Confederation in 1996?

2. How many guns are fired from the Tower of London as a salute to the Sovereign on the occasion of their birthday?

3. In which English city is the Sir John Mills Theatre?

4. In a 1991 census which of these Shetland Islands was more highly populated - Bressay or Whalsay?

5. Which city is home to the G-MEX exhibition centre and Royal Northern College of Music?

6. Which shipping forecast area lies immediately east of Forties?

7. What nationality was the sculptor Marino Marini?

8. In which year did the Thirty Years War begin?

9. Why was John Christopher barred from a carvery in Sheringham, Norfolk in July, 2001?

10. In which year did the actor Sir Alec Guinness become a Companion of Honour?

11. Who wrote the novel About a Boy, which was adapted into a 2002 film starring Hugh Grant?

12. In which year was the Peak District designated a National Park?

13. On which Greek island is the Gramvoussa peninsula?

14. At which sport did Iain Percy win gold at the 2000 Olympics?

15. In which French department is the seaside resort of Trouville?

? GENERAL KNOWLEDGE ?

1. In which English county is Montacute House?

2. In which city was the U.N. Conference on Environment and Development in 1992?

3. What is the colour of the ribbon on a Victoria Cross?

4. Who directed the 1989 film The Tall Guy?

5. In which country was the shipping magnate Aristotle Socrates Onassis born?

6. In which year did Laurence Olivier make his New York stage debut?

7. In which year was Jeffrey Archer made a life peer?

8. Which rank is higher in the Army - Captain or Lieutenant?

9. What is the county town of County Sligo in the Republic of Ireland?

10. In which year did Adrian VI become pope?

11. What was the setting of the television police drama Juliet Bravo?

12. Which former U.S president wrote the 1985 volume No More Vietnams?

13. What did Caleb Bradham rename the beverage known as Brad's Drink?

14. On which island in the British Isles is HMP Albany?

15. What is the name by which members of the Unification Church are known?

ANSWERS: 1 Somerset, 2 Rio de Janeiro, 3 Red, 4 Mel Smith, 5 Turkey, 6 1929, 7 1992, 8 Captain, 9 Sligo, 10 1522, 11 Hartley, Lancashire, 12 Richard Nixon, 13 Pepsi-Cola, 14 Isle of Wight, 15 Moonies.

ENTERTAINMENT

1. Which British animator won an Oscar for his 1993 short film The Wrong Trousers?

2. Who played Maxine Heavey in Coronation Street?

3. Which female vocalist released an album entitled Stardust in 1996?

4. Who starred as the attorney/matchmaker in the 1963 film For Love Or Money?

5. Who was Dick Martin's straight-man and co-host of TV's Laugh-In?

6. Which British singer connects the Seventies band Vinegar Joe and the Eighties band The Power Station?

7. Which 1996 Christmas film starred Arnold Schwarzenegger as a busy Minnesota businessman?

8. Which Friday-night Channel 4 show was written, shot and edited by its presenters from their Brixton bedsit?

9. Which 1996 Chris Rea album featured a collaboration with Shirley Bassey?

10. Which 1953 film starring Marilyn Monroe and Jane Russell featured the song Diamonds Are a Girl's Best Friend?

11. Which popular science TV programme was first screened in 1957 and can still be seen on BBC1?

12. Who had a Christmas number one hit single in 1972 with Long-Haired Lover from Liverpool?

13. Which 1993 Merchant-Ivory film starred Anthony Hopkins and Emma Thompson as a butler and a housekeeper?

14. Who was named the 1996 BBC Sports Personality of the Year?

15. Who had a Christmas number one hit single in 1974 with Lonely This Christmas?

ANSWERS: 1 Nick Park, 2 Tracy Shaw, 3 Natalie Cole, 4 Kirk Douglas, 5 Dan Rowan, 6 Robert Palmer, 7 Jingle All The Way, 8 The Adam and Joe Show, 9 La Passione, 10 Gentlemen Prefer Blondes, 11 Tomorrow's World, 12 Little Jimmy Osmond, 13 The Remains of the Day, 14 Damon Hill, 15 Mud.

GENERAL KNOWLEDGE

1. In Islam, how many surahs are there in the Koran?

2. In which year was the University of Aberdeen founded?

3. In which year was HRH The Prince Philip appointed an Admiral of the Fleet?

4. How much did the Mobira Talkman mobile phone weigh when it was introduced in 1984?

5. In which Russian city is the Harms Festival of performing arts held?

6. In which county is Castle Drogo?

7. Who did EastEnders' Dot Cotton marry in 2002?

8. Which birthday did the city of Riga, Latvia celebrate in 2001?

9. Which writer penned the autobiographical volume Speak, Memory?

10. In which year was the Battle of Vimiero?

11. In which year was the artist Louise Bourgeois born?

12. In a 1991 census which of these Shetland Islands was more highly populated - Fair Isle or Trondra?

13. What is the name given to the flag of Scotland?

14. Which shipping forecast area lies immediately north of Thames?

15. In which religion is the Beth Din the court of judgement?

ANSWERS: 1 114, 2 1495, 3 1953, 4 5kg, 5 St Petersburg, 6 Devon, 7 Jim Branning, 8 800th, 9 Vladimir Nabokov, 10 1808, 11 1911, 12 Trondra, 13 Saltire, 14 Humber, 15 Judaism.

GENERAL KNOWLEDGE

1. Which book of the Bible has more chapters - Jeremiah or Job?

2. What is the name given to the food colouring E174?

3. Which place in the British Isles was known by the Romans as Olicana?

4. In which county are the Mendip Hills, an area of outstanding natural beauty?

5. Which U.S state is larger in area - Arizona or Colorado?

6. What in Buddhism is paritta?

7. What is the plant leontopodium alpinum commonly known as?

8. SU is the symbol for which airline?

9. Of what were the Huronian and Sturtian examples?

10. Which letter of the Greek alphabet is the equivalent of the letter 'z'?

11. In which city are the headquarters of the U.N. agency the IMF?

12. In which year was the University of Exeter founded?

13. What type of creature is an ide?

14. What is the highest rank in the German navy?

15. What is the average gestation period, in days, of a horse?

GENERAL KNOWLEDGE

1. Which French city is famous for its bouillabaisse soup?

2. Which London prison can be found on Du Cane Road, W12?

3. What in Sikhism is a kirpan?

4. Which sea was known by the Romans as mare internum?

5. In which year did Bangladesh enter the Commonwealth?

6. Why might a man not want to hear from the CSA?

7. In which period of geological time was the St David's epoch?

8. Which country's national anthem is entitled Quami Tarana?

9. What is the smallest European bat?

10. How many grand slam singles tennis titles did Steffi Graf win?

11. In which year was Darwin College, Cambridge founded?

12. Which country had the most seats in the European parliament in 1999?

13. What was the most popular name for a girl in England and Wales in the 1960s?

14. In which year did Cyclone Tracy cause the deaths of 65 people?

15. What is the smallest European duck?

ANSWERS: 1 Marseille, 2 Wormwood Scrubs, 3 Small sword, 4 Mediterranean Sea, 5 1972, 6 It's the Child Support Agency, 7 Palaeozoic, 8 Pakistan, 9 Common pipistrelle, 10 22, 11 1964, 12 Germany, 13 Tracey, 14 1974, 15 Common teal.

SPORT

1. Who lost to Stuart Bingham in the first round of the 2000 snooker world championship at the Crucible?

2. With which sport is Murray Walker connected?

3. In which sport does a hooter sound the end of the game?

4. How many players make up a softball team?

5. In which year did Harbhajan Singh become the first Indian bowler to take a hat-trick in Test cricket?

6. Which Portuguese runner smashed his own record in winning the men's race in the 2000 London Marathon?

7. Shinty is a form of which sport?

8. Which ground became the home of Fulham FC in 1896?

9. Which game was invented by Ernest Pitiot?

10. Who was the first bowler in cricket to take 500 Test wickets?

11. Who scored the winning goal of the 1980 F.A. Cup final?

12. Which England cricketer scored 333 against India at Lords in 1990?

13. What fabric covers a snooker table?

14. What is the points value of a converted try in rugby league?

15. Which sport was invented by James Naismith in 1891?

GENERAL KNOWLEDGE

1. Which Channel 4 show shot Zig and Zag to stardom?

2. What is the capital of Norway?

3. In which century did the Crimean War take place?

4. To which novel by David Lodge is Small World a sequel?

5. What was the first name of the 19th-century English cookery writer Mrs Beeton?

6. Which literary figure is portrayed by Geoffrey Rush in the film Quills?

7. In which television series does the radio station KACL appear?

8. Which novel by Ian Fleming was the first to feature James Bond?

9. Which pop star was born Harry Rodger Webb?

10. Which historical event is described in the Thomas Hardy poem The Convergence of the Twain?

11. Which U.S. golfer won the British Open in 1981?

12. Who wrote A Brief History of Time?

13. Which was the first film directed by Jodie Foster?

14. How many sides does a heptagon have?

15. Which author introduced the word 'robot' into the modern vocabulary?

GENERAL KNOWLEDGE

1. Which adjective is used to describe the lungs?

2. What is the middle name of Margaret Thatcher?

3. Who played Little Big Man in 1970?

4. Which TV series introduced us to Windy Miller?

5. In which American state is the city of Tallahassee?

6. Big Kahuna Burgers and Red Apple Cigarettes are screen trademarks of which director?

7. Who appeared in the pocket of David Owen on Spitting Image?

8. How many ounces make up a pound?

9. Which sport is central to the film Escape to Victory?

10. Who directed the Tom Hanks film Cast Away?

11. Which team beat Celtic 9-8 on penalties to win the Scottish Cup in 1990?

12. In which film did Arnold Schwarzenegger first star as a cyborg?

13. What was the name of The Avengers' controller?

14. On what day did 1st January 2002 fall?

15. What nationality was the composer Anton Dvorak?

ANSWERS: 1 Pulmonary, 2 Hilda, 3 Dustin Hoffman, 4 Camberwick Green, 5 Florida, 6 Quentin Tarantino, 7 David Steel, 8 16, 9 Football, 10 Robert Zemeckis, 11 Aberdeen, 12 The Terminator, 13 Mother, 14 Tuesday, 15 Czech.

? GENERAL KNOWLEDGE ?

1. A daddy-longlegs is also known as what?

2. From which club did Leeds United sign Rio Ferdinand?

3. Which was the Oscar-winning song from Mary Poppins?

4. Who, in 1977, became the 39th president of the United States?

5. What is the capital of Queensland?

6. Who played Jane opposite Johnny Weismuller as Tarzan?

7. Who wrote the poem Death Be Not Proud?

8. What would a costermonger sell?

9. Which comedy star was born Arthur S Jefferson?

10. Which team won the F.A. Cup in 1988?

11. Which writer created The Saint?

12. Which actor's real name was Marion Michael Morrison?

13. What is the official language of Mexico?

14. What is the standard monetary unit of Turkey?

15. Who wrote Bleak House?

ANSWERS: 1 Crane fly, 2 West Ham, 3 Chim Chim Cher-ee, 4 Jimmy Carter, 5 Brisbane, 6 Maureen O'Sullivan, 7 John Donne, 8 Fruit and vegetables, 9 Stan Laurel, 10 Wimbledon, 11 Leslie Charteris, 12 John Wayne, 13 Spanish, 14 Lira, 15 Charles Dickens.

ENTERTAINMENT

1. With which rugby-related song did South Africa's Ladysmith Black Mambazo featuring China Black have a U.K. top twenty hit in 1995?

2. Which actor played an advertising executive who pretends to be married to the woman next door in the 1964 film Good Neighbor Sam?

3. What was the name of the ship in the children's series Captain Pugwash?

4. In which European city was the 2001 Rugrats movie set?

5. Which former member of Boyzone hit the U.K. top five with Lovin' Each Day?

6. Which 1977 film was directed and co-written by Terry Gilliam and starred fellow Monty Python member Michael Palin?

7. Which stand-up comedian was the star of the BBC1 sitcom So What Now?

8. Which pop group had a U.K. number one hit (twice) with Don't Stop Movin'?

9. Which actress played the title character in the film adaptation of Bridget Jones's Diary?

10. Of which sitcom was the Seventies series Don't Drink the Water a spin-off?

11. Which long-running U.K. sci fi series was first screened on the day after President Kennedy was assassinated in 1963?

12. Which U.S. girl group hit the U.K. number one spot with Survivor in 2001?

13. Which legendary Hollywood actress and dancer's real name was Margarita Carmen Cansino?

14. Which BBC1 drama series was set in a Manchester factory called Mackintosh Textiles?

15. What was the title of Whitney Houston's debut single in the U.K., which hit the number one spot in 1985?

ANSWERS: 1 Swing Low Sweet Chariot, 2 Jack Lemmon, 3 The Black Pig, 4 Paris, 5 Ronan Keating, 6 Jabberwocky, 7 Lee Evans, 8 S Club 7, 9 Renee Zellweger, 10 On the Buses, 11 Doctor Who, 12 Destiny's Child, 13 Rita Hayworth, 14 Clocking Off, 15 Saving All My Love For You.

? GENERAL KNOWLEDGE ?

1. How many yards make up a mile?

2. Who went Solo on TV for 13 episodes in 1981?

3. Which country visited by Gulliver during his travels was populated by giants?

4. Who starred in An Unseen Enemy in 1912 and The Whales of August in 1987?

5. Who was the first president of the United States?

6. Who had a U.K. number one hit in 1979 with I Will Survive?

7. What relation is Frodo to Bilbo Baggins in stories by J.R.R. Tolkien?

8. Which actor connects Dave with A Fish Called Wanda?

9. George is an informal name for what feature of an aircraft?

10. Who was the youngest member of the Beatles?

11. Without what was Joe 90 just an ordinary boy?

12. By what name are non-wizards known in the Harry Potter books?

13. What do the French call La Manche?

14. Which was the first film to feature Lauren Bacall?

15. In which modern-day country was Doris Lessing born?

ANSWERS: 1 1760, 2 Felicity Kendal, 3 Brobdingnag, 4 Lillian Gish, 5 George Washington, 6 Gloria Gaynor, 7 Cousin, 8 Kevin Kline, 9 Automatic pilot, 10 George Harrison, 11 His glasses, 12 Muggles, 13 English Channel, 14 To Have and Have Not, 15 Iran.

GENERAL KNOWLEDGE

1. Which animal is the adjective equine used to describe?

2. In which continent are the Atlas Mountains?

3. Who wrote The Loneliness of the Long Distance Runner?

4. Who had a U.K. number one hit in 1994 with Saturday Night?

5. What is the nontechnical name for the talus?

6. Tamale is a dish native to which country?

7. Who starred as James Bond in the movie Moonraker?

8. What is the name of the dog belonging to Dorothy in The Wizard of Oz?

9. What is the real name of The Scarlet Pimpernel?

10. Who played The Incredible Shrinking Man?

11. Who learnt how to play the cello for the 1999 biopic Hilary and Jackie?

12. Which British author wrote Whisky Galore?

13. How is Sarah Michelle Gellar better known to millions?

14. Which band sang the theme song to The World is Not Enough?

15. What does Jack exchange for magic beans in the fairy story Jack and the Beanstalk?

ANSWERS: 1 Horse, 2 Africa, 3 Alan Sillitoe, 4 Whigfield, 5 Anklebone, 6 Mexico, 7 Roger Moore, 8 Toto, 9 Sir Percy Blakeney, 10 Grant Williams, 11 Emily Watson, 12 Sir Compton Mackenzie, 13 Buffy, 14 Garbage, 15 A cow

GENERAL KNOWLEDGE

1. Ganymede is a satellite of which planet?

2. Who played DI Frances O'Neil in the Lynda La Plante drama Mind Games?

3. Who are Milo, Bella, Fizz and Jake?

4. Who did Margaret Thatcher replace as leader of the Conservative Party in 1975?

5. Where would a stevedore be employed?

6. Which of the original U.K. Big Brother contestants was first to be evicted?

7. What nationality was the composer Wolfgang Amadeus Mozart?

8. Who directed Rosemary's Baby?

9. Lake Garda is the largest lake in which country?

10. What is Co the chemical symbol for?

11. What does the Latin phrase vox populi mean?

12. In the TV sitcom Porridge what was the middle name of Norman Fletcher?

13. Who followed William Taft as U.S. president?

14. Anton Meyer is a character in which TV medical drama?

15. Who was forced to decline the Nobel prize for literature in 1958?

ANSWERS: 1 Jupiter, 2 Fiona Shaw, 3 The Tweenies, 4 Edward Heath, 5 Dockyard, 6 Sada, 7 Austrian, 8 Roman Polanski, 9 Italy, 10 Cobalt, 11 Voice of the people, 12 Stanley, 13 Woodrow Wilson, 14 Holby City, 15 Boris Pasternak.

ENTERTAINMENT

1. In which Anglo-American film did Alan Rickman and Natasha Richardson play a hairdressing ex-husband and wife?

2. Which Coronation Street character was played by Bernard Youens for twenty years until his death in 1984?

3. Which 1962 film was directed and written by Orson Welles from a novel by Franz Kafka?

4. Which pop star had a 2001 U.K. top ten hit with Let Love Be Your Energy?

5. Which actor played 1950s filmmaker David Merrill in the 1991 movie Guilty By Suspicion?

6. Whose gun was used to shoot EastEnders' Phil Mitchell?

7. In 2001, which trio released their first studio album in four years, This is Where I Came In?

8. Which BBC 1 documentary series about the life of Jesus was presented by BBC Breakfast's Jeremy Bowen?

9. Which actress and singer played The Wedding Planner in the movie of that name?

10. Which TV chef became the new presenter of BBC 2's Masterchef 2001?

11. Who played the second Doctor Who on TV from 1966 to 1969?

12. Which U.K. top five hit by Gabrielle featured in the film Bridget Jones's Diary?

13. Which Hollywood star once said "Young actors love me. They think if that big slob can make it, there's a chance for us."?

14. Which 2001 three-part ITV series used the histories of three families to depict the course of life in Britain since 1945?

15. How many weeks did Bryan Adams's (Everything I Do) I Do It For You spend at the U.K. number one spot in 1991?

ANSWERS: 1 Blow Dry, 2 Stan Ogden, 3 The Trial, 4 Robbie Williams, 5 Robert De Niro, 6 Steve Owen's, 7 The Bee Gees, 8 Son of God, 9 Jennifer Lopez, 10 Gary Rhodes, 11 Patrick Troughton, 12 Out of Reach, 13 Robert Mitchum, 14 Time of Our Lives, 15 16.

GENERAL KNOWLEDGE

1. Sid Waddell is most famous for commentating on which sport?

2. When did the Titanic sink?

3. Jacqueline Pirie played which character in Coronation Street?

4. When was U.S. Democrat politician Al Gore born?

5. What is a diadem?

6. The adjective ursine describes which animal?

7. Crotchet Castle, Headlong Hall and Gryll Grange are all titles of novels by which author?

8. From which country does paella originate?

9. What is the capital of Sri Lanka?

10. Which TV series about an oil company became The Troubleshooters?

11. The characters Roderick Random, Peregrine Pickle and Humphry Clinker appear in novels by whom?

12. Who succeeded Jeremy Beadle as presenter of You've Been Framed?

13. Which actor was born Archibald Alexander Leach?

14. Which of these birds can fly; kookaburra, ostrich, kiwi or cassowary?

15. Who have Robert Donat, Kenneth More and Robert Powell all played on film?

ANSWERS: 1 Darts, 2 1912, 3 Linda Baldwin, 4 1948, 5 Crown, 6 Bear, 7 Thomas Love Peacock, 8 Spain, 9 Colombo, 10 Mogul, 11 Tobias Smollett, 12 Lisa Riley, 13 Cary Grant, 14 Kookaburra, 15 Richard Hannay of The Thirty-Nine Step.

GENERAL KNOWLEDGE

1. What was the name of the daughter of Samantha and Darrin in Bewitched?

2. In which country is To Catch a Thief set?

3. Which member of The Dirty Dozen was also in The Magificent Seven?

4. Who wrote the autobiography The Moon's a Balloon?

5. What is Roquefort a type of?

6. Which island group is Ibiza in?

7. Which D.H. Lawrence novel concerns several generations of the Brangwen family?

8. Aconcagua is the highest peak in which mountain system?

9. Cyberphobia is the irrational fear of what?

10. Who wrote the story Where the Wild Things Are?

11. The adjective vulpine relates to which animal?

12. In which century was the French writer Voltaire born?

13. What was the name of the boy who befriended ET in the film of that name?

14. Which comedy duo had the theme song Bring Me Sunshine?

15. What is Low Sunday also known as?

ANSWERS: 1 Tabitha, 2 Monaco, 3 Charles Bronson, 4 David Niven, 5 Cheese, 6 Balearics, 7 The Rainbow, 8 Andes, 9 Computers, 10 Maurice Sendak, 11 Fox, 12 17th, 13 Elliott, 14 Morecambe and Wise, 15 The first Sunday after Easter.

GENERAL KNOWLEDGE

1. Who was president of the United States from 1963-69?

2. Whom did Sue Barker succeed as presenter of A Question of Sport?

3. How many eggs had to be eaten as a bet in Cool Hand Luke?

4. Which poet claimed - "Love is my religion - I could die for that"?

5. From which film does the song White Christmas come?

6. What is the capital of Paraguay?

7. What is the chemical symbol for gold?

8. The Crocodile River is another name for which river?

9. What is another name for mother-of-pearl?

10. Which film was based on the Joseph Conrad story Heart of Darkness?

11. Who was the 42nd president of the United States?

12. Which medical TV series is set in Cardale?

13. What was The Pink Panther?

14. Who was the first male centrefold in Cosmopolitan magazine?

15. What was the first name of A.A. Milne?

ANSWERS: 1 Lyndon Baines Johnson, 2 David Coleman, 3 50, 4 John Keats, 5 Holiday Inn, 6 Asuncion, 7 Au, 8 Limpopo, 9 Nacre, 10 Apocalypse Now, 11 Bill Clinton, 12 Peak Practice, 13 A jewel, 14 Burt Reynolds, 15 Alan.

ENTERTAINMENT

1. What was the title of the Shamen's 1992 U.K. number one hit?

2. Which 2000 mock-documentary film was set in the world of dog-fancying?

3. Which children's programme of the '60s and '70s aimed to cater for both hearing and non-hearing viewers and featured the talents of Tony Hart?

4. Which British male singer hit the U.K. top ten in 2001 with Rendezvous?

5. Which American composer won Oscars for his work on 1961's Breakfast at Tiffany's and 1982's Victor/Victoria?

6. Which former docu-soap star hosted the BBC1 talent show Star for a Night?

7. Which actress played evil Elektra King in the 1999 Bond film The World is Not Enough?

8. Which BBC1 series followed a group of recruits at the Metropolitan Police Service's training school?

9. Which Welsh rock band released an album entitled Know Your Enemy?

10. Which veteran TV actor appeared in ITV's Peak Practice as Dr Alex Redman's dad?

11. What type of creature was Brian in the children's TV show The Magic Roundabout?

12. The male members of which squeaky-clean British pop band were cautioned by the police in 2001 for being in possession of cannabis?

13. Which actor said, "I have played three presidents, three saints and two geniuses. If that doesn't create an ego problem, nothing does."?

14. Which comic actor explored the intricacies of The Human Face on BBC1?

15. Which Sixties band's members were Steve Marriott, Ronnie Lane, Kenny Jones and Ian McLagen?

ANSWERS: 1 Ebeneezer Goode, 2 Best In Show, 3 Vision On, 4 Craig David, 5 Henry Mancini, 6 Jane McDonald, 7 Sophie Marceau, 8 Raw Blues, 9 Manic Street Preachers, 10 Frank Windsor, 11 A snail, 12 S Club 7, 13 Charlton Heston, 14 John Cleese, 15 Small Faces.

GENERAL KNOWLEDGE

1. What nationality was the explorer Mungo Park?

2. Hibernia was the Roman name for which country?

3. What is a clavichord?

4. Is a meerkat diurnal or nocturnal?

5. Who painted The Last Supper?

6. Who was Chancellor of the Exchequer from 1993-97?

7. Who connects the television series The Good Life and Monarch of the Glen?

8. What is the standard monetary unit of Bulgaria?

9. How many pounds make up a stone?

10. Which English town is at the head of the Orwell estuary?

11. Who holds the record of most Jackanory appearances with 111?

12. The Sierra Madre is the main mountain system of which country?

13. Which novelist wrote Heart of Darkness?

14. The tiger snake is native to which country?

15. What was Russian Anna Pavlova best known as?

ANSWERS: 1 Scottish, 2 Ireland, 3 Musical instrument, 4 Diurnal, 5 Leonardo da Vinci, 6 Kenneth Clarke, 7 Richard Briers, 8 Lev, 9 14, 10 Ipswich, 11 Bernard Cribbins, 12 Mexico, 13 Joseph Conrad, 14 Australia, 15 Ballerina.

GENERAL KNOWLEDGE

1. QANTAS is the national airline of which country?

2. What nationality are the Manic Street Preachers?

3. The adjective lupine describes which animal?

4. In which century was Sir Isaac Newton born?

5. What in communications is a code word for the letter q?

6. Who was the first Englishman to sail around the world?

7. What does the word cachinnate mean?

8. Where are the headquarters of the United Nations?

9. Where are the islets of Langerhans situated?

10. What links the Mediterranean with the Atlantic?

11. Julian and Gregorian are types of what?

12. Who directed the 1965 film Cat Ballou?

13. Gerlachovka is the highest peak in which mountain system?

14. Carriage dog was a former name for which breed of dog?

15. In which city was John F Kennedy assassinated?

ANSWERS: 1 Australia, 2 Welsh, 3 Wolf, 4 17th, 5 Quebec, 6 Francis Drake, 7 Laugh loudly, 8 New York, 9 Pancreas, 10 Strait of Gibraltar, 11 Calendar, 12 Elliot Silverstein, 13 Carpathians, 14 Dalmatian, 15 Dallа.

GENERAL KNOWLEDGE

1. Chinese gooseberry is another name for which fruit?

2. Which animated children's characters were In Paris in a 2000 film sequel?

3. In which British city was the TV series GBH set?

4. Who is the most-capped Scotland footballer?

5. What was the capital of India from 1833-1912?

6. Which author wrote A Town Like Alice?

7. Which of the Marx Brothers was born first?

8. Who was the only Aston Villa player selected to join the England squad for the 2002 World Cup finals?

9. A henbit is a type of what?

10. Who created Sanders of the River?

11. Which Neighbours role was originally played by Kylie Flinker?

12. Who wrote The Ipcress File?

13. How many megabytes are there in a gigabyte?

14. Where is the holy city of Medina?

15. In which country was the British Survivor 2 reality TV series filmed?

GENERAL KNOWLEDGE

1. Who wrote the 1970 one-act play After Magritte?

2. In which year did British iron manufacturer Abraham Darby die?

3. Which tennis player won the 1998 Australian Open women's doubles title with Martina Hingis?

4. Which city in California is the 'city of angels'?

5. Who was the 1972 Wimbledon men's singles tennis champion?

6. Who directed the 1983 film Gorky Park?

7. The French port of St-Nazaire is at the mouth of which river?

8. Which saint and Roman monk was the first archbishop of Canterbury?

9. What is the name of the central character in the play Death of a Salesman?

10. What is the capital of Nicaragua?

11. How many first-class wickets did cricketer Fred Trueman take in his career?

12. Stoop Memorial Ground is the home ground of which rugby union club?

13. What is the name of the newspaper which features in Evelyn Waugh's novel Scoop?

14. 'Old Rowley' was the nickname of which king of England?

15. Who was president of Zambia from 1964-91?

ANSWERS 1. Tom Stoppard 2. 1717 3. Mirjana Lucic 4. Los Angeles 5. Stan Smith 6. Michael Apted 7. Loire 8. St. Augustine 9. Willy Loman 10. Managua 11. 2,304 12. Harlequins 13. The Beast 14. Charles II 15. Kenneth Kaunda.

ENTERTAINMENT

1. Which comedian impersonated Elvis Costello in a Stars in Their Eyes celebrity special?

2. On which island is the 1949 British film If This Be Sin set?

3. Who has played PC Natalie Metcalf in the television series The Cops?

4. Who played Joe Purvis in the television series Grafters?

5. Who directed the 1983 film Daniel, based on the novel The Book of Daniel?

6. Who plays King Louis XI of France in the 1938 film If I Were King?

7. Who has played school librarian Giles in television's Buffy the Vampire Slayer?

8. At which London Underground station was the picture Deathline filmed?

9. Which member of The Fast Show team presented the television fashion show She's Gotta Have It?

10. Which comedienne played Mrs. Leo Hunter in the 1952 film The Pickwick Papers?

11. Who played Stuart in the television drama Queer as Folk?

12. Who directed the 1996 film Unforgettable, which starred Ray Liotta?

13. Who occasionally plays Terry Duckworth in Coronation Street?

14. Which actress played John Gordon-Sinclair's girlfriend in the 1991 sitcom An Actor's Life For Me?

15. What is James Stewart's profession in the 1953 film The Naked Spur?

ANSWERS 1. Frank Skinner 2. Capri 3. Clare McGlinn 4. Robson Green 5. Sidney Lumet 6. Basil Rathbone 7. Anthony Stewart Head 8. Russell Square 9. Arabella Weir 10. Joyce Grenfell 11. Aiden Gillen 12. John Dahl 13. Nigel Pivaro 14. Gina McKee 15. Bounty hunter.

SPORT

1. Who won the Isle of Man Senior TT in 1991 and 1992?

2. Which team won the 1999 county cricket championship?

3. How many times have Bolton been placed third in the Football League Division 1?

4. Who took over captaincy of Northamptonshire C.C.C. in 1996?

5. Who won the 1975 Boston men's marathon?

6. Who was named top male athlete of the 20th century by the I.A.A.F. in November 1999?

7. Which horse won the 1971 Prix de l'Arc de Triomphe?

8. What nationality is high jumper Javier Sotomayor?

9. Which rowing club won the 1989 and 1990 Grand Challenge Cup at Henley?

10. Which football club won the 1999/00 League Cup?

11. Which country were the 1996 world champions at speedway?

12. Which country won the golf World Cup in November 1999?

13. In his 36,012 first-class runs scored from 1894-1928, how many double centuries did Billy Quaife make?

14. For which rugby league team did Gavin Wood and Dan Potter play?

15. At which sport have Eirik Kvalfoss and Frank Ullrich been world champions?

ANSWERS 1. Steve Hislop 2. Surrey 3. Three 4. R.J. Bailey 5. Bill Rodgers 6. Carl Lewis 7. Mill Reef 8. Cuban 9. Hansa Dortmund RC 10. Leicester City 11. Poland 12. U.S.A. 13. Four 14. Dewsbury Rams 15. Biathlon.

POP MUSIC

1. Which reggae legend recorded the 1999 album Living in the Flood?

2. From which group did drummer John Hinch join Judas Priest?

3. Which solo artist had a 2000 Top 10 hit with Dolphins Were Monkeys?

4. In which year did Black Lace first hit the Top 10 with the single Agadoo?

5. Greg Ginn was the frontman of which 1980s band?

6. On which label did Rich Kids have a 1978 Top 30 hit with Rich Kids?

7. In which year did Roxy Music have a Top 10 single with Both Ends Burning?

8. Which female singer recorded the 1956 Top 20 single Jimmy Unknown?

9. Who produced Talk Talk's 1991 album Laughing Stock?

10. Who recorded the 1977 album Before and After Science?

11. Which band did Caravan's Dave Sinclair join after leaving the group in 1971?

12. Which member of Depeche Mode recorded the album Liquid under the name Recoil?

13. Which reggae artist had a posthumous 1999 Top 10 single with Sun is Shining?

14. In which city was country star Kenny Rogers born?

15. For how many years did Lionel Ritchie front The Commodores before going solo in 1982?

ART & LITERATURE

1. Who wrote the 1966 novel The Fixer?

2. Which French painter was born in Le Cateau in 1869?

3. Whose novels include 1946's The Member of the Wedding?

4. Who wrote the 1944 play The Man Who Had All the Luck?

5. Who wrote the 1959 novel The Apprenticeship of Duddy Kravitz?

6. Whose paintings included 1804's The Old Pier?

7. Who wrote the 2001 children's book Mortal Engines?

8. Which sculptor created the 1936 work Fruit de la Lune?

9. Who wrote the book Alice's Adventures in Wonderland?

10. Which writer penned the poem The Rhyme of the Flying Bomb?

11. Who wrote the 2001 book The Dying Animal?

12. Who wrote the 1978 novel Requiem For A Dream?

13. Who wrote the science fiction novel The Door Into Summer?

14. Which author wrote the 1991 novel Jernigan?

15. Who wrote the 1974 novel The Rachel Papers?

ANSWERS 1. Bernard Malamud 2. Henri Matisse 3. Carson McCullers 4. Arthur Miller 5. Mordecai Richler 6. J.M.W. Turner 7. Philip Reeve 8. Jean Arp 9. Lewis Carroll 10. Mervyn Peake 11. Philip Roth 12. Hubert Selby Jr. 13. Robert A. Heinlein 14. David Gates 15. Martin Amis.

? **GENERAL KNOWLEDGE** ?

1. Which word used in signalling indicates that a message received will be complied with?

2. Who was 1974-7 champion flat race jockey?

3. The 1964 film Woman of Straw, starring Sean Connery, was based on a novel by which writer?

4. In which year did British sculptor, typographer and engraver Eric Gill die?

5. Which tennis player won the 1980 Wimbledon men's doubles title with Paul McNamee?

6. In which year was German painter Max Ernst born?

7. Which Russian revolutionary leader became premier in July 1917?

8. The 1978 film The Shout, starring Alan Bates, was based on a short story by which writer?

9. In which year was American avant-garde pianist and jazz composer Cecil Taylor born?

10. At which racecourse is the English Grand National run?

11. What was Honor Blackman's character called in the television show The Avengers?

12. Which unit of area is equivalent to 2.471 acres?

13. Ac is the symbol of which radioactive element?

14. The port of Salto is the second-largest city in which South American country?

15. Who was the English soldier who commanded the British capture of Quebec in the 18th century?

ENTERTAINMENT

1. What is Tony Curtis's character's name in the 1957 film Sweet Smell of Success?

2. Who wrote and directed the 1999 film Boys Don't Cry?

3. What is the television presenter Graham Norton's real surname?

4. Which 1970s television star has appeared in the hospital drama Holby City as Professor Alan Fletcher?

5. Who played Mrs. Anna Madrigal in the television series Tales of the City?

6. In which country was the 1960s series Whiplash, starring Peter Graves, set?

7. Who took over from Hugh Paddick as the genie in the 1970s children's show Pardon My Genie?

8. Who played Gary Winston in the 2001 Peter Howitt film AntiTrust?

9. Which 1970s BBC drama series was set in Gallowshield?

10. In which year did the television contractor TWW lose its franchise to Harlech Television?

11. Who play the male and female leads in the 2000 film Autumn in New York?

12. Who played Hollywood executive Griffin Mill in the 1992 film The Player?

13. Who directed the 2000 film American Psycho?

14. Who plays journalist Lester Bangs in the 2000 film Almost Famous?

15. Who directed the 2000 film Under Suspicion, which stars Gene Hackman and Morgan Freeman?

ANSWERS 1. Sidney Falco 2. Kimberly Peirce 3. Walker 4. David Soul 5. Olympia Dukakis 6. Australia 7. Arthur White 8. Tim Robbins 9. When the Boat Comes In 10. 1967 11. Richard Gere and Winona Ryder 12. Tim Robbins 13. Mary Harron 14. Philip Seymour Hoffman 15. Stephen Hopkins.

SPORT

1. By what score did Germany beat Mexico in the 1998 football World Cup finals second round?

2. Who coached Scotland to their 1990 rugby union Grand Slam?

3. At which sport were Teresa Andersen and Gail Johnson 1973 world champions?

4. What nationality is golfer John Cook, who has earned more than $6m on the U.S. tour?

5. Who was named as coach of France's rugby union team in November 1999?

6. How many runs did Graham Thorpe score in his three Tests against South Africa in 1998?

7. Which horse was leading moneywinner in Britain in 1967?

8. Who did Todd Martin beat in the quarter-finals of the 1999 U.S. Open tennis singles championship?

9. Zhanna Pintusevich was women's 200m champion at the 1997 World Championships. Which country did she represent?

10. Who partnered Arantxa Sanchez to victory in the 1992 French Open mixed doubles championship?

11. Which Finn was the 1998 Australian Grand Prix winner in Formula 1?

12. In cricket, who scored 160 for Lancashire versus Yorkshire in the first innings of their 1999 county championship match?

13. Which club have played in the most rugby league Challenge Cup finals?

14. In which year did tennis player Wilfred Baddeley die?

15. What nationality were the 1968 Olympic two-man bobsleigh champions?

POP MUSIC

1. What was the title of the debut album by the group Cousteau?

2. Who produced the 1987 album Little Baby Buntin' by Killdozer?

3. In which year did Tom Petty & the Heartbreakers release their debut album?

4. Which group recorded the album The Evil Powers of Rock 'N' Roll?

5. What was the title of The Penguin Café Orchestra's second album?

6. Ed Kuepper and Chris Bailey were members of which Australian punk band?

7. In which U.S. city did Pere Ubu form in 1975?

8. Who replaced Dave Krusen as drummer in the group Pearl Jam?

9. Who comprised the 'Million Dollar Quartet' at Sun Records?

10. Which of the Pet Shop Boys is older - Chris Lowe or Neil Tennant?

11. Which female singer recorded the song I Belong to a World That's Destroying Itself in 1968?

12. Which band recorded the 1999 album The Science of Things?

13. Which Irish solo artist once fronted the group Ten Past Seven?

14. Which two musicians recorded the 1966 album Bert and John?

15. In which year did Paul McCartney have a Top 10 single with No More Lonely Nights?

GEOGRAPHY

1. In which U.S. state is the Kilauea volcano?

2. Which sea is larger in area, the Black Sea or the North Sea?

3. Of which country is Funafuti the capital?

4. Which African capital has the larger population - Nairobi or Tunis?

5. On which holiday island are the peaks of Ruivo and Arieiro?

6. On which Caribbean island are the holiday resorts of Gosier and Saint François?

7. Which is the second-largest desert in the world?

8. Of which country is Dushanbe the capital?

9. On which Mediterranean island is the Karpas peninsula?

10. In which African country are the Karuru and Gura waterfalls?

11. Which sea is larger in area, the Red Sea or the Yellow Sea?

12. In which Asian country is the Roman city of Jerash?

13. In which European country is the ski resort of Sölden?

14. Of which African country is Malabo the capital?

15. Which country is larger in area - Uruguay or Venezuela?

ANSWERS 1. Hawaii 2. Black Sea 3. Tuvalu 4. Tunis 5. Madeira 6. Guadeloupe 7. Australian Desert 8. Tajikistan 9. Cyprus 10. Kenya 11. Red Sea 12. Jordan 13. Austria 14. Equatorial Guinea 15. Venezuela.

GENERAL KNOWLEDGE

1. Which king did Elizabeth Woodville marry?

2. In which year on Memorial Day did New York's Madison Square Gardens open?

3. Which car manufacturer makes the Assetto Corsa model?

4. In which European country is the ski resort of Baqueira-Beret?

5. In which English county is Prince Charles's home Highgrove?

6. In which U.S. state is the Spurr volcano?

7. On what day of the week did New Year's Day fall in 1905?

8. In which Yorkshire town is the Magna science adventure centre?

9. On which island is the poet Rupert Brooke buried?

10. In which year did the programme Top Gear begin on network television?

11. Gethin Price is the central character in which 20th century stage play?

12. What is the plant Dicksonia squarrosa better known as?

13. Which European river does the Ponte 25 de Abril bridge span?

14. What animal represents the year 2002 in the Chinese calendar?

15. On which mountain in Ireland, also known as The Reek, did St. Patrick fast for 40 days and nights in 441?

ANSWERS 1. Edward IV 2. 1879 3. Maserati 4. Spain 5. Gloucestershire 6. Alaska 7. Sunday 8. Rotherham 9. Skyros 10. 1978 11. Comedians by Trevor Griffiths 12. Wheki 13. Tagus 14. Horse 15. Croagh Patrick.

ENTERTAINMENT

1. Who plays Geoff, Vinnie and Olive in television's The League of Gentlemen?

2. In which opera by Rimsky-Korsakov does King Dodon appear?

3. Who directed the 2000 film The Beach?

4. Which actress played Vera Hopkins in Coronation Street?

5. Who directed the 2000 film The End of the Affair?

6. What is comedienne Dora Bryan's real name?

7. Who directed the 1922 film Nanook of the North?

8. Who stars in the title role of the 2000 film Erin Brockovich?

9. Which Hollywood actress was born Ruby Stevens?

10. Who directed the film Pi?

11. Who plays Rita Sullivan in Coronation Street?

12. Who played the female lead in the 1998 film You've Got Mail?

13. Who appeared as Jill, Rachel's younger sister, in the sitcom Friends in 2000?

14. Who composed the 1872 opera Djamileh?

15. Who are the two female leads in the 1998 film Practical Magic?

ANSWERS 1. Reece Shearsmith 2. The Golden Cockerel 3. Danny Boyle 4. Kathy Staff 5. Neil Jordan 6. Dora Broadbent 7. Robert Flaherty 8. Julia Roberts 9. Barbara Stanwyck 10. Darren Aronofsky 11. Barbara Knox 12. Meg Ryan 13. Reece Witherspoon 14. Bizet 15. Sandra Bullock and Nicole Kidman.

SPORT

1. Who beat Lindsay Davenport in the 1999 U.S. Open tennis singles semi-final?

2. How many dismissals did South African wicket-keeper Richard Ryall make in his career from 1980-95?

3. Which city is the location of the headquarters of the World Professional Billiards and Snooker Association?

4. Which female golfer won the 1955 Du Maurier Classic?

5. In which sport do Britons Carolyn Wilson and Amanda Dodd compete?

6. What time did Claudia Pechstein take to win the 1994 Olympic 5000m speed skating gold?

7. What nationality is motorcyclist Alex Criville?

8. What nationality was sprinter Ray Stewart?

9. How many gold medals did Kenya win at the 1999 World Athletics Championships?

10. Who was men's long jump champion at the 1991 World Indoor Championships?

11. What nationality is tennis player Juan Carlos Ferrero?

12. Who rode the 1978 Epsom Derby winner Shirley Heights?

13. Who knocked Castleford Lock Lane out of the 2000 Silk Cut Challenge Cup in rugby league?

14. How many medals did gymnast Larisa Latynina win at the Olympics from 1956-64?

15. Which golfer was the 1957 B.B.C. Sports Personality of the Year?

ANSWERS 1. Serena Williams 2. 422 3. Bristol 4. Jenny Lidback 5. Synchronised swimming 6. 7:14.37 7. Spanish 8. Jamaican 9. One 10. Dietmar Haaf 11. Spanish 12. Greville Starkey 13. Villeneuve 14. 18 15. Dai Rees.

POP MUSIC

1. Which group recorded the 2001 album Our Kid Eh?

2. Which group recorded the 1970 album Fire and Water?

3. What is the name of the band in which Jakob Dylan, son of Bob, plays?

4. Whose debut album was 1997's Baduizm?

5. Which studio album by the group the Fall includes the track Iceland?

6. Rabbit Songs was the 2001 debut album of which group?

7. Which group recorded the 1990 album Ritual De Lo Habitual?

8. Which group's second album was 1987's Engine?

9. Which album by The Prodigy went straight to No. 1 in the U.S. charts in 1997?

10. In which year did The Byrds release their album The Notorious Byrd Brothers?

11. Which former singer with the group Steeleye Span recorded the 2001 album Arthur the King?

12. Which group recorded the 1976 album Rastaman Vibration?

13. In which year did The Damned first release the single New Rose?

14. Which group did Richard Hell form after leaving The Heartbreakers in 1976?

15. What is the full surname of singer-songwriter Ed Harcourt?

ANSWERS 1. Shirehorses 2. Free 3. The Wallflowers 4. Erykah Badu 5. Hex Enduction Hour 6. Hem 7. Jane's Addiction 8. American Music Club 9. Fat of the Land 10. 1968 11. Maddy Prior 12. Bob Marley and the Wailers 13. 1976 14. The Voidoids 15. Harcourt-Smith.

HISTORY

1. What was the Prisoners (Temporary Discharge for Ill-Health) Act of 1913 better known as?

2. In which English county was Sir Walter Raleigh born?

3. In which year did British naval officer George Vancouver die?

4. At what age did Edward I marry Eleanor of Castile?

5. Who was U.S. secretary of state from 1977-80?

6. In which year did President Nixon resign?

7. Who was vice-president of the U.S. from 1825-32?

8. What was the Barebones Parliament of 1653 previously known as?

9. In which year did Thomas Paine emigrate to Philadelphia?

10. In which year of World War One was the Battle of Caporetto?

11. Who led the Russian army in the Battle of Borodino?

12. In which month of 1909 did Louis Blériot cross the English Channel in an aeroplane?

13. In which year was the Battle of Friedland?

14. Who did Louis VII of France marry in 1137?

15. In which year did the Free-Soil Party originate in the U.S.?

ANSWERS 1. Cat and Mouse Act 2. Devon 3. 1798 4. Fifteen 5. Cyrus Vance 6. 1974 7. John Caldwell Calhoun 8. Parliament of Saints 9. 1774 10. 1917 11. Marshal Kutuzov 12. July 13. 1807 14. Eleanor of Aquitaine 15. 1848.

GENERAL KNOWLEDGE

1. Who was 1984 and 1988 Olympic men's springboard diving champion?

2. Who was the Mogul emperor of India from 1556-1605?

3. How many wickets did Alec Bedser take in his England Test career?

4. Who was the goddess of youth and spring in Greek mythology?

5. In which year did Roman historian Livy die?

6. Which city in central India was the site of a poisonous gas leak in 1984?

7. Which English soldier became military governor of Montreal in 1760?

8. Which actor's television roles included McLaren in the sitcom Porridge?

9. Who was a Best Supporting Actor Oscar nominee for the film Driving Miss Daisy?

10. Who wrote the 1965 novel The Looking-Glass War?

11. What was the name of the U.S. secretary of state who purchased Alaska?

12. What was the name of the chief of the Ottawa Indians, who led a rebellion against the British from 1763-6?

13. Who was the author of the novel The Cloister and the Hearth?

14. Which 18th century composer and organist composed the oratorio Jephtha?

15. Which Norwegian painter's works include 1893's The Scream?

ANSWERS 1. Greg Louganis 2. Akbar 3. 236 4. Hebe 5. 17 A.D. 6. Bhopal 7. Thomas Gage 8. Tony Osoba 9. Dan Aykroyd 10. John Le Carré 11. William Henry Seward 12. Pontiac 13. Charles Reade 14. John Stanley 15. Edvard Munch.

ENTERTAINMENT

1. Which Scot stars in the 1986 film The Name of the Rose?

2. Which comedienne was one of the six main cast members in the Channel Four sketch show Absolutely?

3. Which Hollywood director's animated creations include The Stain Boy?

4. What nationality is the tenor Giuseppe Di Stefano?

5. Which two comic actors star in the show The Strangerers on satellite television?

6. In which television puppet series did the character Atlanta Shore appear?

7. Who directed the 1961 film Underworld USA?

8. Which Emergency - Ward 10 actress replaced Ray Martine as presenter of the 1960s variety show All Stars and Garters?

9. Who won a Best Supporting Actor Oscar for the film Unforgiven?

10. Who did Grace Lee Whitney play in the 1960s television series Star Trek?

11. Which actor directed and starred in the 1966 film The Naked Prey?

12. In which year was comedian Lou Costello born?

13. Which film won Best Picture (Comedy/Musical) at the 2000 Golden Globes?

14. Who played Linda Sykes, later Baldwin, in Coronation Street?

15. Which musician directed and starred in the 1986 film Under the Cherry Moon?

ANSWERS 1. Sean Connery 2. Morwenna Banks 3. Tim Burton 4. Italian 5. Jack Docherty and Mark Williams 6. Stingray 7. Samuel Fuller 8. Jill Browne 9. Gene Hackman 10. Yeoman Janice Rand 11. Cornel Wilde 12. 1906 13. Toy Story 2 14. Jacqueline Pirie 15. Prince.

SPORT

1. What nationality was Olympic shooting champion Gudbrand Skatteboe?
2. How many laps did Jenson Button complete in his Formula 1 Grand Prix debut at Melbourne in 2000?
3. What nationality are Olympic canoeists Ulrich Papke and Ingo Spelly?
4. For which international Test cricket side does Trevor Gripper play?
5. Who was the 1980 men's world cross-country champion?
6. Cindy Devine was the 1990 women's downhill mountain biking champion. Which country did she represent?
7. Which sport do Will Green, Spencer Brown and Roy Winters play?
8. Mahmoud Karim was the 1946-9 British Open squash champion. Which country did he represent?
9. Which team won the 1980 Scottish F.A. Cup Final?
10. Which Australian motorcyclist is manager of the Nastro Azzurro Honda team?
11. At what weight does boxer Joe Calzaghe fight?
12. Which horse won the 1990 Cheltenham Gold Cup?
13. What nationality is cyclist Tom Steels?
14. Balazs Kiss was the 1996 Olympic hammer champion. Which country did he represent?
15. Which country won the 1975 Davis Cup in tennis?

POP MUSIC

1. Which member of Canned Heat died of a drug overdose in 1970?

2. What has been David Lee Roth's only U.K. Top 30 single?

3. In which year did blues singer Howlin' Wolf die?

4. What is the real name of Diana Ross?

5. In which year did Ron Wood join the Rolling Stones?

6. What was the lead track on the 1976 No. 1 The Roussos Phenomenon E.P.?

7. Who was the original drummer with the group The House of Love?

8. Who recorded the 1989 Top 10 single I Feel the Earth Move?

9. Which female singer had a 1995 hit single with Sexual?

10. Who played bass in The Housemartins?

11. In which year did blues singer Lightnin' Hopkins die?

12. Which reggae artist released the 1984 album Statement?

13. Marie Fredriksson and Per Gessle comprise which duo?

14. Damo Suzuki left the German group Can in 1973 to join which religious organisation?

15. What was the title of the debut album by Hothouse Flowers?

WORDS

1. What is a diaphone - a fog or a foghorn?

2. What might you do in the U.S. with a quirley?

3. Split pea is old rhyming slang for which beverage?

4. If you had the woofits, would you be happy or sad?

5. If something is clavate, what shape is it?

6. Soldan is an archaic word for what type of person?

7. Of what is a shoji made?

8. Where would you find a butt plate?

9. What is the U.S. name for the garment known in the U.K. as tights?

10. What does a prelector do?

11. Why might a surveyor use a fanion?

12. What length of imprisonment is implied by the term 'double sawbuck' in the U.S.?

13. Prad is a slang word for which animal?

14. What is aba - a type of wood or cloth?

15. What would a dapifer bring to a table?

ANSWERS 1. Foghorn 2. Smoke it, it's a cigarette 3. Tea 4. Sad, it's a slang term for depression 5. Club-shaped 6. Sultan 7. Rice paper 8. On a gun 9. Pantihose 10. Lecture in public 11. It's a small flag used to mark stations 12. Twenty years 13. Horse 14. Cloth 15. Meat.

GENERAL KNOWLEDGE

1. Who was a Best Actor Oscar winner for the film Scent of a Woman?

2. Who was the composer of the oratorio The Dream of Gerontius?

3. Who was 1990 and 1991 World Fresh Water angling individual champion?

4. In classical mythology, which princess of Tyre founded Carthage?

5. In which year did British landscape painter J.M.W. Turner die?

6. Who authored the 1960 play Ross?

7. In mathematics, what is the name given to an angle of less than 90°?

8. Who was the author of the novel The Girls of Slender Means?

9. What is the 22nd letter of the Greek alphabet?

10. Flush was the dog of which 19th century writer?

11. Which horse won the 1979 Epsom Derby?

12. Who was British prime minister from 1804-6?

13. Which food fish is also called an eulachon?

14. Which town in N.E. Iran was the birthplace of Omar Khayyam?

15. Who was a Best Actress Oscar nominee for the film The L-Shaped Room?

ANSWERS 1. Al Pacino 2. Sir Edward Elgar 3. Bob Nudd 4. Dido 5. 1851 6. Terence Rattigan 7. An acute angle 8. Muriel Spark 9. Chi 10. Elizabeth Barrett Browning 11. Troy 12. William Pitt (the Younger) 13. Candlefish 14. Nishapur 15. Leslie Caron.

ENTERTAINMENT

1. Under what name do the opera singers Karen England and Rebecca Knight perform?

2. Which actress played Empress Savina in the 2000 film Dungeons & Dragons?

3. Which 2001 film starred Morgan Freeman as Detective Alex Cross?

4. Who's the Boss was the U.S. version of which ITV sitcom?

5. Who played Roy Tate in the television drama series The Men From Shiloh?

6. Which character in the television drama EastEnders famously shot Phil Mitchell in 2001?

7. Who directed the 2001 film Mulholland Drive?

8. Who played Uncle Ernie in a 1973 Australian stage production of the rock opera Tommy?

9. What is Kirk Douglas's character's name in the 1949 film Champion?

10. Which Hollywood actor starred in the play Edward II in Sheffield in March 2001?

11. Who wrote and directed the 2000 film George Washington?

12. Julian Barratt and Noel Fielding comprise which comedy duo?

13. Who plays casino owner Terry Benedict in the 2001 film Ocean's Eleven?

14. Who directed the 2000 film Chopper?

15. Who directed the 2000 film The Original Kings of Comedy?

ANSWERS 1. Opera Babes 2. Thora Birch 3. Along Came a Spider 4. The Upper Hand 5. Lee Majors 6. Lisa 7. David Lynch 8. Keith Moon 9. 'Midge' Kelly 10. Joseph Fiennes 11. David Gordon Green 12. The Boosh 13. Andy Garcia 14. Andrew Dominik 15. Spike Lee.

SPORT

1. Who won the 1952 French Grand Prix in Formula 1?

2. By what score did Italy beat Scotland in the 2000 Six Nations tournament in rugby union?

3. How many goals did Jim Sullivan score for Wigan against Flimby and Fothergill in a 1925 rugby league Challenge Cup?

4. Who knocked Sheffield out of the 2000 Silk Cut Challenge Cup in rugby league?

5. Who won the professional Bowlers' Association's Tournament of Champions in 1987?

6. Which German cyclist won the 2000 Paris-Nice 'race to the sun'?

7. Who scored 917 runs in the Refuge Assurance League for Warwickshire in 1991?

8. How old was Andre Agassi when he first won a Wimbledon singles title?

9. Who was the men's combined exercises champion in gymnastics at the 1956 Olympic Games?

10. How many nations contested the men's events at the 1993 Taekwondo World Championships?

11. At what sport have Michel Daignault and Maryse Perreault been world champions?

12. What nationality is tennis player Hicham Arazi?

13. Which teams met in the 1984 U.E.F.A. Cup Final?

14. Who was the women's singles champion at the All-England Badminton Championships in 2000?

15. Which country's team won the men's I.A.A.F. world half-marathon championship in 1992 and 1993?

ANSWERS 1. Alberto Ascari 2. 34-20 3. 22 4. Thornhill 5. Pete Weber 6. Andreas Klöden 7. Tom Moody 8. 22 9. Viktor Chukarin 10. 82 11. Short-track speed skating 12. Moroccan 13. RSC Anderlecht and Tottenham Hotspur 14. Gong Zhichao 15. Kenya.

POP MUSIC

1. To which label did John Lee Hooker sign in 1955?

2. Which reggae artist released the 1979 compilation album Harder Than the Best?

3. What was the title of the second album by EMF?

4. Who had a 1999 No. 1 single with Blue (Da Ba Dee)?

5. What was The Royal Guardsmen's April 1967 follow-up to the single Snoopy vs. the Red Baron?

6. Which 1986 hit single featured the lyrics "We don't have the time for psychological romance"?

7. Who had a No.1 single in 1989 with All Around the World?

8. In which Australian city were the group The Hoodoo Gurus formed?

9. Which progressive rock group recorded the 1978 album Love Beach?

10. Who had a No. 1 single in 2000 with Pure Shores?

11. Who had a 2000 Top 10 single with Girl on TV?

12. Who recorded the 1968 solo album Oar?

13. Who recorded the 1999 album Approaching Silence?

14. Why did Nick Lowe entitle an E.P. of his Bowi?

15. Who had a No. 1 single in 2002 with The Hindu Times?

ANSWERS 1. Veejay 2. Burning Spear 3. Stigma 4. Eiffel 65 5. Return of the Red Baron 6. Word Up by Cameo 7. Lisa Stansfield 8. Sydney 9. E.L.P. 10. All Saints 11. Lyte Funkie Ones 12. Alexander Spence 13. David Sylvian 14. Because David Bowie entitled one of his albums Low 15. Oasis.

SCIENCE

1. In which century did French neurologist Jean Martin Charcot live?

2. What is SETI an acronym for?

3. What in computer science is OCR?

4. In which Australian city is the Powerhouse Museum?

5. Which company originally developed the computer mouse?

6. What is the only known satellite of the planet Pluto?

7. In which year did German scientist Franz Joseph Müller discover tellurium?

8. In which European capital was surgeon Sir Charles Bell born in 1774?

9. In which year was engineer Sir Clive Sinclair knighted?

10. Which British optician invented the achromatic object glass in 1757?

11. In which year did scientist André Marie Ampère die?

12. Which branch of physical science deals with the behaviour of light?

13. In which year was computer company Sun Microsystems Inc. founded?

14. What was the middle name of scientist James Joule?

15. In which year was the first smart card introduced, in France?

GENERAL KNOWLEDGE

1. Who was Chairman of the Parliamentary Labour Party from 1992-7?

2. Which city was known by the Romans as Lutetia?

3. Which actress in the television programme EastEnders won Sexiest Female prize at the 2001 British Soap Awards?

4. In which year did the aircraft designer Reginald Mitchell die?

5. From which country was the fifth secretary-general of the United Nations?

6. LC is the symbol for which airline?

7. In which city is Napier University?

8. What is the highest rank in the U.S. navy?

9. What was the 1998 BAFTA Best Film award winner?

10. Who is Conservative M.P. for Bromley and Chislehurst?

11. In which period of geological time was the malm epoch?

12. What was Emmeline Pankhurst's maiden name?

13. Which actor's volumes of memoirs include 1975's Bring on the Empty Horses?

14. Of which Nobel prize was Gunnar Myrdal a joint-winner in 1974?

15. In a 1991 census which of these Shetland Islands was more highly populated - Fetlar or Housay?

ANSWERS 1. Doug Hoyle 2. Paris 3. Tamzin Outhwaite 4. 1937 5. Peru 6. Loganair 7. Edinburgh 8. Fleet admiral 9. Shakespeare in Love 10. Eric Forth 11. Jurassic 12. Goulden 13. David Niven 14. Economics 15. Fetlar.

ENTERTAINMENT

1. Who directed the 1996 film Carla's Song?

2. Which two actors fight for the love of Elsa Martinelli in the 1963 film Rampage?

3. Who directed 1999 film Flawless starring Robert De Niro?

4. Which comedian voiced the role of Jasper the Owl in the children's television drama The Magician's House?

5. Which Oscar-nominated actress played Alison Little in the sitcom Chance in a Million?

6. Who directed the 1970 film Take a Girl Like You?

7. Which actress starred in the 1981 sitcom Chintz?

8. How much did the film The Blair Witch Project take at the U.K. box office in the first weekend of its release?

9. Which duo dance and sing the number At the Codfish Ball in the 1936 film Captain January?

10. Who created the television show Dawson's Creek?

11. Which political figure did Robert Donat play in the 1947 film Captain Boycott?

12. The 1986 film Tai-Pan is based on whose novel?

13. Which mother and daughter team were in the 1991 film Rambling Rose?

14. Which Scottish actor is associated with the company Fountainbridge Films?

15. Which duo wrote the sitcom Chelmsford 123?

ANSWERS 1. Ken Loach 2. Robert Mitchum and Jack Hawkins 3. Joel Schumacher 4. Stephen Fry 5. Brenda Blethyn 6. Jonathan Miller 7. Michele Dotrice 8. £5.87m 9. Buddy Ebsen and Shirley Temple 10. Kevin Williamson 11. Charles Parnell 12. James Clavell 13. Diane Ladd and Laura Dern 14. Sean Connery 15. Rory McGrath and Jimmy Mulville.

SPORT

1. Who succeeded Ellery Hanley as coach of St. Helens rugby league team in 2000?

2. How many times did trainer John Scott win the St. Leger?

3. What nationality is tennis player Lleyton Hewitt?

4. Between 1948 and 1973, how many classic races did trainer Noel Murless win?

5. For which rugby league side does Brett Goldsprink play?

6. Which county were women's world champions in pétanque in 1996?

7. Flintshire Fleece and Whitley Warriors compete at which sport?

8. Which country won the women's K1 team event from 1989-95 at the Canoe Slalom World Championships?

9. What nationality is skier Bente Martinsen?

10. Finn Kobbero and Per Neilsen were 1960 All-England Championships men's doubles badminton champions. Which country did they represent?

11. Who was men's show jumping champion at the 1957 European championships?

12. What nationality is runner Charles Kamathi?

13. Who was 1920 Olympic men's 400m freestyle swimming champion?

14. Which Aberdeen footballer was 1971 Scottish P.F.A. Player of the Year?

15. Which women's tennis players met in the final of the Champions Cup at Indian Wells in March 2000?

POP MUSIC

1. Which British songwriter's debut album is called Burning Dorothy?

2. Who is the lead singer in the group The Cardigans?

3. Who recorded the 1976 album Rock and Roll Heart?

4. In which year did XTC have a Top 20 hit with the single Making Plans For Nigel?

5. Which group recorded the 2001 single Getting Away With It?

6. Which rock group recorded the 1999 album Twisted Tenderness?

7. Which group recorded the 2001 album Cydonia?

8. In which year did M/A/R/R/S have a No. 1 single with the song Pump Up the Volume?

9. Which group recorded the 1996 album Crow Pot Pie?

10. Who were voted Rock 'N' Roll Group of the Year for 1967 by Rolling Stone magazine?

11. Which group recorded the 2000 album The Facts of Life?

12. Who recorded the 2001 chart single Daydream in Blue?

13. What was the debut album from the chart act Backyard Dog?

14. Who is the frontman of the group Elbow?

15. Who sings with P.J. Harvey on the track This Mess We're In from her album Tales From The City, Tales From The Sea?

ANSWERS 1. Thea Gilmore 2. Nina Persson 3. Lou Reed 4. 1979 5. James 6. Electronic 7. The Orb 8. 1987 9. Slobberbone 10. The Who 11. Black Box Recorder 12. I Monster 13. All in a Day 14. Gus Garvey 15. Thom Yorke.

PEOPLE

1. Which Radio 1 disc jockey was shot in July 1999?

2. Which illness did actor Michael J. Fox announce he had in 1999?

3. In which country was writer Jonas Lie born?

4. Which actress wrote the book How Was It For You?

5. Which architect did Harry Kendall Thaw murder in 1906?

6. Who was Foreign Secretary from 1989-95?

7. Who was married from 1973-8 to actress Ali McGraw?

8. Irish nationalist Charles Gavan Duffy became prime minister of which Australian state in 1871?

9. In which year did actor John Wells die?

10. Which football club does actor Joseph Fiennes support?

11. In which year did actor Burgess Meredith die?

12. What was the middle name of U.S. union leader Jimmy Hoffa?

13. In which year did alleged murderess Lizzie Borden die?

14. In which year did Johnny Depp and Kate Moss start dating?

15. In which year was the Duke of Edinburgh born?

ANSWERS 1. Tim Westwood 2. Parkinson's Disease 3. Norway 4. Maureen Lipman 5. Stanford White 6. Douglas Hurd 7. Steve McQueen 8. Victoria 9. 1998 10. Chelsea 11. 1997 12. Riddle 13. 1927 14. 1994 15. 1921.

ENTERTAINMENT

1. Which US female vocalist had a U.K. top five hit in 1982 with Heartbreaker?

2. Which 2000 Barry Levinson film featured Billy Connolly as a wig seller turned lunatic?

3. Which fictitious village was the setting for TV's Noel's House Party?

4. Which group, a front for Blur's Damon Albarn, released a self-titled album in 2001, featuring their top five hit, Clint Eastwood?

5. Which 1950s rock 'n' roller was immortalised by Lou Diamond Phillips in the 1987 movie La Bamba?

6. Which Emmerdale character stood trial for the murder and attempted murder of his wife and her lover in 2001?

7. Which member of the Jackson family hit the U.K. top five with the single All For You?

8. Which BBC1 drama featured Keith Barron as Superintendent Beausoleil and David Suchet as Inspector Borne?

9. Which 2001 film followed a girl from inner-city Chicago in her quest to study ballet at the Juilliard in New York?

10. What was the first album to be recorded on Richard Branson's Virgin label?

11. Which film featured Robert De Niro as a New York cop and Kelsey Grammer as a TV presenter?

12. Which US sitcom, based on a 1968 film, starred Tony Randall and Jack Klugman as incompatible friends?

13. Which Spice Girl hit the U.K. number one spot with her solo single What Took You So Long??

14. Which BBC2 series about the police force starred Katy Cavanagh as Mel?

15. Which Irish band's first U.K. top ten single was 1983's New Years Day?

GENERAL KNOWLEDGE

1. Who said "Any girl can look glamorous: all you have to do is stand still and look stupid"?

2. What is the name of the omnipotent head of state in 1984 by George Orwell?

3. What is the Red Planet better known as?

4. What is infectious mononucleosis more commonly known as?

5. Which American novelist wrote The Virginian?

6. Which zodiac sign is represented by the Archer?

7. From which country does Valpolicella wine originate?

8. Who wrote Swallows and Amazons?

9. Kym Marsh was the first member to leave which manufactured pop group?

10. Who wrote the books which were adapted for the TV series Jeeves and Wooster?

11. Who connects The Royle Family and Brookside?

12. Who was poet laureate from 1984-98?

13. Who created Chief Inspector Roderick Alleyn?

14. What is a flycatcher?

15. The Blue Ridge Mountains form part of which mountain system?

GENERAL KNOWLEDGE

1. What is the name of the summer camp featured in the Friday the 13th movies?

2. How many white stars are on the national flag of the United States of America?

3. In which year did the Gulf War take place?

4. Where was the soap opera Eldorado set?

5. Fitch is another name for which animal?

6. What is the name of the the captain in the novel Moby-Dick?

7. What word means the faculty of making fortunate discoveries accidentally?

8. In which country is Transylvania?

9. Which space shuttle exploded in 1986?

10. How many Pink Panther films did Peter Sellers appear in?

11. In which ocean does The Hunt For Red October take place?

12. In which century did the Gunpowder Plot take place?

13. Which novelist had the forename Huffam?

14. What was the name of the inept British agent in the comedy series 'Allo 'Allo!?

15. A howdah is a seat used for riding on the back of which animal?

ANSWERS: 1 Camp Crystal Lake, 2 50, 3 1991, 4 Spain (Los Barcos), 5 Polecat, 6 Ahab, 7 Serendipity, 8 Romania, 9 Challenger, 10 6, 11 The Atlantic, 12 17th, 13 Charles Dickens, 14 Officer Crabtree, 15 Elephant.

GENERAL KNOWLEDGE

1. What is another term for lockjaw?

2. Where is The French Lieutenant's Woman set?

3. The town of Glastonbury is in which English county?

4. In which country is The Good Earth by Pearl S Buck set?

5. In which country is the Tiber river?

6. What is the name of the family featured in the John Ford film The Grapes of Wrath?

7. Cumulus is a type of what?

8. Which horror film first featured the character Pinhead?

9. What is the name of the newspaper in the novel Scoop by Evelyn Waugh?

10. Which comedian played alongside Judi Dench in the film Mrs Brown?

11. How many novels did Emily Bronte write?

12. Who was the first American astronaut in space?

13. How many months do not have 31 days?

14. The adjective leonine refers to which animal?

15. Who wrote The Remains of the Day?

ANSWERS: 1 Tetanus, 2 Dorset, 3 Somerset, 4 China, 5 Italy, 6 Joad, 7 Cloud, 8 Hellraiser, 9 The Beast, 10 Billy Connolly, 11 One, 12 Alan Shepard, 13 Five, 14 Lion, 15 Kazuo Ishiguro

ENTERTAINMENT

1. Which blue cartoon stars had a 1996 U.K. top five hit with I've Got a Little Puppy?

2. Which 2000 film, set during the Cuban missile crisis in 1962, featured Kevin Costner as presidential advisor Kenny O'Donnell?

3. Who originally made up the Rainbow musical trio in the children's series along with Rod and Jane?

4. Which Parisian duo released an album entitled Discovery, featuring their hit One More Time?

5. In which 1968 film did Peter O'Toole play Henry II opposite Katharine Hepburn as Eleanor of Aquitaine?

6. Who was the presenter of the 2001 Channel 5 endurance game show Touch the Truck?

7. Which legendary actress is quoted as saying, "I never said I want to be alone. I only said I want to be let alone."?

8. Who presented Planet for the Apes, a three-part BBC 2 documentary about primates?

9. What was the title of the debut album by the manufactured group Hear'Say?

10. What was the name of the institution in the ITV drama series Bad Girls?

11. Which film, set during the siege of Stalingrad, starred British actors Jude Law, Rachel Weisz and Joseph Fiennes?

12. What sort of animal was 'Rag' in the 1950s children's series Rag, Tag and Bobtail?

13. Who had a UK top five single with Butterfly in 2001?

14. Which late British actor once said, "I have a face that's a cross between two pounds of halibut and an explosion in an old-clothes closet."?

15. Which TV presenting duo had a 1994 U.K. top ten hit with Let's Get Ready to Rhumble under the guise of PJ & Duncan?

ANSWERS: 1 The Smurfs, 2 Thirteen Days, 3 Matthew (Corbett), 4 Daft Punk, 5 The Lion in Winter, 6 Dale Winton, 7 Greta Garbo, 8 Charlotte Uhlenbroek, 9 Popstars, 10 Larkhall (Women's) Prison, 11 Enemy at the Gates, 12 A hedgehog, 13 Crazy Town, 14 David Niven, 15 Ant & Dec.

? GENERAL KNOWLEDGE ?

1. What is the chemical symbol for tungsten?

2. Which then chancellor of the exchequer introduced old age pensions in 1908?

3. Which gangland movie was based on Shakespeare's Macbeth?

4. Who wrote the novel Castle Rackrent?

5. What was the job of the Nicolas Cage character Ronny Cammareri in Moonstruck?

6. Who directed the 1973 film The Exorcist?

7. What nationality was the composer Edward Elgar?

8. What was The Beast in the 1988 film?

9. Cicely Fairfield took the name Rebecca West from a play by which dramatist?

10. How many sides does a nonagon have?

11. Which former Tomorrow's World presenter previously appeared on Multi-Coloured Swap Shop?

12. The Thomas Hardy novel title Far From The Madding Crowd is a quotation from which poet?

13. Which Last of the Summer Wine actor provided voices for animated film The Wrong Trousers?

14. The film O Brother Where Art Thou contains references to which classical text?

15. Which well-known actress is quoted as saying "I am a woman who is unfaithful to a million men."?

ANSWERS: 1 W, 2 David Lloyd George, 3 Men of Respect, 4 Maria Edgeworth, 5 Baker, 6 William Friedkin, 7 English, 8 A tank, 9 Henrik Ibsen, 10 9, 11 Maggie Philbin, 12 Thomas Gray, 13 Peter Sallis, 14 The Odyssey, 15 Greta Garbo.

GENERAL KNOWLEDGE

1. What is the first sign of the zodiac?

2. What is the surname of Rabbit in books by John Updike?

3. Game for a Laugh was based on which American TV show?

4. The plot of which film was relocated to Asia for the 1982 remake Far East?

5. What country did the cricketer Sunil Gavaskar play for?

6. Who wrote the autobiography My Left Foot?

7. In which game might one encounter a zugzwang?

8. What is the capital of Indonesia?

9. Which veteran actor played the Dad of Ted Danson in the 1989 film?

10. Jean Valjean is the hero of which novel?

11. Which actress had the original name Mary Cathleen Collins?

12. Who wrote the novel The Newcomes?

13. What is the standard monetary unit of Spain?

14. Who devised the TV series Thunderbirds?

15. Who created the detective Adam Dalgliesh?

ANSWERS: 1 Aries, 2 Angstrom, 3 People Are Funny, 4 Casablanca, 5 India, 6 Christy Brown, 7 Chess, 8 Jakarta, 9 Jack Lemmon, 10 Les Miserables, 11 Bo Derek, 12 William Makepeace Thackeray, 13 Peseta, 14 Gerry Anderson, 15 P D James.

GENERAL KNOWLEDGE

1. Who wrote The Wind in the Willows?

2. What does the word moribund mean?

3. What was the surname of the Little Women in the book by Louisa M Alcott?

4. Who plays the part of Phil Mitchell in EastEnders?

5. Which novel by Charles Kingsley is set in the 16th century?

6. What is the first name of Gulliver in the book by Jonathan Swift?

7. What is the technical name for the human thighbone?

8. The sweetheart of Yogi Bear in the cartoon was called what?

9. In which country is Yellowstone National Park?

10. Soap opera Knots Landing was a spin-off from which other soap?

11. Which future prime minister wrote the 1832 novel Contarini Fleming?

12. Who directed the 1941 film Citizen Kane?

13. Who was the first Tudor king of England?

14. What is the capital of Wales?

15. Who wrote All Quiet on the Western Front?

ANSWERS: 1 Kenneth Grahame, 2 Near death, 3 March, 4 Steve McFadden, 5 Westward Ho, 6 Lemuel, 7 Femur, 8 Cindy Bear, 9 USA, 10 Dallas, 11 Benjamin Disraeli, 12 Orson Welles, 13 Henry VII, 14 Cardiff, 15 Erich Maria Remarque.

SPORT

1. Which country denied England's rugby union team a Six Nations Championship grand slam in 2000?

2. What is the maximum number of clubs a player is allowed to carry on a round of golf?

3. What nationality was legendary motor racing driver Juan Manuel Fangio?

4. What did Stephen Roche become the first Irishman to win in 1987?

5. Of which TV sports chat show was John Inverdale the host?

6. Which country beat Italy in the final to win football's Euro 2000?

7. Who was the first British golfer to win the U.S. Masters?

8. What is the highest score possible with three darts?

9. Who is the only player to skipper two British Lions tours?

10. At which course did Europe famously win the Ryder Cup in 1985?

11. Who won the women's singles title at the 2000 Wimbledon tennis championships?

12. Which bowler took a wicket with his first-ever delivery in an Ashes Test in 1993?

13. Jose Napoles and John H Stracey are former champions from which sport?

14. From which club did Liverpool sign Stan Collymore for £8.5m in 1995?

15. At which course is the Derby held?

GENERAL KNOWLEDGE

1. Which state is the biggest producer of oil and gas in the USA?

2. Which Star Trek film has the subtitle The Voyage Home?

3. Paul Keating was prime minister of which country from 1991-96?

4. Which Channel 5 game show featured a hidden saboteur?

5. Richard Hadlee and Dennis Lillee are former players of which sport?

6. What type of instrument is a xylophone?

7. In which country was Treasure of the Sierra Madre set?

8. The bacterial disease glanders can be passed on to humans from which animal?

9. What was the first novel by Martin Amis?

10. For which series did ex-Mission Impossible stars Martin Landau and Barbara Bain team up again?

11. Which bejewelled item was the target of the thieves in Topkapi?

12. In which novel by Charles Dickens does Captain Cuttle appear?

13. Which film star was born Julia Turner?

14. What name does Trigger insist on calling Rodney in Only Fools and Horses?

15. Who wrote the Goosebumps series of novels for children?

ANSWERS: 1 Texas, 2 IV, 3 Australia, 4 The Mole, 5 Cricket, 6 Percussion, 7 Mexico, 8 Horse, 9 The Rachel Papers, 10 Space 1999, 11 A dagger, 12 Dombey and Son, 13 Lana Turner, 14 Dave, 15 R L Stine.

GENERAL KNOWLEDGE

1. Who wrote the novel Oranges Are Not the Only Fruit?

2. What was the first name of Mr Smart in Get Smart?

3. Which composer is associated with the film The Sting?

4. Which film told the story of Billy Hayes and his stay in a Turkish jail?

5. Which house does Harry Potter belong to in the novels by J. K. Rowling?

6. Which Morgan Freeman film is a remake of the 1981 film Garde A Vue?

7. Who sang the theme song for The Adventures of Champion?

8. Which feminist author wrote The Second Sex?

9. Which original Charlie's Angel played Mrs King in The Scarecrow and Mrs King?

10. What is the first novel of the Alexandria Quartet by Lawrence Durrell?

11. Who wrote the TV series Only Fools And Horses?

12. Pulque is a light alcoholic drink from which country?

13. Who wrote The Catcher in the Rye?

14. Which Bond film was the last to use a title written by Ian Fleming?

15. What is the chemical symbol for zinc?

GENERAL KNOWLEDGE

1. Where was Gilligans Island?

2. Dabs is a slang name for what?

3. Who directed the 1993 film Schindlers List?

4. Who is the subject of the novel Rookwood by Harrison Ainsworth?

5. Which is the first book of the Old Testament?

6. How many people make up an octet?

7. What is the largest city in Australia?

8. What was the name of the road where the cartoon character Mr Benn lived?

9. Who wrote the novel Stuart Little?

10. Who was the first Hanoverian king of Great Britain and Ireland?

11. The title of the ecological documentary Koyaanisqatsi comes from the Hopi for what?

12. A rickshaw would typically be used in parts of which continent?

13. Who wrote the novel Manhattan Transfer?

14. Who wrote the novel The Murder of Roger Ackroyd?

15. In which year was British entrepreneur Richard Branson born?

ANSWERS: 1 South Pacific, 2 Fingerprints, 3 Steven Spielberg, 4 Dick Turpin, 5 Genesis, 6 Eight, 7 Sydney, 8 Festive Road, 9 E B White, 10 George I, 11 Crazy life, 12 Asia, 13 John Dos Passos, 14 Agatha Christie, 15 1950.

ENTERTAINMENT

1. Which actress followed in her late father's footsteps by starring in the BBC1 series Ballykissangel?

2. Which British group had U.K. number one hits in the '70s with Tiger Feet and Oh Boy?

3. Which 2000 Oscar-nominated film starred Juliette Binoche as the owner of a chocolate shop?

4. Which member of the Monkees played Ena Sharples' grandson Colin Lomax in Coronation Street in 1961?

5. Who had a U.K. top ten hit with the dance track I Wanna Be U in 2001?

6. Which two actors teamed up to star in films including Silver Streak, Stir Crazy and Another You?

7. Which young yachtswoman was the subject of a BBC1 documentary following her progress in the Vendee Globe round-the-world race?

8. Which Welsh band had a U.K. top five hit with Mr Writer?

9. Which ITV soap opera returned to our screens in 2001 after a thirteen year break?

10. Which actor played a serial killer being pursued by James Spader's FBI agent in the 2000 film The Watcher?

11. Who played Welsh Sergeant Major B.L. Williams in the TV sitcom It Ain't Half Hot Mum?

12. Which Billy Joel song was taken to the U.K. number one spot by Westlife in aid of Comic Relief 2001?

13. Which 1986 film featured Richard Gere as Eddie Jillette, an undercover cop?

14. Which duo presented The Brit Awards 2002, shown on ITV?

15. What was the first name of Sigourney Weaver's character Ripley in the Alien series of films?

ANSWERS: 1 Susannah Doyle, 2 Mud, 3 Chocolat, 4 Davy Jones, 5 Chocolate Puma, 6 Richard Pryor & Gene Wilder, 7 Ellen MacArthur (Sailing Through Hell), 8 Stereophonics, 9 Crossroads, 10 Keanu Reeves, 11 Windsor Davies, 12 Uptown Girl, 13 No Mercy, 14 Frank Skinner and Zoe Ball, 15 Ellen.

GENERAL KNOWLEDGE

1. Where was The Jewel in the Crown set?

2. Who took over the role of The Saint from Roger Moore?

3. How many minutes are there in a day?

4. Who wrote the autobiographies Present Indicative and Future Indefinite?

5. What is the twelfth sign of the zodiac?

6. Which American city is nicknamed the Windy City?

7. What does a fletcher make?

8. How many inches make up a yard?

9. How many pints make up a gallon?

10. Jigsaw was the first book by which prolific novelist?

11. What sort of animal is Snowball in Animal Farm by George Orwell?

12. Take My Breath Away was the 1986 Oscar-winning song from which film?

13. What was the maiden name of former prime minister Margaret Thatcher?

14. In which government ministry was Yes Minister set?

15. Mount Logan is the highest peak in which country?

ANSWERS: 1 India, 2 Ian Ogilvy, 3 1440, 4 Noel Coward, 5 Pisces, 6 Chicago, 7 Arrows, 8 36, 9 8, 10 Barbara Cartland, 11 A pig, 12 Top Gun, 13 Roberts, 14 Administrative Affairs, 15 Canada.

GENERAL KNOWLEDGE

1. Which Bond film title was taken from a seventeenth century Japanese poem?

2. Which university broadcasts through the night on BBC2?

3. What nationality was Sigrid Undset who won the Nobel Prize for literature in 1928?

4. What is the capital of the Bahamas?

5. What was the name of the Charlie Chaplin role in most of his films?

6. What was the name of the car in The Love Bug?

7. The gestation period of an elephant lasts approximately how many days?

8. What pen name does J K Rowling use as the author of Fantastic Beasts and Where to Find Them?

9. Children's TV favourite Pingu was created in which country?

10. In which year was the X certificate introduced?

11. Who directed the 1991 film The Commitments?

12. Who wrote Finnegans Wake?

13. A griffin has the body of which animal?

14. What is the highest ranking officer in the British army?

15. Which pop star appeared in the 1992 film Freejack?

ANSWERS: 1 You Only Live Twice, 2 Open University, 3 Norwegian, 4 Nassau, 5 Little Tramp, 6 Herbie, 7 624, 8 Newt Scamander, 9 Norway, 10 1950, 11 Alan Parker, 12 James Joyce, 13 Lion, 14 Field Marshal, 15 Mick Jagger.

GENERAL KNOWLEDGE

1. Who was the first wife of Henry VIII?

2. Who played Fred in the 1994 film The Flintstones?

3. What type of animal is a pointer?

4. Who created the detective Sam Spade?

5. What is another name for the aurora borealis?

6. Which member of the Ingalls family was the narrator of Little House on the Prairie?

7. In which American state is Silicon Valley?

8. Which rock star was born Reginald Dwight?

9. When did Tony Blair become leader of the Labour Party?

10. Which classic film was based on the play Everybody Goes To Ricks?

11. Which child star sued Graham Greene for libel?

12. The novel Wide Sargasso Sea by Jean Rhys is a prequel to which classic novel?

13. Who had a U.K. number one hit in 1996 with Spaceman?

14. On television, who was smarter than the average bear?

15. In which war did the battle of Leyte Gulf take place?

ANSWERS: 1 Catherine of Aragon, 2 John Goodman, 3 Dog, 4 Dashiell Hammett, 5 Northern lights, 6 Laura, 7 California, 8 Elton John, 9 1994, 10 Casablanca, 11 Shirley Temple, 12 Jane Eyre, 13 Babylon Zoo, 14 Yogi, 15 World War II.

ENTERTAINMENT

1. Which veteran entertainer was the host of the ITV show Tonight at the London Palladium?

2. Who played Maximus Decimus Meridius in the 2000 film epic Gladiator?

3. Which BBC1 series starred Dervla Kirwan as Emma Rose, a woman in love with her husband's brother?

4. What was the title of Britney Spears' second album release?

5. Which actress played Sister Anna Kirkwall in ITV's drama series Where the Heart Is?

6. Which U.S. teen singer released an album in 2000 entitled I Wanna Be With You, featuring the hit single Candy?

7. Which actress played Freddie's wife in the Sixties sitcom Meet the Wife?

8. Which former Hollywood couple appeared in the 1967 film version of Doctor Faustus?

9. Which ITV drama series featured James Fox as the billionaire Milton Friedkin?

10. Who had Lovesick Blues at number one in 1962?

11. Which U.S. girl group had a 1963 top five hit with Da Doo Ron Ron?

12. Which comic actor played the late stand-up comedian Andy Kaufman in the 1999 film Man on the Moon?

13. Which BBC1 documentary series followed the progress of the inhabitants of the remote island of Taransay during 2000?

14. Which legendary U.S. vocalist had a top five single in 1969 with Lay Lady Lay?

15. Which giant actor played the title role in the 1983 film Hercules?

ANSWERS: 1 Bruce Forsyth, 2 Russell Crowe, 3 Hearts and Bones, 4 Oops!...I Did It Again, 5 Lesley Dunlop, 6 Mandy Moore, 7 Thora Hird, 8 Richard Burton & Elizabeth Taylor, 9 Metropolis, 10 Frank Ifield, 11 The Crystals, 12 Jim Carrey, 13 Castaway 2000, 14 Bob Dylan, 15 Lou Ferrigno.

? **GENERAL KNOWLEDGE** ?

1. What is the plant osmunda regalis commonly known as?

2. As at April 1st, 1998, what were the three Trident submarines in HM Fleet?

3. In which city is the University of Strathclyde?

4. Which country was known by the Romans as Lusitania?

5. Rickets is a symptom of which vitamin deficiency?

6. From which country is the seventh secretary-general of the United Nations, Kofi Annan?

7. Where in the body would you find the sartorius muscle group?

8. How many hours ahead of G.M.T. is Brunei?

9. What is the meaning of the common abbreviation B.D.A.?

10. What does a hippophile have a love of?

11. Which gas forms a larger percentage of the air by volume - hydrogen or krypton?

12. Which was the busiest international airport in the world in 2000?

13. Which is the only native tree squirrel in Europe?

14. In which year did the footballer Bobby Moore win his first international cap?

15. What is the house plant peltiphyllum peltatum commonly known as?

ANSWERS: 1 Royal fern, 2 Vanguard, Vigilant and Victorious, 3 Glasgow, 4 Portugal, 5 D, 6 Burma, 7 Thigh, 8 Eight, 9 British Dental Association, 10 Horses, 11 Krypton, 12 Atlanta (80 million passengers), 13 Red squirrel, 14 1962, 15 Umbrella plant.

GENERAL KNOWLEDGE

1. Who is the Hindu god of fire?

2. In which European country might one be awarded the Order of the Elephant?

3. What is the correct form of spoken address to a viscount?

4. Which country had the larger estimated population in 1998 - France or Turkey?

5. SK is the abbreviation of which Canadian province?

6. In which year was the University of East Anglia founded - 1963, 1973 or 1983?

7. What in Islam is the difference between an Imam and an imam?

8. In which month does the Spanish fir flower - May or June?

9. In which U.S city is the Henry Ford Museum?

10. Why is a honey-buzzard so called?

11. In heraldry, what colour is sable?

12. Of what is tachophobia the fear?

13. What is the meaning of the common abbreviation D.F.C.?

14. How many hours behind G.M.T. is Venezuela?

15. In which decade did Japan join the United Nations?

ANSWERS: 1 Agni, 2 Denmark, 3 My Lord, 4 Turkey, 5 Saskatchewan, 6 1963, 7 The former is a descendant of Ali, the latter is a prayer leader, 8 May, 9 Detroit, 10 It feeds at the nests of bees and wasps, 11 Black, 12 Speed, 13 Distinguished Flying Cross, 14 Four, 15 The 1950s.

GENERAL KNOWLEDGE

1. Where are the headquarters of the European Investment Bank?

2. In which city is the independent Clifton College?

3. Which shipping forecast area lies immediately east of Shannon - Fastnet or Dogger?

4. In which group of islands would you find Stronsay or Shapinsay?

5. Which place in the British Isles was known by the Romans as Dubris?

6. Which book of the Bible has more chapters - Exodus or Genesis?

7. Which country had the larger estimated population in 1998 - Japan or Pakistan?

8. Which letter of the Greek alphabet is the equivalent of the letter e?

9. What does a bibliophile have a love of?

10. What is the correct form of spoken address to a cardinal?

11. Which children's television series featured the characters King Dithers and Squish?

12. Which treaty ended the Thirty Years' War in 1648?

13. Who was the first President of Wolfson College, Oxford?

14. In which month is Tynwald Day on the Isle of Man?

15. Which U.S. state is larger in area - Connecticut or Hawaii?

SPORT

1. In which U.S. state was Maurice Greene born?

2. A scrum half in rugby union would wear which number on his back?

3. Which country hosted the 1968 Olympic Games?

4. Who was the Formula One world champion in 1996?

5. Which country won the rugby union World Cup in 1991?

6. Which horse won the 2000 Grand National at Aintree?

7. Which boxer was known as the Brown Bomber?

8. What nationality is cricketer Shaun Pollock?

9. Which team won the F.A. Cup in 1979?

10. With which sport is the Queensberry rules associated?

11. In which field event did Jonathan Edwards claim Olympic gold in Sydney?

12. Which country won the cricket World Cup in 1996?

13. What nationality is tennis player Lleyton Hewitt?

14. Which Spanish team lost to Manchester United in the final of the European Cup Winners Cup in 1991?

15. How many majors did golfer Tony Jacklin win?

ANSWERS: 1 Kansas, 2 Nine, 3 Mexico, 4 Damon Hill, 5 Australia, 6 Papillon, 7 Joe Louis, 8 South African, 9 Arsenal, 10 Boxing, 11 The triple jump, 12 Sri Lanka, 13 Australian, 14 Barcelona, 15 Two.

GENERAL KNOWLEDGE

1. In which year was the U.N. Earth Summit in Rio?

2. Which U.S. state is larger in area - Iowa or Georgia?

3. Which political party did Millard Fillmore represent as U.S. president from 1850-3?

4. Scurvy is a symptom of which vitamin deficiency?

5. What is the name given to the red food colouring E120?

6. In 20th century politics, what was the meaning of the common abbreviation A.N.C.?

7. What material is traditionally associated with a 13th wedding anniversary?

8. What does a philatelist collect?

9. What is the highest civilian peacetime decoration in the United States?

10. What in heraldry is a pile?

11. Which period of geological time saw the appearance of the first insects?

12. Which U.S. state did Hurricane Carla devastate in 1961, killing 50 people?

13. Which is closest to the approximate driving distance in miles between London and Berlin - 568 miles, 658 miles or 865 miles?

14. Which European airline is sometimes represented by the initials EI?

15. Who wrote the science fiction classic I, Robot?

ANSWERS: 1 1992, 2 Georgia, 3 Whig, 4 C, 5 Cochineal, 6 African National Congress, 7 Lace, 8 Stamps, 9 Presidential Medal of Freedom, 10 Inverted pyramid, 11 Devonian, 12 Texas, 13 658 miles, 14 Aer Lingus, 15 Columbia University, Isaac Asimov.

GENERAL KNOWLEDGE

1. Why is a barnacle goose so called?

2. Which British king led his army against France in 1743 at Dettingen?

3. Which London theatre was founded by entrepreneur Richard Sadler in 1683?

4. In which U.S. state was the athlete Jesse Owens born?

5. Who penned the book Angus, Thongs and Full-Frontal Snogging: Confessions of Georgia Nicolson?

6. What is the plant tellima grandiflora commonly known as?

7. In which month does the silver fir tree flower - April or August?

8. In which city is the Central Ballet of China located?

9. What was the 1997 BAFTA Best Film award winner?

10. BY is the symbol for which airline?

11. In which period of geological time was the wenlock epoch?

12. What is the highest rank in the German air force?

13. What was the most popular name for a boy in England and Wales in the 1990's?

14. Which letter of the Greek alphabet is the equivalent of the letter t?

15. How many hours behind GMT is Panama?

ANSWERS: 1 From the old belief that the bird hatched from goose barnacles, 2 George II, 3 Sadler's Wells, 4 Alabama, 5 Louise Rennison, 6 Fringe cups, 7 April, 8 Beijing, 9 The Full Monty, 10 Britannia Airways, 11 Silurian, 12 General, 13 Daniel, 14 Tau, 15 Five.

GENERAL KNOWLEDGE

1. What is the average gestation period, in days, of a sheep - 28 weeks or 21 weeks?

2. Who took over as president of the European Union Commission in 1985?

3. In which year did Israel join the United Nations?

4. Which place in the British Isles was known by the Romans as Luguvalium?

5. In which city was the playwright Christopher Marlowe born?

6. In which English city is the independent Repton School?

7. Which English national newspaper did William Deedes edit?

8. From which country was the maidenhair-tree introduced into Europe?

9. Which country's national anthem is entitled La Brabançonne?

10. Which gas forms a larger percentage of the air by volume - helium or neon?

11. In heraldry, if an animal is statant how is it represented?

12. What would you have if you were awarded a D.C.M.?

13. What is the most frequently used word in the spoken English language?

14. Which country had the least seats in the European Parliament in 1999?

15. What is the common name for the tree Quercus?

ENTERTAINMENT

1. In which year did Free have a U.K. hit for the second time with All Right Now?

2. What type of animals were the title characters of the 2000 film The Adventures of Rocky and Bullwinkle?

3. What was the British title of the manic gameshow Jeux Sans Frontieres?

4. Which Spice Girl hit the U.K. top five in 2001 with Feels So Good?

5. In which 1975 film did Michael Caine and Glenda Jackson star as husband and wife?

6. Which Emmerdale character married mysterious hosiery salesman Bob in 2001?

7. With whom did Ricky Martin collaborate on the 2001 U.K. top five single Nobody Wants to be Lonely?

8. Which actress took on the role of FBI agent Clarice Starling in the 2001 film sequel Hannibal?

9. What was the title of the 2001 hit single by Shaggy featuring Rikrok, which knocked Atomic Kitten off the U.K. number one spot?

10. Which actor played Detective Chief Inspector Jim Taggart in the TV drama series Taggart until his death in 1994?

11. Which actor appeared as Dithers the gardener to Ronnie Barker's Lord Rustless in the sitcom Hark at Barker?

12. Which song provided U.K. number one hits for both Tab Hunter in 1957 and Donny Osmond in 1973?

13. Which 1989 baseball movie featured Tom Berenger and Charlie Sheen as team-mates?

14. In which Channel 4 series did Goodness, Gracious Me star Sanjeev Bhaskar search for the truth about the Kama Sutra?

15. Which Irish singer had a 2001 U.K. top five hit with Always Come Back to Your Love?

ANSWERS: 1 1991, 2 A moose & a flying squirrel, 3 It's a Knockout, 4 Melanie B, 5 The Romantic Englishwoman, 6 Viv Windsor, 7 Christina Aguilera, 8 Julianne Moore, 9 It Wasn't Me, 10 Mark McManus, 11 David Jason, 12 Young Love, 13 Major League, 14 Position Impossible, 15 Samantha Mumba.

GENERAL KNOWLEDGE

1. What in computing does the abbreviation GIF stand for?

2. Who became leader of the Labour Party in 1980?

3. What is the colour of the head of a male mallard?

4. Which ocean is larger - the Indian or Atlantic?

5. In which European country are the provinces of Has and Mat?

6. In which group of islands would you find Benbecula and Harris?

7. Which Australian cricketer scored 152 against England in the 1st innings of the 1st Test in 2001?

8. What is the plant taraxacum officinale commonly known as?

9. In which period of geological time was the miocene epoch?

10. How many hours ahead of GMT is Estonia?

11. Which European city was known by the Romans as Olisipo?

12. How much did Nokia's first mobile phone, the Mobira Senator, weigh when it was introduced in 1982 - 1.7 kg or 9.8 kg?

13. As what is Schubert's 1819 Quintet in A major known?

14. Who was Secretary of State for Scotland from 1986-90?

15. What type of creature is a wels?

ANSWERS: 1 Graphic Image Format, 2 Michael Foot, 3 Dark green, 4 Atlantic, 5 Albania, 6 The Hebrides, 7 Adam Gilchrist, 8 Dandelion, 9 Tertiary, 10 Two, 11 Lisbon, 12 9.8kg, 13 The Trout Quintet, 14 Malcolm Rifkind, 15 Fish.

GENERAL KNOWLEDGE

1. In which month does the Corsican pine flower - June or September?

2. Which U.S. state did Hurricane Juan devastate in 1985?

3. Which period of geological time saw the extinction of dinosaurs?

4. How many hours ahead of GMT is Cambodia?

5. What is the average gestation period, in days, of an African elephant - 26 weeks or 91 weeks?

6. Which country was known by the Romans as Caledonia?

7. Which racehorse won the 2001 Epsom Derby?

8. Who succeeded Lord Parkinson as Chairman of the Conservative Party in 1998?

9. What is the plant onopordum acanthium commonly known as?

10. AF is the symbol for which European airline?

11. In a car, what is an A.B.S.?

12. Which country had the larger estimated population in 1998 - Egypt or Vietnam?

13. In which year was Snowdonia designated a National Park - 1951 or 1926?

14. In the Bible, who was the first-born son of Isaac?

15. What colour is the crown of a green woodpecker?

ANSWERS: 1 June, 2 Louisiana, 3 Cretaceous, 4 Seven, 5 640 days, 6 Scotland, 7 Galileo, 8 Michael Ancram, 9 Scottish thistle, 10 Air France, 11 Anti-locking braking system, 12 Vietnam, 13 1951, 14 Esau, 15 Red.

GENERAL KNOWLEDGE

1. What nationality is the sculptor Oscar Niemeyer?

2. Which rank is higher in the Army - Colonel or Major?

3. Of which country did Silvio Berlusconi become prime minister in 2001?

4. In which decade did United Arab Emirates join the United Nations?

5. What is the meaning of the common abbreviation C.A.B.?

6. What is the correct form of spoken address to a Roman Catholic archbishop?

7. Which country's national anthem is entitled La Concorde?

8. How many M.P.s were elected at the 2001 general election - 622 or 659?

9. What is the name of the twin rotor transport helicopter used by the R.A.F.?

10. In which city is the independent Bootham School?

11. Which book of the Bible has more chapters - Jonah or Micah?

12. From which country was the first secretary-general of the United Nations?

13. What was the most popular name for a boy in England and Wales in the 1960s?

14. In heraldry, if an animal is sejant how is it represented?

15. What is the smallest European owl?

ANSWERS: 1 Brazilian, 2 Colonel, 3 Italy, 4 1970s, 5 Citizens Advice Bureau, 6 Your Grace, 7 Gabon, 8 659, 9 Chinook, 10 York, 11 Jonah, 12 Norway, 13 Paul, 14 Sitting, 15 Pygmy owl.

ENTERTAINMENT

1. What was the name of the cook in the Nineties sitcom You Rang M'Lord?

2. Which British band entered the U.K. top ten with two different singles in the same week in 2001?

3. Which British author wrote the book upon which the 1984 film The Little Drummer Girl was based?

4. Which Brookside character married Fred, the Brazilian lover of her friend Lance, in 2001?

5. Which controversial rap star appeared at the 2001 Brit Awards with a mask and chainsaw?

6. Who has presented the TV series Don't Try This At Home and and The Vault?

7. Which vocalist had a 2001 U.K. top five hit with I'm Like a Bird?

8. In which BBC1 series did Alice Evans play Diane, an air stewardess leading two lives?

9. Which sport featured in the 2000 film The Legend of Bagger Vance?

10. Which Eighties television series starred Wendy Craig as Barbara Gray?

11. Which late British actor starred in the title role of the 1973 film Hitler - The Last Ten Days?

12. Who presented the BBC 1 Comic Relief quiz show 1000 to One in 2001?

13. Which anarchic punk band had a U.K. top five hit in 1977 with God Save the Queen?

14. What type of animal is the Emperor turned into in the 2000 Disney movie The Emperor's New Groove?

15. Which BBC2 series followed horticulturalists Gordon Taylor and Guy Cooper on their travels around Britain?

GENERAL KNOWLEDGE

1. What colour legs has a rock partridge?

2. Who became Secretary of State for International Development following the 2001 general election?

3. Which pair starred in the 2001 romantic comedy film Sweet November?

4. In which year was Melvyn Bragg made a life peer?

5. What in Sikhism is a kara?

6. Who wrote the novel The Mystery of Edwin Drood?

7. In which city are the headquarters of the U.N. agency UNESCO?

8. In which decade did Jamaica enter the Commonwealth?

9. What in heraldry is the chief?

10. Where does the stripe run on a striped field mouse?

11. What is the plant ranunculus acris commonly known as?

12. In which U.S. state was the jazz composer Thelonious Monk born?

13. In which year did Kingston upon Hull achieve city status - 1963 or 1897?

14. Which Yorkshire town was known by the Romans as Danum?

15. How many hours ahead of GMT is Guam - 10 or 12?

ANSWERS: 1 Red, 2 Clare Short, 3 Keanu Reeves and Charlize Theron, 4 1998, 5 Steel bangle, 6 Charles Dickens, 7 Paris, 8 1960s, 9 The top third of a shield, 10 From the nape of the neck to the base of the tail, 11 The common buttercup, 12 North Carolina, 13 1897, 14 Doncaster, 15 Ten.

GENERAL KNOWLEDGE

1. Which letter of the Greek alphabet is the equivalent of the letter p?

2. What is the meaning of the common abbreviation CCTV?

3. AI is the symbol for which airline?

4. Which country's national anthem is entitled Hymne Monegasque?

5. In which city was president Ronald Reagan shot in 1981?

6. Who was Secretary of State for Health from 1997 to 1999?

7. In the Bible, who was the sixth son of Jacob?

8. In which African country is the state of Ebonyi?

9. What is the plant primula variabilis commonly known as?

10. In which European country might you find a spectacled salamander?

11. Which letter in Morse code is indicated by two dashes?

12. Which U.S. state did Hurricane Hilda affect in 1964 - Louisiana or Florida?

13. In which period of geological time was the Caradoc epoch?

14. In which South American country is the Itatinga waterfall?

15. As what has crystallophobia been defined - the fear of crystals or the fear of the colour green?

ANSWERS: 1 Pi, 2 Closed-circuit television, 3 Air India, 4 Monaco, 5 Washington, 6 Frank Dobson, 7 Naphtali, 8 Nigeria, 9 Polyanthus, 10 Italy, 11 M, 12 Louisiana, 13 Ordovician, 14 Brazil, 15 Crystals.

? GENERAL KNOWLEDGE ?

1. Of what is doraphobia the fear - doors or fur?

2. Which playwright authored Major Barbara?

3. Which country administers the Queen Charlotte Islands?

4. What was the 1996 BAFTA Best Film award winner?

5. How many digits does a bear have on each foot?

6. In which English county is HMP Blundeston?

7. In which group of islands would you find Tresco and St. Mary's

8. Which country was known by the Romans as Dania?

9. Which book of the Bible has more chapters - Esther or Ruth?

10. Which international organization goes by the acronym CARICOM?

11. What is the average gestation period of a camel - 28 weeks or 58 weeks?

12. Where in the body would you find the muscle group called the pectoralis major?

13. What substance is associated with a 14th wedding anniversary?

14. What is the premier honour awarded in Japan to men?

15. In which country is the Batmanhole cave?

ANSWERS: 1 Fur or animal skins, 2 George Bernard Shaw, 3 Canada, 4 The English Patient, 5 Five, 6 Suffolk, 7 The Scilly Islands, 8 Denmark, 9 Esther, 10 Caribbean Community and Common Market, 11 58 weeks, 12 Chest, 13 Ivory, 14 Order of the Chrysanthemum, 15 Austria.

GENERAL KNOWLEDGE

1. Who succeeded Paddy Ashdown as leader of the Liberal Democrat Party?

2. Who replaced Glenn Hoddle as England football coach?

3. Who was 1999 French Open women's singles tennis champion?

4. Who authored the 1999 children's book Harry Potter and the Prisoner of Azkaban?

5. Who is the wife of Prince Edward?

6. In which year was American silent film producer Hal Roach born?

7. Who was 1999 U.S. Open women's singles tennis champion?

8. Which Brit was Best Supporting Actress Oscar winner in 1999?

9. Who was men's 400m hurdles champion at the 1999 I.A.A.F. World Championships in Seville?

10. Who was elected Labour M.P. for Cardiff West in May 1997?

11. Who was winner of the 1999 British Grand Prix in Formula 1 motor racing?

12. Who directed the Best Picture Oscar nominee The Thin Red Line?

13. Which golf club hosted the 1999 Qatar Masters which was won by Paul Lawrie?

14. What nationality was chemist and philanthropist Alfred Nobel?

15. What was Kirstie Alley's character name in the sitcom Cheers?

ANSWERS 1. Charles Kennedy 2. Kevin Keegan 3. Steffi Graf 4. J.K. Rowling 5. Sophie Rhys-Jones 6. 1892 7. Serena Williams 8. Judi Dench 9. Fabrizio Mori 10. Rhodri Morgan 11. David Coulthard 12. Terrence Malick 13. Doha Golf Club 14. Swedish 15. Rebecca Howe.

ENTERTAINMENT

1. In which film comedy does the character Osgood E. Fielding appear?

2. Which Spanish actor was a Best Actor Oscar nominee in 2001?

3. Which 2001 television comedy drama series featured a Kung-Fu Nurse Bear?

4. Akira Kurosawa's film Throne of Blood is a retelling of which Shakespeare play?

5. Who played the title role in the 1968 film Madigan?

6. Who played Deputy Emmett Ryker in the television drama series The Virginian?

7. Who co-starred with Marilyn Monroe in the 1957 film The Prince and the Showgirl?

8. Which 2001 film set in London starred Paul Nicholls and featured Dani Behr?

9. Which Oscar-winner made his Broadway debut in the play Picnic in 1953?

10. Who choreographed the 1913 ballet Jeux?

11. With which theatre company did Laurence Olivier work from 1926-8?

12. Who in 1994 became the youngest recipient of the American Film Institute's Life Achievement Award?

13. Which pianist composed the 1901 opera Manru?

14. Who played the fishmarket worker Reg Furnell in the television sitcom Down the Gate?

15. Who played the sorcerer Simon De Belleme in the 1980s adventure series Robin of Sherwood?

ANSWERS 1. Some Like It Hot 2. Javier Bardem 3. Happiness 4. Macbeth 5. Richard Widmark 6. Clu Gulager 7. Laurence Olivier 8. Goodbye Charlie Bright 9. Paul Newman 10. Nijinsky 11. Birmingham Repertory Company 12. Jack Nicholson 13. Ignacy Jan Paderewski 14. Reg Varney 15. Anthony Valentine.

SPORT

1. Which snooker player won the Rothman's Grand Prix in 1984?

2. Who did Llanelli play in the quarter-finals of the 2000 Heineken Cup?

3. For which country did Test cricketer Ravi Shastri play?

4. Which Australian was succeeded by Steve McCormack as coach of Salford rugby league side?

5. Who won the Cy Young Award as outstanding pitcher in baseball's American League in 1987?

6. Aldo Montano was 1938 men's sabre world champion in fencing. Which country did he represent?

7. What is the nickname of rugby league player Jason Robinson?

8. What distance did John Jarvis swim in 58 minutes 24 seconds to take the gold medal in the 1900 Olympic Games?

9. Which UK golfer was the runner-up to Greg Norman in the 1980 world matchplay championship?

10. In which year did Paul Laurie first take part in the Ryder Cup?

11. What nationality is golfer Jarrod Moseley?

12. How many winning rides did Fred Archer have in 1877?

13. Which team signed Canadian ice hockey player Marc Hussey in August 1999?

14. Who was the men's 800m champion at the 1987 world championships?

15. Who was the 1974 Australian men's singles tennis champion?

ANSWERS 1. Dennis Taylor 2. Cardiff 3. India 4. John Harvey 5. Roger Clemens. 6. Italy 7. Billy Whizz 8. 4,000m 9. Sandy Lyle 10. 1999 11. Australian 12. 218 13. London Knights 14. Billy Konchellah 15. Jimmy Connors.

POP MUSIC

1. In which year was Spirit in the Sky a No. 1 hit for Norman Greenbaum?

2. Who was the guitarist in the group Bow Wow Wow?

3. Which duo formed the group The Lovin' Spoonful in 1965?

4. Whose country albums include 1970's Okie from Muskogee?

5. In which U.S. state was singer Sheryl Crow born?

6. On which studio album by Boston does No. 1 single Amanda appear?

7. Which jazz guitarist died in December 1999, aged 74?

8. On which label did the Chemical Brothers release their 1999 hit single Let Forever Be?

9. Which U.S. group had a 1966 U.S. hit with The Eggplant That Ate Chicago?

10. Which girl group recorded the 1999 single Jesse Hold On?

11. Which rock star authored the 1989 autobiography Long Time Gone?

12. Who was the drummer with the Boomtown Rats?

13. In which city was singer Lene Lovich born?

14. Which female singer had a 2000 No. 1 with Born To Make You Happy?

15. Which group's singles include 2000's The Facts of Life?

ANSWERS 1. 1970 2. Matthew Ashman 3. Zal Yanovsky & John Sebastian 4. Merle Haggard 5. Missouri 6. Third Stage 7. Charlie Byrd 8. Virgin 9. Dr. West's Medicine Show and Junk Band 10. B*witched 11. David Crosby 12. Simon Crowe 13. Detroit 14. Britney Spears 15. Black Box Recorder.

ART & LITERATURE

1. Who wrote the 1902 play Monna Vanna?

2. Who penned the one-act play Bobby Gould in Hell?

3. Gustav von Aschenbach is the central character in which novella?

4. Who authored the short-story collection The Dove's Nest?

5. Who wrote the 1992 crime novel Long-Legged Fly?

6. Who authored the 1974 novel Dog Soldiers?

7. Who wrote the graphic novel Ghost World?

8. Who penned the 2001 novel Choke?

9. Who authored the 1978 novel Running Dog?

10. In which year did the artist Paul Guigou die?

11. Which poet wrote the 1908 play The Tragedy of Nan?

12. Who painted the 1866 work Monna Vanna?

13. What nationality is the painter Jan van Imschoot?

14. In which novel is Tyler Durden the central character?

15. What nationality is the painter Olav Christopher Jenssen?

ANSWERS 1. Maeterlinck 2. David Mamet 3. Death in Venice by Thomas Mann 4. Katherine Mansfield 5. James Sallis 6. Robert Stone 7. Daniel Clowes 8. Chuck Palahniuk 9. Don Delillo 10. 1871 11. John Masefield 12. Dante Gabriel Rossetti 13. Belgian 14. Fight Club by Chuck Palahniuk 15. Norwegian.

GENERAL KNOWLEDGE

1. What is the name of the U.S. rap group whose albums include It Takes a Nation of Millions to Hold Us Back?

2. Who was chancellor of West Germany from 1969-74?

3. Who wrote the 1950 book I, Robot?

4. In Greek mythology, which of the three Fates was the spinner of the thread of life?

5. In which year was Irish disc jockey and TV presenter Terry Wogan born?

6. Who was the 1999 U.S. P.G.A. golf champion?

7. Which ancient Egyptian god was ruler of the underworld?

8. Who wrote the play Steaming which was filmed in 1985 by Joseph Losey?

9. Mount Smolikas is the highest peak in which mountain range in Greece?

10. In which year was the town of Guernica in Northern Spain destroyed by German bombers during the Spanish Civil War?

11. Who was the scorer of the winning goal for West Bromwich Albion in the 1968 F.A. Cup Final?

12. Which wine bottle holds the equivalent of twenty normal bottles?

13. On which island is the sitcom Father Ted set?

14. Who was 1987 Australian Open women's singles tennis champion?

15. Whose volume of poetry, The Birthday Letters, won the 1999 Whitbread Book of the Year Award?

ANSWERS 1. Public Enemy 2. Willy Brandt 3. Isaac Asimov 4. Clotho 5. 1938 6. Tiger Woods 7. Osiris 8. Nell Dunn 9. Pindus 10. 1937 11. Jeff Astle 12. Nebuchadnezzar 13. Craggy Island 14. Hana Mandlikova 51. Ted Hughes.

ENTERTAINMENT

1. Who did Hervé Villechaize play in the Bond film The Man with the Golden Gun?

2. Who won the Best Supporting Actress Oscar in 2000 for her role in Girl, Interrupted?

3. Who played Fidgit in the film Time Bandits?

4. Which actor played Joseph Valachi in the 1972 film The Valachi Papers?

5. Which actor played Pancho Villa in the 1972 film?

6. What is the 1993 follow-up to Wim Wenders's film Wings of Desire?

7. Which actor played the owner of Empire Industries in the 1984 sitcom Empire?

8. Who played Professor X in the 2000 film The X-Men?

9. In which year was the actor Verne Troyer born?

10. Who did Jacqueline Pirie play in Emmerdale?

11. Who played Dawson in Dawson's Creek?

12. Who directed the 1991 film The People Under the Stairs?

13. Who played Marmalade Atkins in the children's TV series Educating Marmalade?

14. What was comedian Dick Emery's middle name?

15. In which year did Zoë Ball and Kevin Greening first co-host the Radio 1 Breakfast Show on a regular basis?

ANSWERS 1. Nick-Nack 2. Angelina Jolie 3. Kenny Baker 4. Charles Bronson 5. Telly Savalas 6. Faraway, So Close 7. Patrick Macnee 8. Patrick Stewart 9. 1969 10. Tina Dingle 11. James Van Der Beek 12. Wes Craven 13. Charlotte Coleman 14. Gilbert 15. 1997.

SPORT

1. In which year was the Trials Riding world championship for motorbikes inaugurated?

2. Who did Stephen Hendry beat in the quarter-finals of the 1999 British Open in snooker?

3. Which English football team won the 1999/00 Premier League?

4. In which year did Australian tennis player Daphne Akhurst die?

5. What nationality were the 1992 & 1994 Olympic two-man bob champions?

6. Who finished third in the 1999 Belgian Grand Prix in Formula 1?

7. How many matches did Tom Richardson take to grab 1000 first-class wickets from 1892-6?

8. In which city is the headquarters of the Badminton Association of England Ltd.?

9. Which golfer won the 1993 U.S. Women's Open?

10. In cricket, who scored 111 for Glamorgan against Northants in the 2nd innings of their 1999 county championship game?

11. At what sport was John Shea a 1932 Olympic champion?

12. How many golds did Italy win at the 1999 World Athletics Championships?

13. In which city was the 1977 U.E.F.A. Champion Clubs' Cup Final played?

14. In which sport is the Swaythling Cup competed for?

15. Who was women's 200m champion at the 1985 world indoor athletics championships?

POP MUSIC

1. Which singer's albums include Atlantic Crossing and A Night on the Town?

2. Who recorded the 1993 Top 20 single What's My Name?

3. In which year was John Lennon's album Double Fantasy released?

4. Who recorded the 2001 album of cover versions entitled Strange Little Girls?

5. In which year was the album Fisherman's Blues released by The Waterboys?

6. Who produced the album Searching for the Young Soul Rebels by Dexy's Midnight Runners?

7. Which male artist recorded the albums Ramblin' Boy and Ain't That News?

8. Which former member of the group The Mekons formed the group The Waco Brothers?

9. Which duo recorded the 2001 single Pretender Got My Heart?

10. Which male singer recorded the 2001 single Close To You?

11. What is the title of the third album by the Spice Girls?

12. Which group released the 1977 single Jocko Homo?

13. Which act had a 1998 chart hit with the single Music Sounds Better With You?

14. In which year did singer Jeff Buckley die?

15. Who recorded the album Born Again Savage?

ANSWERS 1. Rod Stewart 2. Snoop Doggy Dogg 3. 1980 4. Tori Amos 5. 1988 6. Pete Wingfield 7. Tom Paxton 8. Jon Langford 9. Alisha's Attic 10. Marti Pellow 11. Forever 12. Devo 13. Stardust 14. 1997 15. Steve Van Zandt.

GEOGRAPHY

1. In which county is St. Albans?

2. What is the capital of the French department of Val d'Oise?

3. What is the county town of the Irish county of Wexford?

4. What is the highest peak of the Rhaetian Alps?

5. On which river is the Illinois port of Peoria?

6. Which is the largest of the Azores group of islands?

7. The Belgian town of Namur lies on a promontory between which two rivers?

8. Helena is the capital of which U.S. state?

9. Mount Vancouver is a mountain on the border between Canada and which U.S. state?

10. On which river is the city of Semipalatinsk in Kazakhstan?

11. What is the capital of the Italian region of Campania?

12. In which South American country is Mount Sorata?

13. Which river separates the Bronx from Manhattan in New York City?

14. On which river is the German town of Esslingen?

15. The Japanese port of Shimonoseki is on which island?

GENERAL KNOWLEDGE

1. In which U.S. state was the bandleader Glenn Miller born?

2. Which actress wrote the 1971 autobiography I Was Born Greek?

3. Which musical instrument is known as a liquorice-stick?

4. In which year did Italy, France, Spain and Portugal adopt the Gregorian calendar?

5. Which girl group had a 2000 No. 1 single with the song Black Coffee?

6. How many points is the green ball worth in snooker?

7. What part of a ship is known as a mud-hook?

8. In which month of 1936 did King Edward VIII abdicate?

9. In which country is the highest waterfall in the British Isles?

10. In which year did the Showa epoch end in Japan?

11. Which country is larger in area - Norway or Belarus?

12. How many arches does the Ribblehead Viaduct have?

13. In which country is the town of Tequila?

14. Which female author's plays for television have included 1967's Poor Cherry?

15. In which year did Soho club The Wag open?

ANSWERS 1. Iowa 2. Melina Mercouri 3. Clarinet 4. 1582 5. All Saints 6. 3 points 7. Anchor 8. December 9. Scotland 10. 1989 11. Norway 12. 24 13. Mexico 14. Fay Weldon 15. 1981.

ENTERTAINMENT

1. Who starred in the 1928 film Pandora's Box?

2. In which year was the pilot for the sitcom The Dustbinmen shown?

3. Which actress played Christian Bale's wife in the 1997 film Metroland?

4. In which country was the 1971 film Valdez is Coming shot?

5. Who played The President's Analyst in the 1967 film?

6. Who starred as Joan of Arc in a 2000 Luc Besson film?

7. Who played the lead in the film Whatever Happened to Harold Smith?

8. What is Charlie's surname in TV's Ground Force?

9. Who played an ambitious weathergirl in the 1995 film To Die For?

10. In which year was comedian Charlie Drake born?

11. Who played Damien Day in the sitcom Drop the Dead Donkey?

12. Which pop singer appeared as Micky Shannon in a 2000 episode of the drama series Heartbeat?

13. Who did Ian Moor impersonate to win Stars in Their Eyes in 1998?

14. Who drove the Ring-a-Ding Convert-a-Car in the cartoon series Wacky Races?

15. Which former EastEnders star headed the cast in the ITV drama Hero of the Hour?

ANSWERS 1. Louise Brooks 2. 1968 3. Emily Watson 4. Spain 5. James Coburn 6. Milla Jovovich 7. Tom Courtenay 8. Dimmock 9. Nicole Kidman 10. 1925 11. Stephen Tompkinson 12. Gary Barlow 13. Chris De Burgh 14. Professor Pat Pending 15. Ross Kemp

SPORT

1. What nationality is tennis player Andreas Vinciguerra?

2. In which year did Spion Kop win the Epsom Derby?

3. By what score did Dewsbury beat Stanley Rangers in the 2000 Silk Cut Challenge Cup in rugby league?

4. How many golds have China won at the summer Olympics from 1896-1996?

5. Which athlete was 1963 BBC Sports Personality of the Year?

6. With what sport is Austrian Mathias Zdarsky associated?

7. In which city was Welsh rugby union player Simon Easterby's mother born?

8. What nationality is canoeist Renn Crichlow?

9. For which team did Giancarlo Fisichella drive in the 2000 Formula 1 season?

10. Between 1978-84, how many times did Grete Waitz finish in the first three of the world cross country championships?

11. How many kilometres did cyclist Jules Dubois ride in an 1894 1 hour speed record?

12. For which club side does French rugby union player Abdelatif Benazzi turn out?

13. At which sport was Dugald McPherson British Amateur champion in 1928?

14. Who did Rangers beat in the 1930 Scottish F.A. Cup Final?

15. How many runs did W. W. Hinds score on his debut Test innings for the West Indies against Zimbabwe in 2000?

ANSWERS 1. Swedish 2. 1920 3. 66-0 4. 52 5. Dorothy Hyman 6. Alpine skiing 7. Dublin 8. Canadian 9. Benetton 10. Seven 11. 38.22 km 12. Agen 13. Squash 14. Partick Thistle 15. 46

POP MUSIC

1. In which town did the group Meat Beat Manifesto form in 1986?

2. Who had a 1990 hit single with the song Elephant Stone?

3. Who had a 1999 Top 10 single with I Knew I Loved You?

4. Which member of Nick Cave's backing group leads the combo Dirty Three?

5. On which label did the Waterboys record the album Room to Roam?

6. Which Goth group recorded the live album Gotham?

7. In which year did Faust sign to Virgin Records?

8. From which country do the group Daryll Ann hail?

9. Who co-produced the Tom Waits album Mule Variations with the singer?

10. Which heavy metal band recorded the 2000 album Q2k?

11. Which group recorded the 1990 album Goodbye Jumbo?

12. Which group recorded the album MACHINA/the machines of god?

13. Which solo artist had a 1999 Top 10 single with Waiting For Tonight?

14. Which group recorded the 2000 mini-album Hotel Baltimore?

15. Whose debut solo album was Raw Like Sushi?

HISTORY

1. The burning of whose house in 1847 in Athens led to Lord Palmerston sending a fleet to Piraeus, Greece in 1850?

2. In which year did Russia's Lunik III first send back pictures of the dark side of the moon?

3. Who was appointed Chancellor of the German Reich in 1930?

4. In which year did poet and soldier Sir Philip Sidney die?

5. In which year of the 1960s was the Sino-Indian War?

6. With which country did Britain engage in a Cod War in 1958?

7. In which month of 1967 was the Six-day War between Israel and the Arab nations?

8. Who, in 1947, organized the R.P.F. movement in France?

9. In which year did Olof Palme first become Prime Minister of Sweden?

10. Who served as Minister of Housing from 1951-54?

11. Who succeeded General MacArthur in 1951 as Commander-in-Chief of U.N. forces in Korea?

12. What was Fidel Castro's father's occupation?

13. In which year did Alfred the Great die?

14. In which year did Martin Bormann become chief of staff to Rudolf Hess?

15. In which year was the Challenger space shuttle disaster?

ANSWERS 1. Don Pacifico 2. 1959 3. Heinrich Brüning 4. 1586 5. 1962 6. Iceland 7. June 8. Charles de Gaulle 9. 1969 10. Harold Macmillan 11. General Matthew Ridgway 12. Sugar planter 13. 899 14. 1933 15. 1986.

? GENERAL KNOWLEDGE ?

1. Which European country houses the Rhodope Mountains and Balkan Mountains?

2. Who was King of Mercia from 757-796?

3. What novel is the second part of Roddy Doyle's Barrytown Trilogy?

4. Who was a Best Actor Oscar nominee for his role as composer Chopin in the film A Song to Remember?

5. On which river is the new town of Newtown in central Wales?

6. What is the comic alter ego of actor Patrick Fyffe?

7. Who was a Best Actor Oscar winner for the 1944 film Going My Way?

8. Who wrote the novel Life and Loves of a She-Devil?

9. Who is the aunt and guardian of Lydia Languish in the play The Rivals?

10. Which 19th-century statesman led the Anti-Corn-Law League with Richard Cobden?

11. Who was a Best Actor Oscar nominee for the 1985 film Murphy's Romance?

12. Who wrote the 1916 novel The Brook Kerith?

13. Who was 1939 Wimbledon women's singles tennis champion?

14. Which Turkey-born shipowner married Jackie Kennedy in 1968?

15. Who wrote the 1929 novel The Seven Dials Mystery?

ANSWERS 1. Bulgaria 2. Offa 3. The Snapper 4. Cornel Wilde 5. River Severn 6. Hilda Bracket 7. Bing Crosby 8. Fay Weldon 9. Mrs. Malaprop 10. John Bright 11. James Garner 12. George Moore 13. Alice Marble 14. Aristotle Onassis 15. Agatha Christie

ENTERTAINMENT

1. Which 2000 film comedy starred Tim Meadows as Leon Phelps?

2. In which 1998 film did George Clooney star as Jack Foley?

3. Which Coronation Street actress won the Best Dramatic Performance prize at the 2001 British Soap Awards?

4. Which 2001 animated film featured the voices of comedians Mike Myers and Eddie Murphy?

5. In which city is the the Australian Ballet based?

6. What was the 1999 BAFTA Best Film award winner?

7. Which BBC television drama series stars Trevor Eve as DCI Peter Boyd?

8. Who directed the 1994 film Radioland Murders?

9. Which 2001 film comedy starred Heather Graham and Chris Klein?

10. In which city is the National Ballet company of the Netherlands located?

11. Who scored the American musical West Side Story?

12. Which 2000 John Fawcett film starred Katharine Isabelle and Emily Perkins?

13. Which three characters did Chris Rock play in the 2001 film Down to Earth?

14. Who played Angel in a television spin-off series from the show Buffy: the Vampire Slayer?

15. Which 2001 film comedy starred Luke de Woolfson and James Lance?

ANSWERS 1. The Ladies Man 2. Out of Sight 3. Georgia Taylor 4. Shrek 5. Melbourne 6. American Beauty 7. Waking the Dead 8. Mel Smith 9. Say It Isn't So 10. Amsterdam 11. Leonard Bernstein 12. Ginger Snaps 13. Lance Barton, Charles Wellington III and Joe Guy 14. David Boreanaz 15. Late Night Shopping.

SPORT

1. Which horse won the 1979 Grand National?

2. How many golds did Ethiopia win in the 1999 World Athletics Championships?

3. Which athlete was 1993 BBC Sports Personality of the Year?

4. Who was 1980 Olympic women's long jump champion?

5. Bob Howe and Mary Hawton won the 1958 Australian Open mixed doubles tennis title. What nationality were they?

6. Which Briton won the 1971 British Grand Prix in Formula 1?

7. Which women's golfer won the Compaq Open in August 1999?

8. In April 1994, who scored a record 375 runs against England in one innings?

9. Who was women's single-seater winner in luge tobogganing at the 1983 World Cup?

10. By what score did Wales beat Canada at rugby union in August 1999?

11. Who won the women's 100m at the 1999 World Athletics Championships?

12. In cricket, which wicketkeeper made eight catches for Somerset against Combined Universities in their 1982 Benson & Hedges Cup?

13. By what score did England beat the United States at rugby union in August 1999?

14. For which sport is the Espirito Santo Trophy awarded?

15. Which English rugby union side are nicknamed the Tigers?

ANSWERS 1. Rubstic 2. Two 3. Linford Christie 4. Tatyana Kolpakova 5. Australian 6. Jackie Stewart 7. Laura Davies 8. Brian Lara 9. Ute Weiss 10. 33-19 11. Marion Jones 12. Derek Taylor 13. 106-8 14. Golf (it's a women's world amateur team trophy) 15. Leicester.

POP MUSIC

1. In which year was Tracy Chapman's album Tracy Chapman released?

2. Who produced the first album by Family, Music in a Doll's House?

3. Which Rolling Stones studio album includes the track Start Me Up?

4. Who recorded the 1984 album Fans?

5. On which label did Supergrass record their Top 10 single Moving?

6. Which female vocal group had a 1966 hit single with Attack?

7. Which group had a 1980 Top 10 single with Someone's Looking At You?

8. Which female singer had a 1999 Top 10 single with Sunshine?

9. In which city was guitarist Nils Lofgren born?

10. New York band Blue Oyster Cult were the brainchild of which journalist?

11. Which jazz artist recorded the album Classics in the Key of G?

12. Which Van Morrison studio album features the songs Precious Time and Philosopher's Stone?

13. Who had a 1989 hit single with Dear Jessie?

14. With which 1970s rock band did John Bonham play the drums?

15. Which member of the band Blood, Sweat & Tears wrote the much-covered song Spinning Wheel?

ANSWERS 1. 1988 2. Dave Mason 3. Tattoo You 4. Malcolm McLaren 5. Parlophone 6. Toys 7. Boomtown Rats 8. Gabrielle 9. Chicago 10. Sandy Perlman 11. Kenny G 12. Back On Top 13. Madonna 14. Led Zeppelin 15. David Clayton-Thomas.

WORDS

1. What does the prefix onto- mean?

2. Where would an ecclesiastic wear a zucchetto?

3. What is homiletics?

4. Louping ill is a disease of which animal?

5. What does the Yiddish phrase meshuga mean?

6. What is foxing to a cobbler?

7. What does the prefix agro- denote?

8. Who would perform a pas seul?

9. What in India is alap?

10. In Egypt, what would a canopic jar have contained?

11. Who might wear a rochet?

12. Who would use the technique of effleurage?

13. In zoology, if something is acuadal, what does it lack?

14. What would you have done with a tickey in South Africa until 1961?

15. In which gambling game is the phrase à cheval used?

GENERAL KNOWLEDGE

1. Which chesspiece moves in an L-shaped direction?

2. On which river is the market town of Settle in North Yorkshire?

3. Who was a Best Actor Oscar nominee for his role in the 1984 film Under the Volcano?

4. In which year was the poet Ezra Pound indicted for treason by the U.S. government?

5. Who was 1932-3 world heavyweight boxing champion?

6. Port Blair is the capital of which territory of India?

7. Which former standard monetary unit of Thailand was replaced in 1928 by the baht?

8. Which port in central Vietnam was the former capital of the kingdom of Annam?

9. Who wrote the 1932 novel Tobacco Road?

10. Munich is the capital of which state of Germany?

11. Who was the French author of the novel Eugénie Grandet?

12. Who was the 1986 Commonwealth women's 100m hurdles champion?

13. In which year was veteran Northern Ireland politician Ian Paisley born?

14. Which industrial city and port in Belgium is at the confluence of the Rivers Lys and Scheldt?

15. Of which U.S. state is Boise the capital?

ANSWERS 1. Knight 2. River Ribble 3. Albert Finney 4. 1945 5. Jack Sharkey 6. The Andaman and Nicobar Islands 7. Tical 8. Hué 9. Erskine Caldwell 10. Bavaria 11. Honoré de Balzac 12. Sally Gunnell 13. 1926 14. Ghent 15. Idaho.

ENTERTAINMENT

1. Who directed the 1999 film The Straight Story?

2. Who is the male lead in the 1952 swashbuckling film Against All Flags?

3. Who is the female star of the 1996 film Last Dance?

4. Which actress directed the 1990 film Impulse starring Theresa Russell?

5. What is Eddie Murphy's character name in the 1996 film The Nutty Professor?

6. Which stand-up comedian made the show Bring the Pain for U.S. cable channel H.B.O.?

7. Which comic actor assisted in the 1983 sketch series Michael Barrymore?

8. What is Robert Carlyle's character name in the Bond film The World Is Not Enough?

9. In which city is the 1986 film Echo Park set?

10. Who played an astronaut in the 1999 film The Astronaut's Wife?

11. Who played a robot in the 1999 film Bicentennial Man?

12. Which playwright scripted the 1966 comedy film After the Fox?

13. Who left The Big Breakfast as a regular presenter in July 1999?

14. Louise McClatchy and Jai Simeone comprise which comedy duo?

15. What do the main protagonists attempt to build in the 1986 film Eat the Peach?

ANSWERS 1. David Lynch 2. Errol Flynn 3. Sharon Stone 4. Sondra Locke 5. Sherman Klump 6. Chris Rock 7. Nicholas Lyndhurst 8. Renard 9. Los Angeles 10. Johnny Depp 11. Robin Williams 12. Neil Simon 13. Kelly Brook 14. Supergirly 15. A 'wall of death' ride.

SPORT

1. Which British side lost the 1961 Fairs Cup in football?

2. What nationality is golfer David Park?

3. With which sport would you associate the names Michael Hadschieff and Ye Qiaobo?

4. Who was women's 10,000m champion at the 1994 I.A.A.F. World Cup?

5. Which football team's home ground is called Bloomfield Road?

6. Which sport do Canterbury Crusaders and Auckland Blues play in New Zealand?

7. Which 19th-century horserace trainer won the Oaks 12 times?

8. In which city was Australian cricketer Michael Bevan born?

9. Which country were women's relay orienteering world champions in 1997?

10. In which sport might the Sheffield Sharks play the Chester Jets?

11. At what sport did Otto Furrer win a world title in 1932?

12. In which sport were Hui Jun and Geng Lijuan world champions in 1987?

13. In canoeing, what does C4 stand for?

14. Which Welsh rugby union side play at the Gnoll?

15. Steen Stovgaard and Lene Køppen were 1977 world badminton mixed doubles champions. Which country were they from?

POP MUSIC

1. Which group's debut album was entitled Faithless Street?

2. Which female singer recorded the 2000 album Gung Ho?

3. In which year did The Jam first release the single Eton Rifles?

4. Which group's albums include Deliverance and Panorama?

5. Which rapper recorded the 2000 album Roc La Familia?

6. Which chart group recorded the 2001 single So Fresh, So Clean?

7. Which pop group recorded the 2001 album Outrospective?

8. Which pop group recorded the 2001 single Broke?

9. Which group did The Who support on their first major U.S. tour in 1967?

10. OX4 is a 'Best of' album by which group?

11. Which girl group recorded the 1978 single Typical Girls?

12. Which U.S. group recorded the 2000 album Chore of Enchantment?

13. What is the name of the 2001 studio album by Frank Black and the Catholics?

14. Which group did J. Mascis disband to form Dinosaur in 1984?

15. Which group recorded the album Never Loved Elvis?

ANSWERS 1. Whiskeytown 2. Patti Smith 3. 1979 4. The Cosmic Rough Riders 5. Jay-Z 6. Outkast 7. Faithless 8. The Beta Band 9. Herman's Hermits 10. Ride 11. The Slits 12. Giant Sand 13. Dog in the Sand 14. Deep Wound 15. The Wonder Stuff.

SCIENCE

1. Which Japanese physicist won a Nobel prize in 1949?

2. Which company did chemist Paul J. Flory join in 1934 as a researcher?

3. Which chemist was President of the British Chess Federation from 1950-3?

4. Which has the higher melting point - aluminium or barium?

5. With whom did scientist Alexis Carrel devise a respiratory machine for removed organs in 1935?

6. Which Luxembourg-born scientist was appointed President of the Paris Academy of Sciences in 1912?

7. In which European country was the Nobel prize-winning chemist A.I. Virtanen born?

8. At what temperature in degrees centigrade does zinc boil?

9. Who won the 1926 Nobel prize in chemistry for his work on disperse systems?

10. Which of these is not a prime number - 547, 557 or 567?

11. Which Nobel prize winner invented the sun-valve?

12. In which European country was the chemist Gerhard Herzberg born?

13. Of what is seismology the scientific study?

14. Who was awarded the 1939 Nobel prize in medicine?

15. Who was awarded the 1944 Nobel prize in chemistry for his discovery of the fission of heavy nuclei?

GENERAL KNOWLEDGE

1. In which year did U.S. singer and jazz pianist Nat 'King' Cole die?

2. Which U.S. food manufacturer invented the advertising slogan '57 Varieties'?

3. Which city in New South Wales, Australia, was the scene of a gold rush in 1851?

4. Who wrote the 1978 novel The Sea, the Sea?

5. Which imaginary creature is depicted as a white horse with one long spiralled horn growing from its forehead?

6. In ancient Greek drama what was the name given to the first of two movements made by a chorus during the performance of a choral ode?

7. What was the name of the character played by Ronald Allen in the TV soap Crossroads?

8. Who was the 1997 Wimbledon women's singles tennis champion?

9. Who wrote the 1978 play Plenty?

10. Which TV conjuror is married to his former assistant Debbie McGee?

11. Who wrote the 1963 novel Inside Mr. Enderby?

12. Who wrote the 1970 novel The Naked Face?

13. Who directed the 1985 comedy film After Hours?

14. In which year was Radio Gaga a Top 10 single for the group Queen?

15. Which Polish-born British property developer was involved in the Profumo scandal?

ENTERTAINMENT

1. Who directed the 2000 film American Psycho?

2. Who directed the 1952 film The Importance of Being Earnest?

3. Which comedy team wrote the 1960s sitcom Barney is my Darling?

4. Who made his debut as Tarzan in the 1955 film Tarzan's Hidden Jungle?

5. The 1999 movie The Insider is based on whose life story?

6. Who played Moriarty in the 1939 film The Adventures of Sherlock Holmes?

7. Who played Duggie Ferguson in Coronation Street?

8. Which actor played the lead in the 1958 film I, Mobster?

9. Who directed the 1961 film A Taste of Honey?

10. Who wrote and directed the 1997 film Afterglow?

11. What nationality is stage actress Zoë Caldwell?

12. Which star of the 1992 sitcom The Big One co-wrote the series?

13. What was the maiden name of actress Mrs. Patrick Campbell?

14. Who played Simon Sparrow in the 1954 film Doctor in the House?

15. Who played Jane in the 1934 film Tarzan and his Mate?

ANSWERS 1. Mary Harron 2. Anthony Asquith 3. Marty Feldman and Barry Took 4. Gordon Scott 5. Jeffrey Wigand 6. George Zucco 7. John Bowe 8. Steve Cochran 9. Tony Richardson 10. Alan Rudolph 11. Australian 12. Sandi Toksvig 13. Beatrice Stella Tanner 14. Dirk Bogarde 15. Maureen O'Sullivan.

SPORT

1. On which horse did Alwin Schockemöhle win the 1976 Olympic individual show jumping gold?

2. In golf, which U.S. city hosted the Bay Hill Invitational Tournament in March 2000?

3. At what sport is Australian Kieren Perkins a former world record holder?

4. Which Italian was 1993 World Footballer of the Year?

5. In which year was boxer Naseem Hamed born?

6. In which year was athlete Tim Montgomery born?

7. In which sport is the James Norris Memorial Trophy awarded?

8. In which city are American football team the Carolina Panthers based?

9. Which country does athlete Mel Lattany represent?

10. Which duo were U.S. Open women's doubles tennis champions in 1993?

11. Which American won the 1953 and 1954 Indianapolis 500 race?

12. In which year did French tennis player Rene Lacoste die?

13. Which country were 1996 Olympic yachting champions at soling class?

14. In which year was athlete Jon Drummond born?

15. Who was 1984 Olympic super-heavyweight boxing champion?

POP MUSIC

1. Which member of The Farm was killed in a car crash in 1986?

2. In which year did the Mahavishnu Orchestra form?

3. What was the title of Martine McCutcheon's 1999 debut album?

4. What is the name of the dog on wheels on the sleeve of Belle and Sebastian's single Dog on Wheels?

5. Which group covered Everything I Do (I Do It For You) in 1992, reaching the Top 10?

6. Which group recorded the soundtrack to the film The Virgin Suicides?

7. In which year did Black Box have a No. 1 single with Ride On Time?

8. In which city were the group Rip, Rig & Panic based?

9. Who recorded the 2000 album And Then Nothing Turned Itself Inside Out?

10. Who played drums on Joe Jackson's album Body and Soul?

11. Which group recorded the album Aion?

12. Who had a Top 10 hit in February 2000 with Adelante?

13. Which 1980s band released the album Pelican West?

14. Who had a 1990 Top 10 hit single with Enjoy the Silence?

15. Which member of The Jam produced the single Tom Verlaine by The Family Cat?

ANSWERS 1. Andy McVann 2. 1971 3. You, Me & Us 4. Patch 5. Fatima Mansions 6. Air 7. 1989 8. Bristol 9. Yo La Tengo 10. Gary Burke 11. Dead Can Dance 12. Sash! 13. Haircut 100 14. Depeche Mode 15. Rick Buckler.

PEOPLE

1. In which year did the former Chancellor of the Exchequer Iain Macleod die?

2. The founder of the Consumers' Association died in 2002. Who was he?

3. In which year did the actor Walter Matthau first suffer a heart attack?

4. The 1997 film Year of the Horse is a rockumentary about which musician?

5. In which year was the actor Christopher Walken born?

6. In which country was the television talk show host Jerry Springer born?

7. Which fashion designer married Andreas Kronthaler in 1992?

8. In which year did the singer Björk famously attack a reporter at Bangkok Airport?

9. What nationality is the jazz pianist Olga Konkova?

10. Which painter does the American writer Patricia Cornwell believe to have been the murderer Jack the Ripper?

11. In which year was the philosopher Friedrich Nietzsche born?

12. Where was Meredith Hunter beaten to death in 1969?

13. Who won the 2000 Nobel prize for literature?

14. In which year did the radio pioneer Marconi die?

15. What item of clothing did Ellery Chun famously invent?

ANSWERS 1. 1970 2. Lord Young of Dartington 3. 1966 4. Neil Young 5. 1943 6. England 7. Vivienne Westwood 8. 1996 9. Russian 10. Walter Sickert 11. 1844 12. The Altamont music festival 13. V.S. Naipaul 14. 1937 15. The Hawaiian or 'Aloha' Shirt.

ENTERTAINMENT

1. Which British female vocalist claimed I Only Want to Be With You in the U.K. top five in 1963?

2. Which actor played author William Forrester in the 2000 film Finding Forrester?

3. What was the name of Paul Nicholas' character in the eighties series Just Good Friends?

4. With which band is John Frusciante, who released a solo album in 2001 entitled To Record Only Water For Ten Days, also a guitarist with?

5. Who wrote, directed, produced and starred in the 1990 film Mo' Better Blues?

6. Which Channel 4 comedy series was co-written by, and starred, Jessica Stevenson, aka Cheryl in The Royle Family?

7. Which band, the product of the ITV series Popstars, hit the U.K. number one spot with their debut single Pure and Simple?

8. Which comedian and writer presided over The British Academy Film Awards in 2001?

9. Which 2000 film starred Russell Crowe as Terry Thorne, a professional negotiator?

10. Which BBC 2 comedy series featured two Royle Family stars and two former Hollyoaks stars?

11. How old was reggae legend Bob Marley when he died - 36 or 42?

12. What was the name of Mel Gibson's character in the Lethal Weapon movies?

13. Which British band looking to build on U.S. success had a 2001 hit in the U.K. with Back Here?

14. Whose Amazing World of Animals appeared on BBC 1?

15. Which US vocalist had a U.K. number one hit in 1963 with Devil in Disguise?

ANSWERS: 1 Dusty Springfield, 2 Sean Connery, 3 Vince Pinner, 4 The Red Hot Chili Peppers, 5 Spike Lee, 6 Spaced, 7 Hear'Say, 8 Stephen Fry, 9 Proof of Life, 10 Two Pints of Lager (and a Packet of Crisps), 11 36, 12 Martin Riggs, 13 BBMak, 14 Rolf's (Rolf Harris), 15 Elvis Presley.

? GENERAL KNOWLEDGE ?

1. What is the name of the captain in The Caine Mutiny by Herman Wouk?

2. Who links The Bed-Sit Girl and The Rag Trade?

3. Who was the founder of the Mormon Church?

4. Who appeared on television as Nicodemus and Lord Marchmain?

5. Who was the subject of the novel Lust for Life by Irving Stone?

6. What was the nationality of the character played by Ralph Fiennes in The English Patient?

7. Where in England is Greenham Common?

8. What is a klipspringer?

9. Who played The Last Action Hero?

10. Which member of the Monty Python team wrote The Saga of Erik the Viking?

11. In which game is a flat stone bounced across the surface of water?

12. Which Australian author won the Nobel Prize for literature in 1973?

13. Who was represented in Greek mythology as wearing winged sandals?

14. As what did the Englishman Thomas Sheraton make his name?

15. What was the middle name of the rock singer and songwriter Jim Morrison?

ANSWERS: 1 Queeg, 2 Sheila Hancock, 3 Joseph Smith, 4 Laurence Olivier, 5 Vincent van Gogh, 6 Hungarian, 7 Berkshire, 8 Antelope, 9 Arnold Schwarzenegger, 10 Terry Jones, 11 Ducks and drakes, 12 Patrick White, 13 Hermes, 14 Furniture maker, 15 Douglas.

GENERAL KNOWLEDGE

1. Who wrote The Four Feathers?

2. Which American economist wrote The Affluent Society?

3. After which poet was the Russian town Detskoe Selo renamed in 1937?

4. Which American statesman and renowned orator claimed 'There is always room at the top'?

5. What name was given to supporters of the exiled Stuart king James II?

6. Which English poet wrote the sonnet collection Delia?

7. Which pop star appeared in the 1976 film The Man Who Fell to Earth?

8. What is the common name for pyrite or iron pyrites?

9. Which English Cavalier poet wrote To Althea, from Prison?

10. What name is given to the permanent freezing of the ground in areas bordering on ice sheets?

11. Which British crown colony reverted to Chinese rule in 1997?

12. On which island was the detective series Bergerac set?

13. Which popular travel author won a W H Smith Book Award for his book Down Under?

14. What is the capital of Indonesia?

15. Who directed the films Manhattan and Radio Days?

ANSWERS: 1 A E W Mason, 2 John Kenneth Galbraith, 3 Aleksandr Pushkin, 4 Daniel Webster, 5 Jacobites, 6 Samuel Daniel, 7 David Bowie, 8 Fool's gold, 9 Richard Lovelace, 10 Permafrost, 11 Hong Kong, 12 Jersey, 13 Bill Bryson, 14 Jakarta, 15 Woody Allen.

?

GENERAL KNOWLEDGE

1. In which city are the V I Warshawski novels by Sara Paretsky set?

2. Which German composer wrote the opera Der Rosenkavalier?

3. Who replaced Sir Iain Vallance as chairman of British Telecom?

4. Which founder of the Pre-Raphaelite Brotherhood painted Beata Beatrix and The Blessed Damozel?

5. In which country is the port of Jaffna?

6. Which Irish political leader was known as the Liberator?

7. Which ex-Blue Peter presenter is the daughter of Gloria Hunniford?

8. Which Colombian novelist won the 1982 Nobel Prize for Literature?

9. What was the name of the official bodyguard of Roman emperors created by Augustus?

10. Which archangel announced the birth of John the Baptist to Zechariah?

11. Which British novelist wrote Mansfield Park and Northanger Abbey?

12. Who starred in the title role of the 1922 film Robin Hood?

13. In which London church is Poets' Corner?

14. David Starkey has won a W H Smith Book Award for his biography of which British monarch?

15. Which unit of weight for precious stones is equal to 0.20 grams?

ANSWERS: 1 Chicago, 2 Richard Strauss, 3 Sir Christopher Bland, 4 Dante Gabriel Rossetti, 5 Sri Lanka, 6 Daniel O'Connell, 7 Caron Keating, 8 Gabriel Garcia Marquez, 9 Praetorian Guard, 10 Gabriel, 11 Jane Austen, 12 Douglas Fairbanks, 13 Westminster Abbey, 14 Elizabeth I, 15 Carat.

ENTERTAINMENT

1. Which BBC 1 comedy series set in a toy company starred Pauline Quirke and Robert Daws?

2. What was the debut single of the Pet Shop Boys, which hit the U.K. number one spot in 1985?

3. Who played actor Max Schreck in the 2000 film Shadow of the Vampire?

4. Which science fiction series of the Sixties featured Oliver Reed as scientist Dr Richard Franklin?

5. What was the title of the 2001 U.K. top five hit by Jakatta?

6. Which 1990 film starred Gene Hackman and Anne Archer as a deputy district attorney and his key witness?

7. Which Coronation Street character discovered the existence of his 12-year-old son in 2001?

8. Which legendary actor and dancer's first screen appearance came in 1933's Dancing Lady, in which he played himself?

9. Who had a 2001 U.K. top five hit with Ms Jackson?

10. Which 2000 film earned Goldie Hawn's daughter Kate Hudson an Oscar nomination?

11. Which actor played Detective Chief Inspector Ross Tanner in the crime drama series Second Sight?

12. Which British female vocalist had a 2001 U.K. top five hit with Here With Me?

13. Which former Goon fronted the surreal Sixties comedy sketch show It's a Square World?

14. Which 1973 film featured Jack Nicholson as a sailor escorting a thief to naval prison?

15. Which ITV comedy series set in the 1970s featured Slade's Noddy Holder as headmaster Neville Holder?

ANSWERS: 1 Office Gossip, 2 West End Girls, 3 Willem Dafoe, 4 R3, 5 American Dream, 6 Narrow Margin, 7 Mike Baldwin, 8 Fred Astaire, 9 Outkast, 10 Almost Famous, 11 Clive Owen, 12 Dido, 13 Michael Bentine, 14 The Last Detail, 15 The Grimleys.

GENERAL KNOWLEDGE

1. What was the full name of author Nevil Shute?

2. Which African country was formerly known as Dahomey?

3. In which Sheridan play does the character Mrs Malaprop appear?

4. Which German driver achieved his first Formula 1 victory in the 2001 San Marino Grand Prix?

5. What is the largest of the United Arab Emirates?

6. Which Austrian-born composer is credited with the invention of 12-tone music?

7. Who presented the TV series Civilisation?

8. Dagestan is an autonomous republic of which country?

9. Which actress received an Oscar nomination for her performance in the title role of the 1954 film Carmen Jones?

10. What is the largest lake in the British Isles?

11. Who was the first murder victim in the Bible?

12. In which film did the song Moon River appear?

13. What was the name of the Lone Ranger's Indian companion?

14. Which British boxer lost his world heavyweight title to Hasim Rahman in 2001?

15. What is the capital of Uruguay?

ANSWERS: 1 Nevil Shute Norway, 2 Benin, 3 The Rivals, 4 Ralf Schumacher, 5 Abu Dhabi, 6 Arnold Schoenberg, 7 Kenneth Clark, 8 Russia, 9 Dorothy Dandridge, 10 Lough Neagh, 11 Abel, 12 Breakfast at Tiffany's, 13 Tonto, 14 Lennox Lewis, 15 Montevideo.

? GENERAL KNOWLEDGE ?

1. Who wrote Zen and the Art of Motorcycle Maintenance?

2. Which English critic wrote the five volume work Modern Painters?

3. What was the stage name of Harold Jenkins, who had a hit with the song It's Only Make Believe in 1958?

4. Which football team won the 2000/01 Nation wide League First Division championship?

5. From which Rossini opera does the Lone Ranger TV theme music come?

6. Which Australian city is named after the queen consort of William IV?

7. What profession did the character played by Jack Nicholson have in Terms of Endearment?

8. By what name was the only English pope, Nicholas Breakspear, known?

9. Which New Zealand-born actress played Irene in the BBC series The Forsyte Saga?

10. Who was the sixth president of the United States?

11. Which vehicle derives its name from the U.S. Army's General Purpose vehicle or GP?

12. Margaret Dumont was the long-suffering stooge to which comedy team?

13. In the Old Testament, who received the Ten Commandments?

14. Which Spanish actor played the father of the Spy Kids in the 2001 film?

15. Of which Irish rock group are Bono and The Edge members?

GENERAL KNOWLEDGE

1. In which TV series for children did the Soup Dragon appear?

2. Which sea lies between the Italian mainland and the islands of Sicily, Sardinia and Corsica?

3. What is the name of the Earl of Wessex's film company?

4. Which American hurdler was undefeated in 107 meetings between 1977 and 1987?

5. In which U.S. state are the Adirondack Mountains?

6. Which French priest founded the Lazarists?

7. Who played Norma Desmond in the 1950 film Sunset Boulevard?

8. Which poet is the subject of the poem Adonais by Percy Bysshe Shelley?

9. What nationality is the actress Liv Ullmann?

10. Which Shakespeare play is subtitled What You Will?

11. Which actress starred in the films Body Heat, Romancing the Stone and Peggy Sue Got Married?

12. What is the surname of Lucky Jim in the novel by Kingsley Amis?

13. Who wrote The Tale of Jeremy Fisher?

14. What name is given to a Muslim place of worship?

15. What is the only venomous snake found wild in the British Isles?

ANSWERS: 1 The Clangers, 2 12 Tyrrhenian Sea, 3 Ardent Productions, 4 Edwin Moses, 5 New York, 6 St Vincent de Paul, 7 Gloria Swanson, 8 John Keats, 9 Norwegian, 10 Twelfth Night, 11 Kathleen Turner, 12 Dixon, 13 Beatrix Potter, 14 Mosque, 15 Adder.

SPORT

1. In the summer of 2000, which cricket side was beaten by England in a Test series for the first time in 31 years?

2. Who refereed the 2001 Worthington Cup Final between Birmingham City and Liverpool?

3. A professional boxer between 112 and 118 pounds fights in which weight division?

4. Which horse won the Grand National in 1994?

5. Which number lies between 20 and 12 on a dartboard?

6. In January 2000, who became the youngest Briton and the fifth-youngest person of all time to be chosen as a Formula 1 driver?

7. Who was the first batsman to score his 100th first-class century during a Test match?

8. Who became Britain's most expensive goalkeeper in May 2000?

9. What is the maximum length in inches of a baseball bat?

10. In which sport do England and Scotland compete for the Calcutta Cup?

11. Which cyclist won Great Britain's first gold medal at the Sydney Olympics?

12. A professional boxer between 140-147 pounds fights in which weight division?

13. Which tennis player won the French Open in 1991 and 1992?

14. In which sport would the Nottingham Panthers play the Sheffield Steelers?

15. What colour ring on an archery target is worth seven points?

GENERAL KNOWLEDGE

1. Who played Harry O on television?

2. Which French monarch was married to Marie-Antoinette?

3. Who wrote the short story collection Guys and Dolls?

4. Which country beat American Samoa by a world record score of 31-0 in a World Cup qualifying game in 2001?

5. What is the shallowest of the Great Lakes?

6. Which American composer wrote the opera Nixon in China?

7. Who wrote the war-time trilogy Sword of Honour?

8. Which 60s group had hits with White Rabbit and Somebody to Love?

9. Which U.S. novelist wrote The Accidental Tourist?

10. What is the stage name of Marshall Bruce Mathers III?

11. Which English swimmer won the men's 100m breaststroke at the Seoul Olympics?

12. Who wrote the novel Mary Barton?

13. What does the Ugly Duckling grow into in Hans Christian Andersen's fairy tale?

14. Which 2001 film starred Renée Zellweger in the title role?

15. With which singing group did Diana Ross find fame?

GENERAL KNOWLEDGE

1. Which American author created the detective Philip Marlowe?

2. Which opera by Donizetti was based on a novel by Sir Walter Scott?

3. What name is given to a boundary between air masses having different temperature and humidity?

4. Which horse won the 2001 Grand National?

5. What was the name of Dustin Hoffman's character in The Graduate?

6. Which English dramatist wrote Hobson's Choice?

7. Which Monty Python star sang the theme song for One Foot in the Grave?

8. According to legend, at whom did Peeping Tom peep?

9. Who wrote the novel Jane Eyre?

10. Which Irish monk founded the monastery at Lindisfarne?

11. Which Roman emperor ordered the building of a wall between Solway Firth and the Tyne?

12. What is the name of the cat in The Simpsons?

13. In the Old Testament, who was the twin brother of Jacob?

14. Which former member of the Goons died in 2001 at the age of 79?

15. How many heads of U.S. presidents are carved into Mount Rushmore?

GENERAL KNOWLEDGE

1. Who wrote the novel National Velvet?

2. Which Essex town was sacked by the Iceni led by Boudicca in 60 A.D.?

3. What name is given to a negatively charged particle that is a constituent of all atoms?

4. In which French city was Joan of Arc burned at the stake?

5. For which gemstones is the Australian mining town of Coober Pedy famous?

6. Which American novelist wrote Imaginary Friends and Foreign Affairs?

7. The Day of the Jackal centres on the attempted assassination of which leader?

8. Which British boxer lost his world title to Marco Antonio Barrera in 2001?

9. Who produced the Star Wars and Indiana Jones series of films?

10. Which German tennis player won five successive Grand Slam tournaments in the 1980s?

11. Which American actor starred in High Noon and Mr Deeds Goes to Town?

12. With which radio station is TV's Alan Partridge associated?

13. Who replaced Peter Gabriel as lead singer of Genesis in 1975?

14. Which team won the 2000/01 Scottish Premier League title?

15. Of which African country is Lusaka the capital?

ANSWERS: 1 Enid Bagnold, 2 Colchester, 3 Electron, 4 Rouen, 5 Opals, 6 Alison Lurie, 7 General De Gaulle, 8 Naseem Hamed, 9 George Lucas, 10 Steffi Graf, 11 Gary Cooper, 12 Radio Norwich, 13 Phil Collins, 14 Celtic, 15 Zambia

ENTERTAINMENT

1. Which ITV comedy drama series starred Ardal O'Hanlon as magazine journalist Eamon?

2. With whom did UB40 collaborate on the 1990 U.K. top ten hit I'll Be Your Baby Tonight?

3. Which actress starred as a Brazilian chef in the 1999 film Woman on Top?

4. Which comedy writer was behind series such as Butterflies, Luv and Bread?

5. Which U.S. band had a 2001 U.K. top five hit with Loco?

6. Which member of the team played King Arthur in 1975's Monty Python and the Holy Grail?

7. Which BBC1 fly-on-the-wall documentary series followed a team of U.S. lawyers and their clients in Massachusetts?

8. Who had a 2001 U.K. top five hit with Teenage Dirtbag?

9. Which member of Blue Watch became a dad to baby Eve in the 2001 series of London's Burning?

10. Which actor starred as advertising executive Nick Marshall in the 2000 film What Women Want?

11. Which city was the setting for the Channel 4 comedy drama series Sex and the City, starring Sarah Jessica Parker?

12. In which 2000 film did Michael Douglas play a judge turned drugs 'czar'?

13. Which actress played Edie Pegden in the TV sitcom Last of the Summer Wine?

14. Which song by British band Toploader reached the U.K. top ten in 2001 after being released for the third time?

15. Which actor played the first black U.S. president in the 1972 film The Man?

ANSWERS: 1 Big Bad World, 2 Robert Palmer, 3 Penelope Cruz, 4 Carla Lane, 5 Fun Lovin' Criminals, 6 Graham Chapman, 7 Boston Law, 8 Wheatus, 9 Geoffrey Pearce, 10 Mel Gibson, 11 New York, 12 Traffic, 13 Thora Hird, 14 Dancing in the Moonlight, 15 James Earl Jones.

GENERAL KNOWLEDGE

1. What was the first full-length film by Walt Disney?

2. Which comic strip detective was created by Chester Gould in 1931?

3. What was the adopted name of Canadian-born beauty expert Florence Nightingale Graham?

4. Which team beat Tottenham Hotspur in the 2000/01 F.A. Cup semi-finals?

5. What is the lightest metal?

6. Which composer wrote the opera Elektra?

7. What nationality is the author Margaret Atwood?

8. What name for the devil means 'light-bearer' in Latin?

9. Which forename is shared by Prince Andrew and Prince Harry?

10. Which French-born actress won an Oscar for It Happened One Night?

11. Which poet is best known for his Elegy Written in a Country Churchyard?

12. Which film star is an international bridge player?

13. Who succeeded Richard Nixon as U.S. President?

14. Which singer and actress starred in the film The Wedding Planner?

15. Of which U.S. state is Denver the capital?

ANSWERS: 1 Snow White, 2 Dick Tracy, 3 Elizabeth Arden, 4 Arsenal, 5 Lithium, 6 Richard Strauss, 7 Canadian, 8 Lucifer, 9 Albert, 10 Claudette Colbert, 11 Thomas Gray, 12 Omar Sharif, 13 Gerald Ford, 14 Jennifer Lopez, 15 Colorado.

GENERAL KNOWLEDGE

1. Where was the film Purely Belter set?

2. Which British dramatist wrote Look Back in Anger and The Entertainer?

3. Who directed the Carry On series of films?

4. Who won the Best Supporting Actor Oscar for his performance in Traffic at the 2001 Oscars?

5. Who was principal conductor of the Hallé Orchestra until his death in 1970?

6. Which passenger ship was sunk by a German U-boat on May 7 1915?

7. Which was the second film in which Clint Eastwood played Harry Callaghan?

8. Who is the only woman to have been chosen as a running mate in a U.S. presidential election?

9. What is the real first name of blues guitarist B B King?

10. Which 2001 film starred Robert De Niro and Cuba Gooding Jr?

11. Which flower is used as a symbol of remembrance for the dead of the World Wars?

12. For which novel did Kingsley Amis win the Booker Prize?

13. What is the diameter of a compact disc - 15 cm or 12 cm?

14. Which former captain became England's leading run-scorer in Test cricket in 1993?

15. How many horses finished the 2001 Grand National - eight or four?

ANSWERS: 1 Newcastle, 2 John Osborne, 3 Gerald Thomas, 4 Benicio Del Toro, 5 Sir John Barbirolli, 6 The Lusitania, 7 Magnum Force, 8 Geraldine Ferraro, 9 Riley, 10 Men of Honour, 11 Poppy, 12 The Old Devils, 13 12 cm, 14 Graham Gooch, 15 Four.

GENERAL KNOWLEDGE

1. Who took over from Julie Walters as the mother of Adrian Mole on TV?

2. Which series of novels by James Fenimore Cooper includes The Last of the Mohicans?

3. Who won the Best Supporting Actress Oscar for her performance in Pollock at the 2001 Oscars?

4. Which poet wrote the lyric drama Prometheus Unbound?

5. What is the trade name of the antidepressant drug fluoxetine?

6. Which American talk show host was born Lawrence Harvey Zeiger in 1933?

7. Which TV series was set in Royston Vasey?

8. With which English king is the Authorised Version of the Bible associated?

9. Which English admiral was known as 'Old Grog'?

10. What term for an unconventional individual is named after a 19th-century American lawyer who failed to brand his cattle?

11. Which singer-songwriter recorded the album Tapestry in 1971?

12. Who wrote the autobiography Angela's Ashes?

13. Which Hollywood actor played a cocaine trafficker in the 2001 film Blow?

14. Which country held the crew of a U.S. spy plane after it made an emergency landing in 2001?

15. In computing, what does the abbreviation AI stand for?

ENTERTAINMENT

1. Which British group had a 1990 U.K. top five hit with I'm Free?

2. Which 1991 film featured a family of giant beetles disguised as humans in order to save the Brazilian rain forest?

3. Which 2001 ITV series revealed the process involved in the formation of a manufactured music group?

4. What was the title of Wet Wet Wet's second number one single, which reached the top of the U.K. charts in 1992?

5. Which 2000 British film featured Ben Kingsley and Ian McShane as gangsters?

6. Which original Star Trek character was played by DeForest Kelley?

7. Which Donna Summer song provided Martine McCutcheon with a 2001 U.K. top ten hit?

8. Which U.S. comic actor played a Russian circus musician in the 1984 film Moscow on the Hudson?

9. Which Channel 4 comedy series was set in a northern nightclub owned by wheelchair-bound Brian Potter?

10. Which girl band had a 2001 U.K. number one hit with Whole Again?

11. Which Scottish estate was the setting for the BBC1 series Monarch of the Glen?

12. Which U.S. country singer released the acoustic album Little Sparrow in 2001?

13. Who was the presenter of Channel 4's Time Team?

14. Which Oscar-winning actor was Cast Away in the 2000 film?

15. Which former musical quiz show was presented by both Tom O'Connor and Lionel Blair?

ANSWERS: 1 Soup Dragons, 2 Meet the Applegates, 3 Popstars, 4 Goodnight Girl, 5 Sexy Beast, 6 Dr Leonard McCoy (Bones), 7 On the Radio, 8 Robin Williams, 9 Peter Kay's Phoenix Nights, 10 Atomic Kitten, 11 Glenbogle, 12 Dolly Parton, 13 Tony Robinson, 14 Tom Hanks, 15 Name That Tune.

? ?

GENERAL KNOWLEDGE

1. The cast of which TV series were reunited to make Mirrorball?

2. Which character in Greek mythology was able to charm all living things with his lyre playing?

3. What is the first novel in Paul Scott's Raj Quartet?

4. Which film directed by Ang Lee was named Best Foreign Film at the 2001 Oscars?

5. What was the nickname of American gangster Charles Arthur Floyd?

6. Which French dramatist wrote A Flea in Her Ear?

7. Who played Will Scarlett in the film Robin Hood - Prince of Thieves?

8. Which French racing driver was world champion in 1985, 1986, 1989 and 1993?

9. Which American orchestra did Eugene Ormandy conduct from 1936 to 1980?

10. Which important fuel gas has the chemical formula C_3H_8?

11. Which film dog was played by a male collie called Pal?

12. What was the first novel by John Grisham?

13. What is the name of Fred Flintstone's wife?

14. Which golfer added the Players Championship, the so-called 'fifth major', to his collection of titles in March 2001?

15. Who played the young starlet in the 1933 film King Kong?

GENERAL KNOWLEDGE

1. Who wrote the novel Room at the Top?

2. Which author wrote Cakes and Ale and The Moon and Sixpence?

3. By what name was 16th-century Italian artist Paolo Caliari known?

4. Which driver halted Michael Schumacher's run of six successive victories by winning the 2001 Brazilian Grand Prix?

5. Of which county in Northern Ireland is Enniskillen the county town?

6. Which king was the subject of Shakespeare's first history play?

7. Which Michael Caine film ends with a bus on the edge of a cliff?

8. In which African country did the Mau Mau operate in the 1950s?

9. In which African country is the city of Fez?

10. Which Italian dramatist won the Nobel prize for literature in 1997?

11. Which famous first-class train was inaugurated in 1883, running from Paris to the Black Sea?

12. After whom is the Harvard lampoon Worst Actress of the Year Award named?

13. What name is given to the breakdown of sugar to alcohol by the action of yeast?

14. Which comedian hosted the 2001 Oscars?

15. Who played Sir Thomas More in the 1966 film A Man for All Seasons?

ANSWERS: 1 John Braine, 2 W Somerset Maugham, 3 Paolo Veronese, 4 David Coulthard, 5 Fermanagh, 6 King John, 7 The Italian Job, 8 Kenya, 9 Morocco, 10 Dario Fo, 11 Orient Express, 12 Natalie Wood, 13 Fermentation, 14 Steve Martin, 15 Paul Scofield.

GENERAL KNOWLEDGE

1. Which chieftain united the Gauls against Julius Caesar in 52 BC?

2. Of which country was Daniel Ortega head of state?

3. What is the name of the gang William is a member of in stories by Richmal Crompton?

4. What was the name of the motorist whose beating at the hands of the LAPD led to five days of rioting in 1992?

5. Which lyricist wrote the words to On the Sunny Side of the Street and The Way You Look Tonight?

6. What is the second period of the Palaeozoic Era called?

7. Who played eight members of the same family in Kind Hearts and Coronets?

8. On which Shakespeare play is Akira Kurosawa's film Ran based?

9. What was the first name of actor Lon Chaney?

10. Which character in Greek mythology sacrificed his daughter Iphigenia?

11. Which creatures does an ornithologist study?

12. What name is given to goods thrown overboard to lighten a ship in distress?

13. Which football team did Alf Garnett support?

14. In which European country is the city of Verona?

15. Who recorded the albums Look Sharp, Jumpin' Jive and Night and Day?

ANSWERS: 1 Vercingetorix, 2 Nicaragua, 3 The Outlaws, 4 Rodney King, 5 Dorothy Fields, 6 Ordovician Period, 7 Alec Guinness, 8 King Lear, 9 Alonso, 10 Agamemnon, 11 Birds, 12 Jetsam, 13 West Ham United, 14 Italy, 15 Joe Jackson.

ENTERTAINMENT

1. What was the title of the BBC1 comedy drama which starred Billy Connolly as Kingdom Swann, Edwardian photographer?

2. What was the title of Sonia's debut single, which hit the U.K. number one spot in 1989?

3. Which horror film actor played Prince Prospero in 1964's The Masque of the Red Death?

4. Which former EastEnder starred as single mum Abby in the BBC1 drama series 2,000 Acres of Sky?

5. Which U.S. vocalist had a U.K. top five hit in 1976 with Theme From Mahogany (Do You Know Where You're Going To)?

6. Which 2000 film set in an American high school was based on a novel by Dostoevsky?

7. What did Del and Raquel name their son in the sitcom Only Fools and Horses?

8. Which girl group had a 2001 U.K. top ten hit with All Hooked Up?

9. Which future James Bond star appeared as French anthropologist Pommier in the 1985 film Nomads?

10. Which decade was revisited by Channel 4 in its follow-up to the series The 1900s House?

11. Which comedian starred in the BBC1 collection of sketches In Pieces?

12. Which sportz-metal band hit the UK number one spot in 2001 with Rollin'?

13. Which famous Flowerpot Men returned to TV in 2001, this time in full colour and without strings?

14. Which Oscar-winning film starred Chow Yun Fat and Zhang Zi Yi

15. Which actor played Indian reporter Hari Kumar in the Eighties TV drama The Jewel in the Crown?

GENERAL KNOWLEDGE

1. Which 19th-century British artist painted Christ in the House of His Parents?

2. Who connects Star Trek and T J Hooker on TV?

3. Which American author wrote The Holcroft Covenant and The Icarus Agenda?

4. In what year did the English Civil War end?

5. Which African lake is the second deepest in the world?

6. In Arthurian legend, which knight of the Round Table was the son of King Lot?

7. In which country is the Shakespeare play A Midsummer Night's Dream set?

8. Of which Himalayan kingdom is Thimbu or Thimphu the capital?

9. Which American astronomer predicted the existence of a planet beyond Neptune?

10. Of which Irish county is Mullingar the county town?

11. Which scavenging doglike mammal has striped, spotted and brown varieties?

12. Who made up The Odd Couple with Jack Lemmon?

13. Which country was the first to use 'gunboat diplomacy'?

14. A portrait of which American president was sold for $20 million in March 2001?

15. Which Scottish village hosts the best-known Highland Games?

ANSWERS: 1 Sir John Everett Millais, 2 William Shatner, 3 Robert Ludlum, 4 1651, 5 Lake Tanganyika, 6 Gawain, 7 Greece, 8 Bhutan, 9 Percival Lowell, 10 Westmeath, 11 Hyena, 12 Walter Matthau, 13 Germany, 14 George Washington, 15 Braemar.

GENERAL KNOWLEDGE

1. Which system of healing is based on the belief that disease results from a lack of normal nerve function?

2. Who presented the quiz show 3-2-1?

3. Which dancer and choreographer died in 2001 at the age of 102?

4. What is the only seal that feeds on penguins?

5. Which English dramatist wrote The Lady's Not for Burning?

6. In which English county is the town of Chippenham?

7. Who provided the voice of the dragon in the Disney film Mulan?

8. The Fédération Colombophile Internationale is the world governing body of which sport?

9. Which English novelist wrote New Grub Street?

10. Who was the first prime minister to use Chequers as his country residence?

11. Which international environmental pressure group was founded in British Columbia in 1971?

12. What name is given to tissue damage caused by exposure to extreme cold?

13. Which 2001 film set in Mexico starred Penelope Cruz and Matt Damon?

14. Who sailed around the world in Gipsy Moth IV?

15. Which collection of fairy tales includes Hansel and Gretel and Rumpelstiltskin?

ANSWERS: 1 Chiropractic, 2 Ted Rogers, 3 Dame Ninette de Valois, 4 Leopard seal, 5 Christopher Fry, 6 Wiltshire, 7 Eddie Murphy, 8 Pigeon racing, 9 George Gissing, 10 David Lloyd George, 11 Greenpeace, 12 Frostbite, 13 All the Pretty Horses, 14 Sir Francis Chichester, 15 Grimm's Fairy Tales.

GENERAL KNOWLEDGE

1. Which religious group featured in the film Witness?

2. Which French actor starred in the Hollywood films Algiers and Gaslight?

3. With which boy band did Ritchie Neville spring to fame?

4. Which English poet wrote Stone and Flower and Farewell Happy Fields?

5. In radio, what does A.M. stand for?

6. Which U.S. nuclear-powered submarine was the first vessel to circumnavigate the world underwater?

7. How many films did Fred Astaire make with Ginger Rogers?

8. Whitefish Bay is the south-eastern arm of which of the Great Lakes?

9. Which star of Fawlty Towers presented The Human Face on TV?

10. What was the real first name of the spy Kim Philby?

11. Which British athlete won the women's long jump at the 1964 Olympics?

12. Who wrote The Thirty-Nine Steps?

13. Which English king abdicated in 1936?

14. Who won a Best Actress Oscar for her performance in Erin Brockovich?

15. How many millimetres are there in a kilometre?

ENTERTAINMENT

1. Who played Calamity Jane in the 1953 film musical of the same name?

2. Which female vocalist had a U.K. top five hit in 1989 with The Best?

3. Which 1992 film featured James Belushi and Cybill Shepherd as husband and wife?

4. Which Hollywood actor made an appearance in BBC2's The Last Fast Show Ever?

5. Which glamrock group had a U.K. number one hit in 1973 with See My Baby Jive?

6. In which 2000 film did Winona Ryder appear as a former victim of demonic possession?

7. Which Sixties sitcom starring Arthur Lowe was a spin-off from Coronation Street?

8. Which British group had a 2001 U.K. top ten hit with Inner Smile?

9. What was the name of Arnold Schwarzenegger's character in the 1987 film Predator?

10. Which BBC1 drama, based on Don Quixote, starred Colin Firth in the title role?

11. Which actor played Jeremy Stickles in the 2000 BBC1 dramatlsation of Lorna Doone?

12. Which US actress/singer scored a U.K. number one hit with Love Don't Cost a Thing in 2001?

13. Which Star Trek: the Next Generation actor played Ebenezer Scrooge in a 2000 TV movie version of A Christmas Carol?

14. Which 2000 film by M. Night Shyamalan starred Bruce Willis as a security guard who escapes a fatal train derailment?

15. Which 1970s drama series starring Edward Woodward as a newspaper reporter provided a depressing vision of the future?

ANSWERS: 1 Doris Day, 2 Tina Turner, 3 Once Upon a Crime, 4 Johnny Depp, 5 Wizzard, 6 Lost Souls, 7 Pardon the Expression, 8 Texas, 9 Dutch, 10 Donovan Quick, 11 Martin Clunes, 12 Jennifer Lopez, 13 Patrick Stewart, 14 Unbreakable, 15 1990.

GENERAL KNOWLEDGE

1. What is the name of the language used in the Anthony Burgess novel A Clockwork Orange?

2. Which French monarch was known as the Sun King?

3. Of which newspaper was Ben Bradlee executive editor from 1968 to 1991?

4. Which veteran singer-songwriter won the award for Best Original Song at the 2001 Oscars?

5. What sort of glassware has a name meaning 'a thousand flowers' in Italian?

6. Which English runner won the 800m at the 1924 and 1928 Olympics?

7. In which TV series did the character Frasier first appear?

8. What name is given to a star that explodes and increases in brightness by a million times or more?

9. With what sort of books is author Louis L'Amour chiefly associated?

10. Which Essex town was called Caesaromagus by the Romans?

11. Which bridge was re-erected as a tourist attraction at Lake Havasu City in Arizona?

12. Which former pop star starred in the TV series Budgie?

13. Which university won the 2001 Boat Race?

14. With which sport is Kareem Abdul-Jabbar associated?

15. Which German city was the venue for the trials of Nazi war criminals after World War II?

ANSWERS: 1 Nadsat, 2 Louis XIV, 3 Washington Post, 4 Bob Dylan, 5 Millefiori, 6 Doug Lowe, 7 Cheers, 8 Supernova, 9 Westerns, 10 Chelmsford, 11 London Bridge, 12 Adam Faith, 13 Cambridge, 14 Basketball, 15 Nuremberg.

GENERAL KNOWLEDGE

1. Who wrote the book The Cat in the Hat?

2. Which Shakespeare play features Ferdinand, the king of Navarre?

3. Who won a Best Actor Oscar for his performance in Gladiator?

4. Which community for homeless boys was founded by Father Edward Flanagan in Nebraska in 1917?

5. What was the pen name of the author John Griffith Chaney?

6. Abigail was one of the wives of which Biblical king of Israel?

7. Who was the winner of Big Brother in the 2001 UK series?

8. Which gas is synthesised using the Haber-Bosch process?

9. By what name is the central keep of the Tower of London known?

10. Which British author created the detective Albert Campion?

11. Which comic strip features Snoopy, Charlie Brown and Linus?

12. Which jazz musician is the subject of the novel Young Man with a Horn by Dorothy Baker?

13. Which title was conferred on Princess Anne in 1987?

14. In which European country is the port La Coruña?

15. Which athletics field event was formerly known as the hop, step and jump?

GENERAL KNOWLEDGE

1. To which film was The Jewel of the Nile a sequel?

2. Which Russian-born U.S. novelist wrote The Fountainhead?

3. General Sani Abacha became president of which African country in 1993?

4. Which pilot flew the first British Concorde in 1969?

5. Who wrote The Unbearable Lightness of Being?

6. Which Italian actor starred in A Fistful of Dollars and Lucky Luciano?

7. What relation was novelist Isabel Allende to the overthrown Chilean president Salvador Allende?

8. By what name was Haitian president Jean-Claude Duvalier known?

9. Which 2001 film starred Robert De Niro and Kelsey Grammer?

10. What is the technical name for weakening of the bones?

11. Which prolific U.S. inventor invented the electric light bulb?

12. Whose first film appearance was as second welder in the 1957 film Time Lock?

13. Which film was named Best Picture at the 2001 Oscars?

14. In which constellation are the stars Castor and Pollux?

15. Which country singer and actor married Julia Roberts in 1993?

ANSWERS: 1 Romancing the Stone, 2 Ayn Rand, 3 Nigeria, 4 Brian Trubshaw, 5 Milan Kundera, 6 Gian Maria Volonté, 7 Niece, 8 Baby Doc, 9 15 Minutes, 10 Osteoporosis, 11 Thomas Edison, 12 Sean Connery, 13 Gladiator, 14 Gemini, 15 Lyle Lovett.

SPORT

1. Which country did Britain's men beat by half a point to win athletics' European Cup at Gateshead in July 2000?

2. Wayne Gretzky is a legend in which sport?

3. Which country won the 1970 football World Cup?

4. In rugby union, who did the Newcastle Falcons beat in the Tetleys Bitter Cup final in February 2001?

5. What is the minimum number of darts required to finish from a 501 start?

6. Which British football manager was born in Glasgow in 1941?

7. In which month is Royal Ascot traditionally held?

8. Former middle-distance runner Steve Ovett was born in which year - 1945 or 1955?

9. How many pieces does a player start a game of chess with?

10. Which legendary cricketer had a Test batting average of 99.94?

11. Which South American country knocked Great Britain out of the Davis Cup world group in July 2000?

12. Which British golfer lost in a play-off for the 1995 U.S. Open title to Steve Elkington?

13. Who won the F.A. Cup in 2000?

14. In which country is the Magny-Cours motor racing circuit?

15. What nationality is 1976 Olympic Games double gold medallist Alberto Juantorena?

? GENERAL KNOWLEDGE ?

1. Michael Barrymore was formerly what to Shirley Bassey and others?

2. Which team game was originally called Mintonette?

3. In Greek mythology, which merman is traditionally shown blowing on a conch shell?

4. Which This Life actor starred in the TV drama series Teachers?

5. Tammany Hall is the executive committee of which U.S. political party in New York?

6. Which Italian physicist gave his name to the S.I. unit of electromotive force?

7. Which director released the album You Made Me Love You?

8. By what name was the Russian city of Volgograd known from 1925 to 1961?

9. What form of Indian cookery takes its name from the cylindrical clay oven used?

10. Which American novelist wrote Player Piano and God Bless You, Mr Rosewater?

11. Which narcotic drug obtained from opium is used in medicine for the relief of severe pain?

12. Which child star was born Joe Yule?

13. What is the longest river in Europe?

14. Who was the first bowler to take 500 wickets in Test cricket?

15. Which English novelist wrote She and King Soloman's Mines?

ANSWERS: 1 Hairdresser, 2 Volleyball, 3 Triton, 4 Andrew Lincoln, 5 Democratic Party, 6 Alessandro Volta, 7 Orson Welles, 8 Stalingrad, 9 Tandoori, 10 Kurt Vonnegut Jr, 11 Morphine, 12 Mickey Rooney, 13 The Volga, 14 Courtney Walsh, 15 H Rider Haggard.

? **GENERAL KNOWLEDGE** ?

1. The title of the TV series Triangle described the route between Gothenburg, Rotterdam and which English port?

2. Which Shakespeare play is about one of King Priam's sons?

3. What is the name of the petrol-thickening jelly used in incendiary bombs and flame-throwers?

4. Which golfer became the oldest winner in the history of the European tour when he won the 2001 Madeira Island Open?

5. What sort of creature is a tanager?

6. Which French author was born François-Marie Arouet?

7. Who provided the voice for Jessica Rabbit in the film Who Framed Roger Rabbit?

8. Which South African dramatist wrote the play No-Good Friday?

9. Which Welsh rugby player scored in every possible way in their 2001 Six Nations win against France?

10. Agate is a semi-precious variety of what form of quartz?

11. Which Canadian singer recorded the albums Blue and Miles of Aisles?

12. What number was The Prisoner in the television series of that name?

13. Which Irish adventurer attempted to steal the crown jewels from the Tower of London in 1671?

14. Who was sacked as manager of Tottenham Hotspur in 2001?

15. Which device in a jet engine provides extra thrust for take off or supersonic flight?

ANSWERS: 1 Felixstowe, 2 Troilus and Cressida, 3 Napalm, 4 Des Smyth, 5 A bird, 6 Voltaire, 7 Kathleen Turner, 8 Athol Fugard, 9 Neil Jenkins, 10 Chalcedony, 11 Joni Mitchell, 12 Six, 13 Colonel Blood, 14 George Graham, 15 Afterburner.

GENERAL KNOWLEDGE

1. The film Jerry Maguire featured which sport?

2. Which 16th-century English composer wrote the 40-part motet Spem in alium?

3. What is the chief river of Ghana?

4. Which 2001 film about the Cuban missile crisis starred Kevin Costner?

5. Of which organisation was Oliver Tambo president general from 1969 to 1991?

6. Which U.S. shot-putter developed the style in which the putter turns 180 degrees?

7. In which country did television's Reilly - Ace of Spies operate?

8. Which epic poem by Dante begins on Good Friday in 1300?

9. Which 19th-century British philosopher wrote the essay On Liberty?

10. Who was the first direct descendant of Queen Elizabeth II not to bear a royal title?

11. Which German motor manufacturer was set up in 1937 to produce a 'people's car'?

12. The River Tamar forms a historic boundary between which two counties?

13. What is the profession of Nick in the sitcom Beast?

14. Who played Sally Bowles in the film Cabaret?

15. Which fish is smoked and sold as finnan haddie?

GENERAL KNOWLEDGE

1. Who was the 1982 U.S. Open golf champion?

2. Who was the 1994 Commonwealth women's 10,000m champion?

3. Which city in the Netherlands was the residence of Charles II of England during his exile?

4. Which 1960s rock group comprised Eric Clapton, Jack Bruce and Ginger Baker?

5. Matilda Alice Victoria Wood was the real name of which English music-hall entertainer?

6. Who wrote the 1906 novel The Man of Property?

7. What is a vaporetto?

8. Who wrote the 1968 novel Only When I Larf?

9. On which lake is the Scottish village and fishing port of Ullapool?

10. Which English naval officer was chief minister of Naples from 1779-1806?

11. Who was the 1996 world Formula 1 motor racing champion?

12. Which city in Switzerland was the headquarters of the League of Nations?

13. Who wrote the 1953 novel After the Funeral?

14. Who wrote the 1939 novel No Orchids for Miss Blandish?

15. Which 1969 film starring Richard Burton and Rex Harrison was based on a play by Charles Dyer?

ANSWERS 1. Tom Watson 2. Yvonne Murray 3. Breda 4. Cream 5. Marie Lloyd 6. John Galsworthy 7. A steam-powered passenger boat used on the canals in Venice 8. Len Deighton 9. Lake Broom 10. Sir John Acton 11. Damon Hill 12. Geneva 13. Agatha Christie 14. James Hadley Chase 15. Staircase.

ENTERTAINMENT

1. Which comedian featured a spoof version of Who Wants to be a Millionaire on his TV show, called Who Wants to Win an Ounce?

2. Which husband and wife team played David and Mary Caxton in the 1958 sitcom Caxton's Tales?

3. Who directed the 1999 film Random Hearts?

4. Who played Alec Picton-Jones in the sitcom Hippies?

5. Who played Candyman in the 1992 film?

6. Which comedienne was born Lynne Shepherd in 1945?

7. Who wrote and directed the film comedy Fanny and Elvis?

8. Who plays an orphan in the 1978 film Candleshoe?

9. Who plays Christmas Jones in the Bond film The World is Not Enough?

10. Which actress plays Annie Spadaro in the sitcom Caroline in the City?

11. Who directed the 1974 film The Taking of Pelham One Two Three?

12. Which comedian stars in the 1972 film Cancel My Reservation?

13. Who directed the 1979 film Cuba starring Sean Connery?

14. What is the real first name of entertainer Max Bygraves?

15. Who won Best Female Artist at the 1999 European MTV Awards?

ANSWERS 1. Ali G 2. Wilfred and Mabel Pickles 3. Sydney Pollack 4. Julian Rhind-Tutt 5. Tony Todd 6. Marti Caine 7. Kay Mellor 8. Jodie Foster 9. Denise Richards 10. Amy Pietz 11. Joseph Sargent 12. Bob Hope 13. Richard Lester 14. Walter 15. Britney Spears.

SPORT

1. Which Briton won the 1962 South African Grand Prix in Formula 1?

2. In which city were the 1987 World Student games held?

3. Which country did rugby union's British Lions tour in 1997?

4. In which county is the Grand National Archery Society based?

5. Christophe Tiozzo was 1990 WBA super-middleweight champion. Which country did he represent?

6. Which stadium was built to host the 1908 Olympic Games?

7. Which woman took a hat-trick for Australia against England in a Test match in February 1958?

8. In which city was cricketer James Boiling born?

9. How many gold medals did gymnast Vitaliy Scherbo win at world championships from 1992-5?

10. In which year did U.S. tennis player Dwight Davis die?

11. At what sport have Keiji Okada and Yuko Hasama been world champions?

12. Which cricketer was 1975 B.B.C. Sports Personality of the Year?

13. For which two clubs did Scot Jimmy McGrory net 410 league goals from 1922-38?

14. For which Premier League side did veteran goalie Neville Southall appear in the 1999/00 season?

15. Which man set a world record of 10.2 seconds for the 100m on 20th June 1936?

POP MUSIC

1. Which group recorded the 1985 album The Clock Comes Down the Stairs?

2. To which label did Furniture sign in 1986?

3. In which year did Sad Café have a Top 10 single with Every Day Hurts?

4. Who recorded the 1982 album 10,9,8,7,6,5,4,3,2,1?

5. Which duo recorded the album Freeze Frame?

6. Which Australian entertainer recorded the 1965 single Linda?

7. Which funk group recorded the 1970 album Osmium?

8. On which label did Feeder record the album Yesterday Went Too Soon?

9. Which Dutch group recorded the 1978 single Rock 'N Roll?

10. Who produced Ian Gomm's 1978 single Hold On?

11. Who had a 1985 Top 10 single with Material Girl?

12. In which year did the Jesus and Mary Chain release the Some Candy Talking E.P.?

13. Which studio album by Fun Boy Three features the song The Farm Yard Connection?

14. Who produced the Jam's 1980 single Goin' Underground?

15. Who recorded the 1977 album Bullinamingvase?

ART & LITERATURE

1. Which Australian author wrote the 2001 novel Dark Palace?

2. In which year was the author George MacDonald Fraser born?

3. Who wrote the 2000 novel The Corrections?

4. What nationality is the artist Roman Signer?

5. In which city was the U.S. artist Frank Stella born?

6. Who wrote the 1977 book The Condition of Muzak?

7. Who wrote the 2000 book Walking the Dog?

8. Who wrote the 2001 children's book A Land Without Magic?

9. Which author penned the 2000 novel The PowerBook?

10. Which crime writer's books include Lestrade and the Kiss of Horus?

11. Who wrote the novel A Long and Happy Life?

12. Who penned the novel The Fourth Protocol?

13. In which N.E. town is the Baltic Centre for Contemporary Art?

14. Which crime writer wrote the novel Pagan Babies?

15. Which Australian writer won the 2001 Commonwealth Writers' Prize Best Book Award?

ANSWERS 1. Frank Moorhouse 2. 1925 3. Jonathan Franzen 4. Swiss 5. Boston 6. Michael Moorcock 7. Walter Mosley 8. Stephen Elboz 9. Jeanette Winterson 10. M.J. Trow 11. Reynolds Price 12. Frederick Forsyth 13. Gateshead 14. Elmore Leonard 15. Peter Carey.

GENERAL KNOWLEDGE ?

1. Who was the mother of the English king Richard I?

2. Which comedy actor played Charles Brown in the television sitcom Sykes?

3. Which actor played Hoss Cartwright in the television western show Bonanza?

4. Which actress played Meg Richardson in the television soap Crossroads?

5. Who was the 1987 world Formula 1 motor racing champion?

6. Which German philosopher's works included The World as Will and Idea?

7. Ljubljana is the capital of which republic in central Europe?

8. Which fish is also called a long-fin tunny?

9. Which genus of plants includes the wood sorrel?

10. What is the basic SI unit of amount of substance?

11. Which actor played Max in the television series Hart to Hart?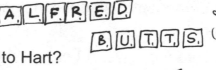

12. Who directed the 1955 film The Long Gray Line?

13. Which principality in S.W. Europe includes the port La Condamine?

14. Which board game was invented by Alfred M. Butts?

15. Which actress starred in the title role of the 1968 Robert Aldrich film The Legend of Lylah Clare?

ANSWERS 1. Eleanor of Aquitaine 2. Richard Wattis 3. Dan Blocker 4. Noele Gordon 5. Nelson Piquet 6. Arthur Schopenhauer 7. Slovenia 8. Albacore 9. Oxalis 10. Mole 11. Lionel Stander 12. John Ford 13. Monaco 14. Scrabble 15. Kim Novak.

ENTERTAINMENT

1. Who played Holly Goodhead in the Bond film Moonraker?

2. Who played Governor Earl Kemp Long in the 1989 film Blaze?

3. What is the name of the malfunctioning penguin in the film Toy Story 2?

4. In which comedy show do the characters Papa Lazarou and Hilary Briss appear?

5. Who plays W.S. Gilbert in the film Topsy Turvy?

6. Who plays a sideshow ventriloquist in the 1925 film The Unholy Three?

7. Who starred as a film producer in the 1991 film Grand Canyon?

8. In which city did Placido Domingo make his debut as a baritone?

9. Who directed the 1980 film Scanners?

10. Who won Best Director at the 2000 Golden Globes?

11. What is Kim Basinger's profession in the 1987 film Nadine?

12. What is the nickname of headmaster Harry Andrews in the 1980s sitcom A.J. Wentworth, B.A.?

13. Which actor presented the 2000 Channel Four series Six Experiments that Changed the World?

14. Who does Liz Dawn play in Coronation Street?

15. Who directed the 1956 film Trapeze?

SPORT

1. Who replaced Robert Howley as Welsh rugby union captain in 2000?

2. Who rode Wolfhound to victory in the 1993 Haydock Park Sprint Cup?

3. In cricket, who scored 117 for Essex against Northants in the 1st innings of their 1999 county championship game?

4. In which year was the Tennis & Rackets Association formed?

5. Who knocked Eccles out of the 2000 rugby league Silk Cut Challenge Cup?

6. By what score did England beat Ireland in the 2000 Six Nations rugby union tournament?

7. In which year did cricketer Timothy Bloomfield make his county debut for Middlesex?

8. How many times did Kapil Dev take 5 or more wickets in an innings in his 131 Tests?

9. Who took 7-73 for Nottinghamshire against Somerset at Taunton in 1998?

10. Which baseball player had the best batting average in 1962?

11. In which year were the Endurance Riding World Championships in equestrianism first held?

12. In which year was boxer Julius Francis born?

13. What country did champion Nordic skier Lyubov Korzyryeva represent?

14. Who was 1924 Olympic women's 200m breaststroke swimming champion?

15. Which Spanish golfer won the 1983 U.S. Masters?

POP MUSIC

1. Which group had a 1982 Top 20 hit with the song Promised You A Miracle?

2. Which band fronted by Justine Frischmann had a Top Twenty hit single in 1995 with Waking Up?

3. Which John Lennon song is covered on the 2001 album Love, Shelby by Shelby Lynne?

4. Who produced the 1991 record album Seamonsters by The Wedding Present?

5. Which male singer recorded the 2001 single I Forgot?

6. Which group recorded the 2001 single The Way To Your Love?

7. In which year did John Martyn record the album Solid Air?

8. Which group's hit singles include The Universal and Beetlebum?

9. Which group recorded the 1993 Top 10 single Little Fluffy Clouds?

10. What do the initials of the New York club CBGB's stand for?

11. What nationality is the songwriter Howie Beck?

12. Which punk musician composed the soundtrack for Alex Cox's film Walker?

13. Who recorded the 1985 album Behind the Sun?

14. Which group recorded the 1983 album Torment and Toreros?

15. Who had a 1989 Top 20 single with the song Voodoo Ray?

ANSWERS 1. Simple Minds 2. Elastica 3. Mother 4. Steve Albini 5. Lionel Richie 6. Hearsay 7. 1973 8. Blur 9. The Orb 10. Country, Bluegrass & Blues 11. Canadian 12. Joe Strummer 13. Eric Clapton 14. Marc and the Mambas 15. A Guy Called Gerald.

GEOGRAPHY

1. On which Greek island is the resort of Batsi?

2. In which vale is the market town of Sevenoaks in Kent?

3. In which sea are the Kerkennah Islands?

4. On which river is the market town of Welshpool?

5. In which European capital city are the districts of Nørrebro and Vesterbro?

6. Which West Yorkshire town is situated at the confluence of the Rivers Ryburn and Calder?

7. In which gulf is the island of Socotra?

8. In which U.S. state is the port of Tarpon Springs?

9. In which English county is the seaside resort of Holkham?

10. In which European country is the ski resort of Barèges?

11. In which English county is Abbots Bromley?

12. Valence is the capital of which French department?

13. The Whitsunday Islands lie off the coast of which Australian state?

14. Of which country is Thimphu the capital?

15. Which is Germany's highest mountain?

ANSWERS 1. Andros 2. Vale of Holmesdale 3. Mediterranean Sea 4. Severn 5. Copenhagen 6. Sowerby Bridge 7. Gulf of Aden 8. Florida 9. Norfolk 10. France 11. Staffordshire 12. Drôme 13. Queensland 14. Bhutan 15. Zugspitze.

GENERAL KNOWLEDGE

1. In which year did the Italian operatic tenor Enrico Caruso die?

2. What is the name of the female reproductive part of a flower?

3. Which genus of woodland plants includes the windflower?

4. Which French novelist authored François le Champi?

5. Who were the male and female leads in the 1974 film The Night Porter?

6. What is the name given to the mass of lymphoid tissue at the back of the throat behind the uvula?

7. In which Italian city is La Scala opera house?

8. What was the former name from 1940-62 for the Russian port of Perm?

9. Who wrote the 1969 play Breath?

10. In which year did U.S. aviator and polar explorer Richard Byrd die?

11. Who was the 1954 winner of the British Open golf tournament?

12. Which actress played Purdey in the television show The New Avengers?

13. Who had a 1973 No. 1 single with Can the Can?

14. Which Phoenician prince in Greek mythology slew the dragon guarding the spring of Ares?

15. What was the name given to the army established in 1645 during the Civil War by the English parliamentarians?

ANSWERS 1. 1921 2. Pistil 3. Anemone 4. George Sand 5. Dirk Bogarde and Charlotte Rampling 6. Adenoids 7. Milan 8. Molotov 9. Samuel Beckett 10. 1957 11. Peter Thomson 12. Joanna Lumley 13. Suzi Quatro 14. Cadmus 15. New Model Army

ENTERTAINMENT

1. Which comedy duo impersonate pop stars in the television series Rock Profile?

2. Who directed and starred in the 2001 film Freddy Got Fingered?

3. Who plays a military prison governor in the 2001 film The Last Castle?

4. Who directed the 1968 film Finian's Rainbow?

5. Who directed the 2001 film Serendipity?

6. Who played boxer James J. Corbett in the 1942 film Gentleman Jim?

7. In which year was Caryl Churchill's play Top Girls first produced in London?

8. Who played Prince Salina in the 1963 film The Leopard?

9. Who directed the 2000 film Book of Shadows: Blair Witch 2?

10. Who plays the beatnik Jon Rubin in the 1968 film Greetings?

11. Which rapper co-stars with Steven Seagal in the film Exit Wounds?

12. Which English actor stars in the 2001 film In the Bedroom?

13. What was Al Pacino's reported fee for the film The Godfather?

14. Who directed the 2001 film Artificial Intelligence: AI?

15. Who is the male lead in the 2000 film Romeo Must Die?

ANSWERS 1. Matt Lucas and David Walliams 2. Tom Green 3. James Gandolfini 4. Francis Ford Coppola 5. Peter Chelsom 6. Errol Flynn 7. 1982 8. Burt Lancaster 9. Joe Berlinger 10. Robert De Niro 11. DMX 12. Tom Wilkinson 13. $35,000 14. Steven Spielberg 15. Jet Li.

SPORT

1. Which rugby league club signed Keith Senior in September 1999?

2. Which horse won the 1917 Grand National?

3. From which country is runner Maria Mutola?

4. How many Olympic gold medals did Lasse Viren win from 1972-6?

5. Which Swedes won the 1987 Australian Open men's doubles tennis title?

6. Which Frenchman won the 1987 Belgian Grand Prix in Formula 1?

7. Who finished second in the men's 100m at the 1999 World Athletics Championships?

8. Who won the Harry Sunderland Trophy in 1980 whilst with Widnes?

9. How many golds did Romania win at the 1999 World Athletics Championships?

10. With which winter sport are Anton Fischer and Jeffrey Jost associated?

11. By what score did Lindsay Davenport beat Martina Hingis in the 2000 Australian Open singles tennis championship final?

12. In which year were Surrey crowned the first official cricket county championship winners?

13. Which sport is played by the New Jersey Devils?

14. What nationality is golfer Colleen Walker?

15. Who was 1954 Sports Illustrated Sportsman of the Year?

ANSWERS 1. Leeds Rhinos 2. Ballymacad 3. Mozambique 4. Four 5. Stefan Edberg and Anders Järryd 6. Alain Prost 7. Bruny Surin 8. Mal Aspey 9. Two 10. Bobsleigh 11. 6-1,7-5 12. 1890 13. Ice hockey 14. American 15. Roger Bannister.

POP MUSIC

1. Which singer guests on the song First Man in Space by the group The All Seeing I?

2. What is the title of George Michael's debut solo L.P.?

3. Who featured on Technotronic's 1990 hit single Get Up (Before the Night Is Over)?

4. What is the title of the second album by the group The Fugs?

5. Which ex-soap actress had a 1999 Top 10 single with I've Got You?

6. Which group had a 1986 hit with the single All Fall Down?

7. In which year did The Tourists have a Top 10 single with I Only Want to Be With You?

8. Which female singer had a 1983 Top 10 hit with the song Move Over Darling?

9. In which year did Gary Numan first have a hit single with Cars?

10. In which year did Elvis Costello have a Top 10 single with I Can't Stand Up For Falling Down?

11. Which singer featured on Y-Tribe's 1999 hit Enough is Enough?

12. Gore, Fletcher, Gahan. Which pop group?

13. What was Piero Umiliani's only hit single?

14. On which label did George Michael record his album Songs from the Last Century?

15. Which group did Ian Broudie form in 1982?

HISTORY

1. In which year of World War II was Coventry Cathedral destroyed?

2. In which year did Cory Aquino become president of the Philippines?

3. In which year was the Battle of Towton in the Wars of the Roses?

4. In which year did Edward Heath become M.P. for Bexley?

5. In which year was English Roman Catholic prelate Reginald Pole born?

6. In which year did Dick Turpin die?

7. Which treaty, signed in 1360, ended the first phase of the Hundred Years' War?

8. In which year did Jacques Chirac first become prime minister of France?

9. In which month of 1981 was Pope John Paul II shot?

10. In which year did the Seven Years' War end?

11. Who was elected vice-president of the U.S. in 1852 but died six weeks after being sworn in?

12. Who was mayor of West Berlin from 1957-66?

13. In which year was the Philippeville Massacre in Algeria?

14. In which year did Hosni Mubarak become president of Egypt?

15. The War of the Bavarian Succession was fought between which two countries?

GENERAL KNOWLEDGE

1. In which year was Brunel's Clifton Suspension Bridge completed?

2. Who succeeded Franklin Pierce in 1857 as U.S. president?

3. What is the plant convallaria majalis commonly known as?

4. Who was president of the European Union Commission from 1977-81?

5. In which year was the University of Wales, Cardiff founded?

6. What is the correct form of spoken address to a countess?

7. In which year did the Tay Road Bridge open?

8. What is the approximate driving distance in miles between London and Paris - 157, 207 or 257?

9. What are the four colours on the flag of Sudan?

10. Which writer's volumes include 1900's The Shadowy Waters?

11. Where did the poet William Wordsworth die in 1850?

12. What in martial arts is an ashi gatami?

13. Who wrote the 1936 novel Flowers for the Judge?

14. In which year did Theodore Roosevelt die?

15. Who wrote the 1947 book Gimlet Mops Up?

ANSWERS 1. 1864 2. James Buchanan 3. Lily of the Valley 4. Roy Jenkins 5. 1893 6. Madam 7. 1966 8. 257 miles 9. Green, black, red and white 10. W.B. Yeats 11. Rydal Mount, Ambleside 12. Leg lock 13. Margery Allingham 14. 1919 15. Capt. W.E. Johns.

ENTERTAINMENT

1. Who composed the 1919 opera Fennimore and Gerda?

2. Which Monty Python member played Yellowbeard in a 1983 film?

3. Who directed the 1949 film western The Walking Hills?

4. Who won the Best Actor in a Drama award at the 2000 Golden Globes?

5. Who starred as Alex in a 1989 stage production of A Clockwork Orange?

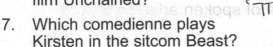

6. What is the theme song to the 1955 prison drama film Unchained?

7. Which comedienne plays Kirsten in the sitcom Beast?

8. Who directed the 1947 film Unconquered?

9. In which year did opera singer Stafford Dean make his debut at Glyndebourne?

10. Who stars as film star Nick Lang in the 1991 film The Hard Way?

11. What is the name of Woody's horse in the film Toy Story 2?

12. Who has played Alan Turner in Emmerdale?

13. Who directed the film Double Jeopardy, which stars Ashley Judd?

14. Who was the male lead in the 1988 film The Unbearable Lightness of Being?

15. What anniversary did news programme Newsnight celebrate in 2000?

ANSWERS 1. Frederick Delius 2. Graham Chapman 3. John Sturges 4. Denzil Washington 5. Phil Daniels 6. Unchained Melody 7. Doon Mackichan 8. Cecil B. De Mille 9. 1964 10. Michael J. Fox 11. Bullseye 12. Richard Thorp 13. Bruce Beresford 14. Daniel Day-Lewis 15. 20th.

SPORT

1. Michael Staksrud was 1973 world men's speed skating champion. What country did he represent?

2. With which field event would you associate Philippa Roles and Judy Oakes?

3. Who were Everton's three scorers in their 1985 European Cup-Winners' Cup Final win?

4. What nationality is swimmer Lars Frolander?

5. Who was men's 100m champion at the 1977 I.A.A.F. World Cup?

6. In which sport were Ichiro Ogimura and Yoshio Tomita world champions in 1956?

7. Who rode the 1953 winner of the Oaks, Ambiguity?

8. For which county did cricketer Darren Bicknall make his debut in 1987?

9. How many gold medals have Lithuania won at the summer Olympics from 1896-1996?

10. Who is the mother of athlete Daniela Caines?

11. What nationality is skier Christl Cranz?

12. In which Australian city is the Albert Park Formula 1 racetrack?

13. What nationality are canoeists Beniamino Bonomi and Daniele Scarpa?

14. For which team did Formula 1 driver Jenson Button compete in the 2000 Grand Prix season?

15. Which state withdrew from the National Football League in Australian Rules Football in 1977-8?

ANSWERS 1. Norway 2. Shot 3. Gray, Steven & Sheedy 4. Swedish 5. Steve Williams 6. Table tennis 7. Joe Mercer 8. Surrey 9. One 10. Blondelle Thompson 11. German 12. Melbourne 13. Italian 14. Williams 15. Victoria.

POP MUSIC

1. Which group had a 1993 Top 10 single with The Key the Secret?

2. Which group had a 1999 Top 10 single with Steal My Sunshine?

3. Which group had a 1996 hit single with Pearl's Girl?

4. Which Scottish group were dropped from an Alice Cooper tour in the early 1980s for reportedly being 'too weird'?

5. On which label did the Undertones record the 1981 hit Julie Ocean?

6. On which label did Vengaboys release the 1999 album The Party Album!?

7. Which group had a 1994 Top 40 hit with Girl You'll Be A Woman Soon?

8. Which hip-hop group recorded the song Millie Pulled a Pistol on Santa?

9. Which male singer had a 1991 hit with Cold Cold Heart?

10. Which veteran rock 'n' roller recorded the 1995 album Young Blood?

11. Which group recorded the song I Want a New Drug on the 1983 album Sports?

12. Who had a 1954 No. 1 single with Finger of Suspicion?

13. Which group had a 1992 hit with Who's Gonna Ride Your Wild Horses?

14. Which group recorded the 1968 album Cheap Thrills?

15. In which year was U.S.A. for Africa's We Are the World a No. 1 hit?

ANSWERS 1. Urban Cookie Collective 2. Len 3. Underworld 4. Big Country 5. Ardeck 6. Positiva 7. Urge Overkill 8. De La Soul 9. Midge Ure 10. Jerry Lee Lewis 11. Huey Lewis and the News 12. Dickie Valentine 13. U2 14. Big Brother & the Holding Company 15. 1985.

WORDS

1. What might you do in an estaminet?

2. What drugs are known in the U.S. as splash?

3. Flowery is British rhyming slang for which type of room?

4. What on an insect is a forfex?

5. What type of creature is a cleg?

6. What is dactylography?

7. For which part of the body is a filbert a slang word?

8. What in North American slang is a sky bear?

9. What type of performer is an equilibrist?

10. Snotty is British nautical slang for which crew member?

11. What is lincrusta?

12. What does the Latin phrase ut infra mean?

13. What might you do in East Africa with a kanzu?

14. What type of creature is a carabid - an antelope or a beetle?

15. What is the name given to a plunger in a churn?

ANSWERS 1. Eat or drink, it's a small bar or bistro 2. Amphetamines 3. A cell As below 4. Pair of pincers 5. Horsefly 6. The scientific study of fingerprints 7. Head 8. Police helicopter 9. Tightrope walker 10. Midshipman 11. A type of wallpaper 12. As below 13. Wear it, it's a garment 14. Beetle 15. Dasher.

GENERAL KNOWLEDGE

1. Who directed the 1940 film Christmas in July?

2. In which year was the actress Ava Gardner born?

3. By which name is the Eurasian plant cleavers also known?

4. Which 17th century Dutch portrait painter was born Pieter van der Faes?

5. What was the name of the world's security command in children's television puppet show Captain Scarlet and the Mysterons?

6. Which bird makes its first appearance on the seventh day of Christmas in the song Twelve Days of Christmas?

7. Who was the director of the 1966 film The Bible?

8. What type of creature is a nilgai?

9. In which year did stage and film comedian Charlie Chaplin die?

10. In which year was world light-heavyweight boxing champion Archie Moore born?

11. Who was elected M.P. for Cardiff South and Penarth in May 1997?

12. Who was elected Israeli prime minister in May 1999?

13. Which comedian won the Perrier Award at the 1999 Edinburgh Festival in his guise as 'The Pub Landlord'?

14. Which island of the Mediterranean is separated from Italy by the Strait of Messina?

15. Who did Monty Woolley play in the 1942 film The Man Who Came To Dinner?

ANSWERS 1. Preston Sturges 2. 1922 3. Goosegrass 4. Peter Lely 5. Spectrum 6. Swan 7. John Huston 8. A large Indian antelope 9. 1977 10. 1913 11. Alun Michael 12. Ehud Barak 13. Al Murray 14. Sicily 15. Sheridan Whiteside.

ENTERTAINMENT

1. Which comedian thinks he has only two weeks to live in the 1939 comedy Never Say Die?

2. Who directed the 1967 film Ulysses, based on the novel by James Joyce?

3. Who wrote the 1970s sitcom Alexander the Greatest?

4. Which author does Ewan McGregor play in the 2000 film Nora?

5. In which city is the 1973 film The Sting set?

6. During the making of which film was Montgomery Clift disfigured in a car crash?

7. Who played Stacey Sutton in the Bond film A View to a Kill?

8. Who is the female star of the 1942 film musical Iceland?

9. Who directed and starred in the 1969 comedy Take the Money and Run?

10. Who directed 1932 film I Am a Fugitive from a Chain Gang?

11. Who wrote the 1999 Channel Four drama Kid in the Corner?

12. Who played headmaster Richard Nixon in the 1997 sitcom Chalk?

13. Who played cyborg T-1000 in the 1991 film Terminator 2: Judgement Day?

14. What is Brad Pitt's character name in the film Fight Club?

15. Who directed the 1991 film Jungle Fever?

SPORT

1. In which city was the 1978 BDO world professional darts championship held?

2. What is the full name of Welsh rugby union player Rupert Moon?

3. Briton Martin Potter was a world professional champion in 1989. At what sport?

4. In which year did VfB Leipzig first win the German League?

5. What nationality is swimmer Brendon Dedekind?

6. In cricket, who scored 201 for Hampshire against Sussex in the 2nd innings of their 1999 county championship game?

7. Which U.S. jockey earned over $203m from 1974-96?

8. In cricket, who scored 111 n.o. for Hampshire against Sussex in the 2nd innings of their 1999 county championship game?

9. Which nation were men's team winners in the 1982 World Freshwater Championships in angling?

10. Which American pair won the 1938 and 1939 Wimbledon women's doubles title?

11. Who was runner-up in the 1966 Formula 1 world championship?

12. In cricket, who scored 105 for Durham against Essex in the 1st innings of their 1999 county championship game?

13. Which club won the Welsh league in rugby union in 1997/8?

14. Which motor racer was 1973 Sports Illustrated Sportsman of the Year?

15. What nationality was WBC super-featherweight boxing champion Cornelius Boza Edwards?

ANSWERS 1. Nottingham 2. Rupert Henry St. John Barker Moon 3. Surfing 4. 1903 5. South African 6. William Kendall 7. Chris McCarron 8. Adrian Aymes 9. Holland 10. Alice Marble and Sarah Fabyan 11. John Surtees 12. James Daley 13. Swansea 14. Jackie Stewart 15. Ugandan.

POP MUSIC

1. Which group recorded the 2001 single Turn?

2. Which girl group recorded the 2001 single All I Want?

3. Which boy band recorded the 2001 single More Than That?

4. Which female singer sang the song Djini Judy on the 1968 album The Wind in the Willows by the group The Wind in the Willows?

5. Which singer-songwriter recorded the 2001 album Gold?

6. Which record by Staff Sgt. Barry Sadler was a U.S. No. 1 single in 1966?

7. Which group recorded the 2001 album Souljacker?

8. Beautiful Day is the opening track on which U2 studio album?

9. In which year was the Bruce Springsteen album Nebraska released?

10. Which duo left the group the Human League to form the band Heaven 17?

11. Who recorded the 1977 No. 1 single Way Down?

12. Which double A-side was a December 1962 No. 1 single for Cliff Richard?

13. Which female singer recorded the 1999 album Telegram?

14. Which group recorded the 1988 album 16 Lovers Lane?

15. Which female artist recorded the 1990 album Love in a Small Town?

SCIENCE

1. What does MS-DOS stand for in computing?

2. Which chemical element has the symbol Hs?

3. What nationality was nuclear physicist Horni Bhabha?

4. What is the largest of Neptune's moons?

5. Whose greatest published work was De Re Metallica?

6. Of which planet is Desdemona a satellite?

7. What is the name given to the point at which the three phases of water: vapour, liquid and ice, are in equilibrium?

8. Which German physicist discovered the 'uncertainty principle' in quantum theory in 1927?

9. What is the average diameter in miles of Neptune's moon Galatea?

10. What organization in the U.S. is the A.A.A.S.?

11. What nationality was pioneer photographer Nadar?

12. Which element did Otto Hahn and Lise Meitner discover in 1918?

13. In which European capital was Jacques Lucien Monod born?

14. Who became Professor of Mathematics at the University of Pisa in 1589?

15. What colour is pitchblende?

ANSWERS 1. Microsoft Disk Operating System 2. Hassium 3. Indian 4. Triton 5. Georgius Agricola 6. Uranus 7. The triple point 8. Werner Heisenberg 9. 108 miles 10. American Association for the Advancement of Science 11. French 12. Proactinium 13. Paris 14. Galileo 15. Black.

? **GENERAL KNOWLEDGE** ?

1. Which comedian starred in the film The Debt Collector?

2. Which celebrity got married in to DJ Fatboy Slim?

3. Who was winner of the 1999 French Open men's singles tennis championship?

4. Who was men's marathon winner at the 1999 I.A.A.F. World Championships?

5. Which boardgame features two kings, two queens and sixteen pawns?

6. Which actor played Death in the film Meet Joe Black?

7. Who wrote the 1999 novel The Alibi?

8. Which tennis player knocked Martina Hingis out of the 1999 ladies singles tournament at Wimbledon?

9. Who was author of the 1999 novel Inconceivable?

10. Which new minister was put in charge of the Greenwich Dome following the departure of Peter Mandelson?

11. In which year was Saint Ignatius Loyola born?

12. What is the name given to a calendar year of 366 days?

13. Which actor voiced the Genie in the 1992 animated film Aladdin?

14. Which Italian football team were the winners of the 1999 U.E.F.A. Cup?

15. Which manager of Newcastle United resigned early in the 1999/2000 season?

ENTERTAINMENT

1. Who directed the 1927 film The Unknown starring Lon Chaney?

2. In which Australian city was actor-manager Sydney W. Carroll born?

3. Who stars as a boys' school teacher in the 1971 film Unman, Wittering and Zigo?

4. Which American actress stars in Kenneth Branagh's film Love's Labours Lost?

5. Who directed the film Holy Smoke starring Kate Winslet?

6. Who did Patrick Cargill play in the 1971 film version of Up Pompeii?

7. In which Verdi opera does Elisabeth de Valois appear?

8. Who directed the 1939 film Union Pacific?

9. Who composed the 1832 opera The Love Potion?

10. In which Mozart opera does the character Don Alfonso appear?

11. What is Roger Moore's profession in the 1985 film The Naked Face?

12. What is Russ Abbot's real name?

13. Who plays Mr. Blume in the film Rushmore?

14. Which actress played Winnie Purvis in Emmerdale Farm?

15. Who won the 1992 Perrier Award at the Edinburgh Festival for Best Newcomer?

SPORT

1. How many Tests did cricketer David Capel play for England?

2. Ron Northcott was winning skip three times at the curling world championships. For which country?

3. In cricket, who scored 265 for Surrey vs. Middlesex in the 1st innings of their 1999 county championship game?

4. In which year was the European Cup-Winners' Cup in men's handball first held?

5. In which year did British tennis player Dora Boothby die?

6. What was unusual about the weapon Boris Onischenko used in fencing at the 1972 Olympics?

7. How many golds did Germany get in the 1999 World Athletics Championships?

8. Which Scottish football team entered the 1871/2 F.A. Cup in England?

9. Which ice hockey player is known as the 'Russian Rocket'?

10. Yuriy Sedykh set a world record for hammer throw on 30th August 1986. How far was it?

11. What do the initials TKO stand for?

12. Who rode Diesis to victory in the 1982 Dewhurst Stakes?

13. Is cricketer J.J. Bates a right-handed or left-handed bat?

14. Who won the roller hockey title when it was a demonstration sport at the 1992 Olympic Games?

15. At what sport have Emma Carney and Chris McCormack been world champions?

ANSWERS 1. 15 2. Canada 3. Alistair Brown 4. 1976 5. 1970 6. It registered hits when no contact had occurred 7. Four 8. Queen's Park 9. Pavel Bure 10. 86.74m 11. Technical knock-out 12. Lester Piggott 13. Right-handed 14. Argentina 15. Triathlon.

POP MUSIC

1. Which Smokey Robinson song did Japan release as a single in 1982?

2. In which year did R & B singer Billy Stewart die?

3. Which Neil Young song did Jason and the Scorchers record on the B-side of the single White Lies?

4. Which artist recorded the 1988 album Born 2B Blue?

5. Which two singers appear on album sleeves on the cover of Jilted John's single Jilted John?

6. Which Richard Thompson song features on the reverse of the single Peace in Our Time by The Imposter?

7. Which group's debut album in 1992 was You, the Night and the Music?

8. Who wrote the Jam song Innocent Man?

9. Who had a 1994 Top 10 single with Confide in Me?

10. Who recorded the 1984 album Medicine Show?

11. Who composed the soundtrack for the 1985 film Birdy?

12. On which label was Haircut Onc Hundred's single Prime Time released?

13. Who is credited with vocals on the single I Don't Want To Live With Monkeys by the Higsons?

14. How old was Rory Gallagher when he died in 1995?

15. What is the B-side of the Human League's 1978 single Being Boiled?

PEOPLE

1. In which year did the author Richard Brautigan commit suicide?

2. Actress Talia Shire is the sister of which film director?

3. Actress Kate Hudson is the daughter of which other actress?

4. How old was the actor Richard Farnsworth when he died in 2000?

5. What nationality is the jazz pianist Bugge Wesseltoft?

6. Which recording artist was the subject of the song Chuck E's in Love by Rickie Lee Jones?

7. Which musician did the actress Liv Tyler believe her father to be until the age of 10?

8. In which year did the playwright Lorraine Hansberry die?

9. In which year did the explorer George Mallory disappear on Mount Everest?

10. Who was the second person to win the top prize on the U.K. quiz show Who Wants To Be A Millionaire?

11. What is the third name of Britain's Prince Edward?

12. Who took over as director of the National Theatre in 2001?

13. Ron Peel was the main shareholder of which late 20th century U.S. manufacturing company?

14. Who did the singer Jennifer Lopez marry in 2001?

15. Who stepped down as leader of Northern Ireland's SDLP in September, 2001?

ANSWERS 1. 1984 2. Francis Ford Coppola 3. Goldie Hawn 4. 80 5. Norwegian 6. Chuck E. Weiss 7. Todd Rundgren 8. 1965 9. 1924 10. David Edwards 11. Richard 12. Nicholas Hytner 13. Ronco 14. Chris Judd 15. John Hume.

ENTERTAINMENT

1. On which Nineties panel game show were Eddie Large and Phill Jupitus team captains?

2. Who is the lead singer with Everything but the Girl?

3. Who starred as the psychiatrist in the 1992 film Final Analysis?

4. Which monarch did Dame Peggy Ashcroft play in the Seventies TV drama Edward and Mrs Simpson?

5. Which father and daughter had a U.K. number one hit single in 1967 with Somethin' Stupid?

6. Which Hollywood star directed the 1987 film version of The Glass Menagerie?

7. Which ex-Blue Peter presenter was the host of the TV series Backdate?

8. Who hit the U.K. number one spot in 1996 with Jesus to a Child?

9. Which singer played Anita in the drama series Band of Gold?

10. Which 1995 film starred Julia Roberts and Dennis Quaid as husband and wife?

11. Who starred as the adopted American Indian Jack Crabb in the 1970 film Little Big Man?

12. Which Coronation Street character was played by Peter Baldwin?

13. Which husband and wife vocal duo had a U.K. top ten hit in 1985 with Solid?

14. Who played Chief Inspector Wexford in The Ruth Rendell Mysteries on TV?

15. Which 1995 French film starred Juliette Binoche and Olivier Martinez as aristocrats fleeing a cholera epidemic?

ANSWERS: 1 Gag Tag, 2 Tracey Thorn, 3 Richard Gere, 4 Queen Mary, 5 Nancy and Frank Sinatra, 6 Paul Newman, 7 Valerie Singleton, 8 George Michael, 9 Barbara Dickson, 10 Something to Talk About, 11 Dustin Hoffman, 12 Derek Wilton, 13 Ashford and Simpson, 14 George Baker, 15 The Horseman on the Roof.

GENERAL KNOWLEDGE

1. Which gas forms a larger percentage of the air by volume - ozone or neon?

2. DX is the symbol for which airline?

3. What is the colour of the patch on the face of a goldfinch?

4. In which year was Colin Cowdrey made a life peer - 1958 or 1997?

5. What is sawm, one of the 'five pillars of Islam'?

6. In which Midlands city is the independent Bablake School?

7. Which shipping forecast area lies immediately north of Shannon?

8. Who succeeded James Polk in 1849 as U.S president?

9. In which year did Malta join the United Nations - 1964 or 1978?

10. How many hours ahead of GMT is Botswana - nine or two?

11. Which letter of the Greek alphabet is the equivalent of the letter k?

12. What is the meaning of the common abbreviation CD-ROM?

13. What was the most popular name for a girl in England and Wales in the 1990s?

14. Which period of geological time saw the appearance of humans?

15. In which bay was the Diamond Grace oil tanker grounded in 1997?

ANSWERS: 1 Neon, 2 Danair, 3 Red, 4 1997, 5 Fasting during Ramadan, 6 Coventry, 7 Rockall, 8 Zachary Taylor, 9 1964, 10 Two, 11 Kappa, 12 Compact disc read-only memory, 13 Emma, 14 Quaternary, 15 Tokyo Bay.

GENERAL KNOWLEDGE

1. Which Texas town was established in 1849 to protect settlers from attacks by the Comanche tribe?

2. Which country's national anthem is entitled La Dessalinienne - Haiti or El Salvador?

3. What colour feet and legs has a greylag goose?

4. In the Bible, who was the elder brother of Moses?

5. What in computing does the abbreviation MIDI stand for?

6. What was the professional name of the Russian-born designer Romain de Tirtoff?

7. Which Secretary of State for Wales from 1993-5 had trouble singing?

8. About which historical figure is the opera Tsar and Carpenter by Albert Lortzing?

9. What in Sikhism is a kangha?

10. In which east coast English city is the independent Hymers College?

11. Which shipping forecast area lies immediately north of Fitzroy - Fastnet or Sole?

12. In which year was Brecon Beacons designated a National Park - 1935 or 1957?

13. MB is the abbreviation of which Canadian province?

14. How many hours behind GMT is Nicaragua - eight or six?

15. What does a plangonologist collect?

GENERAL KNOWLEDGE

1. Which American playwright authored the 2000 play Jitney?

2. What nationality was the 17th century painter Jacob van Ruisdael?

3. In which year did Kenya enter the Commonwealth - 1954 or 1963?

4. What is the average gestation period of a lion - 15 weeks or 26 weeks?

5. Who authored the 1971 play Butley, which has famously starred Alan Bates?

6. Where in the body would you find the anterior tibialis muscle group?

7. How many hours ahead of GMT is Austria?

8. In which play by Shakespeare does the character Petruchio appear?

9. In which month does the leyland cypress flower?

10. What is the plant muscari armeniacum commonly known as?

11. Whose paintings include Parnassus which hangs in the Prado?

12. Which Mexican painter's works include the 1937 watercolour Head of a Peasant Girl?

13. Who authored the 2000 novel Sushi for Beginners?

14. Who penned the poem The Village Blacksmith?

15. Who wrote the 1950 play The Country Girl?

ANSWERS: 1 August Wilson, 2 Dutch, 3 1963, 4 15 weeks, 5 Simon Gray, 6 Shin, 7 One, 8 The Taming of the Shrew, 9 March, 10 Grape hyacinth, 11 Nicolas Poussin, 12 Diego Rivera, 13 Marian Keyes, 14 Henry Wadsworth Longfellow, 15 Clifford Odets.

ENTERTAINMENT

1. In which city is the grave of the Doors singer Jim Morrison?

2. Who played Easy Rawlins in the 1995 film Devil in a Blue Dress?

3. Which ex-Pixies singer/guitarist released an album in 1996 entitled The Cult of Ray?

4. Which Italian city was the scene of the heist in the 1969 film The Italian Job?

5. Which action-packed Sunday tea-time drama series of the Nineties starred Celia Imrie and Ronald Pickup?

6. What was the title of the 1996 album release by Tori Amos?

7. Which Waterworld star played a traumatised war-hero in the 1994 film The War?

8. Which actor played Mr Swindley in Coronation Street before starring in the comedy series Dad's Army?

9. Which singer had a U.K. number one in 1960 with Please Don't Tease?

10. Which Four Weddings and a Funeral star played Clive Durham in the 1987 film Maurice?

11. Which Have I Got News For You star appeared in a series of eight comedies in the Nineties based on scripts by Ray Galton and Alan Simpson?

12. Who directed the last segment of the 1995 film Four Rooms?

13. Who played Larry Sanders in TV's The Larry Sanders Show?

14. Which German-born singer released an album entitled Deadline For My Memories in 1996?

15. Which Brookside character was played by Susan Twist?

ANSWERS: 1 Paris, 2 Denzel Washington, 3 Frank Black, 4 Turin, 5 Black Hearts In Battersea, 6 Boys For Pele, 7 Kevin Costner, 8 Arthur Lowe, 9 Cliff Richard, 10 Hugh Grant, 11 Paul Merton, 12 Quentin Tarantino, 13 Garry Shandling, 14 Billie Ray Martin, 15 Rosie Banks.

GENERAL KNOWLEDGE

1. In which city are the headquarters of the U.N. agency the World Health Organisation?

2. What is the correct form of spoken address to a pope?

3. Is Cleethorpes north or south of Grimsby?

4. Who penned the autobiographical work The Flame Trees of Thika?

5. How many hours ahead of GMT is Bahrain?

6. What in heraldry is the base?

7. In the Bible, who was the fifth son of Jacob?

8. What in computing does the abbreviation LSI stand for?

9. What is the plant fritillaria imperialis commonly known as?

10. Who was Chairman of the Conservative Party from 1983-5?

11. In which U.S. city is the Bass Museum of Art?

12. Which poet's works include 1815's The White Doe of Rylstone?

13. Which former Secretary of State for Northern Ireland famously admitted smoking cannabis?

14. What date is St. George's Day?

15. In which year was the fat dormouse introduced to Britain - 96 A.D. or 1902?

ANSWERS: 1 Geneva, 2 Your Holiness, 3 South, 4 Elspeth Huxley, 5 Three, 6 The lowest part of a shield, 7 Dan, 8 Large Scale Integration, 9 Crown imperial, 10 John Selwyn Gummer, 11 Miami, 12 William Wordsworth, 13 Mo Mowlam, 14 23rd April, 15 1902.

GENERAL KNOWLEDGE

1. From which country was the sixth secretary-general of the United Nations, Boutros Boutros-Ghali?

2. Which political party did John Tyler represent as U.S president from 1841-5?

3. What is the meaning of the common abbreviation BAFTA?

4. What is the approximate driving distance in miles between London and Madrid - 959, 1059 or 1159?

5. What is the colour of the cross on the flag of Finland?

6. Who was the famous singer son of Gladys Love Smith?

7. What is banshay?

8. Who launched the feminist publication The Woman Rebel in 1914?

9. What was actress Jane Danson's character name in the television show Coronation Street?

10. In which year did Boris Becker first play Stefan Edberg in the Wimbledon men's singles tennis championship?

11. Which future French president became Keeper of the Seals and Justice Minister in 1956?

12. In which year did the Nuremberg trial begin?

13. Which side won the 1461 Battle of Mortimer's Cross in the Wars of the Roses?

14. By what name were the bodyguards of Roman emperor's known?

15. In which year did Oswald Mosley organise the British Union of Fascists - 1932 or 1939?

ANSWERS: 1 Egypt, 2 Whig, 3 British Academy of Film and Television Arts, 4 1059 miles, 5 Blue, 6 Elvis Presley, 7 A Burmese martial art, 8 Margaret Sanger, 9 Leanne Battersby, 10 1988, 11 François Mitterrand, 12 1945, 13 Yorkists, 14 The Praetorian Guard, 15 1932.

GENERAL KNOWLEDGE

1. In which century did the Spanish painter Bartolemé Estéban Murillo live?

2. Who became Secretary of State for Work and Pensions following the 2001 general election?

3. Which author worked for two years in the early 20th century at the Hong Kong and Shanghai Bank?

4. Which island is further north - Ibiza or Minorca?

5. Who wrote the 1956 novel Anglo-Saxon Attitudes?

6. Name one of the five Foreign Secretaries who served under Mrs Thatcher?

7. What is a gyoji?

8. How old was jazz musician Charlie Parker when he died in 1955 - 69 or 34?

9. Which pop group recorded the 2001 single Get a Grip?

10. Which Duke was defeated at the Battle of Sedgemoor in 1685?

11. Who presided over the Bloody Assizes?

12. What was the profession of the father of racing driver Stirling Moss?

13. Which battle initiated the Wars of the Roses in 1455?

14. In which state of the U.S.A. is the city of Amarillo?

15. In which U.S. city is the de Young Museum which closed its doors in 2000 until a planned reopening in 2005?

ANSWERS: 1 17th century, 2 Alistair Darling, 3 P.G Wodehouse, 4 Minorca, 5 Angus Wilson, 6 Peter Carrington, Francis Pym, Geoffrey Howe, John Major and Douglas Hurd, 7 The referee of a sumo match, 8 34, 9 Semisonic, 10 Duke of Monmouth, 11 Judge Jeffreys, 12 Dentist, 13 Battle of St Albans, 14 Texas, 15 San Francisco.

ENTERTAINMENT

1. What was the title of Dennis Potter's sequel to the TV drama Karaoke?

2. Which folk-rock band were named after an island off Northumberland?

3. Who played Annalise Hartman in Neighbours?

4. Who played the wheelchair-bound Man With A Plan in the film Things To Do In Denver When You're Dead?

5. Which band released an album in 1996 entitled Everything Must Go?

6. Who played Henry Willows in the sitcom Home to Roost?

7. Which Monty Python star wrote and played the lead role in the 1983 film The Missionary?

8. Which of Batman's enemies was portrayed on the small screen by Burgess Meredith?

9. In which European country did glam-rock group Hanoi Rocks originate?

10. Which actor played the father of a clairvoyant child in the 1980 film The Shining?

11. From which country did the group Men At Work come?

12. Who starred as the magician's assistant in the 1996 film Rough Magic?

13. Who presented the golfing gameshow Full Swing?

14. Which rapper released an album in 1996 entitled The Return Of The Real?

15. Who played the assassin hired to kill President Charles de Gaulle in the 1973 film The Day of the Jackal?

ANSWERS: 1 Cold Lazarus, 2 Lindisfarne, 3 Kimberley Davies, 4 Christopher Walken, 5 Manic Street Preachers, 6 John Thaw, 7 Michael Palin, 8 The Penguin, 9 Finland, 10 Jack Nicholson, 11 Australia, 12 Bridget Fonda, 13 Jimmy Tarbuck, 14 Ice T, 15 Edward Fox.

GENERAL KNOWLEDGE

1. Which European city is further west - Genoa or Munich?

2. Which German artist's works include the 1920 oil painting Prague Street?

3. In which city are the headquarters of the U.N. agency the International Labour Organisation?

4. How many hours ahead of GMT is Iraq?

5. In heraldry, if an animal is rampant how is it represented?

6. In which U.S. state would you find the Everglades?

7. VS is the symbol for which airline?

8. Which country's national anthem is entitled Kimigayo - South Korea or Japan?

9. What type of creature is a slow worm?

10. Who became Secretary of State for Health following the 2001 general election?

11. In which U.S. city is the Currier Gallery of Art?

12. Who became leader of the Picts and Scots in 844?

13. Which pop group recorded the 2001 single Hard to Explain?

14. Which composer did the sculptress Anne Marie Brodersen marry in 1891?

15. Which London-born painter's works include the 2000 oil Dirty Mirror?

ANSWERS: 1 Genoa, 2 Otto Dix, 3 Geneva, 4 Three, 5 On hind legs, 6 Florida, 7 Virgin Atlantic Airways, 8 Japan, 9 A legless lizard, 10 Alan Milburn, 11 Manchester, 12 Kenneth MacAlpin, 13 The Strokes, 14 Carl Nielsen, 15 Howard Hodgkin.

GENERAL KNOWLEDGE

1. In which play by Shakespeare does the character Leontes appear?

2. How many hours behind GMT is Martinique - seven or four?

3. Which Switzerland-born artist's works include Temple Gardens, painted in 1920?

4. What in martial arts is a hanbo?

5. Which German city is further west - Bonn or Düsseldorf?

6. Who wrote the 1931 novel Police at the Funeral?

7. In which year did Cyprus enter the Commonwealth?

8. In which city was the 17th century Dutch painter Gerrit Dou born?

9. Who was the author of the 1886 novel The Mayor of Casterbridge?

10. Who became General Secretary of the T.U.C. in 1973?

11. What bird features on the national flag of Albania?

12. What is the meaning of the common abbreviation CBI?

13. In which group of Islands would you find West Burra and East Burra?

14. Who became Leader of the House of Commons after the 2001 general election?

15. Which country's national anthem is entitled Jana Gana Mana - India or Burma?

ANSWERS: 1 The Winter's Tale, 2 Four, 3 Paul Klee, 4 A wooden staff, 5 Düsseldorf, 6 Margery Allingham, 7 1961, 8 Leiden, 9 Thomas Hardy, 10 Len Murray, 11 Eagle, 12 Confederation of British Industry, 13 The Shetland Islands, 14 Robin Cook, 15 India.

GENERAL KNOWLEDGE

1. In U.S. slang, what is an "ambulance chaser"?

2. Of which country is Douala the capital?

3. Which Scottish painter's works include 1804's Pitlessie Fair?

4. Who wrote the 2001 novel Running in Heels?

5. What is the official language of El Salvador?

6. Who was Secretary of State for Defence from 1995-7?

7. What is the colour of the star central to the flag of Burkina Faso?

8. Of which martial art is fu jya a style?

9. Which author's first novel, published in 1922 under the pseudonym William Earle, was Mossyface?

10. Dutchy Lion is the mascot of which country's international football team?

11. In which year did the character Dev Alahan first appear in the television show Coronation Street?

12. In which U.S. city is the Everson Museum of Art?

13. What is the meaning of the common abbreviation ABTA?

14. What substance is usually associated with a 15th wedding anniversary?

15. Who wrote the 1983 novel Stick?

ANSWERS: 1 A lawyer who seeks to profit from lawsuits of accident victims, 2 Cameroon, 3 David Wilkie, 4 Anna Maxted, 5 Spanish, 6 Michael Portillo, 7 Yellow, 8 Kung fu, 9 Captain W E Johns, 10 Netherlands, 11 1999, 12 Syracuse, New York, 13 Association of British Travel Agents, 14 Crystal, 15 Elmore Leonard.

ENTERTAINMENT

1. Which U.S. group claimed It's a Love Thing in the U.K. charts in 1981?

2. Which Friends actor starred in the 2000 film Three to Tango?

3. Which former EastEnder played barrister Sam Lucas in ITV's drama series In Defence?

4. Which British group had a Rock 'n' Roll Winter in the U.K. top ten in 1974?

5. Which Irish actor played the Black Prince in the 1987 film Lionheart?

6. Who presented the BBC1 quiz show The Syndicate?

7. Which sex symbol made her film debut as Javotte Lemoine in 1952's Le Trou normand?

8. Which 2000 film adaptation of a Noel Coward comedy starred Julie Andrews and Colin Firth?

9. Which Seventies sitcom starring Terry Scott and June Whitfield preceded Terry and June?

10. Which Australian pop star had a 2000 number one hit with Spinning Around?

11. Which actress played the lead in the 1962 film The Roman Spring of Mrs Stone?

12. Which EastEnders teenager accused her maths tutor of attacking her in 2000?

13. Which New Jersey teenage rap duo released the debut album We Didn't Say That!?

14. Which comedian and actor played headmaster Ian George in the BBC1 drama series Hope & Glory?

15. Which Hollywood actor provided the voice of Rocky the Rooster in the animated film Chicken Run?

ANSWERS: 1 Whispers, 2 Matthew Perry, 3 Ross Kemp, 4 Wizzard, 5 Gabriel Byrne, 6 Nick Ross, 7 Brigitte Bardot, 8 Relative Values, 9 Happy Ever After, 10 Kylie Minogue, 11 Vivien Leigh, 12 Nicky diMarco, 13 Daphne & Celeste, 14 Lenny Henry, 15 Mel Gibson.

GENERAL KNOWLEDGE

1. What is the collective noun for kittens?

2. What is the largest lake in South America?

3. What type of creature is a bleak?

4. In which year did Mike Baldwin marry Jackie Ingram in the television show Coronation Street?

5. Who wrote the 1942 play The Skin of Our Teeth?

6. Which English author was known by the nickname Plum?

7. In which city is the University of Ulster?

8. Who wrote the novels Jamaica Inn and Rebecca?

9. What is the plant erythronium dens-canis commonly known as?

10. Name one of the three Home Secretaries who served under John Major?

11. What type of creature is a moderlieschen?

12. Who was the author of the 1934 novel Murder on the Orient Express?

13. What is the meaning of the common abbreviation APR?

14. Who was the author of the 1982 novel The Mosquito Coast?

15. Which country's national anthem is entitled Arise, O Compatriots?

ANSWERS: 1 A kindle, 2 Lake Titicaca, 3 Fish, 4 1991, 5 Thornton Wilder, 6 P.G Wodehouse, 7 Coleraine, 8 Daphne Du Maurier, 9 Dogtooth violet, 10 Kenneth Baker, Kenneth Clarke and Michael Howard, 11 Fish, 12 Agatha Christie, 13 Annual Percentage Rate, 14 Paul Theroux, 15 Nigeria.

GENERAL KNOWLEDGE

1. What is the meaning of the common abbreviation B.E.M.?

2. Who was Chancellor of the Exchequer from 1990-3?

3. What is the collective noun for locusts

4. In which U.S. city is the photography and film gallery called George Eastman House?

5. In which country are the Ilopango and Izalco volcanoes?

6. Of which country did Kjell Magne Bondevik become prime minister in 1997?

7. JG is the symbol for which airline?

8. Who was Chairman of the Conservative Party from 1995-7?

9. Which Leeds-born abstract painter's works include 1956's Azalea Garden?

10. Who wrote the 1963 novel The Girls of Slender Means?

11. Which poet's volumes include 1899's The Wind Among the Reeds?

12. Who wrote the 1862 play Love's Comedy?

13. What was former England cricketer Martyn Moxon's highest Test score?

14. Which Italian composed the 1960 work Circles?

15. On which bay is the Spanish port of Gijon?

GENERAL KNOWLEDGE

1. Which comic actor played P.C Wilcox in the television show Coronation Street in 1969?

2. What does a tegestologist collect - beer-mats or hair?

3. Of what is clinophobia the fear?

4. Which Scottish author wrote the science fiction novel Inversions?

5. In which year of the 1970s was Mrs Thatcher elected leader of the Conservative Party?

6. Which English city was known by the Romans as Vigornia?

7. What colour legs has a grey partridge?

8. Which country's national anthem is entitled Oms Hemecht?

9. Who wrote the 1967 novel The Pyramid?

10. In which novel by Charles Dickens does the character Mercy Pecksniff appear?

11. Who painted Interior in Paddington?

12. In which English city is the independent Perse School?

13. Which shipping forecast area lies immediately north of Dogger?

14. What is photophobia?

15. In which year did Brian Faulkner become prime minister of Northern Ireland - 1960 or 1971?

SPORT

1. Who became the first European Open snooker champion by beating Terry Griffiths?

2. Who knocked Tim Henman out of the men's singles at Wimbledon in 1998 and 1999?

3. Which U.S. golfer won the British Open in 1970?

4. What is the name of rugby union side Richmond's home ground?

5. What is the nickname of Bristol City football club?

6. In which year were the summer Olympic Games held in Seoul?

7. At which cycling event did Chris Boardman become Olympic champion in 1992?

8. Which football club bought David Batty from Newcastle United in 1998?

9. Which team won 15 of the 16 Formula 1 Grands Prix in 1988?

10. In which event did Carl Lewis win a fourth consecutive Olympic gold medal in 1996?

11. Which British cyclist crashed out of the 1998 Tour de France whilst wearing the Yellow Jersey?

12. Which cricketer captained Yorkshire from 1971 to 1978?

13. Which football club signed Alan Kennedy from Newcastle United?

14. Which rugby union club side did Phil de Glanville captain in the 1995 Pilkington Cup final?

15. Which jockey rode Mark of Esteem to victory in the 1996 2000 Guineas?

ANSWERS: 1 John Parrott, 2 Pete Sampras, 3 Jack Nicklaus, 4 The Madejski Stadium, 5 The Robins, 6 1988, 7 4,000m individual pursuit, 8 Leeds United, 9 McLaren, 10 Long jump, 11 Chris Boardman, 12 Geoffrey Boycott, 13 Liverpool, 14 Bath, 15 Frankie Dettori.

GENERAL KNOWLEDGE

1. What was the name of the white calf that survived two attempts to cull it during the 2001 foot-and-mouth epidemic?

2. Which American-born British sculptor created The Rock Drill and St Michael and the Devil?

3. What name was given to the tax levied in Anglo-Saxon Britain to buy off Viking invaders?

4. Who wrote the book on which the film Hannibal was based?

5. What is the largest and most luminous type of star?

6. Which lake in Israel is also called the Sea of Galilee?

7. What sort of bird is a gadwall?

8. The film A Man For All Seasons was set during the reign of which monarch?

9. Which rare-earth metal has the symbol La?

10. How many wickets did Courtney Walsh take in his Test career?

11. Who played Rhett Butler in the film Gone With the Wind?

12. Who wrote the novel Mr Midshipman Easy?

13. Which adjective refers to the reign of James I?

14. Which shrub is also called furze or whin?

15. Which London street is synonymous with the British diamond trade?

ANSWERS: 1 Phoenix, 2 Sir Jacob Epstein, 3 Danegeld, 4 Thomas Harris, 5 Supergiant, 6 Lake Tiberias, 7 A duck, 8 Henry VIII, 9 Lanthanum, 10 519, 11 Clark Gable, 12 Frederick Marryat, 13 Jacobean, 14 Gorse, 15 Hatton Garden.

GENERAL KNOWLEDGE

1. Which art movement took its name from a childish French word for hobby-horse?

2. Which member of the Have I Got News for You team also presented the TV chat show Room 101?

3. Which hunter in Greek mythology was changed into a stag by Artemis and killed by his own hounds?

4. Who won her sixth London Marathon wheelchair race in 2002?

5. Which Palestinian terrorist leader has a name which means 'Father of Struggles'?

6. What musical term indicates that a work is to be sung without accompaniment?

7. Who wrote the powerful novel The Grapes of Wrath?

8. Which French composer is best known for his Requiem of 1887?

9. What the largest New World member of the cat family?

10. Which famous keeper of Leicester Gaol weighed over 52 stone when he died in 1809?

11. In which American city were the 1984 summer Olympics held?

12. Which film first made a star of juvenile actor Macaulay Culkin?

13. Who was the first man in the Bible?

14. What name is given to scurf that forms on the scalp and comes off in flakes?

15. In which musical did Denise Van Outen make her West End debut in 2001?

ANSWERS: 1 Dada, 2 Paul Merton, 3 Actaeon, 4 Tanni Grey-Thompson, 5 Abu Nidal, 6 A cappella, 7 John Steinbeck, 8 Gabriel Fauré, 9 Jaguar, 10 Daniel Lambert, 11 Los Angeles, 12 Home Alone, 13 Adam, 14 Dandruff, 15 Chicago.

GENERAL KNOWLEDGE

1. Which Finnish runner won the 5,000m and 10,000m at the 1972 and 1976 Olympics?

2. Who was the second president of the United States?

3. For which film did Elizabeth Taylor receive an Oscar?

4. Who wrote Goblin Market and Other Poems?

5. Which English king was known as Harefoot?

6. On which river does the German city of Ulm stand?

7. Which TV series is set on Craggy Island?

8. Of which American city was Richard Daley mayor from 1955 to 1976?

9. Which Algerian-born author wrote The Outsider?

10. In what year was the Glorious Revolution in English history?

11. Which Italian dictator was known as Il Duce?

12. Which Mel Brooks film featured the song Springtime For Hitler?

13. Of which rock group was Francis Rossi lead singer?

14. Which football team clinched the 2000/01 Premiership title with five games still to play?

15. What name is given to the offspring of a male donkey and a female horse?

ANSWERS: 1 Lasse Viren, 2 John Adams, 3 Butterfield 8, 4 Christina Rossetti, 5 Harold I, 6 Danube, 7 Father Ted, 8 Chicago, 9 Albert Camus, 10 1688, 11 Benito Mussolini, 12 The Producers, 13 Status Quo, 14 Manchester United, 15 Mule.

ENTERTAINMENT

1. Which 2000 film version of a children's cartoon series featured the evil Lawrence III?

2. Which Emmerdale character ended his stag night by being tied to a telegraph pole wearing his underwear and dog collar?

3. Which British group had a U.K. top ten hit with Sale of the Century in 1996?

4. Which 1974 film directed by, and starring, Sidney Poitier, also featured Bill Cosby and Richard Pryor?

5. Which U.S. girl group had a 1974 U.K. number one hit with When Will I See You Again?

6. Which British comic actor played the title role in the 2000 film Merlin: The Return?

7. Which member of The Goodies appeared in the Eighties sitcom Me and My Girl?

8. What was the title of the 2001 U.K. top five hit by Fragma featuring Maria Rubia?

9. In which African country was the 1988 film A World Apart set?

10. Who played Barry in Auf Wiedersehen Pet?

11. Which film was awarded the best picture Oscar at the Academy Awards in 2002?

12. What was the title of the 2001 U.K. number one hit by Rui Da Silva featuring Cassandra?

13. Which actor was the subject of The BBC and BAFTA Tribute in 2000 after receiving a knighthood earlier in the year?

14. In which 2000 film did Nicolas Cage star as a wealthy stockbroker who finds himself in a parallel life?

15. Which former soap actor played Eddie Scrooge in ITV's contemporary version of A Christmas Carol in 2000?

ANSWERS: 1 Pokemon the Movie 2000, 2 Ashley, 3 Sleeper, 4 Uptown Saturday Night, 5 Three Degrees, 6 Rik Mayall, 7 Tim Brooke-Taylor, 8 Everytime You Need Me, 9 South Africa, 10 Timothy Spall, 11 A Beautiful Mind, 12 Touch Me, 13 Michael Caine, 14 The Family Man, 15 Ross Kemp.

GENERAL KNOWLEDGE

1. In which century was the diary of Samuel Pepys first published?

2. Which Scottish golfer won the British Open five times in the first decade of the 20th century?

3. Who wrote the novels Tropic of Cancer and Tropic of Capricorn?

4. Which 2001 film starred Keanu Reeves, James Spader and Marisa Tomei?

5. What name is given to the mark under the c in words such as façade and Français?

6. Which former West German chancellor was born Herbert Frahm?

7. Which poet wrote the verse collection A Martian Sends a Postcard Home?

8. Who was allowed to help Jesus to carry the cross?

9. Which Second Division team reached the 2000/01 F.A. Cup semi-finals by beating Leicester City?

10. Which very hard metal has the chemical symbol Ta?

11. Which jockey won the Derby a record nine times between 1954 and 1983?

12. In which of his own films does Wes Craven appear as Fred the janitor?

13. Which member of the Royal Family was fined for driving her Bentley at 93 mph in 2001?

14. How many years are there in a century?

15. Which Conservative politician married Jennie Jerome in 1874?

ANSWERS: 1 19th, 2 James Braid, 3 Henry Miller, 4 The Watcher, 5 Cedilla, 6 Willy Brandt, 7 Craig Raine, 8 Simon of Cyrene, 9 Wycombe Wanderers, 10 Tantalum, 11 Lester Piggott, 12 Scream, 13 The Princess Royal, 14 100, 15 Randolph Churchill.

GENERAL KNOWLEDGE

1. What was the name of the song chosen as the U.K. entry for the 2001 Eurovision Song Contest?

2. Which American poet wrote the verse collections A Boy's Will and North of Boston?

3. Villette is based on the experiences of Charlotte Bronte as a governess in which foreign city?

4. Which spy was released in 2001 after serving 19 years for betraying secrets during the Cold War?

5. The former duchy of Brabant is divided between which two countries?

6. Which 15-year-old U.S. gymnast won five medals at the Barcelona Olympics?

7. In which country was Braveheart mostly filmed?

8. Of which element is tritium a radioactive isotope?

9. Which 3rd-century Roman martyr was condemned to be killed by a squad of archers?

10. Who succeeded to the U.S. presidency in 1850 on the death of Zachary Taylor?

11. Which 19th-century French educator developed a system of writing for the blind?

12. What was the name given to the series of disputes over fishing between Britain and Iceland?

13. Which American trombonist and bandleader disappeared on a flight in 1944?

14. After appearing together in which film did Tom Hanks and Rita Wilson get married?

15. Which creature has between 14 and 177 pairs of legs?

ANSWERS: 1 No Dream Impossible, 2 Robert Frost, 3 Brussels, 4 Geoffrey Prime, 5 Belgium and the Netherlands, 6 Shannon Miller, 7 Ireland, 8 Hydrogen, 9 Saint Sebastian, 10 Millard Fillmore, 11 Louis Braille, 12 The 'Cod Wars', 13 Glenn Miller, 14 Volunteers, 15 Centipede.

GENERAL KNOWLEDGE

1. What was the first programme to appear on the British TV station Channel Four?

2. Which French painter founded Cubism with Pablo Picasso?

3. What sort of creature is a trogon?

4. Which controversial road safety device was invented by the Dutchman Maus Garsonides

5. What is the SI unit of frequency?

6. Which German poet wrote The Ship of Fools?

7. Who won a Best Song Oscar for the film Philadelphia?

8. In the Stations of the Cross, what number is the picture in which Jesus dies on the cross?

9. What name is given to a Hindu of the highest caste?

10. Which English art critic coined the term Post-Impressionism?

11. Which American dramatist wrote The Crucible?

12. By what name is nacre popularly known?

13. Where was the children's TV show Words and Pictures set?

14. What name is given to a stand or support for utensils before or on a fire?

15. Which British naval explorer landed at Botany Bay in 1770?

ANSWERS: 1 Countdown, 2 Georges Braque, 3 A bird, 4 The Gatso speed camera, 5 Hertz, 6 Sebastian Brant, 7 Bruce Springsteen, 8 Twelve, 9 Brahman, 10 Roger Fry, 11 Arthur Miller, 12 Mother-of-pearl, 13 A public library, 14 Trivet, 15 Captain James Cook.

ENTERTAINMENT

1. In which 2000 film did Johnny Depp appear as a gypsy called Cesar?

2. Which EastEnders character was sent to prison in 2000 for being in contempt of court?

3. Which British duo had a U.K. top five hit with Sowing the Seeds of Love in 1989?

4. Which 1988 Alan Parker film starred Gene Hackman and Willem Dafoe as FBI agents?

5. What nationality was Emmerdale's Joe, who married Tricia in 2000 in order to escape deportation?

6. What was the title of Diana Ross' 1971 U.K. number one hit?

7. Who directed the 2000 film satire Cecil B. Demented?

8. What was the alter ego of Wonder Woman in the TV series?

9. Who won a Best Actor Oscar for his performance as reporter Mike Connor in the 1940 film The Philadelphia Story?

10. Which Australian singer had a 2000 U.K. top ten hit with Please Stay?

11. Which 2000 film starring Val Kilmer was based around a expedition to Mars?

12. What was the name of Roddy McDowall's chimpanzee character in the TV series The Planet of the Apes?

13. Which British singer had a U.K. top five hit in 2000 with Supreme?

14. What condition does Dustin Hoffman's character suffer from in the 1988 film Rain Man?

15. Which soap celebrated its 40th birthday in December 2000?

GENERAL KNOWLEDGE

1. To which Robert Louis Stevenson novel is Catriona the sequel?

2. Which state unilaterally declared independence from Nigeria in May 1967?

3. What is the subtitle of Dvorák's Symphony No 9 in E minor?

4. Which rugby union team won the 2001 Tetley's Bitter Cup?

5. In which English county is the town of Bicester?

6. Which Irish novelist wrote At Swim-Two-Birds?

7. In the film Men of Honour Cuba Gooding Jnr plays what?

8. Which Hebrew prophet picked up the mantle as successor to Elijah?

9. John Dryden's All For Love is a reworking of which Shakespeare play?

10. Which U2 song won three Grammy awards in 2001?

11. Which atoll in the Marshall Islands gave its name to a form of swimwear?

12. In children's television programme The Hoobs what are Tiddlypeeps?

13. Which actor and rapper stars in the film The Legend of Bagger Vance?

14. What is the first name of Dr Frankenstein in Mary Shelley's novel?

15. Which joint is formed by the meeting of the humerus, radius and ulna?

ANSWERS: 1 Kidnapped, 2 Biafra, 3 From the New World, 4 Newcastle, 5 Oxfordshire, 6 Flann O'Brien, 7 A navy diver, 8 Elisha, 9 Antony and Cleopatra, 10 Beautiful Day, 11 Bikini, 12 Children, 13 Will Smith, 14 Victor, 15 Elbow.

GENERAL KNOWLEDGE

1. Which island is also called Rapa Nui and Isla de Pascua?

2. Who played bashful bachelor David in the televison series A Life of Bliss?

3. Which actor plays William Forrester in the film Finding Forrester?

4. What name is given to a tree of the genus Taxus?

5. Which sparrow is also called a dunnock?

6. What is the only form of gambling permitted in the British armed forces?

7. Which actress became a star after playing an Amazon princess in 1932?

8. Which former Kent and England left-handed batsman took 1,018 first-class catches?

9. What is the name of Katharina's younger sister in Shakespeare's The Taming of the Shrew?

10. Of which U.S. state is Frankfort the capital?

11. What name is given to the Saturday before Easter Sunday?

12. What nickname was given to any one of four large German guns produced by the Krupp works in World War I?

13. Who played Little Lord Fauntleroy in the 1921 film?

14. What is the name of the hero of The Pilgrim's Progress?

15. In which novel by George du Maurier does the character Svengali appear?

? GENERAL KNOWLEDGE ?

1. Which English novelist wrote The Children of the New Forest?

2. What was the first Sunday newspaper published in Britain?

3. Let the River Run was the 1988 Oscar-winning song from which film?

4. On which Thomas Hardy novel is the film The Claim based?

5. Which fibrous protein is found in hair, nails, horns, hoofs and skin?

6. What was the first name of the founder of Lord's Cricket Ground?

7. Which chemical element has the symbol Se?

8. What was the occupation of Clarence in the 1988 sitcom?

9. Which English logician and philosopher wrote The Principles of Mathematics in 1903?

10. Against which king was the Rye House Plot directed?

11. Which member of the Kennedy family drove his car off a bridge in 1969?

12. What is the profession of the character played by Bob Hope in the film The Paleface?

13. Which glamorous Hollywood couple announced their separation after 11 years of marriage in February 2001?

14. What nationality were most of the pop group Abba?

15. Which singer was billed as 'the Last of the Red Hot Mamas'?

ANSWERS: 1 Frederick Marryat, 2 The Observer, 3 Working Girl, 4 The Mayor of Casterbridge, 5 Keratin, 6 Thomas, 7 Selenium, 8 Removals man, 9 Bertrand Russell, 10 Charles II, 11 Teddy (Edward) Kennedy, 12 Dentist, 13 Tom Cruise and Nicole Kidman, 14 Swedish, 15 Sophie Tucker.

ENTERTAINMENT

1. Which children's TV character had the U.K. Christmas number one in 2000 with Can We Fix It?

2. Which TV family lived on a smallholding in Walnut Grove, Plum Creek, Minnesota?

3. Who directed and starred in the 1984 film Harry & Son?

4. Which flamboyant U.S. pianist successfully sued the Daily Mirror in 1959?

5. Which British actress played Woody Allen's wife in his 2000 film Small Time Crooks?

6. What was the Nashville Teens' biggest hit, which reached number six in the U.K. charts in 1964?

7. What was the venue for Miss World 2000, screened by Channel 5?

8. Which British group had a U.K. number one hit in 1963 with Do You Love Me?

9. Which 1984 film starred Jon Cryer and Demi Moore?

10. Which Beatles track provided Candy Flip with a 1990 U.K. top five single?

11. What was the title of the 1988 U.K. number one hit by Enya?

12. Which 2000 film featuring David Arquette and Oliver Platt was set in the world of wrestling?

13. Which Star Trek actor played disguise expert Paris in the Seventies TV series Mission: Impossible?

14. What was the title of the Backstreet Boys' fourth album, released in 2000?

15. Which actress starred in the title role of the 1985 film Marie?

ANSWERS: 1 Bob the Builder, 2 The Ingalls of Little House on the Prairie, 3 Paul Newman, 4 Liberace, 5 Tracey Ullman, 6 Tobacco Road, 7 The Millennium Dome, 8 Brian Poole & the Tremeloes, 9 No Small Affair, 10 Strawberry Fields Forever, 11 Orinoco Flow, 12 Ready to Rumble, 13 Leonard Nimoy, 14 Black & Blue, 15 Sissy Spacek.

GENERAL KNOWLEDGE

1. Which French composer wrote the opera Lakmé?

2. Who played Juliet in John Gielgud's celebrated 1935 production of Romeo and Juliet?

3. Of which novel by Jane Austen is Anne Elliot the heroine?

4. Who led the British Labour Party from 1931 to 1935?

5. Which assault rifle adopted by the U.S. Army in 1967 is also called AR-15?

6. From which English king's visit did Bognor Regis derive its royal suffix?

7. Which 2001 film starred Kevin Spacey, Helen Hunt and Haley Joel Osment?

8. The title of the film Fifteen Minutes is a reference to a famous quote by Andy Warhol about what?

9. Which American dramatist wrote Who's Afraid of Virginia Woolf?

10. In which Scottish city is Marischal College?

11. Which character in the Old Testament derived his strength from his long hair?

12. In which borough of New York City are Wall Street and Broadway?

13. What was the name of the bear in television's The Life and Times of Grizzly Adams?

14. What is the surname of the star of the sitcom Ellen?

15. Which former Wimbledon champion died of AIDS in 1993?

ANSWERS: 1 Leo Delibes, 2 Peggy Ashcroft, 3 Persuasion, 4 George Lansbury, 5 M16 rifle, 6 George V, 7 Pay It Forward, 8 Fame, 9 Edward Albee, 10 Aberdeen, 11 Samson, 12 Manhattan, 13 Ben, 14 DeGeneres, 15 Arthur Ashe.

GENERAL KNOWLEDGE

1. What was the title of the theme tune of Minder?

2. Which American dramatist wrote the play Waiting for Lefty?

3. Who played Lieutenant Norman Buntz in Hill Street Blues?

4. Which Japanese detective did Peter Lorre play in a series of films?

5. In which U.S. state is Kent State University?

6. Which French novelist wrote Bonjour Tristesse?

7. The film Anne of the Indies was about a female pirate known as what?

8. Which German astronomer discovered the three principles of planetary motion?

9. What was the first name of FBI agent Starling in the films Silence of the Lambs and Hannibal?

10. Which Disney film features the voices of John Goodman and Eartha Kitt?

11. Which prayer is also called Pater Noster or Our Father?

12. Which American television series set in a hospital won eight Emmy Awards in 1995?

13. Which highly infectious disease of animals was discovered in Britain in 2001 for the first time in 20 years?

14. Marie Byrd Land is an unclaimed region of which continent?

15. Which Asian city hosted the 1988 Olympics?

ANSWERS: 1 I Could Be So Good For You, 2 Clifford Odets, 3 Dennis Franz, 4 Mr Moto, 5 Ohio, 6 Françoise Sagan, 7 Captain Providence, 8 Johannes Kepler, 9 Clarice, 10 The Emperor's New Groove, 11 Lord's Prayer, 12 ER, 13 Foot-and-mouth, 14 Antarctica, 15 Seoul.

? GENERAL KNOWLEDGE ?

1. Who played nurse Hilda Price in General Hospital?

2. Which well-known nursery rhyme was written by U.S. poet Sarah Josepha Hale in 1830?

3. Who played Cathy to Laurence Olivier's Heathcliff in the 1939 film Wuthering Heights?

4. Which British tennis player won the Copenhagen Open in 2001?

5. In which New Mexico city was the atomic bomb developed in the Manhattan Project?

6. Which canal extends 36 miles from Eastham on Merseyside?

7. Who is the heroine of the novel Far from the Madding Crowd by Thomas Hardy?

8. Which English conductor founded the Academy of St Martin-in-the-Fields?

9. To which English king was Margaret of Anjou queen?

10. What sort of creature is a loon?

11. Which Brazilian racing driver was killed at Imola in 1994?

12. What is the capital of Argentina?

13. Which novelist wrote The Young Caesar and The Aerodrome?

14. Who was the first female swimmer to win gold medals in three successive Olympics?

15. Which of the gifts brought by the Magi is also known as olibanum?

ANSWERS: 1 Linda Bellingham, 2 Mary Had a Little Lamb, 3 Merle Oberon, 4 Tim Henman, 5 Los Alamos, 6 Manchester Ship Canal, 7 Bathsheba Everdene, 8 Neville Marriner, 9 Henry VI, 10 A bird, 11 Ayrton Senna, 12 Buenos Aires, 13 Rex Warner, 14 Dawn Fraser, 15 Frankincense.

GENERAL KNOWLEDGE

1. Who authored the farce The Magistrate and the play Two Hundred A Year?

2. What was the name of Lord Howard of Effingham's flaghip against the Spanish Armada?

3. In which year was Newgate, the famous London prison, demolished?

4. Who was the son of Chingachgook in the novel The Last of the Mohicans?

5. What is the name given to the leader of congregational prayer in a mosque?

6. Who was the French composer of the 1884 opera Manon?

7. Who was Secretary-General of the Commonwealth from 1975-89?

8. Which novel by Iain Banks features the character Uncle Rory?

9. In which year was the siege at the mission in San Antonio, Texas, called the Alamo?

10. Which country was formerly known as Siam?

11. Who directed the 1935 film Captain Blood starring Errol Flynn?

12. What is the German name for the Polish port Gdansk?

13. Who became the first Aboriginal member of the Australian parliament in 1971?

14. Who wrote the 1922 novel Huntingtower?

15. Who directed the 1972 film The Mechanic starring Charles Bronson?

ANSWERS 1. Arthur Wing Pinero 2. The Ark Royal 3. 1902 4. Uncas 5. Imam 6. Jules Massenet 7. Sonny Ramphal 8. The Crow Road 9. 1836 10. Thailand 11. Michael Curtiz 12. Danzig 13. Neville Thomas Bonner 14. John Buchan 15. Michael Winner.

ENTERTAINMENT

1. Who directed the 1981 film Southern Comfort?

2. Which character has been played by Deena Payne in Emmerdale?

3. In which U.S. state is the 1980 film Heaven's Gate set?

4. Who plays the lead in the 1981 film An Unsuitable Job for a Woman?

5. Who plays Albert Einstein in the 1994 film I.Q.?

6. Who played Hector in the 2000 BBC TV drama Monarch of the Glen?

7. Which former Coronation Street actress played Dolly in Dinnerladies?

8. Who played Dr. Chase Meridian in the film Batman Forever?

9. Who plays Gale Weathers in the film Scream 3?

10. Who directed the 1948 film Call Northside 777?

11 Who plays detective Philo Vance in the 1940 film Calling Philo Vance?

12. Director Jack Fisk's wife took the lead in the 1981 film Raggedy Man. Who is she?

13. Which child actor played the lead in the 1950 film Kim?

14. Who is the stepfather of Cenerentola in Rossini's opera La Cenerentola?

15. Who directed the 1981 film Raiders of the Lost Ark?

SPORT

1. Who was the 1997 FIA Formula 3000 champion?

2. After Western Province, which team have won the Currie Cup in South African rugby union the most times?

3. Which French woman won the 2000 Paris Open singles tennis title?

4. Where were the 1990 Asian Games held?

5. How long did Don Ritchie take to run 100 miles on 15th October, 1977?

6. Which country have been men's volleyball world champions the most times?

7. What country did cyclist Nikolay Makarov represent?

8. Which sport is played by the London Leopards?

9. Which country won the 1975 women's world championships in hockey?

10. In which year did French tennis player André Gobert die?

11. Who was the 1953-5 world 500cc motorcycling champion?

12. What nationality is judo player Eva Bisseni?

13. Who scored Manchester United's two goals in their 1979 F.A. Cup Final defeat?

14. Who scored both goals in Liverpool's 2-1 win at Wimbledon in April, 2000?

15. Which Briton was WBC flyweight boxing champion in 1983?

ANSWERS 1. Ricardo Zonta 2. Northern Transvaal 3. Nathalie Tauziat 4. Beijing 5. 11 hours 30 minutes 51 seconds 6. USSR 7. USSR 8. basketball 9. England 10. 1951 11. Geoff Duke 12. French 13. McQueen & McIlroy 14. Emile Heskey 15. Charlie Magri.

POP MUSIC

1. Who recorded the 1999 album Maybe You've Been Brainwashed Too?
2. Which artist directed Blur's video for the single Country House?
3. Who recorded the 1999 album Sleepless?
4. Who recorded the 2000 Top 10 single U Know What's Up?
5. In which year did Ian Dury and the Blockheads have a Top 10 hit with Reasons To Be Cheerful, Pt. 3?
6. Which female singer had a 1994 No. 1 single with Saturday Night?
7. Which group recorded the 1983 mini-album 10-4-60?
8. On which label was the Manic Street Preachers' number one single, The Masses Against the Classes?
9. Who recorded the 1999 dance hit Madagascar?
10. Who recorded the 1999 album I See a Darkness?
11. Mark Morris and Scott Morris are members of which 1990s group?
12. Which punk group released the 1980 record The Black Album?
13. In which year did PJ And Duncan have a Top 10 single with Let's Get Ready To Rhumble?
14. Which female singer had a 1999 Top 10 single with I Try?
15. Which rap group released the 1996 album Temples of Boom?

ANSWERS 1. New Radicals 2. Damien Hirst 3. Kate Rusby 4. Donell Jones 5. 1979 6. Whigfield 7. The Long Ryders 8. Epic 9. Art of Trance 10. Bonnie 'Prince' Billy 11. The Bluetones 12. The Damned 13. 1994 14. Macy Gray 15. Cypress Hill.

ART & LITERATURE

1. Who wrote the 2001 novel Love Stuck?

2. Who wrote the 1923 play The Great Broxopp?

3. Who wrote the 2001 novel He Kills Coppers?

4. In which European city is the Marino Marini Museum?

5. Who is author of the novels Beneath the Blonde and Eating Cake?

6. Which painter's works include 1912's Still Life with Ginger Pot?

7. Who wrote the 1970 novel The Bluest Eye?

8. Whose volumes of short stories include The Casuarina Tree?

9. What is the collective name for Henry Miller's novels Sexus, Nexus, and Plexus?

10. Who wrote the 2000 novel MotherKind?

11. Which comedienne penned the 1999 novel Whistling for the Elephants?

12. Which playwright wrote the drama Fool For Love?

13. Which English playwright authored the drama The Party?

14. Which poet wrote the 2001 collection Stonepicker?

15. Which comedian's debut novel was 2000's Shopgirl?

ANSWERS 1. Susie Gilmour 2. A.A. Milne 3. Jake Arnott 4. Florence 5. Stella Duffy 6. Piet Mondrian 7. Toni Morrison 8. W. Somerset Maugham 9. The Rosy Crucifixion 10. Jayne Anne Phillips 11. Sandi Toksvig 12. Sam Shepard 13. Trevor Griffiths 14. Frieda Hughes 15. Steve Martin.

GENERAL KNOWLEDGE

1. In which year did sculptor Sir Jacob Epstein die?

2. What is the name given to the books The Military Orchid, The Goose Cathedral and A Mine of Serpents by author Jocelyn Brooke?

3. Which city is capital of Northern Ireland?

4. Who was a Best Actor Oscar nominee for the film The Hasty Heart?

5. On which Hawaiian island is the town of Wahiawa?

6. What is the name given to the chisel-edged tooth at the front of the mouth?

7. In which U.S. city was Barnett Newman, Abstract Impressionist painter and founder of the "Subject of the Artist' school of 1948 born?

8. Who is the suitor of Bianca in the play The Taming of the Shrew?

9. Giacomo Balla, Italian artist, was one of the founders of which art movement?

10. Who wrote the novel Oscar and Lucinda?

11. Which actor's television roles included The Six Million Dollar Man?

12. In which market place was German 'wild boy' Kaspar Hauser found in 1928?

13. Which Russian statesman's original surname was Ulyanov?

14. In which year did country singer Patsy Cline die in an air crash?

15. What is the name given to the volume of water that would cover an area of 1 acre to a depth of 1 foot?

ANSWERS 1. 1959 2. The Orchid Trilogy 3. Belfast 4. Richard Todd 5. Oahu 6. Incisor 7. New York 8. Lucentio 9. Futurism 10. Peter Carey 11. Lee Majors 12. Nuremberg 13. Lenin 14. 1963 15. An acre-foot.

ENTERTAINMENT

1. In which year was the television programme What the Papers Say first broadcast?

2. Who directed the 2001 film Behind Enemy Lines?

3. Who created and latterly presented the television quiz show Winner Takes All?

4. Which poet does John Hannah portray in the 2001 film Pandaemonium?

5. Who wrote the 2001 television play Vacuuming Completely Nude in Paradise?

6. In which city is the 1999 film Women Talking Dirty set?

7. In which country was the television series Xena: Warrior Princess filmed?

8. Who directed the 1967 film In the Heat of the Night?

9. What was Bill Pertwee's character name in the sitcom You Rang, M'Lord?

10. Who directed the 1956 boxing film Somebody Up There Likes Me?

11. In which year was the first Glyndebourne opera festival?

12. Which duo star in the 2000 film What Lies Beneath?

13. Which former actress in the television soap Dallas appeared on the London stage as Mrs. Robinson in a production of The Graduate in 2001?

14. Who plays the character Thade in the 2001 film Planet of the Apes?

15. Who directed the 2001 film Enigma?

ANSWERS 1. 1956 2. John Moore 3. Geoffrey Wheeler 4. Wordsworth 5. Jim Cartwright 6. Edinburgh 7. New Zealand 8. Norman Jewison 9. PC Wilson 10. Robert Wise 11. 1934 12. Michelle Pfeiffer and Harrison Ford 13. Linda Gray 14. Tim Roth 15. Michael Apted.

SPORT

1. In which year were the first World Championships in korfball?

2. Where were the 1959 Pan-American Games held?

3. Who were 1980/1 First Division champions in football in England?

4. At what sport was Vadim Krasnochapka world champion in 1988?

5. Who was the 1996 U.S. PGA golf champion?

6. In which year did Jesper Parnevik first play in the Ryder Cup?

7. Which jockey rode Embassy to victory in the 1997 Cheveley Park Stakes?

8. Which tennis player won the ATP Hamlet Cup in August, 1999?

9. In which year was real tennis included in the Olympic Games?

10. How many golds did China get in the 1999 World Athletics Championships?

11. In what sport would you encounter the terms ballet, moguls and aerials?

12. Who did Toulouse play in the quarter-finals of the Heineken Cup in rugby union in 2000?

13. Which wicket-keeper made 22 dismissals for Sri Lanka in the 1985 three match series against India?

14. How many Tests did Ian Botham play for England at cricket?

15. In baseball, who hit the most home runs in the 1949 season?

POP MUSIC

1. Who recorded the album Niun Niggung?

2. Who recorded 1999's Utopia Parkway?

3. On which Bon Jovi studio album does the song Bad Medicine feature?

4. Which band released the 1999 album 60 Second Wipeout?

5. Who recorded the 2000 Top 10 single More Than I Needed To Know?

6. Which U.S. group recorded the album Black Foliage?

7. Which Scottish group's debut L.P. was 1989's C86?

8. Who recorded the 1999 album The Amateur View?

9. Which group recorded 1994 Top 10 single Steam?

10. Which track from Los Lobos' E.P. ...And A Time To Dance won a Grammy?

11. Which guitarist recorded the 1965 Capitol album Summer Surf?

12. Who recorded the 1999 album Carboot Soul?

13. Which group's debut album was 1986's Heaven's End?

14. Who recorded the 1999 album Suicaine Gratifaction?

15. On which label did Sting record the album Brand New Day?

ANSWERS 1. Mouse on Mars 2. Fountains of Wayne 3. New Jersey 4. Atari Teenage Riot 5. Scooch 6. Olivia Tremor Control 7. BMX Bandits 8. To Rococo Rot 9. East 17 10. Anselma 11. Dick Dale 12. Nightmares in Wax 13. Loop 14. Paul Westerberg 15. A & M.

GEOGRAPHY

1. In which English county is Blithfield Reservoir?

2. Of which country is Vilnius the capital?

3. On which European island are Malia and Sitia?

4. Walachia is a region of which European country?

5. Which country is larger in area - Puerto Rico or El Salvador?

6. Which Asian country houses the Musandam penisula?

7. In which sea is the island of Zakynthos?

8. The Tacana volcano straddles the border between which two countries?

9. In which European country is the Corno alle Scale mountain?

10. The town of Napier is on which bay in New Zealand?

11. On which Caribbean island is the resort of Negril?

12. The Alpujarra are a system of hills in which European country?

13. In which Canadian province might you ski at the Kicking Horse Mountain Resort?

14. On which lake is the Michigan port of St. Joseph?

15. On which European island is the port of Sciacca?

GENERAL KNOWLEDGE

1. Who wrote the 1980 novel Princess Daisy?

2. Where would an Edwardian woman have worn a toque?

3. Which singer starred in the 1957 film Jailhouse Rock?

4. Who won a Best Actor Oscar for the film The Godfather?

5. Which British philosopher's books include Principles of Mathematics?

6. In which continent is the mountain system of the Andes?

7. What is the name of the Mediterranean coastal region between Cannes in France and La Spezia in Italy?

8. What was the name of Lady Chatterley's Lover?

9. Who was 1989 Wimbledon men's singles tennis champion?

10. What was the name of the French underground movement that fought against the Germans in World War II?

11. The heavy woollen cloth with a thick nap called duffel is named after a town in which European country?

12. Who is the author of the play The Quare Fellow?

13. What is the name of the Sunday preceding Ash Wednesday?

14. Who wrote the novel The Ipcress File?

15. What is the motto of the British Royal Air Force?

ANSWERS 1. Judith Krantz 2. On the head - it was a small brimless hat 3. Elvis Presley 4. Marlon Brando 5. Bertrand Russell 6. South America 7. The Riviera 8. Oliver Mellors 9. Boris Becker 10. The Maquis 11. Belgium 12. Brendan Behan 13. Quinquagesima 14. Len Deighton 15. 'Per ardua ad astra'.

ENTERTAINMENT

1. Whose television roles include Zoë in Coronation Street and Rachel in Bad Girls?

2. In which country is the 1957 film Campbell's Kingdom set?

3. Which actress plays Rita in the BBC TV drama Playing The Field?

4. Who directed the 1972 film The Railway Children?

5. How many million dollars did Ben Affleck earn for making the film Forces Of Nature?

6. In which town was the film The Blair Witch Project shot?

7. Which sculptor does Gérard Depardieu play in the 1988 film Camille Claudel?

8. Who played Egg in This Life on television?

9. What is the name of the God of Thunder in Wagner's opera Das Rheingold?

10. Who plays an oil heiress in the 1929 film Untamed?

11. Which actress stars as a singer-songwriter in the 1994 film Camilla?

12. Which Lloyd Webber musical closed on Broadway in 2000, after more than 7,000 performances?

13. Who directed the 1996 film Sleepers?

14. Which boxer plays himself in the film Black and White, during which he beats up Robert Downey Jr.?

15. Which actress stalks Clint Eastwood in the 1971 film Play Misty For Me?

SPORT

1. In which city were the 1973 World Student Games held?

2. Diminuendo and Melodist dead-heated in which 1988 Irish Classic?

3. In which city were the 1991 Pan-American Games held?

4. At what sport were François Brandt and Roelof Klein Olympic champions in 1900?

5. Who won the women's London Marathon in 2000?

6. How much did Steve Davis win for taking the 1988 World Matchplay title in snooker?

7. At what sport has Peter Knowles been a No. 1 in England?

8. Who won the 1965 golf World Cup?

9. What nationality is runner Gabriela Szabo?

10. With which sport are Elgin Baylor and Hakeem Olajuwan associated?

11. By what score did Uruguay beat Argentina in the 1930 World Cup Final in football?

12. On which horse did Tony McCoy win his 200th race of the 1999/00 season?

13. Who was men's 100m breaststroke swimming world champion in 1998?

14. Who in 1977 became the youngest player to appear in a Ryder Cup?

15. Who is the Olympic silver medal-winning father of runner Inger Miller?

ANSWERS 1. Moscow 2. Irish Oaks 3. Havana 4. Rowing 5. Tegla Loroupe 6. £100,000 7. Badminton 8. South Africa 9. Romanian 10. Basketball 11. 4-2 12. Mr. Cool 13. Frédéric Deburghgraeve 14. Nick Faldo 15. Lennox Miller.

POP MUSIC

1. On which Neil Young studio album does the song Buffalo Springfield Again appear?

2. Which singer recorded the 2001 album Music of the Spheres?

3. The 1986 album The Moon and the Melodies was a collaboration between composer Harold Budd and which group?

4. Which group's albums include Bang! and Egyptology?

5. Which rap band were formerly known as Spectrum City?

6. Which group recorded the 2000 album Secret South?

7. Who collaborated with Peter Buck of the group R.E.M. on the 1997 album West?

8. Which punk group released the 1979 compilation album Singles Going Steady?

9. Which group recorded the 2000 album 100 Broken Windows?

10. In which year was Radiohead's Paranoid Android a Top 5 single hit?

11. Which male singer recorded the 2001 single Perfect Gentleman?

12. Who had a 1976 No. 1 single with the song Dancing Queen?

13. Which rock group recorded the 2001 single New Born?

14. Which group had a 1985 No. 1 single with the song I'm Your Man?

15. Which group recorded the 2001 single Juxtapozed with U?

ANSWERS 1. Silver and Gold 2. Ian Brown 3. The Cocteau Twins 4. World Party 5. Public Enemy 6. 16 Horsepower 7. Mark Eitzel 8. The Buzzcocks 9. Idlewild 10. 1997 11. Wyclef Jean 12. Abba 13. Muse 14. Wham! 15. Super Furry Animals.

HISTORY

1. Who was the father of Carolingian ruler Charles Martel?

2. In which year was the Good Friday Agreement signed in Ireland?

3. In which year was General Pinochet made commander-in-chief of the Chilean Army?

4. In which year did Scottish theologian John Duns Scotus die?

5. In which year did Edward Gierek become First Secretary of the Communist Party in Poland?

6. Which future prime minister was President of the Board of Trade from 1921-22?

7. In which year was John F. Kennedy elected U.S. president?

8. Which Spanish prime minister was murdered by ETA in 1973?

9. The Clayton-Bulwer Treaty signed in 1850 concerned the construction of what?

10. In which year was Patrice Lumumba, first prime minister of the Republic of the Congo, assassinated?

11. Who instigated the Third Servile War in 73 B.C.?

12. In which year was the Treaty of Adrianople, which ended war between Russia and Turkey, signed?

13. In which battle did General Albert S. Johnston die in 1862?

14. Which king of Denmark introduced Christianity into the country in 960?

15. In which year did Sir Alec Douglas-Home die?

ANSWERS 1. Pepin of Herstal 2. 1998 3. 1972 4. 1308 5. 1970 6. Stanley Baldwin 7. 1960 8. Carrero Blanco 9. Panama Canal 10. 1961 11. Spartacus 12. 1829 13. Battle of Shiloh 14. Harold Bluetooth 15. 1995.

GENERAL KNOWLEDGE

1. For which 1957 film did Joanne Woodward win a Best Actress Oscar?

2. Who authored the 1835 novel The Yemassee?

3. What is the capital of the state of Penang in Peninsular Malaysia?

4. Who was the 1970 world matchplay golf champion?

5. Which order of mammals includes the anteaters and sloths?

6. Which theatre on Bankside in Southwark, London, was erected in 1599?

7. Who is the author of the novel The House of the Spirits?

8. Which British architect is noted for his planning of New Delhi, India?

9. Who was Soviet president from 1985-8?

10. In which African country is the city of Umtata?

11. Who was the U.S. author of poetry collection I Shall Not Be Moved?

12. Who authored the novel Redgauntlet which was published in 1824?

13. Which town in S. England is the administrative centre of the Isle of Wight?

14. Which Los Angeles-born singer-songwriter's albums include Little Criminals?

15. Who wrote the 1882 play An Enemy of the People?

ANSWERS 1. The Three Faces of Eve 2. William Gilmore Simms 3. George Town 4. Jack Nicklaus 5. Edentata 6. The Globe 7. Isabel Allende 8. Edwin Lutyens 9. Andrei Gromyko 10. South Africa 11. Maya Angelou 12. Sir Walter Scott 13. Newport 14. Randy Newman 15. Henrik Ibsen

ENTERTAINMENT

1. Who directed the 1992 film The Hand that Rocks the Cradle?

2. What was Lady Penelope's surname in Thunderbirds?

3. In which year did the panel game Through the Keyhole first appear on television?

4. What is Linda Darnell's profession in the 1951 film The Lady Pays Off?

5. Which Hollywood actress appeared as Angie Tyler in the 1980s sitcom Three Up, Two Down?

6. Who plays a Broadway priest getting mixed up with a chorus girl in the 1959 film Say One For Me?

7. In which year is the 1990 film Total Recall set?

8. Who played Bert in the sitcom Till Death Us Do Part?

9. Who plays Johnny Depp's uncle in the 1993 film Arizona Dream?

10. Who played 1996's The Cable Guy on screen?

11. What is Carole Lombard's profession in the 1935 film Hands Across The Table?

12. Who voiced Thomas O'Malley Cat in the Disney film The Aristocats?

13. Who directed the 1943 musical Cabin in the Sky?

14. Who played Bill Haydon in the 1979 BBC TV drama Tinker Tailor Soldier Spy?

15. Which sitcom featured the characters Lady Patience Hardacre and Henri Lecoq?

ANSWERS 1. Curtis Hanson 2. Creighton-Ward 3. 1987 4. Schoolteacher 5. Lysette Anthony 6. Bing Crosby 7. 2084 8. Alfie Bass 9. Jerry Lewis 10. Jim Carrey 11. Manicurist 12. Phil Harris 13. Vincente Minnelli 14. Ian Richardson 15. Brass.a

SPORT

1. Laura Badea was the 1996 Olympic women's individual foil champion in fencing. Which country did she represent?

2. Golfer Lee Westwood withdrew from the Los Angeles Open in 2000. Why?

3. Who was the 1992 Olympic women's 400m individual medley swimming champion?

4. Which 48-year-old won the 1968 U.S. PGA golf title?

5. Who replaced Danny Wilson as the boss of Sheffield Wednesday in 2000?

6. What nationality is golfer Elisabeth Esterl?

7. Which horse won the 1998 Hennessy Cognac Gold Cup at Leopardstown?

8. Who was the 1988 Olympic men's tennis champion?

9. In which year was automatic timing first used in athletics at the Olympic Games?

10. Who was the 1911 Wimbledon women's singles tennis champion?

11. Who won the 1958 Moroccan Grand Prix in F1?

12. Which golfer was the 1996 Sports Illustrated Sportsman of the Year?

13. Which country won rugby union's 1993 World Cup Sevens?

14. What nationality is swimmer Michael Klim?

15. At what weight was Virgil Hill a WBA world champion from 1987-91?

ANSWERS 1. Romania 2. He had flu 3. Krisztina Egerszegi 4. Julius Boros 5. Peter Shreeves 6. German 7. Dorans Pride 8. Miloslav Mecir 9. 1932 10. Dorothea Lambert 11. Stirling Moss 12. Tiger Woods 13. England 14. Australian 15. Light-heavyweight.

POP MUSIC

1. In which year did The Dooleys have a Top 10 single with Chosen Few?

2. On which label did The Fall record the single The Man Whose Head Expanded?

3. Which performer recorded the song Hitler's Liver for the E.P. A Factory Sampler?

4. Which rock group released the 1973 album In a Glass House?

5. Which saxophone player fronted group Essential Logic?

6. Who replaced John Towe as drummer of Generation X?

7. Who played drums on Bryan Ferry's The Price Of Love E.P.?

8. Who recorded the 1984 album Raining Pleasure?

9. On which label did Adam Faith release the 1959 single What Do You Want?

10. On which label was The Silent Sun single by Genesis released?

11. On which label did the Fire Engines release the 1981 single Candyskin?

12. Under what name does Richard Melville Hall record?

13. By what name was guitarist Eddie Jones known?

14. Chris Stamey and Peter Holsapple were members of which 1980s U.S. group?

15. Which singer's albums include 1969's Joy Of A Toy?

ANSWERS 1. 1979 2. Rough Trade 3. John Dowie 4. Gentle Giant 5. Lora Logic 6. Mark Laff 7. Paul Thompson 8. The Triffids 9. Parlophone 10. Decca 11. Pop Aural 12. Moby 13. Guitar Slim 14. The dB's 15. Kevin Ayers.

WORDS

1. What in airforce slang is a kiwi or penguin?

2. What would a bellarmine contain?

3. Which military body was known as the Wavy Navy?

4. What might you do with Kate and Sidney according to its translation from British rhyming slang?

5. What is badigeon used for?

6. What might you do with a calamus, write with it or read with it?

7. What status has an Oink in the U.S.?

8. Which drug is known in the U.S. as doobie?

9. What type of creature is a balisaur?

10. Tomato sauce is Australian rhyming slang for which animal?

11. What is conium - a plant or one of the chemical elements?

12. How many sides does an enneagon have?

13. To what former British coin does the slang term Tosheroon refer?

14. What in boxing parlance is a pug?

15. To which foodstuff does the adjective butyric apply?

ANSWERS 1. A non-flying member of the airforce 2. Liquid, it's a type of jug 3. Royal Naval Volunteer Reserve 4. Eat it, it's steak and kidney 5. Repairing masonry 6. Write, it's a quill-pen 7. One income no kids 8. Marijuana 9. Badger 10. Horse 11. Plant 12. Nine 13. Half-crown 14. A boxer 15. Butter.

GENERAL KNOWLEDGE

1. In which radio drama does the character Captain Cat appear?

2. Which book did Ebenezer Cobham Brewer famously publish in 1870?

3. What was the Roman name for Ireland?

4. Who wrote the 1957 novel Gidget?

5. In which year was Dutch abstract expressionist painter Karel Appel born?

6. Who was world middleweight boxing champion from 1941-7?

7. What is the capital of Jordan?

8. In which year did U.S. aviator Amelia Earhart disappear?

9. Who wrote the 1939 novel Finnegans Wake?

10. Which bone in the ear is also called the incus?

11. Which comic actor played the title role in the film Wayne's World?

12. What is the capital of Azerbaijan?

13. Who was the 1976 Olympic men's downhill skiing champion?

14. Who wrote the 1974 novel Shardik?

15. What was the setting of the 1948 film The Snake Pit starring Olivia de Havilland?

ANSWERS 1. Under Milk Wood 2. Brewer's Dictionary of Phrase and Fable 3. Hibernia 4. Frederick Kohner 5. 1921 6. Tony Zale 7. Amman 8. 1937 9. James Joyce 10. Anvil 11. Mike Myers 12. Baku 13. Franz Klammer 14. Richard Adams 15. A mental institution.

ENTERTAINMENT

1. Who directed the 2001 film The Fast and the Furious?

2. Who plays the matriarchal Peggy Mitchell in the television soap EastEnders?

3. What was the name of Yogi Bear's girlfriend in the popular television cartoon series?

4. What was Clint Eastwood's first film with the director Don Siegel?

5. What was the name of Orson Welles's character in the 1958 film Touch of Evil?

6. Who directed the 2000 film Wonder Boys?

7. Who directed the 2001 film Joy Ride which stars Steve Zahn?

8. What was the codename of John Mills's character Tommy Devon in the 1970s television series The Zoo Gang?

9. Who narrated the 1970s documentary series The World at War?

10. On which novel is Alfred Hitchcock's 1936 film Sabotage based?

11. The 2001 film In the Bedroom is adapted from which short story?

12. In which year was the children's television programme Blue Peter first broadcast?

13. Which politician did Peter Barkworth portray in the 1981 drama series Winston Churchill - the Wilderness Years?

14. Which two actresses played Emma Harte in the 1985 television series A Woman of Substance?

15. Who provided the vocals for George Clooney on the song I Am A Man Of Constant Sorrow from the film O Brother, Where Art Thou?

ANSWERS 1. Rob Cohen 2. Barbara Windsor 3. Cindy Bear 4. Coogan's Bluff 5. Hank Quinlan 6. Curtis Hanson 7. John Dahl 8. Elephant 9. Laurence Olivier 10. Joseph Conrad's Secret Agent 11. Killings by Andre Dubus 12. 1958 13. Stanley Baldwin 14. Jenny Seagrove and Deborah Kerr 15. Dan Tyminski.

SPORT

1. What nationality is Nordic skier Matti Raivo?

2. Who was captain of the 1999 European Ryder Cup team?

3. How many runs did Don Bradman make for Australia in the 1930 five match series against England?

4. Who finished third in the 1999 German F1 Grand Prix?

5. By what score did San Francisco Giants lose the 1989 World Series in baseball?

6. Which rider was individual dressage champion at the 1928 Olympics?

7. Which four teams played in Pool 2 of the 1999/00 Heineken Cup in rugby union?

8. Who was the 1968 Olympic women's 400m freestyle swimming champion?

9. Which golfer won the 1946 U.S. Open?

10. What nationality is golfer Jarmo Sandelin?

11. For which Test cricket side does Sadagopan Ramesh play?

12. Who did the U.S.A. beat in the 1996 ice hockey World Cup Final?

13. What nationality is skater Irina Slutskaya?

14. Which was voted outstanding college American Football team in 1971 by United Press?

15. Who was the 1964 U.S. men's singles tennis champion?

ANSWERS 1. Finnish 2. Mark James 3. 974 4. Heinz-Harald Frentzen 5. 4-0 6. Carl von Langen 7. Bath, Padova, Swansea, Toulouse 8. Debbie Meyer 9. Lloyd Mangrum 10. Swedish 11. India 12. Canada 13. Russian 14. Nebraska 15. Roy Emerson

POP MUSIC

1. Which studio album by Motörhead features the songs Jailbait and The Hammer?

2. From which city were vocal group The Orioles?

3. What is guitarist Bram Tchaikovsky's real name?

4. Who was the original lead singer in the group which became Mott The Hoople?

5. Who recorded the 1999 single Once Around the Block?

6. Which actress-model recorded the 1999 single Oh Yeah?

7. In which city were the group Flaming Lips formed in 1983?

8. In which year did Mega City Four release the album Sebastopol Road?

9. The lead singer of Mother Love Bone died in 1990. What was his name?

10. Which group reformed in 1993 to play at Bill Clinton's inauguration party?

11. Which group recorded the 1971 album Teenage Head?

12. In which year did Then Jericho have a Top 20 hit with Big Area?

13. In which year did singer Laura Nyro die?

14. Which group's singles included 1991's Tingle and Sensitize?

15. What is Morrissey's full name?

ANSWERS 1. Ace of Spades 2. Baltimore 3. Peter Bramall 4. Stan Tippens 5. Badly Drawn Boy 6. Caprice 7. Oklahoma City 8. 1992 9. Andy Wood 10. Fleetwood Mac 11. The Flamin' Groovies 12. 1989 13. 1997 14. That Petrol Emotion 15. Steven Patrick Morrissey.

SCIENCE

1. In which year was the first atomic bomb detonated?

2. In which year did nuclear physicist Eugene Paul Wigner die?

3. In which year was Nereid, a moon of neptune, discovered?

4. What are the two main types of computers in use today?

5. In which century did U.S. scientist Benjamin Franklin live?

6. In which county was botanist William Withering born?

7. Is fluorine lighter or heavier than air?

8. In computer science, what is pixel short for?

9. Which bird was cosmonaut Valentina Tereshkova's call sign on her Vostok VI space mission?

10. What is the symbol of the element Nobelium?

11. Which English physiologist originated the terms 'synapse' and 'neuron'?

12. What nationality was biologist Ernest Mayr?

13. In which German town is scientist Georgius Agricola buried?

14. Iapetus is a moon of which planet?

15. Approximately how many miles in diameter is Uranus's moon Portia?

ANSWERS 1. 1945 2. 1995 3. 1949 4. Analogue and digital 5. 18th Century 6. Somerset 7. Heavier 8. Picture element 9. Seagull 10. No 11. Charles Scott Sherrington 12. German 13. Zeitz 14. Saturn 15. 66 miles

GENERAL KNOWLEDGE

1. What is the name of the hill on which the city of Jerusalem stands?

2. What in heraldry is the name given to the colour red?

3. Which actor's television credits include the title role in Father Dowling Investigates?

4. Who directed the 1943 film The Outlaw starring Jane Russell?

5. What is the name of the wild mountain sheep of N. Africa, also called an aoudad?

6. In which Shakespeare play does the clown Launcelot Gobbo appear?

7. For which 1950 film by Billy Wilder were both William Holden and Gloria Swanson Oscar-nominated?

8. What is the brightest star in the constellation Lyra?

9. What is a coelacanth?

10. In which U.S. state is the resort town of Aspen, which is noted for its skiing?

11. In which year was Soviet-born Icelandic pianist Vladimir Ashkanazy born?

12. In which African country is the city of Germiston which houses the world's largest gold refinery?

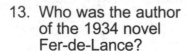

13. Who was the author of the 1934 novel Fer-de-Lance?

14. Which Hebrew patriarch in the Old Testament built an ark?

15. Which annual plant is also called ladies' fingers?

ENTERTAINMENT

1. What is Tobey Maguire's character name in the film The Cider House Rules?

2. Who plays Agent Scully in The X-Files?

3. Who played actress Coral Atkins in the ITV drama Seeing Red in 2000?

4. Which Italian actress starred in the 1953 film Aida?

5. Which actor from the film L.A. Confidential starred in the 1992 film Romper Stomper?

6. Which comedy duo star in the 1942 film A-Haunting We Will Go?

7. Who played Lawrence Bingham in the 1971 sitcom Doctor at Large?

8. Who played George Maple in the 1970s sitcom Don't Forget to Write?

9. Which Top of the Pops presenter also hosted the fashion show She's Gotta Have It in 2000?

10. Who directed the 1977 biopic Valentino?

11. Who directed the 1985 film Agnes Of God?

12. Which comic actor played Clarence Darrow in a one-man show tour of Britain in 2000?

13. What was the name of Peter Perfect's car in the cartoon show Wacky Races?

14. Which contestant won Stars In Their Eyes in 1995?

15. Who does Joshua Jacks play in Dawson's Creek?

ANSWERS 1. Homer Wells 2. Gillian Anderson 3. Sarah Lancashire 4. Sophia Loren 5. Russell Crowe 6. Laurel & Hardy 7. Richard O'Sullivan 8. George Cole 9. Jayne Middlemiss 10. Ken Russell 11. Norman Jewison 12. Leslie Nielsen 13. Turbo Terrific 14. Lee Griffiths 15. Pacey.

SPORT

1. At what sport has Jens Voit competed?

2. In which year was the women's World Cup in cricket first held?

3. What nationality is golfer Marc Farry?

4. Gymnast Junichi Shimizu was 1978 world champion at horse vault. Which country did he represent?

5. Who lost to Ted Hankey in the 2000 Embassy World Darts Championship by 6-0?

6. Sanbon shobu and Ippon shobu are types of championship in which sport?

7. Which snooker player won the 1999 Champions Cup in Croydon?

8. Which football player transferred from PSV Eindhoven to Barcelona in July, 1996 for £13.2m?

9. Who won the 125cc San Marino Grand Prix in motorcycling in 1999?

10. Which women's field event did Ilke Wyludda win at the 1994 European Championships?

11. In tennis, who beat Andre Agassi in the final of the 1999 ATP Mercedes Benz Cup?

12. Who rode Oh So Wonderful to victory in the 1998 Juddmonte Diamond Stakes at York?

13. Which golfer won the European Masters in September, 1999?

14. Sisi Dolman was 1988-91 world women's powerlifting champion. In what weight division?

15. Which female golfer won the Donegal Irish Open in September, 1999?

ANSWERS 1. Cycling 2. 1973 3. French 4. Japan 5. Ronnie Baxter 6. Karate 7. Stephen Hendry 8. Ronaldo 9. Marco Melandri 10. Discus 11. Pete Sampras 12. Pat Eddery 13. Lee Westwood 14. 52kg 15. Sandrine Mendiburu.

POP MUSIC

1. Who is the leader of the group Limp Bizkit?

2. Which guitarist was born John Anthony Genzale Jr. in 1952?

3. From which city do the U.S. band Eleventh Dream Day hail?

4. Which solo artist recorded the 2000 album Pure?

5. Which male artist recorded the albums All the News That's Fit to Sing and I Ain't Marching Anymore?

6. Which guitarist recorded the 1977 album Slowhand?

7. Which Bristol-born recording artist recorded the 2001 album Blowback?

8. Which group recorded the 2001 album Rooty?

9. In which year did the group Amazulu have a Top Five single with the song Too Good To Be Forgotten?

10. Which member of the group The Beautiful South recorded the 2001 solo album Fat Chance under the pseudonym Biscuit Boy (aka Crackerman)?

11. Which singer-songwriter recorded the 2000 album Heliocentric?

12. Which group recorded the 2001 live album Waltz Across America?

13. Which group recorded the live album Familiar to Millions?

14. In which year was singer Sean Lennon born?

15. Which former member of the group Wire went on to run the record label Swim?

ANSWERS 1. Fred Durst 2. Johnny Thunders 3. Chicago 4. Gary Numan 5. Phil Ochs 6. Eric Clapton 7. Tricky 8. Basement Jaxx 9. 1986 10. Paul Heaton 11. Paul Weller 12. The Cowboy Junkies 13. Oasis 14. 1975 15. Colin Newman.

PEOPLE

1. In which year was the actress Claire Bloom born?

2. How many children did Cleopatra VII have by Antony?

3. In which country was fashion designer Oscar de la Renta born?

4. In which country was conductor Karl Böhm born?

5. With which group is Shane Lynch a singer?

6. How many wives did American religious leader Brigham Young have?

7. In which year did U.S. outlaw Belle Starr die?

8. Which French writer authored Clochemerle?

9. What was the middle name of comedian Tommy Handley?

10. Who was the father of Alexander the Great?

11. Camille Donatacci is the third wife of which comedy actor?

12. Which U.S. singer was involved in a fracas at Heathrow Airport in September, 1999?

13. Which actor did Courteney Cox marry in 1999?

14. How old was Clint Eastwood when son Morgan was born in 1996?

15. What age was Lolo Ferrari, a star of television show Eurotrash, when she died in 2000?

ANSWERS 1. 1931 2. Three 3. Dominican Republic 4. Austria 5. Boyzone 6. 27 7. 1889 8. Gabriel Chevallier 9. Reginald 10. Philip II 11. Kelsey Grammer 12. Diana Ross 13. David Arquette 14. 66 15. 30.

SPORT

1. Which World Championship snooker venue is in Sheffield, England?

2. Which rugby union club did Jonathan Sleightholme leave to join Northampton?

3. Which team were captained by Ferenc Puskas at the 1954 football World Cup?

4. Which swimming event did John Naber become the first person to complete in less than two minutes in 1976?

5. Which British driver won the 1989 and 1992 Brazilian Grands Prix?

6. How many players does a beach volleyball team have?

7. Which German player was European Footballer of the Year in 1981?

8. How many caps did rugby union's Gavin Hastings win for Scotland between 1986 and 1995 - 61 or 92?

9. Why was Rhodesia banned from the 1972 Olympic Games?

10. Who captured his second major of 1998 in winning the Open at Royal Birkdale?

11. Who won the men's race in the 2002 London Marathon?

12. What is the name of rugby union club Gloucester's home ground?

13. Which field event title did Jan Zelezny successfully defend at the 1996 Olympic Games?

14. Who knocked France out of the 1986 World Cup?

15. In which year did basketball's Michael Jordan become the NBA's leading scorer for a record tenth time?

GENERAL KNOWLEDGE

1. Which Roman Catholic organisation takes its name from the Latin for 'God's work'?

2. In medicine, what does the abbreviation E.C.G. stand for?

3. Who created the oriental villain Fu Manchu?

4. Bamboozled is a film by which controversial American director?

5. Which prime minister led the republic of Ireland into the Common Market?

6. What is the singular of graffiti?

7. Who won a Best Supporting Actor Oscar for From Here to Eternity?

8. What name was given to the part of Anglo-Saxon England controlled by the Vikings?

9. Which Dutch striker joined Manchester United in a record £19 million transfer deal in 2001?

10. Who wrote the novel Daniel Deronda?

11. Which word meaning 'rebirth' describes the period in European history that began in the 14th century?

12. In which game show did Bernie the Bolt load the crossbow?

13. What was the nickname of U.S. crime boss Charles Luciano?

14. Which Australian city is the state capital of Victoria?

15. Murray Harkin is the former business partner of which member of the Royal Family?

ANSWERS: 1 Opus Dei, 2 Electrocardiogram, 3 Sax Rohmer, 4 Spike Lee, 5 Jack Lynch, 6 Graffito, 7 Frank Sinatra, 8 Danelaw, 9 Ruud Van Nistelrooy, 10 George Eliot, 11 Renaissance, 12 The Golden Shot, 13 Lucky, 14 Melbourne, 15 The Countess of Wessex.

GENERAL KNOWLEDGE

1. What was the name of The Addams Family butler?

2. Which word was originally an abbreviation of the German word Fliegerabwehrkanone?

3. In Greek mythology, who was the father of Icarus?

4. Which German football team knocked Manchester United out of the 2000/01 Champions League?

5. What sort of creature is an accentor?

6. Which Welsh poet wrote A Small Desperation and Funland?

7. What is the name of the local paper in EastEnders?

8. High Willhays is the highest point of which upland region of England?

9. Which theoretical temperature corresponds to minus 273.15 degrees on the Celsius scale?

10. Which Nigerian novelist wrote Things Fall Apart?

11. Which English king was killed at the Battle of Bosworth Field?

12. How many stories are there in the Decameron?

13. By what name was American comedian Louis Francis Cristillo known?

14. Which seven-a-side ball game is played in a swimming pool?

15. What nationality is Derartu Tulu, winner of the women's race in the 2001 London Marathon?

ANSWERS: 1 Lurch, 2 Flak, 3 Daedalus, 4 Bayern Munich, 5 A bird, 6 Dannie Abse, 7 Walford Gazette, 8 Dartmoor, 9 Absolute zero, 10 Chinua Achebe, 11 Richard III, 12 100, 13 Lou Costello, 14 Water polo, 15 Ethiopian.

? **GENERAL KNOWLEDGE** ?

1. Who wrote Anne of Green Gables?

2. Which pianist and conductor was married to the cellist Jacqueline Du Pre?

3. What was the name of the Queen's favourite corgi, who had to be put down in 2001?

4. Which singer-songwriter recorded the albums This Year's Model and Punch the Clock?

5. In which Asian country is the city of Da Nang?

6. Which English historian claimed that 'absolute power corrupts absolutely'?

7. Which Evelyn Waugh novel is a satire on the American way of death?

8. Which Austrian conductor, musical director of the Berlin Philharmonic Orchestra, died in 1989?

9. Who wrote the novel Absolute Beginners?

10. Which British dramatist wrote Equus and Amadeus?

11. Which suffragette founded the Women's Social and Political Union?

12. What feature did silent film comic Ben Turpin have insured?

13. Who wrote Charlie and the Chocolate Factory?

14. Which unit of land measurement is equal to 4840 square yards?

15. What nationality is El Mouaziz, winner of the men's race in the 2001 London Marathon?

ENTERTAINMENT

1. Who presented the BBC2 series The House Detectives?

2. Which pop legend released the live album One Night Only, recorded at Madison Square Garden in 2000?

13. In which seventies sitcom did John Alderton and Hannah Gordon star as a divorced couple?

4. Which 1960 film starred Spencer Tracy as a defence attorney and Gene Kelly as a cynical reporter?

5. Which actor starred as Pete Gifford in ITV's comedy drama series Cold Feet?

6. What was MC Tunes versus 808 State's 1990 U.K. top ten hit?

7. Which 2000 film starring Gwyneth Paltrow as a Las Vegas showgirl was directed by her father Bruce?

8. Whose Wildlife Gardens were created on BBC2?

9. From which film was Olivia Newton-John's 1978 U.K. top five hit Hopelessly Devoted to You taken?

10. Which actress played Harvey Keitel's wife in the 1989 film The January Man?

11. Which BBC1 series about money matters was presented by Sally Magnusson?

12. Which Irish vocalist had a U.K. top five hit in 1988 with Missing You?

13. Which actor played a businessman who comes face to face with himself as a child in the 2000 film Disney's The Kid?

14. Where did The Flintstones live in the cartoon series?

15. Which U.S. singer had a 2000 U.K. number one with Can't Fight the Moonlight?

GENERAL KNOWLEDGE

1. What was the profession of the hero in the 1941 film Pimpernel Smith?

2. Which poet and dramatist was murdered in a Deptford tavern in 1593?

3. Racing driver Dale Earnhardt was killed on the final lap of which well-known race in 2001?

4. Which tailless primate has slender and slow varieties?

5. What name is given to the lower house of the Manx Parliament?

6. Which U.S. pianist and bandleader wrote Artistry in Rhythm?

7. Which poet lived in Dove Cottage?

8. Which director made the films Women in Love, The Boy Friend and Tommy?

9. What sort of house has a name literally meaning in the Bengali style?

10. Which professional team golf event was first contested in 1927?

11. Which American singer-songwriter was born Robert Allen Zimmerman?

12. Where does the television programme name Jackanory come from?

13. Which comic police force did Mack Sennett create in his silent films?

14. Who was elected prime minister of Israel in 2001?

15. Which Irish novelist wrote The Country Girls?

GENERAL KNOWLEDGE

1. What sort of creature is a gurnard?

2. Which Irish dramatist wrote Juno and the Paycock?

3. How many tries did England score in their 2001 Six Nations Championship victory over Italy?

4. Which American architect designed the Guggenheim Museum in New York City?

5. Who was the Greek goddess of the moon?

6. Which U.S. city is bisected by the Santa Monica mountains?

7. Which American author received a law degree from the University of Mississippi in 1981?

8. To which American comedian was Gracie Allen married?

9. Which small crustacean is known as a pill bug in America?

10. Who wrote the novel Fathers and Sons?

11. Which English artist painted Rain, Steam and Speed?

12. Who said "Ask not what your country can do for you - ask what you can do for your country"?

13. Which film received 12 nominations for the 2001 Oscars?

14. What is the capital of Hungary?

15. Which American astronomer presented the TV series Cosmos and wrote the novel Contact?

ANSWERS: 1 A fish, 2 Sean O'Casey, 3 Ten, 4 Frank Lloyd Wright, 5 Selene, 6 Los Angeles, 7 John Grisham 8 George Burns, 9 Woodlouse, 10 Ivan Turgenev, 11 J M W Turner, 12 John F Kennedy, 13 Gladiator, 14 Budapest, 15 Carl Sagan.

GENERAL KNOWLEDGE

1. Who is the author of Lost Boy and A Man Named Dave?

2. Which American neurologist wrote The Man who Mistook His Wife for a Hat and Awakenings?

3. On which asteroid did NASA land an unmanned craft in 2001?

4. Which 18th-century political theorist wrote Reflections on the Revolution in France?

5. What was the real first name of American comedian Bud Abbott?

6. Which English novelist wrote To the Lighthouse?

7. Who did Telly Savalas play in the film The Greatest Story Ever Told?

8. Which Spanish surrealist artist painted The Crucifixion in 1951?

9. Which French nobleman wrote the novel Justine?

10. Which Italian conductor became principal conductor of the Berlin Philharmonic in 1989?

11. Which English actress won an Oscar for her portrayal of the Duchess of Brighton in The VIPs?

12. Who was assassinated while campaigning for the U.S. presidential nomination in 1968?

13. The film The Fighting Prince of Donegal is set during the reign of which English monarch?

14. What is the most common blood group in the world?

15. Which English novelist wrote A Clockwork Orange?

ENTERTAINMENT

1. What was the name of Connie Booth's character in the sitcom Fawlty Towers?

2. Which teenage trio released their debut album, One Touch, in 2000, featuring the U.K. top ten hit Overload?

3. Which 1962 film featured John Wayne as General Sherman and Spencer Tracy's voice in its narration?

4. Which actor played lawyer John Close in the ITV drama series Close & True?

5. Which vocalist had a U.K. top five hit in 1996 with Give Me a Little More Time?

6. In which 2000 film did Robert De Niro star as an ex-cop recovering from a stroke?

7. Which character met a sudden death in the final episode of the sitcom One Foot in the Grave?

8. Which British group had a U.K. number one hit with Start in 1980?

9. Which character did Michael Caine play in the 1965 film The Ipcress File?

10. Which actress starred along with Lucy Liu and Drew Barrymore in the 2000 film remake of Charlie's Angels?

11. What was the title of the final ITV Inspector Morse drama?

12. With whom did the Eurythmics collaborate on the 1985 U.K. top ten hit Sisters Are Doin' it For Themselves?

13. Which Star Wars: Episode 1 actress played a single mother in the 2000 film Where the Heart Is?

14. What was the name of Jimmy Nail's character in the 1980s comedy drama series Auf Wiedersehen, Pet?

15. From which film was Destiny's Child's 2000 U.K. number one single Independent Women taken?

ANSWERS: 1 Polly Sherman, 2 Sugababes, 3 How the West Was Won, 4 Robson Green, 5 Gabrielle, 6 Flawless, 7 Victor Meldrew, 8 The Jam, 9 Harry Palmer, 10 Cameron Diaz, 11 The Remorseful Day, 12 Aretha Franklin, 13 Natalie Portman, 14 'Oz' Osbourne, 15 Charlie's Angels.

GENERAL KNOWLEDGE

1. Which British novelist wrote New Grub Street?

2. Which French theologian was famous for his love for Héloïse?

3. Who defeated Jack Dempsey to become world heavyweight boxing champion in 1926?

4. Which actress, singer and songwriter was married to Roy Rogers?

5. The sackbut was a precursor of which musical instrument?

6. Which African country was formerly called Upper Volta?

7. In which city is the film Bitter Sweet set?

8. Which English poet and novelist wrote The Edwardians and All Passion Spent?

9. Who became the fastest woman to circumnavigate the globe alone in the Vendée Globe 2000 yacht race?

10. Which British novelist wrote Evelina and Camilla?

11. Which classic American horse race is run on the first Saturday in May at Churchill Downs?

12. The title character of the film Jackie Brown was originally called what?

13. Which bird has green, lesser spotted and great spotted varieties?

14. What is the title of the film sequel to The Silence of the Lambs?

15. Which American media mogul founded CNN?

ANSWERS: 1 George Gissing, 2 Peter Abelard, 3 Gene Tunney, 4 Dale Evans, 5 Trombone, 6 Burkina Faso, 7 Vienna, 8 Vita Sackville-West, 9 Ellen MacArthur, 10 Fanny Burney, 11 Kentucky Derby, 12 Jackie Burke, 13 Woodpecker, 14 Hannibal, 15 Ted Turner.

GENERAL KNOWLEDGE

1. Which chat show host appeared in the 1988 film Hairspray?

2. Which British novelist is noted for her Balkan Trilogy and Levant Trilogy?

3. Who directed the films The Last Picture Show and Paper Moon?

4. Which England batsman joined Surrey from Middlesex in 2001?

5. Of which Asian country is Vientiane the capital?

6. Which martial arts actor and director fractured his skull when making the 1986 film Armour of God?

7. Who played televison's Six Million Dollar Man?

8. Which American actress was known as the 'Sweater Girl' in the 1940s?

9. By what first name was the baseball player Henry Aaron known?

10. Which German novelist wrote The Magic Mountain and Buddenbrooks?

11. Which two countries contest The Ashes in cricket?

12. Which American author wrote The Friendly Persuasion?

13. Which actress starred with Bob Hope and Bing Crosby in a series of Road to... films?

14. On which TV show did Nigel Lythgoe and others create a new pop group?

15. Which modern animal is related to the mammoth?

ANSWERS: 1 Ricki Lake, 2 Olivia Manning, 3 Peter Bogdanovich, 4 Mark Ramprakash, 5 Laos, 6 Jackie Chan, 7 Lee Majors, 8 Lana Turner, 9 Hank, 10 Thomas Mann, 11 England and Australia, 12 Jessamyn West, 13 Dorothy Lamour, 14 Popstars, 15 Elephant.

GENERAL KNOWLEDGE

1. Which Italian-American film director trained to be a priest?

2. Which British composer wrote On Hearing the First Cuckoo in Spring?

3. What does a hippologist study?

4. Which cartoon bird was created by Walter Lantz?

5. Of which country is Bangui the capital?

6. Which member of rock group The Faces died in 1997?

7. Who directed the film Back To The Future?

8. Which English novelist wrote A Journal of the Plague Year?

9. Buster Bloodvessel was the frontman of which eighties pop group?

10. What is the capital of the United Arab Emirates?

11. Which actress was known as the 'Jersey Lily'?

12. For which novel is the Spanish author Miguel de Cervantes famous?

13. Michael Praed left the television series Robin of Sherwood to join which 1980s soap?

14. Who won a Best Actor Oscar for The African Queen?

15. Of which country is Managua the capital?

ENTERTAINMENT

1. Which English actress played the Devil in the 2000 film Bedazzled?

2. Which actor played cult hero Reg Holdsworth in Coronation Street?

3. What was the title of the 2000 double live album release by Oasis?

4. Which actor played an android and his creator in the 1987 film Making Mr. Right?

5. In which Airport was BBC1's docusoap set?

6. Which U.S. group had a 1965 U.K. number one hit with Mr Tambourine Man?

7. In which 2000 film did Mark Wahlberg star as a ex-con drifting into gangsterism?

8. Which Peak Practice character, played by Gary Mavers, left the series in 2000?

9. Which Irish punk band's line-up on forming in 1975 was Bob Geldof on vocals, Johnnie Fingers on keyboards, Pete Briquette on bass and Gerry Cott and Garry Roberts on guitar?

10. Which Scots actor starred in the title role of the 1991 film The Pope Must Die?

11. What chart position did Elvis Presley's first U.K. hit, 1956's Heartbreak Hotel, reach?

12. In which 2000 film did Michael Douglas star as a professor of English?

13. Which actor played Detective Dave Starsky in the Seventies U.S. cop series Starsky and Hutch?

14. Which Brighton-based D.J. released his second album, Halfway Between the Gutter and the Stars, in 2000?

15. Which actor played Wall Street vulture Lawrence Garfield in the 1991 film Other People's Money?

ANSWERS: 1 Elizabeth Hurley, 2 Ken Morley, 3 Familiar to Millions, 4 John Malkovich, 5 Heathrow, 6 The Byrds, 7 The Yards, 8 Dr Andrew Attwood, 9 Boomtown Rats, 10 Robbie Coltrane, 11 No. 2, 12 Wonder Boys, 13 Paul Michael Glaser, 14 Fatboy Slim, 15 Danny DeVito.

? GENERAL KNOWLEDGE ?

1. Where was the writer and film director Marguerite Duras born?

2. Which New Zealand-born author wrote The Garden Party and Bliss?

3. Who was known as 'the lady with the lamp'?

4. Which Shakespeare play is partly set in the Forest of Arden?

5. Of which planet is Deimos a moon?

6. What does the C stand for in the computer abbreviation ASCII?

7. Which Scottish novelist wrote Juan in America?

8. Which Italian racing driver was world champion in 1952 and 1953?

9. Of which U.S. state is Lansing the capital?

10. To which continent is the mamba native?

11. Which American jazz musician was known as Satchmo?

12. Which was the first Gerry Anderson television series to use human rather than puppet actors?

13. Which of the British Isles has three legs on its flag?

14. What nationality is Abdul Baset Ali al-Megrahi who was convicted of the Lockerbie bombing?

15. Which Greek philosopher was tutor to Alexander the Great?

ANSWERS: 1 Vietnam, 2 Katherine Mansfield, 3 Florence Nightingale, 4 As You Like It, 5 Mars, 6 Code, 7 Eric Linklater, 8 Alberto Ascari, 9 Michigan, 10 Africa, 11 Louis Armstrong, 12 UFO, 13 Isle of Man, 14 Libyan, 15 Aristotle.

GENERAL KNOWLEDGE

1. Which British novelist wrote The Citadel?

2. Which Indian author created the fictional town of Malgudi?

3. Who won the men's singles at the 2001 Australian Open?

4. Which British folk singer and playwright wrote the song The First Time Ever I Saw Your Face?

5. What sort of creature is a piddock?

6. Which British novelist used the pseudonyms Jean Plaidy and Victoria Holt?

7. What was the name of the character played by Sandra Dickinson in Hitch-Hikers Guide to the Galaxy?

8. Which English actor was the first to play Hamlet, Macbeth, King Lear and Richard III?

9. Who succeeded Chris Woodhead as head of Ofsted?

10. Which English novelist wrote East Lynne?

11. Which race meeting was established by Queen Anne in 1711?

12. Who wrote the television comedy Only Fools and Horses?

13. Which Oscar-winning actor starred in the film What Women Want?

14. Who created the detective Philip Marlowe?

15. On which river does Manchester stand?

ANSWERS: 1 H E Bates, 2 R K Narayan, 3 Andre Agassi, 4 Ewan MacColl, 5 A mollusc, 6 Eleanor Hibbert, 7 Trillian, 8 Richard Burbage, 9 Mike Tomlinson, 10 Mrs Henry Wood, 11 Royal Ascot, 12 John Sullivan, 13 Mel Gibson, 14 Raymond Chandler, 15 River Irwell.

GENERAL KNOWLEDGE

1. In the children's television programme, what was the name of Noggin the Nog's wicked uncle?

2. Which pioneer of paperback publishing founded Penguin Books?

3. What is the meaning of the title 'Fidei Defensor' belonging to English monarchs?

4. Which American football team won Super Bowl XXXV?

5. Who wrote The Day of the Triffids?

6. In what year was Nelson Mandela released from prison?

7. Which fictional bear is a friend of Christopher Robin?

8. In Greek mythology, which mountain nymph fell in love with Narcissus?

9. Which creatures are the principal food of the aardwolf?

10. Which tennis player beat Serena and Venus Williams in consecutive matches at the 2001 Australian Open?

11. Which major upland mass forms the 'backbone of England'?

12. Who was the first man to set foot on the Moon?

13. Who played Mac MacIntyre in the 1983 film Local Hero?

14. In which European country is the city of Maastricht?

15. Which carbohydrate is also called milk sugar?

ANSWERS: 1 Nogbad the Bad, 2 Sir Allen Lane, 3 Defender of the faith, 4 Baltimore Ravens, 5 John Wyndham, 6 1990, 7 Winnie-the-Pooh, 8 Echo, 9 Termites, 10 Martina Hingis, 11 The Pennines, 12 Neil Armstrong, 13 Peter Riegert, 14 The Netherlands, 15 Lactose.

SPORT

1. Which England bowler took four wickets in one over in the Fourth Test against the West Indies at Headingley in August 2000?

2. How many points are awarded for a try in rugby union?

3. Which team knocked Newcastle United out of the Worthington Cup in two successive seasons?

4. How many yards long is a cricket pitch?

5. With which sport are the Harlem Globetrotters famously associated?

6. Who won his seventh men's singles title at Wimbledon in 2000?

7. Who was the first athlete to run 100 sub-four-minute miles?

8. Which boxer was known as the Dark Destroyer?

9. Which player scored the first goal for Manchester United in the 1999 FA Cup Final?

10. For which country does rugby league star Gorden Tallis play?

11. In which sport did Audley Harrison win gold at the Sydney Olympics?

12. How many players make up an ice hockey team?

13. Which country knocked Romania out of Euro 2000?

14. Which horse won the Grand National in 1983?

15. How many Formula One world championships did Jackie Stewart win as a driver?

GENERAL KNOWLEDGE

1. Who wrote the 1934 play Days Without End?

2. What is the meaning of the common abbreviation CIA?

3. Who was Secretary of State for Trade and Industry from 1998-2001?

4. Which surrealist artist's works include 1930's Spectre du Soir?

5. Name one of the four Home Secretaries who served under Mrs Thatcher?

6. In Christianity, what is the period from Ash Wednesday to Easter known as?

7. Which American artist painted the 1940 oil Report from Rockport?

8. Who led the civil rights bus boycott in Montgomery, Alabama in 1955?

9. In which year did the artist Pablo Picasso die - 1987 or 1973?

10. Who wrote the 1941 book Worrals of the W.A.A.F.?

11. In which novel by Charles Dickens does the character Mr Brownlow appear?

12. In which novel by Thomas Hardy does the character Fanny Robin appear?

13. Name one of the three items represented in the centre of the flag of Angola?

14. Who was Secretary of State for the Environment from 1985-6?

15. Who wrote the 1975 novel Sweet William?

ANSWERS: 1 Eugene O'Neill, 2 Central Intelligence Agency, 3 Stephen Byers, 4 Salvador Dali, 5 William Whitelaw, Leon Brittan, Douglas Hurd and David Waddington, 6 Lent, 7 Stuart Davis, 8 Martin Luther King, 9 1973, 10 Capt W.E Johns, 11 Oliver Twist, 12 Far From the Madding Crowd, 13 Machete, golden star and part of a cog wheel, 14 Kenneth Baker, 15 Beryl Bainbridge.

GENERAL KNOWLEDGE

1. What is the main difference between Lataste's viper and a common viper?

2. From which country was Dag Hammarskjold, the second secretary-general of the United Nations?

3. Who was Archbishop of Canterbury from 1903-28?

4. What is the colour of the central stripe on the flag of Mali?

5. At which Oxford college did Oscar Wilde study?

6. Who wrote the 1950 novel The Martian Chronicles?

7. In which year did the character Valerie Barlow die in the television show Coronation Street - 1966 or 1971?

8. Which 2001 serial novel was written by, among others, Roddy Doyle and Frank McCourt?

9. Who wrote the 1939 novel The Confidential Agent?

10. Which 20th century U.S. president was born in Hyde Park, New York?

11. Who authored the 1934 play Within the Gates?

12. Who wrote the 1822 novel The Fortunes of Nigel?

13. Who was Chairman of the Conservative Party from 1992-4?

14. What is the common name of the plant Lonicera?

15 Who wrote the 2001 novel Skipping Christmas?

ANSWERS: 1 The former has a nose horn, 2 Sweden, 3 Randall Davidson, 4 Yellow, 5 Magdalen, 6 Ray Bradbury, 7 1971, 8 Yeats is Dead!, 9 Graham Greene, 10 Franklin Delano Roosevelt, 11 Sean O'Casey, 12 Walter Scott, 13 Norman Fowler, 14 Honeysuckle, 15 John Grisham.

GENERAL KNOWLEDGE

1. What is the approximate driving distance in miles between London and Venice - 919, 1019 or 1119?

2. What is the meaning of the common abbreviation C.J.D.?

3. Who wrote the book Like Water for Chocolate?

4. Which British painter's works included The Music of the Woods in 1906?

5. What is the capital of Belarus?

6. Which writer lived in exile in France under the name Sebastian Melmoth?

7. In which French city was the author Jules Verne born?

8. In which country would you find the volcano Vesuvius?

9. Which comedienne played Julia Stone in the television show Coronation Street?

10. What does an arctophile have a love of?

11. Of which country did Guy Verhofstadt become prime minister in 1999?

12. Which Mexican painter's works include the 1937 watercolour Head of a Peasant Girl?

13. Who wrote the 2000 novel Sushi for Beginners?

14. In which Midlands city is the independent Radcliffe College?

15. Who did Clementine Hozier marry in 1908?

ENTERTAINMENT

1. Who directed and starred in the 1985 film Pale Rider?

2. Who had a U.K. number one hit single in 1972 with Take Me Bak 'Ome?

3. Home Improvement star Tim Allen played a toy salesman in which 1994 Christmas movie?

4. Which presenter of the children's TV show Blue Peter left the show in 1995 to become an early morning host on BBC Radio 2?

5. The attempted assassination of which pop artist and film-maker was the subject of a 1996 film by Mary Harron?

6. Which Boon star played Billy Bones in the 1995 TV movie Ken Russell's Treasure Island?

7. In 1995, Kim Wilde appeared in a production of which rock musical in London's West End?

8. Who wrote and directed the 1995 film In the Bleak Midwinter?

9. Who had a U.K. number one hit single in 1981 with It's My Party?

10. Who won a Best Supporting Actress Oscar in 1984 for her performance in A Passage to India?

11. In the 1995 Bond film GoldenEye, which character was played by Samantha Bond?

12. Which Brookside character was played by Paul Usher?

13. In 1995, which band broke Michael Jackson's record for first-week sales of a double album in America?

14. Who played Jimmy Porter in the 1959 film version of Look Back in Anger?

15. Which Star Trek character was played on TV and film by DeForrest Kelley?

ANSWERS: 1 Clint Eastwood, 2 Slade, 3 The Santa Clause, 4 Diane-Louise Jordan, 5 Andy Warhol (I Shot Andy Warhol), 6 Michael Elphick, 7 Tommy, 8 Kenneth Branagh, 9 Dave Stewart with Barbara Gaskin, 10 Peggy Ashcroft, 11 Miss Moneypenny, 12 Barry Grant, 13 The Beatles, 14 Richard Burton, 15 Dr McCoy.

GENERAL KNOWLEDGE

1. Why is a bird named a hoopoe so called?

2. Who became prime minister of New Zealand in 1999?

3. What sort of animal is a chamois?

4. Which shipping forecast area lies immediately north of Plymouth?

5. From which country was Kurt Waldheim, the fourth secretary-general of the United Nations?

6. In which European city are the headquarters of the International Atomic Energy Association?

7. What are the two colours that make up the background of the flag of Portugal?

8. Who wrote the 1819 poem Peter Bell?

9. Which American writer penned 1900's The Man That Corrupted Hadleyburg?

10. What in martial arts is one's choong sim?

11. In which year did Stefan Edberg first play Tim Henman in the U.S. Open men's singles tennis championship?

12. What is unusual about Commonwealth members Vanuatu, Cameroon and Mozambique?

13. What is the meaning of the common abbreviation C.A.A.?

14. In which country would you find the city of Tbilisi?

15. Who was president of the European Union Commission from 1995-99?

ANSWERS: 1 After its call, 2 Helen Clark, 3 A goat-like antelope, 4 Lundy, 5 Austria, 6 Vienna, 7 Red and green, 8 William Wordsworth, 9 Mark Twain, 10 Centre of gravity, 11 1996, 12 They were never British colonies, 13 Civil Aviation Authority, 14 Georgia, 15 Jacques Santer.

GENERAL KNOWLEDGE

1. Who painted the 1939 work New York Movie?

2. Who directed the 1953 film Johnny Guitar?

3. In which European country are the provinces of Vas and Zala?

4. Who was the Australian prime minister from 1949-66?

5. Where on a ship would you find a cringle?

6. Which has the higher melting point - potassium or sodium?

7. Which member of the Eagles was lead guitarist in the group Barnstorm who released the 1972 album Barnstorm?

8. In which English county is the local government district of Fenland?

9. What weapon was referred to in World War I as a toc emma?

10. Which American artist painted the 1928 oil The Figure 5 in Gold?

11. In which year was H.R.H. the Duke of Gloucester born - 1924 or 1944?

12. Where would you hear an epicede?

13. In which European country is the port of Hämeenlinna?

14. Of what is palaeozoology the scientific study?

15. Which author wrote the 2000 short story collection How It Ended?

ANSWERS: 1 Edward Hopper, 2 Nicholas Ray, 3 Hungary, 4 Robert Menzies, 5 On a sail, 6 Sodium, 7 Joe Walsh, 8 Cambridgeshire, 9 Trench-mortar, 10 Charles Demuth, 11 1944, 12 A funeral, 13 Finland, 14 Fossil animals, 15 Jay McInerney.

GENERAL KNOWLEDGE

1. Who played Stan the Fryer in the 1975 television drama series Trinity Tales?

2. Which painter's works include 1948's La Philosophie dans Le Boudoir?

3. As what is the animal called a chevrotain also known?

4. Which continent is the larger land mass - Africa or North America?

5. Snake is Australian military slang for which rank?

6. Who wrote the 1958 novel I Like It Here?

7. Needle and pin is rhyming slang for which beverage?

8. What are the constituent elements of the alloy steel?

9. Who succeeded Gladstone as prime minister in 1894?

10. At what temperature in degrees centigrade does potassium boil - 130 or 766?

11. Who wrote the novel The Odessa File?

12. In which English county is the town of East Grinstead?

13. Which studio album by The Cocteau Twins features the track The Itchy Glowbo Blow?

14. In which year was the storming of the Bastille?

15. In which African country is the town of Jos?

ANSWERS: 1 Bill Maynard, 2 René Magritte, 3 Mouse deer, 4 Africa, 5 Sergeant, 6 Kingsley Amis, 7 Gin, 8 Iron and carbon, 9 Earl of Rosebery, 10 766, 11 Frederick Forsyth, 12 West Sussex, 13 Blue Bell Knoll, 14 1789, 15 Nigeria.

ENTERTAINMENT

1. Which British group had a U.K. top ten hit in 1986 with Suspicious Minds?

2. Which actor provided the voice of the orphan mouse Stuart Little in the 2000 movie of the same name?

3. What was the title of Jon Secada's 1992 U.K. top five hit?

4. Which English king did Robert Shaw play in the 1966 film A Man For All Seasons?

5. Which ex-EastEnder became the presenter of BBC1's Battersea Dogs' Home in 2000?

6. Which U.S. grunge group had a 1992 U.K. top ten hit with Come As You Are?

7. Which British author wrote the book upon which the 2000 film High Fidelity was based?

8. In which year did Sandie Shaw, representing the U.K., win the Eurovision Song Contest with a rendition of Puppet on a String?

9. What was the name of Prince's character in the 1984 film Purple Rain?

10. Which Irish band had a 2000 U.K. number one hit with Breathless?

11. Which 1990 film starred Steven Seagal as a former Drug Enforcement Agency troubleshooter?

12. Which ITV comedy drama series featured Michelle Collins as ex-dancer Maxine Gaines?

13. Which former boy band member hit the U.K. number one spot in 2000 with Life is a Rollercoaster?

14. Which sports presenter hosted BBC TV's Wimbledon 2000 coverage along with Sue Barker?

15. Who directed the 2000 film sequel Mission: Impossible 2?

ANSWERS: 1 Fine Young Cannibals, 2 Michael J Fox, 3 Just Another Day, 4 Henry VIII, 5 Patsy Palmer, 6 Nirvana, 7 Nick Hornby, 8 1967, 9 The Kid, 10 The Corrs, 11 Marked For Death, 12 Up Rising, 13 Ronan Keating, 14 John Inverdale, 15 John Woo.

? **GENERAL KNOWLEDGE** ?

1. In which European country is the castle town of Detmold?

2. For what discovery was James Chadwick awarded the 1935 Nobel prize in physics?

3. Who directed the 1947 boxing picture Body and Soul?

4. Who wrote the 2001 children's book Witch Hill?

5. Which country administers the Juan Fernandez Islands?

6. Where would you find a bobeche?

7. In which year was the Battle of the Boyne - 1690 or 1715?

8. Which French artist's works include 1921's Woman with a Cat?

9. Which German formulated the third law of thermodynamics?

10. What job would you do in the U.S. if you were known as a swipe?

11. Which is the largest lake in Africa?

12. Which singer had a 1990 Top 10 single with the song Room At The Top?

13. On which part of the body might you wear your petrols, according to Australian slang?

14. Which 19th century Aberdonian painted the 1837 work Francesca da Rimini?

15. What was the middle name of the U.S. general George C. Marshall?

GENERAL KNOWLEDGE

1. What in classical Greece was a discobolous?

2. Which U.S. state is larger in area - Maryland or New Hampshire?

3. What nationality was the landscape painter Meindert Hobbema?

4. What was Victoria Wood's character name in the sitcom Dinnerladies?

5. Which Scottish portrait painter's works include that of Colonel Alastair Ranaldson Macdonell of Glengarry which was first exhibited in 1812?

6. What was the debut record album by the singer Sade?

7. What is a fife?

8. Which country did the British defeat in the Battle of Wandiwash in 1760?

9. In which unitary authority in Wales is the town of Prestatyn?

10. Which U.S. state is larger in area - Utah or Wyoming?

11. What would you do in a balneary?

12. Which Derbyshire town gives its name to a type of jam-filled pastry?

13. Which author penned the 1999 novel Hearts in Atlantis?

14. If something is flagelliform, what is it shaped like?

15. Which of these is not a prime number - 991, 994 or 997?

ANSWERS: 1 A discus thrower, 2 Maryland, 3 Dutch, 4 Bren, 5 Sir Henry Raeburn, 6 Diamond Life, 7 A musical instrument, 8 France, 9 Denbighshire, 10 Wyoming, 11 Take a bath, it's a bathing room, 12 Bakewell, 13 Stephen King, 14 A whip, 15 994.

GENERAL KNOWLEDGE

1. In which English county is the Solway Coast, an area of outstanding natural beauty?

2. What was the 1950's New Zealand equivalent of a Teddy-boy?

3. Of which country was Léon Gambetta premier from 1881-2?

4. Which British chemist evolved the 'Displacement Law'?

5. Who plays a Manhattan psychiatrist in the 2001 film Don't Say a Word?

6. Which country administers the Aeolian Islands?

7. In which play by Shakespeare does the character Dogberry appear?

8. In which mountain range would you find Pico de Aneto and Monte Perdido?

9. Who authored the 2001 novel Spin Cycle?

10. Which musical instrument is known as an axe?

11. In which ocean are the Marshall Islands?

12. Which artist's works include 1945's The Smoker by a Wall?

13. What nationality was the Nobel prize-winning scientist Robert Bárány?

14. What is a dasyure - a carnivorous mammal or an eye disease?

15. Which group recorded the 2000 album Make It Better?

ANSWERS: 1 Cumbria, 2 Bodgie, 3 France, 4 Frederich Soddy, 5 Michael Douglas, 6 Italy, 7 Much Ado About Nothing, 8 The Pyrenees, 9 Nick Duerden, 10 Guitar, 11 Pacific, 12 Jean Dubuffet, 13 Austrian, 14 Carnivorous mammal, 15 Dubstar.

ENTERTAINMENT

1. Which British band hit the U.K. number one spot in 1989 with Belfast Child?

2. Which futuristic 1992 film's cast included Emilio Estevez, Mick Jagger, Rene Russo and Anthony Hopkins?

3. Which U.S. city was the setting for Ross and Rachel's drunken marriage in the sitcom Friends?

4. What was Dusty Springfield's 1966 U.K. number one hit called?

5. Which 2000 children's film based on a series of well-known books starred Alec Baldwin and Peter Fonda?

6. With whom did Freddie Mercury duet on the 1987 and 1992 U.K. top ten hit Barcelona?

7. Which female vocalist returned to the U.K. top five in with a song entitled 2 Faced?

8. Which controversial Channel 4 series began in 2000 with ten volunteers moving in to a house filled with cameras?

9. Which comic actor played Sydney in the ITV comedy series Pay and Display?

10. Which Monty Python team member directed the 1977 film Jabberwocky?

11. Which BBC1 comedy drama series featured former Goodnight Sweetheart star Elizabeth Carling as Charlotte, a superstar pop singer?

12. What was the title of the fourth album by The Corrs, released in 2000?

13. Which film starred Mel Gibson as an 18th-century American landowner?

14. Which Sixties sitcom by Johnny Speight starred Eric Sykes and Spike Milligan?

15. Which 1974 film set in Brooklyn starred Michael Sarrazin and Barbra Streisand as husband and wife?

ANSWERS: 1 Simple Minds, 2 Freejack, 3 Las Vegas, 4 You Don't Have to Say You Love Me, 5 Thomas and the Magic Railroad, 6 Montserrat Caballe, 7 Louise, 8 Big Brother, 9 James Bolam, 10 Terry Gilliam, 11 Border Cafe, 12 In Blue, 13 The Patriot, 14 Curry and Chips, 15 For Pete's Sake.

GENERAL KNOWLEDGE

1. Which sculptor's works include the 1921 bronze Turning Torso?

2. In which Australian state is the seaport of Geraldton?

3. In which decade was the British Secretary for Ireland, Lord Cavendish, assassinated?

4. Which Israeli politician is known as 'BiBi'?

5. What chemical substance does the Haber process produce?

6. Which actress first played Mary Dixon, daughter of Dixon of Dock Green in a BBC television police series?

7. What piece of naval equipment is known as a ham-bone?

8. Who wrote the 2000 novel Fin?

9. What is an entresol?

10. In which county is the seaside resort of Mablethorpe?

11. For which form of therapy is the scientist Niels Ryberg Finsen best remembered?

12. If something is fucoid, what is it shaped like?

13. In which department of France is the town of Gap?

14. Who wrote the 2001 novel The Red Room?

15. Which country music artist recorded the 2000 album of covers Milk Cow Blues?

GENERAL KNOWLEDGE

1. In which year was the song Ghost Town a No. 1 single for The Specials?

2. Who wrote the 1964 novel The Spire?

3. In which country was chemist Lars Onsager born?

4. In which country is the Badalona cave system?

5. If you suffer from balletomania what do you have a passion for?

6. Which German city is further south - Bonn or Cologne?

7. What was the name of the U.S. president in the television comedy show Whoops! Apocalypse?

8. What is a cep?

9. In which country was the artist Anselm Kiefer born?

10. For which political party did Emmeline Pankhurst stand as an electoral candidate in 1926?

11. What is balbriggan - a gypsy or a type of fabric?

12. In which discipline did Robert S. Mulliken win a Nobel prize in 1966?

13. Which poet was born Ricardo Neftali Reyes Basoalto in 1904?

14. In which English county is the town of Thetford?

15. Who wrote the 1853 novel Hypatia?

ANSWERS: 1 1981, 2 William Golding, 3 Norway, 4 Spain, 5 Ballet, 6 Bonn, 7 Johnny Cyclops, 8 An edible mushroom, 9 Germany, 10 Conservative Party, 11 Fabric, 12 Chemistry, 13 Pablo Neruda, 14 Norfolk, 15 Charles Kingsley.

GENERAL KNOWLEDGE

1. On which river is Wimborne Minster, Dorset?

2. Who was elected the president of the Gold Coast in 1952?

3. In which novel by Thomas Hardy does the character Elfride Swancourt appear?

4. Which U.S. state includes the islands Nantucket and Martha's Vineyard?

5. Lemland and Lumparland are islands in which group?

6. Which U.S. prison is nicknamed Big Q?

7. Who wrote the 1971 novel Not To Disturb?

8. What is a cockatoo to an Australian criminal?

9. In which year did the Doors release the album Waiting for the Sun?

10. How did the author Erskine Childers die in 1922?

11. In which South American country is the Pilao waterfall?

12. What nationality was the Nobel prize-winning poet Eugenio Montale?

13. In which U.S. state was the drama series The Waltons set?

14. Which Australian educational establishment is known as 'the shop'?

15. Which river flows through the Austrian capital, Vienna?

ANSWERS: 1 Stour, 2 Kwame Nkrumah, 3 A Pair of Blue Eyes, 4 Massachusetts, 5 Åland Islands, 6 San Quentin, 7 Muriel Spark, 8 A lookout, 9 1968, 10 He was shot by a firing squad, 11 Brazil, 12 Italian, 13 Virginia, 14 University of Melbourne, 15 The Rive Danube.

GENERAL KNOWLEDGE

1. Who was director of the 1946 film Duel in the Sun starring Gregory Peck and Jennifer Jones?

2. What is the name of the nest in which a hare lives?

3. Which novel by John Cleland was subtitled Memoirs of a Woman of Pleasure?

4. In which year did Scottish architect and artist Charles Rennie Mackintosh die?

5. Who wrote the 1941 novel N or M?

6. Who directed the 1992 film satire The Player?

7. Which overture by Mendelssohn was first performed in 1832?

8. Who directed the 1963 film Irma La Douce?

9. Who was the Czech composer of the opera The Bartered Bride?

10. Which U.S. golfer won the 1998 Shell Houston Open?

11. Who was the first wife of Jacob in the Old Testament?

12. Which Brighton-born animator was known as 'Britain's answer to Walt Disney'?

13. Who was the Roman goddess of love?

14. Which tennis player was 1994 French Open men's doubles champion with Jonathan Stark?

15. Who was second son of Noah in the Old Testament?

ANSWERS 1. King Vidor 2. Form 3. Fanny Hill 4. 1928 5. Agatha Christie 6. Robert Altman 7. Fingal's Cave overture 8. Billy Wilder 9. Bedrich Smetana 10. David Duval 11. Leah 12. Anson Dyer 13. Venus 14. Byron Black 15. Japheth.

ENTERTAINMENT

1. Who directed the 1970 film The Arousers?

2. How many million dollars did Mark Wahlberg earn for the film Three Kings?

3. Which Upstairs Downstairs actress played Olivia in the soap Sunset Beach?

4. In which European capital is the 1932 film Arsène Lupin set?

5. Which James Bond actor appears in the film The Long Good Friday as an Irish terrorist?

6. Who plays the lead as a pirate in the 1962 film The Rage of the Buccaneers?

7. Which actor starred in the films The Mummy and George of the Jungle?

8. Who played the lead in the 1952 film Hans Christian Andersen?

9. Who composed the 1825 one-act opera Don Sanche?

10. What nationality is soprano Barbara Bonney?

11. Who directed the 1956 film Around the World in Eighty Days?

12. What is Walter Matthau's profession in the 1969 film Cactus Flower?

13. Who composed the opera La Bohème?

14. Who directed and starred in the 1972 film Rage?

15. Who played Clarice Starling in the film The Silence of the Lambs?

ANSWERS 1. Curtis Hanson 2. $4m 3. Lesley-Anne Down 4. Paris 5. Pierce Brosnan 6. Ricardo Montalban 7. Brendan Fraser 8. Danny Kaye 9. Liszt 10. American 11. Michael Anderson 12. Dentist 13. Puccini 14. George C. Scott 15. Jodie Foster.

SPORT

1. Which tennis player was 1992 Sports Illustrated Sportsman of the Year?

2. Who was women's figure skating champion at the 1998 Olympics?

3. How many golds did Morocco win at the 1999 World Athletics Championships?

4. Who were Eastern Division winners of the NFC Conference in American Football in 1980?

5. In which year did Gottfried Van Cramm win the French Open singles tennis title for the second time?

6. In which vehicle did Gatsonides and Worledge win the 1953 Monte Carlo Rally?

7. Which football team's home ground is at Fratton Park?

8. U.I.T. is the international governing body of which sport?

9. Which Ryder Cup saw Lee Westwood's first appearance?

10. At what weight did Sugar Ray Leonard win a 1976 Olympic boxing title?

11. Who was coach at the L'Aquila rugby club in Italy from 1989-91?

12. Which Italian cyclist won the 1983 Giro d'Italia?

13. At what sport have Jeanette Brown and Guyonne Dalle been world champions?

14. Quick as Lightning won the 1980 1000 Guineas. Who was the rider?

15. With which sport does one associate Jean Daud and Sébastien Chabal?

POP MUSIC

1. Which solo artist had a 1999 Top 10 single with Man! I Feel Like A Woman?

2. With which female singer did Zucchero duet on the 1992 hit Diamante?

3. Which duo recorded the 1991 single Zeroxed?

4. What is the title of the Divine Comedy's 1999 'Greatest Hits' album?

5. Which group's only hit single was 1965's She's Lost You?

6. Who is lead singer with Heaven 17?

7. Which studio album by Laurie Anderson features the song O Superman?

8. Dr. John's album Duke Elegant is an album of whose songs?

9. On which album cover did baby Spencer Elden feature in 1991?

10. Which group recorded the 1993 album Gentlemen?

11. Nick Kane is guitarist with which best-selling group?

12. On which label was Tim Hardin's debut L.P. recorded?

13. Matthew Bellamy is singer with which group?

14. Which group recorded the 1999 Top 10 album Invincible?

15. Who is the female singer with the group Venini?

ANSWERS 1. Shania Twain 2. Randy Crawford 3. Zero Zero 4. A Secret History 5. The Zephyrs 6. Glenn Gregory 7. Big Science 8. Duke Ellington 9. Nevermind by Nirvana 10. The Afghan Whigs 11. The Mavericks 12. Verve 13. Muse 14. Five 15. Debbie Lime.

ART & LITERATURE

1. Who wrote the children's book The Kite Rider?

2. Which member of the comedy team The League of Gentlemen authored a volume of short stories entitled Never Trust A Rabbit?

3. Who wrote the 1988 book Mother London?

4. Who writes the Baby Father series of novels?

5. Who wrote the 2001 children's book At the Crossing Places?

6. Who authored the comic novel The Best a Man Can Get?

7. At which college did the sculptor Henry Moore teach from 1932-39?

8. Who wrote the 1924 play Play at the Castle?

9. Who wrote the 1917 play Wurzel Flummery?

10. Who painted the 1855 work The Porteous Mob?

11. Whose children's books include Lady Lollipop?

12. In which year did the artist Jean Dubuffet hold his first solo art exhibition?

13. Who wrote the novel Utz?

14. Which artist created the piece The Last Thing I Said To You is Don't Leave Me?

15. Who wrote the graphic novel Jimmy Corrigan: The Smartest Kid on Earth?

ANSWERS 1. Geraldine McCaughrean 2. Jeremy Dyson 3. Michael Moorcock 4. Patrick Augustus 5. Kevin Crossley-Holland 6. John O'Farrell 7. Chelsea School of Art 8. Ferenc Molnar 9. A.A. Milne 10. James Drummond 11. Dick King-Smith 12. 1944 13. Bruce Chatwin 14. Tracey Emin 15. Chris Ware.

GENERAL KNOWLEDGE

1. Who directed the 1977 World War II film A Bridge Too Far?

2. What did Melvil Dewey most famously invent?

3. Which arm of the Atlantic Ocean was formerly known as the German Ocean?

4. What is the name of the white two-piece cotton costume worn to play judo?

5. Who was the Dutch painter of The Garden of Earthly Delights?

6. Which port in the Côte d'Ivoire is the legislative capital of the country?

7. In which year did cricket commentator John Arlott die?

8. What is an oenophile?

9. An aberdevine was the former name for which cagebird?

10. Which genus of plants includes dyer's rocket?

11. What is the name of the annual ceremony held on the Queen's Birthday on Horse Guards Parade?

12. Who directed the 1984 film Swann in Love starring Jeremy Irons?

13. For which 1953 film was Richard Burton a Best Actor Oscar nominee?

14. What character did George Raft play in the 1932 film Scarface?

15. Who was German commander-in-chief at the Battle of Jutland in 1916?

ENTERTAINMENT

1. Who plays villainess Fatima Blush in the 1983 Bond film Never Say Never Again?

2. What is the name of the family central to the U.S. sitcom ALF?

3. Who played Sheila Haddon in the 1980s sitcom All At No. 20?

4. Who starred as an American ambassador in the 1963 film The Ugly American?

5. Who is quizmaster on Channel Four's Fifteen to One?

6. What was John Thomson's character name in Steve Coogan's television film Three Fights, Two Weddings and a Funeral?

7. Who played Susie in the 1999 drama series Real Women?

8. Who directed the film The Talented Mr. Ripley?

9. Which cast member played Mr. Creosote in the film Monty Python's Meaning of Life?

10. Who won a Best Director Oscar in 2000 for the film American Beauty?

11. Who directed the film Deep Blue Sea?

12. Which soap opera is set in Albert Square?

13. In which year was comedian Billy Connolly born?

14. Who directed the 1999 film The Green Mile?

15. Which Irish comedian succeeded Ardal O'Hanlon as the host of BBCTV's The Stand-up Show?

ANSWERS 1. Barbara Carrera 2. Tanner 3. Maureen Lipman 4. Marlon Brando 5. William G. Stewart. 6. Fat Bob 7. Michelle Collins 8. Anthony Minghella 9. Terry Jones 10. Sam Mendes 11. Renny Harlin 12. EastEnders 13. 1942 14. Frank Darabont 15. Tommy Tiernan.

SPORT

1. What nationality is golfer Riikka Hakkarainen?

2. Which Spaniard won the 1982 Vuelta a España cycle race?

3. With what sport are Pippa Funnell and Karen Dixon associated?

4. My Babu won the 1948 2000 Guineas. Who was the rider?

5. Which cyclist is known as El Yaya?

6. Who won the Isle of Man senior TT in 1993?

7. How many Tests did cricketer Craig White play for England from 1994-7?

8. How many times have Sheffield United won the 1st Division in football?

9. Who was men's European water-skiing champion in 1974 & 1975?

10. Who won the 1985 Chicago men's marathon?

11. Who scored a 140 break in the 2000 Benson and Hedges Masters snooker tournament to win £19,000?

12. Which jockey won the 1997 Prix Royal Oak on Ebadiyla?

13. Which BNL hockey side signed Canadian Chad MacLeod in September 1999?

14. Which country won the 1975 rugby league World Cup?

15. In which year did Tobin Bailey make his county debut for Northants at cricket?

ANSWERS 1. Finnish 2. Marino Lejaretta 3. Equestrianism 4. Charlie Smirke 5. Laurent Jalabert 6. Phillip McCallen 7. Eight 8. Once 9. Paul Seaton 10. Steve Jones 11. Ken Doherty 12. Gérald Mosse 13. Milton Keynes Kings 14. Australia 15. 1996.

POP MUSIC

1. Which female singer recorded the 1992 album Erotica?

2. Which rock group recorded the 1971 album Islands?

3. Which US heavy metal group recorded the 1981 album Fair Warning?

4. Which group recorded the 1995 Top Five single U Sure Do?

5. Who led the rock groups Jane's Addiction and Porno For Pyros?

6. Which female singer's father sang in a group called The Abbey Folk?

7. Which group recorded the 2001 single Waiting for the Summer?

8. Which singer-songwriter recorded the 2001 album Rockin' the Suburbs?

9. Which funk band recorded the 1972 album Cabbage Alley?

10. Which group recorded the 2001 single Astounded?

11. Which singer had a 1988 No. 2 single with the song Don't Worry Be Happy?

12. Which group recorded the 1994 album Orange?

13. Which group recorded the 2000 album Stankonia?

14. Who recorded the 2000 live album Road Rock Volume One?

15. Which track by the group the Stooges did the Damned cover on their album Damned Damned Damned?

ANSWERS 1. Madonna 2. King Crimson 3. Van Halen 4. Strike 5. Perry Farrell 6. Kathryn Williams 7. Delirious? 8. Ben Folds 9. The Meters 10. Bran Van 3000 11. Bobby McFerrin 12. The Jon Spencer Blues Explosion 13. Outkast 14. Neil Young 15. I Feel Alright.

GEOGRAPHY

1. What is the German village of Blindheim better known as?

2. The former penal colony of Devil's Island belongs to which island group?

3. In which Australian state are the Grampian Mountains?

4. Monte Perdido in Spain is in which mountain range?

5. Georgian Bay is in the N.E. part of which North American Great Lake?

6. The German city of Duisburg lies at the confluence of which two rivers?

7. On which bay is the Spanish town of La Linea?

8. Shaba is a region of which African country?

9. Which river enters the North Sea at Middlesbrough?

10. Which island joined with Tanganyika to form Tanzania?

11. Between which two countries was the former Russian province of Livonia divided in 1918?

12. Paramaribo is the capital of which South American republic?

13. On which French river is the porcelain centre of Limoges?

14. Where are the administrative headquarters of Gwynedd?

15. The city of Laval is a suburb of which Canadian city?

ANSWERS 1. Blenheim 2. Safety Islands 3. Victoria 4. Pyrenees 5. Huron 6. Rhine and Ruhr 7. Bay of Gibraltar 8. Democratic Republic of Congo 9. Tees 10. Zanzibar 11. Estonia and Latvia 12. Surinam 13. Vienne 14. Caernarfon 15. Montreal

GENERAL KNOWLEDGE

1. Which club were winners of the 1997 Courage Clubs championship in rugby union?

2. Which American theatre director and producer collaborated with Orson Welles in running the Mercury Theatre company?

3. Who wrote the 1909 play Strife?

4. Which 18th Century Italian etcher's works include Imaginary Prisons?

5. Who authored the 1881 novel A Laodicean?

6. Kishinev is capital of which republic in S.E. Europe?

7. Who was 1990 Wimbledon women's singles tennis championship runner-up?

8. Who was the author of the short story collection The Day We Got Drunk on Cake?

9. Which symbol of Joan of Arc was adopted by the free French forces' leader Charles de Gaulle in 1940?

10. The Chianti mountain range in Tuscany is part of which mountain group?

11. Who wrote the 1858 novel Doctor Thorne?

12. Who was author of the book I, Claudius?

13. Which plant of the genus Lactuca is cultivated for its large edible leaves?

14. Who played the lead in the 1960s cult science fiction television series Adam Adamant Lives!?

15. What name did pop singer Alvin Stardust use when he led the group The Fentones?

ANSWERS 1. Wasps 2. John Houseman 3. John Galsworthy 4. Giovanni Battista Piranesi 5. Thomas Hardy 6. Moldova 7. Zina Garrison 8. William Trevor 9. Cross of Lorraine 10. Apennines 11. Anthony Trollope 12. Robert Graves 13. Lettuce 14. Gerald Harper 15. Shane Fenton.

ENTERTAINMENT

1. Who star as Robert and Angie Martin in the 2001 film The Martins?

2. Who produced the BBC television comedy series The Young Ones?

3. Who directed the 2001 film The Score which starred Robert DeNiro?

4. Which actress played Dolly Clothes-Peg in the children's television series Worzel Gummidge which began in 1979?

5. What is Burt Lancaster's character name in the 1957 film Sweet Smell of Success?

6. What was the 1989 sequel to the 1983 drama series The Winds of War?

7. Which musician starred in the 1972 film The Harder They Come?

8. Who played DS Tom Stone in the long-running television cop show Z Cars?

9. Who plays James Joyce in the 2000 film Nora?

10. In which year was the television nature programme Survival first broadcast?

11. Who played Blofeld in the 1971 film Diamonds Are Forever?

12. Mark Morris's 1991 ballet The Hard Nut is based on which previous dance work?

13. Who played Annie Mayle in the 1993 BBC television series A Year in Provence?

14. Who plays the impresario Harold Zidler in the 2001 film Moulin Rouge!?

15. Who directed the film Cast Away, which starred Tom Hanks?

SPORT

1. In which city was the 1988 football World Cup Group E game between Belgium and South Korea played?

2. For which country was Linetta Wilson a 1996 Olympic swimming champion?

3. At what sport was Olga Sedakova a 1998 world champion?

4. Who won the Harry Vardon Trophy in golf from 1971-4?

5. In which country was Italy's rugby union player Wilhelmus Visser born?

6. What nationality is golfer Thomas Bjorn?

7. Anna Hübler and Heinrich Burger were pairs figure skating champions at which Olympics?

8. Which golfer was 1978 Sports Illustrated Sportsman of the Year?

9. Who were Eastern Division winners of the NFC Conference in American Football in 1979?

10. Who was 1988 French Open men's singles tennis title winner?

11. In which vehicle did Chiron and Basadonna win the 1954 Monte Carlo rally?

12. What nationality is golfer Nina Karlsson?

13. In which year did shooting become part of the Olympic programme?

14. In cricket, who scored 110 for Northants vs. Hants in the 1st innings of their 1999 county championship game?

15. Aleksandr Lebziak was 1997 world amateur boxing champion. At what weight?

ANSWERS 1. Paris 2. U.S.A. 3. Synchronised swimming 4. Peter Oosterhuis 5. South Africa 6. Danish 7. 1908 8. Jack Nicklaus 9. Dallas Cowboys 10. Mats Wilander 11. Lancia-Aurelia 12. Swedish 13. 1896 14. Russell Warren 15. Light-heavyweight.

POP MUSIC

1. What is Kiss frontman Gene Simmons's real name?

2. Who recorded the 1988 album Bummed?

3. Which group recorded the album Wh'Appen?

4. Which song does Ron Sexsmith sing on the 1999 compilation album Bleeker Street?

5. Who duetted with Tom Jones on the song Baby, It's Cold Outside in 1999?

6. Which studio album by Julian Cope featured the hit single Beautiful Love?

7. Which David Bowie studio album features the single Fashion?

8. Who recorded the 1991 album Mighty Like A Rose?

9. In which year was Beck born?

10. Which song by the Rolling Stones did Tori Amos cover on the 1992 E.P. Crucify?

11. What creature features on the cover of the album The Fat of the Land by the Prodigy?

12. On which label did the group S Club 7 record single S Club Party?

13. Which female singer recorded the 1999 album On the 6?

14. Simon Fowler is lead vocalist with which group?

15. Who had a 2000 No. 1 hit with the song American Pie?

HISTORY

1. Who was made King of Spain in 1808 by Napoleon?

2. Who did John of Gaunt marry in 1396 after the death of his second wife?

3. In which year was the Beer Hall Putsch initiated by Adolf Hitler?

4. In which year did Iraq invade Kuwait, leading to the Gulf War?

5. In which month of 1982 did Argentina first invade the Falkland Islands?

6. Who was U.S. ambassador to the United Nations from 1971-2?

7. In which year did Henry VIII of England die?

8. In which year was Marie Antoinette guillotined?

9. Which womens' rights leader was born Emmeline Goulden in 1858?

10. Who served as Lord Chancellor from 1660-7?

11. The Tripolitan War of 1801-5 was between the North African state of Tripoli and which country?

12. To which islands was Archbishop Makarios of Cyprus exiled in 1956?

13. What was Benito Mussolini's father's occupation?

14. In which month of 1215 did King John sign the Magna Carta?

15. Who was governor of the U.S. state of Georgia from 1971-5?

GENERAL KNOWLEDGE

1. Who was prime minister of New Zealand from 1928-30?

2. On which gulf in Italy is the small port of Imperia?

3. Who was president of the African National Congress from 1977-91?

4. Which Bohemian composer and violinist was Dvorak's son-in-law?

5. Who was 1996 British Open golf champion?

6. Which town in the Ukraine was the site of a nuclear power accident in 1986?

7. Who was Best Actor Oscar winner for the film The Color of Money?

8. Who were the male and female stars of the 1935 film Top Hat?

9. In which year did French impressionist painter and sculptor Edgar Degas die?

10. Who was 1952 Olympic men's 5,000m champion?

11. Who is sister of Meg, Jo and Beth March in the novel Little Women?

12. In which year did British art historian and Soviet spy Anthony Blunt die?

13. What is the third brightest star in the constellation Orion?

14. Which Scottish jockey was 1983 flat racing champion?

15. Which golfer was winner of the 1998 Philips PFA Golf Classic on the PGA European Seniors Tour?

ANSWERS 1. Joseph Ward 2. Gulf of Genoa 3. Oliver Tambo 4. Josef Suk 5. Tom Lehman 6. Chernobyl 7. Paul Newman 8. Fred Astaire and Ginger Rogers 9. 1917 10. Emil Zatopek 11. Amy 12. 1983 13. Bellatrix 14. Willie Carson 15. Neil Coles.

ENTERTAINMENT

1. Who was originally chosen to play Archie Bunker in the U.S. sitcom All in the Family?
2. Who directed the 1975 film French Connection 2?
3. Who played the wife of Robert Donat in the 1939 film Goodbye Mr. Chips?
4. Who directed the 1992 film Lorenzo's Oil?
5. The New Centurions is a 1972 film about which U.S. city's police force?
6. Which actor played Tom Wedloe in the children's TV show Gentle Ben?
7. In which year did conductor Andrew Davis make his debut at Glyndebourne?
8. In which city was the ITV drama At Home with the Braithwaites set?
9. Who plays Dot Cotton in EastEnders?
10. Who directed the 1993 film The Dark Half, which was based on a Stephen King book?
11. In which comedy show did German exchange teacher Herr Lipp appear?
12. Who directed the 1988 film Walker?
13. Which actress played a wheelchair-bound crime writer in the 1994 sitcom All Night Long?
14. Who played Steerpike in the 2000 BBCTV adaptation of Gormenghast?
15. Who played Trudy in the 2000 BBCTV drama Clocking Off?

SPORT

1. Which Briton was part of the team that won the 1998 Le Mans 24-Hour Race?

2. In which city were the 1983 Pan-American Games held?

3. What was the name of the winning boat in the 1886 America's Cup?

4. Which golfer was 1964 Sports Illustrated Sportsman of the Year?

5. Samuth Sithnaruepol was 1988 IBF boxing champion. At what weight?

6. What nationality is golfer Olivier Edmond?

7. What nationality is champion amateur cyclist Bruno Risi?

8. In which year did British tennis player Lottie Dod die?

9. Which club won the men's English National Inter-League in hockey in 1990?

10. Who did Bristol play in the quarter-finals of the Tetley's Bitter Cup in rugby union in 1990?

11. Who was 1954 and 1956 World Sidecar champion in motorcycling?

12. In which European city were the 1981 World Student Games held?

13. Which Second Division team appeared in the 1920 F.A. Cup Final?

14. In which capital city were the 1958 Asian Games held?

15. How long did Lorraine Miller take to run 10 miles on 9th January 1993?

ANSWERS 1. Allan McNish 2. Caracas 3. Mayflower 4. Ken Venturi 5. Strawweight 6. French 7. Swiss 8. 1960 9. Havant 10. Harlequins 11. Wilhelm Noll 12. Bucharest 13. Huddersfield Town 14. Tokyo 15. 54:21.8.

POP MUSIC

1. Who had a 2000 Top 10 single with Show Me the Meaning of Being Lonely?

2. Which studio album by Be-Bop Deluxe contains the song Maid in Heaven?

3. Which two women's names provided Marty Wilde with hit singles?

4. What was Dr. Feelgood drummer John Martin better known as?

5. Which unusual pairing had a 1987 hit with Rockin' Around the Christmas Tree?

6. Which group covered David Bowie's song Ziggy Stardust in 1982?

7. Which studio album by Lambchop features the track Your Life As A Sequel?

8. Which German group released the album Underwater Sunlight?

9. Which solo singer had a 1999 Top 10 single with Wild Wild West?

10. Who produced Meat Loaf's album Bat Out of Hell?

11. Which group recorded the 1991 single My Head's in Mississippi?

12. Two-thirds of which trio used to be in a band called The Jennifers?

13. In which city did Michael Hutchence die?

14. Who recorded the 1969 album Folkjokeopus?

15. In which city was singer Kevin Coyne born?

WORDS

1. The adjective gnathic refers to which part of the body?

2. What does a thurifer carry?

3. What in Scotland is a hoast?

4. What shape is the type of tomb known as a tholos?

5. What word in ballet is used to describe the tip of the toe?

6. What type of bird is a koel?

7. If something is caprine, what creature does it resemble?

8. In New Zealand, what type of food is a cheerio?

9. What is a tenterhook used to hold?

10. What is another name for a fever blister?

11. What is the holding of two nonconsecutive high cards in a suit at bridge called?

12. What type of creature is a goa?

13. What in Canada is muskeg?

14. What would you have done with a johannes in Portugal in the 18th century?

15. A howlet is a poetic name for which bird?

ANSWERS 1. The jaw 2. The censer at a religious ceremony 3. A cough 4. Beehive-shaped 5. Pointe 6. A cuckoo 7. A goat 8. It's a small sausage 9. Cloth 10. Cold sore 11. Tenace 12. A gazelle or antelope 13. Undrained boggy land 14. Spent it 15. An owl.

GENERAL KNOWLEDGE

1. In which month of the year 2000 did Al Gore concede the U.S. presidential election to George W. Bush?

2. Where did John Lennon and Yoko Ono marry in 1969?

3. In which year was the drink Sunny Delight launched in Britain?

4. In which country was Cardiff City F.C. chairman Sam Hammam born?

5. In which year did the car manufacturer Maserati celebrate its 75th anniversary?

6. In which year was Lord Lucan declared dead by the English courts?

7. Which actor did Sheila Ryan marry in 1976?

8. In computing, what is a 'cobweb site'?

9. In which year was the author Hubert Selby Jr. born?

10. Which company was the first to make Worcester sauce-flavoured crisps?

11. In which African country is the town of Binga?

12. In which 1998 children's television show did the characters Stepney and Alderney appear?

13. What instrument does the jazz musician Sonny Rollins play?

14. In which year did the Battle of Jersey take place?

15. In which European city are the Pushkin Museum of Fine Arts and the Kremlin?

ANSWERS 1. December 2. Gibraltar 3. 1998 4. Lebanon 5. 2001 6. 1999 7. James Caan 8. A web site that has not been updated for a long time 9. 1928 10. Seabrook 11. Zimbabwe 12. The Wombles 13. Saxophone 14. 1781 15. Moscow.

ENTERTAINMENT

1. Who played Quaker Jess Birdwell in the 1956 film Friendly Persuasion?

2. In which soap did Joe Absolom play a character called Matthew?

3. Who directed the 1997 film I Know What You Did Last Summer?

4. What was the title of Bill Forsyth's 1999 follow-up to the film Gregory's Girl?

5. The 1956 film Reach for the Sky is based on whose life story?

6. Which comedian played Gudrun in the 1999 comedy show Dark Ages?

7. Which French actor played the lead in the 1982 film Danton?

8. Which Hollywood star played Flynn in the 1997 film Welcome to Sarajevo?

9. Who directed the 1999 film Man on the Moon?

10. The 1987 film Dark Eyes starring Marcello Mastroianni is based on stories by which author?

11. Who play the Three Musketeers in the 1997 film The Man in the Iron Mask?

12. Which comedian sang the title song of the 1960 film Raymie?

13. Who voiced Stinky Pete in the film Toy Story 2?

14. In which city was comedian Brian Conley born?

15. Who plays movie producer Bowfinger in a 1999 film?

SPORT

1. Which country were world team champions at speedway in 1995?

2. What is the profession of Mary Reveley?

3. Who scored two double centuries for Kent against Essex in their cricket match in July 1938?

4. What nationality is golfer Jose Coceres?

5. Which man won the 1984 and 1985 Biathlon World Cup?

6. In football, who did Holland beat in the 1998 World Cup 2nd Round?

7. For which rugby league club have both Richie Blackmore and David Barnhill played?

8. In which year was the World Cup in diving first held?

9. How many times did Bobby Jones win the U.S. Amateur Championship in golf?

10. For which nation has Narbonne rugby union player Stuart Reid played?

11. In cricket, who scored 108 for Middlesex vs. Leicestershire in the 2nd innings of their 1999 county championship game?

12. In which sport is the Conn Smythe Trophy awarded?

13. In which city were the 1983 World Student games held?

14. Who scored a total of five field goals for the San Francisco 49ers in their two Super Bowl games in 1982 and 1985?

15. Which pair were 1997 U.S. Open men's doubles tennis champions?

ANSWERS 1. Denmark 2. Racehorse trainer 3. Arthur Fagg 4. Argentinian 5. Frank-Peter Rötsch 6. Yugoslavia 7. Leeds Rhinos 8. 1979 9. Five 10. Scotland 11. Owais Shah 12. Ice hockey 13. Edmonton 14. Ray Wersching 15. Daniel Vacek and Yevgeny Kafelnikov.

POP MUSIC

1. In which year did Bruce Springsteen first play in the U.K.?

2. Which female singer recorded the 2001 album Read My Lips?

3. Under what name do the twins Dawn and Baz Larder record?

4. Who recorded the 1994 Top 20 single Loser?

5. Which group recorded the 1979 single Death Disco?

6. Which boy band recorded the 2001 single Pop?

7. Which rock group recorded the 2001 single Elevation?

8. Who recorded the 2001 album Beat 'Em Up?

9. Who recorded the album Jesus of Cool?

10. Which group recorded the 1979 single Good Times?

11. Which duo recorded the 2000 album You Win Again?

12. Which U.S. group recorded the 2000 album Alan Freed's Radio?

13. Which former member of the group Hawkwind was once in the Blackpool band The Rockin' Vicars?

14. Which group recorded the 1979 album Voulez-vous?

15. Which singer recorded the 2000 album Holy Wood (In the Shadow of the Valley of Death)?

ANSWERS 1. 1975 2. Sophie Ellis Bextor 3. The Radon Daughters 4. Beck 5. PiL 6. *N Sync 7. U2 8. Iggy Pop 9. Nick Lowe 10. Chic 11. Van Morrison & Linda Gail Lewis 12. Lou Ford 13. Lemmy 14. Abba 15. Marilyn Manson.

SCIENCE

1. Which naturalist's written works include 1869's Malay Archipelago?

2. In which century did British biologist Thomas Henry Huxley live?

3. V is the symbol for which unit of electromotive force?

4. Which British scientist is considered the founder of the science of eugenics?

5. In which century did German physicist Otto von Guericke live?

6. In which year was Dolly the cloned sheep created?

7. Which was the first element to be created artificially?

8. What nationality was botanist Hugo Marie De Vries?

9. In which capital city is the Institut Pasteur based?

10. Which condition does the acronym AIDS stand for?

11. In which European capital was physicist Edward Teller born?

12. Which English scientist discovered benzene in 1825?

13. What, in computing, does ISDN stand for?

14. In which year was J. Robert Oppenheimer awarded the Enrico Fermi Award by the Atomic Energy Commission?

15. What, in computing, does PCMCIA stand for?

ANSWERS 1. Alfred Russel Wallace 2. 19th century 3. Volt 4. Sr Francis Galton 5. 17th century 6. 1997 7. Technetium 8. Dutch 9. Paris 10. Acquired Immune Deficiency Syndrome 11. Budapest 12. Michael Faraday 13. Integrated Services Digital Network 14. 1963 15. Personal Computer Memory Card International Association.

GENERAL KNOWLEDGE

1. Which playwright's works for television include 1991's GBH?

2. Which unit of distance used in astronomy is equal to 0.3066 of a parsec?

3. Which pop group's Top 10 singles included 1971's My Brother Jake?

4. Who is the narrator of the novel Brideshead Revisited?

5. Which 1979 record album by Michael Jackson spent over 170 weeks in the U.K. album chart?

6. The St. John River, which forms part of the international boundary between the U.S. and Canada, rises in which state?

7. Who wrote the 1880 novel The Tragic Comedians?

8. Who was prime minister of Israel from 1977-83?

9. Which British field marshal was commander-in-chief of the British forces in France and Flanders from 1915-18?

10. Which Canada-born revue singer's films included 1967's Thoroughly Modern Millie?

11. Who was the wife of Cronus and mother of Zeus in Greek mythology?

12. What was the nickname of Richard I of England?

13. Who wrote the 1863 novel Hard Cash?

14. Which is the inner and longer of the two bones of the human forearm?

15. Which Argentinian was 1998 W.B.A. flyweight boxing champion?

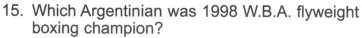

ANSWERS 1. Alan Bleasdale 2. A light year 3. Free 4. Charles Ryder 5. Off the Wall 6. Maine 7. George Meredith 8. Menachim Begin 9. Douglas Haig 10. Beatrice Lillie 11. Rhea 12. The Lion-Heart (or Couer de Lion) 13. Charles Reade 14. Ulna 15. Hugo Soto.

ENTERTAINMENT

1. Who plays disc jockey Eyeball Paul in the 2000 film Kevin & Perry Go Large?

2. Who directed the 1969 film Once Upon A Time In The West?

3. Who directed the 1989 film Say Anything?

4. Who plays Honey Whitlock in the John Waters film Cecil B. Demented?

5. Which newscaster hosted the quiz show The People Versus in 2000?

6. Who plays book dealer Dean Corso in the film The Ninth Gate?

7. Who played Richard Lipton in the television comedy series Hot Metal?

8. Who directed the 1999 film Ghost Dog: The Way of the Samurai?

9. Who directed the 2000 film Scream 3?

10. Who plays the title role in the 2000 film The Grinch?

11. Who directed the 2000 film Small Time Crooks?

12. Who directed the 1983 film The Fourth Man which starred Jeroen Krabbé?

13. Who voices the character Sulley in the 2001 film Monsters, Inc.?

14. Who played Faye Boswell in the 1970s television drama series Within These Walls?

15. In which county was the television police drama Wycliffe set?

SPORT

1. In cricket, who scored 125 for Kent against Somerset in the 2nd innings of their 1999 county championship game?

2. In which year was the French Derby first run?

3. What nationality is boxer Marco Antonio Barrera?

4. In which year were the first world rowing championships held?

5. Which country won the men's water polo title at the 1995 FINA World Cup?

6. In which year did the world championships in snowboarding start?

7. For which side did cricketer Ian Blackwell make his county debut in 1997?

8. In cricket, how many runs did Papua New Guinea score against Gibraltar in their 60 overs match on 18th June 1986?

9. Which rider led Britain to team bronze at the 1998 World Equestrian Games?

10. Michael Jordan was NBA leading scorer in 1993. What was his average per game?

11. Who holds the record of 14 goals scored in World Cup finals tournaments?

12. What nationality is golfer Wayne Riley?

13. Who was 1998 women's 200m freestyle swimming world champion?

14. Which U.S. golfer was leading money winner on the European Tour in 1967?

15. For which international side does winger Liam Botham play?

ANSWERS 1. Robert Key 2. 1836 3. Mexican 4. 1962 5. Hungary 6. 1993 7. Derbyshire 8. 455 runs 9. Polly Phillips 10. 32.6 points 11. Gerd Müller 12. Australian 13. Claudia Poll 14. Gay Brewer 15. England.

POP MUSIC

1. What was the second album by The Beastie Boys?

2. With which group had Abiodun Oyewole been performing prior to his brush with the police in 1970?

3. Which Swedish group had a hit in 1998 with Four Big Speakers?

4. On which label is the album Unplugged by the Corrs?

5. Which girl group had a hit single in 1986 with Love is the Slug?

6. What relationship was Mike Love to Brian, Carl, and Dennis Wilson of the Beach Boys?

7. Which Irish group had a 1996 hit single with Twinkle?

8. Who recorded the 1971 album Sun, Moon and Herbs?

9. Which solo singer had a 1999 Top 10 single with My Love is Your Love?

10. Which female singer had her first solo hit in 1990 with Livin' in the Light?

11. What is unusual about the record player on the back cover of Jethro Tull's album Songs From the Wood?

12. Which mod-revival group recorded the 1981 album Ambience?

13. Which group had a 1975 hit single with Skiing in the Snow?

14. Which U2 studio album includes the song With or Without You?

15. What was Barry White's first Top 30 hit single?

ANSWERS 1. Paul's Boutique 2. The Last Poets 3. Whale 4. Atlantic 5. We've Got A Fuzzbox and We're Gonna Use It 6. Cousin 7. Whipping Boy 8. Dr. John 9. Whitney Houston 10. Caron Wheeler 11. It's made from a tree stump 12. The Lambrettas 13. Wigan's Ovation 14. The Joshua Tree 15. I'm Gonna Love You Just A Little Bit More Baby.

PEOPLE

1. In which year did the theatre critic Kenneth Tynan die?

2. What was the middle name of the U.S. president Warren G. Harding ?

3. In which year was the actor Cuba Gooding Jr. born?

4. In which year did the Russian leader Lenin die?

5. Which actress is part of the clothes design team FrostFrench?

6. Which screen legend was the first centrefold of Playboy magazine in 1953?

7. Which Labour M.P. defected to the Liberal Democrats in December 2001?

8. What nationality is the fashion designer Jean-Charles de Castelbajac?

9. Who penned the book The True Adventures of the Rolling Stones?

10. Who was runner-up in the 2001 BBC Sports Personality of the Year competition?

11. Who in 2001 was awarded a total of six stars for his two restaurants in the Michelin Red Guide?

12. In which year did the violinist Jascha Heifetz die?

13. Who was elected Conservative M.P. for Folkestone and Hythe in 2001?

14. In which year was the sculptor August Rodin born?

15. How old was the biblical character Abraham when he died?

ANSWERS 1. 1980 2. Gamaliel 3. 1968 4. 1924 5. Sadie Frost 6. Marilyn Monroe 7. Paul Marsden 8. French 9. Stanley Booth 10. Ellen MacArthur 11. Marc Veyrat 12. 1987 13. Michael Howard 14. 1840 15. 175.

SPORT

1. Which team won the 2002 Worthington Cup?

2. How many tries did England score in their 80-23 win over Italy in February 2001?

3. Which country won seven gold medals in boxing at the 1992 Olympics?

4. Who was the European footballer of the year in 1968?

5. Which golfer won the U.S. Open in 1994 and 1997?

6. Which boxer took 243 seconds to dispose of British champion Julius Francis in a much-hyped fight in January 2000?

7. Who won the gold medal in the 100m breaststroke event at the 1988 Olympics?

8. Which British stadium hosted the final of the 1976 European Cup?

9. Which word is used to describe any seaside golf course?

10. What nationality is footballer Paolo Di Canio?

11. Who captained the Continental European team to victory in the inaugural golf competition for the trophy that bears his name?

12. Which Japanese city hosted the 1998 Winter Olympics?

13. Who was the first man to win both the 200m and 400m gold medals at the same Olympic Games?

14. Butch Harmon and David Leadbetter are top coaches in which sport?

15. In which city does the Great North Run half-marathon begin?

GENERAL KNOWLEDGE

1. What type of car was Miriam in the TV series Lovejoy?

2. Which German composer wrote A German Requiem?

3. In Greek mythology, which race of creatures were part horse and part man?

4. Which country ended the Australian cricket team's run of 16 successive wins in 2001?

5. What sort of blood cells are also called leucocytes?

6. Which chemical element was discovered by Hennig Brand in the 17th century?

7. What type of building provides refuge from a flood in the film When Tomorrow Comes?

8. Which U.S. folk singer wrote Where Have All the Flowers Gone and Kisses Sweeter Than Wine?

9. In art, what name is given to a depiction of the Virgin Mary supporting the body of the dead Christ?

10. Which motor race takes its name from the Italian for 'thousand miles'?

11. Which British novelist wrote Room at the Top?

12. Who narrated the film The Swiss Family Robinson?

13. Which member of the Beyond the Fringe team trained as a medical doctor?

14. From which lake was Donald Campbell's Bluebird raised in 2001?

15. Which metal is added to copper to make brass?

ANSWERS: 1 A Morris Minor, 2 Johannes Brahms, 3 Centaurs, 4 India, 5 White blood cells, 6 Phosphorus, 7 A church, 8 Pete Seeger, 9 Pieta, 10 Mille Miglia, 11 John Braine, 12 Orson Welles, 13 Jonathan Miller, 14 Coniston Water, 15 Zinc.

GENERAL KNOWLEDGE

1. In which historical period was the televison series By the Sword Divided set?

2. Which English novelist wrote Cold Comfort Farm?

3. Who did Greg Rusedski defeat in the final of the 2001 Sybase Open?

4. Which English mountaineer was the first man to climb the Matterhorn?

5. What is the capital of Canada's Yukon Territory?

6. Which German city was formerly called Karl-Marx-Stadt?

7. In the film Back to the Future III Marty goes on a mission to which year?

8. Which American novelist wrote The Age of Innocence?

9. What is the name of Viola's twin brother in Shakespeare's Twelfth Night?

10. Which former manager of Wolverhampton Wanderers died in 2001 at the age of 85?

11. Which cartoonist created the schoolgirls of St Trinian's?

12. What is kept in television's Veronica's Closet?

13. Which pop star visited Britain in 2001 to address the Oxford Union on the subject of child welfare?

14. Which Welsh actor married Elizabeth Taylor twice?

15. Which king did caricaturist James Gillray portray as Farmer George?

ANSWERS: 1 The English Civil War, 2 Stella Gibbons, 3 Andre Agassi, 4 Edward Whymper, 5 Whitehorse, 6 Chemnitz, 7 1885, 8 Edith Wharton, 9 Sebastian, 10 Stan Cullis, 11 Ronald Searle, 12 Lingerie, 13 Michael Jackson, 14 Richard Burton, 15 George III.

GENERAL KNOWLEDGE

1. Who wrote The Moon and Sixpence?

2. Which American engineer invented the cotton gin?

3. In the Old Testament, which military commander under King David killed Absalom?

4. Which 2001 film starred Juliette Binoche, Leslie Caron, Johnny Depp and Dame Judi Dench?

5. What name is usually given to a holy war waged on behalf of Islam as a religious duty?

6. Which animal was called camelopardalis or spotted camel by the Romans?

7. Which Jane Austen novel begins "It is a truth universally acknowledged that a single man in possession of a good fortune must be in want of a wife"?

8. Which Russian dramatist wrote The Seagull?

9. On which river does Cheltenham stand?

10. Which American Beat poet wrote Howl?

11. Which American comedienne married Desi Arnaz in 1940?

12. What name is given to the promontory of basalt columns on the coast of Antrim in Northern Ireland?

13. What was the family business in the television series The Brothers?

14. Who won the first Grand Prix of the 2001 Formula One season in Melbourne?

15. Which acute respiratory disease is also called pertussis?

ANSWERS: 1 W Somerset Maugham, 2 Eli Whitney, 3 Joab, 4 Chocolat, 5 Jihad, 6 Giraffe, 7 Pride and Prejudice, 8 Anton Chekhov, 9 River Chelt, 10 Allen Ginsberg, 11 Lucille Ball, 12 Giant's Causeway, 13 Haulage, 14 Michael Schumacher, 15 Whooping cough.

ENTERTAINMENT

1. What did C.A.T.S. stand for in the title of the Eighties series C.A.T.S. Eyes?

2. What was the title of Westlife's second album?

3. Which Monty Python member wrote and starred in the 1983 film The Missionary?

4. Which chef presented his Seafood Lovers Guide on BBC2?

5. Who duetted with Deniece Williams on the 1978 UK top five hit Too Much Too Little Too Late?

6. Which actor starred as Englishman turned native American Grey Owl in the film of that name?

7. Which actor narrated the ITV series Britain at War in Colour?

8. Which U.S. group had a 1973 U.K. top ten hit with Love Train?

9. In which U.S. city was the 1970 film The Only Game in Town set?

10. Which former Casualty actor starred as DCI Mortimer Marzec in the Channel 5 drama series Headless?

11. Which 2000 film starred Guy Pearce as amnesiac salesman Leonard Shelby?

12. What type of creature was Ermintrude in the children's TV show The Magic Roundabout?

13. Which model turned actress replaced Kathleen Turner in the role of Mrs Robinson in a West End production of The Graduate in 2000?

14. Which actress starred as teenager Anita in the 1992 film Guncrazy?

15. Which former Casualty star appeared as Rob Maguire in the ITV drama series The Knock?

ANSWERS: 1 Covert Activities Thames Section, 2 Coast to Coast, 3 Michael Palin, 4 Rick Stein, 5 Johnny Mathis, 6 Pierce Brosnan, 7 John Thaw, 8 The O'Jays, 9 Las Vegas, 10 Patrick Robinson, 11 Memento, 12 A cow, 13 Jerry Hall, 14 Drew Barrymore, 15 Jonathan Kerrigan.

GENERAL KNOWLEDGE

1. What was the occupation of the character played by Jack Lemmon in the film How to Murder Your Wife?

2. In Shakespeare's The Tempest, what is the name of the 'airy spirit' that does Prospero's bidding?

3. Who won the Whitbread Book of the Year Award for his novel English Passengers?

4. Which Florentine statesman and author wrote The Prince?

5. What is the state capital of Pennsylvania?

6. Which 17th-century radical sect was led by Gerrard Winstanley?

7. What were The Oddball Couple on television?

8. In which country is Winnipeg?

9. What is the highest mountain in Ireland?

10. Who wrote The Treasure of the Sierra Madre?

11. Which U.S. actor starred in Double Indemnity and The Apartment?

12. Who began presenting Omnibus on television in 1982?

13. What is the name of Bertie Wooster's manservant in P. G. Wodehouse's stories?

14. In Shakespeare's play, who kills Macbeth?

15. Which American tennis player won the women's singles at the 2001 Australian Open?

? GENERAL KNOWLEDGE ?

1. To which prime minister was novelist Lady Caroline Lamb married?

2. Which play by Shakespeare features the characters Leontes and Perdita?

3. Who choreographed the ballet Romeo and Juliet, danced by Margot Fonteyn and Rudolf Nureyev in 1965?

4. Which former MI6 agent is the author of The Big Breach?

5. In which country is the city of Faisalabad?

6. Who was the 14th president of the United States?

7. In which U.S. state was the 1986 film Hoosiers set?

8. Which Japanese city hosted the 1998 Winter Olympics?

9. Clara Furse became the first female chief executive of which institution?

10. Which novelist wrote Whisky Galore?

11. Which famous nanny was created by P. L. Travers?

12. What name is given to the winter dormancy of certain mammals?

13. What is the occupation of Lovejoy in stories by Jonathan Gash?

14. What is the only whale that has been observed to prey on other whales?

15. Which method of relaxation is represented by the letters TM?

ANSWERS: 1 Viscount Melbourne, 2 The Winter's Tale, 3 Sir Kenneth Macmillan, 4 Richard Tomlinson, 5 Pakistan, 6 Franklin Pierce, 7 Indiana, 8 Nagano, 9 The London Stock Exchange, 10 Compton Mackenzie, 11 Mary Poppins, 12 Hibernation, 13 Antiques dealer, 14 Killer whale, 15 Transcendental Meditation.

GENERAL KNOWLEDGE

1. Which gentleman murderer features in five novels by Patricia Highsmith?

2. What was the first name of the Scottish pirate Captain Kidd?

3. Which novel by Charles Dickens features the character Dolly Varden?

4. What is the capital of Namibia?

5. Which French-born conductor was music director of the Cleveland Orchestra from 1972 to 1982?

6. What nationality was the painter Daniel Maclise?

7. In 1933 what was the average time taken to make a film?

8. Who wrote Five Children and It?

9. In which European country is the city of Winterthur?

10. By what name was American rock-and-roll disc jockey Robert Weston Smith known?

11. Which famous building is at 1600 Pennsylvania Avenue, Washington D.C.?

12. Which movie star had wives called Movita and Tarita?

13. Who resigned from the Cabinet for the second time in two years in January 2001?

14. What name is given to members of the Order of the Reformed Cistercians of the Strict Observance?

15. Which Wild West frontiersman was shot dead while playing poker in Deadwood in 1876?

ANSWERS: 1 Tom Ripley, 2 William, 3 Barnaby Rudge, 4 Windhoek, 5 Lorin Maazel, 6 Irish, 7 22 days, 8 Edith Nesbit, 9 Switzerland, 10 Wolfman Jack, 11 The White House, 12 Marlon Brando, 13 Peter Mandelson, 14 Trappists, 15 Wild Bill Hickok.

ENTERTAINMENT

1. Which Irish band released their tenth studio album, All That You Can't Leave Behind, in 2000?

2. Which Joe Orton play was adapted into a 1970 film starring Richard Attenborough and Lee Remick?

3. Which BBC1 sitcom starred Caroline Aherne as Denise?

4. Which member of the Spin City cast provided the voice for Tom in 1992's Tom and Jerry: The Movie?

5. Which British film featured James Bolam as an ageing gangster?

6. Which brash TV interviewer hosted a self-titled BBC 2 dinner party chat show?

7. What was the title of the 1973 U.K. top ten hit by the British group Stealer's Wheel?

8. Which English actor played the mastermind of a London bank heist in the 1981 film Loophole?

9. Which Friends actor starred in the film Lost In Space?

10. Which British group had a U.K. number one hit in 1966 with With a Girl Like You?

11. Which nineties drama series featured a couple played by Adam Faith and Zoe Wanamaker?

12. Which former EastEnder scored a U.K. top five hit with I'm Over You?

13. Which actor played the title role in the 1991 film The Doctor?

14. Which BBC1 sitcom starred Richard Wilson as grumpy Victor Meldrew?

15. What was the title of Steps' 2000 album release?

ANSWERS: 1 U2, 2 Loot, 3 The Royle Family, 4 Richard Kind, 5 It Was an Accident, 6 Ruby Wax (Ruby), 7 Stuck in the Middle With You, 8 Albert Finney, 9 Matt LeBlanc, 10 The Troggs, 11 Love Hurts, 12 Martine McCutcheon, 13 William Hurt, 14 One Foot in the Grave, 15 Buzz.

GENERAL KNOWLEDGE

1. Which 17th-century author wrote the novel Oroonoko?

2. In which decisive naval battle did Octavian defeat Mark Antony in 31 BC?

3. Which Oscar-winning actor played a murder suspect in the film Under Suspicion?

4. Who wrote the novel White Teeth?

5. Of which U.S. state is Madison the capital?

6. By what name is Vittorio de Sica's film Ladri di Biciclette known in Britain?

7. What is Paul McCartney's real first name?

8. Which German physicist formulated the quantum theory?

9. In which film did Clint Eastwood co-star with his son Kyle?

10. Which British tenor sang in the first performances of all Benjamin Britten's operas?

11. What number is between five and one on a dartboard?

12. In Greek legend, by what part of his body was Achilles held when he was dipped in the River Styx?

13. Who was the top money-making film star in 1970?

14. What do the initials GCSE stand for?

15. Which musical term literally means 'beautiful singing' in Italian?

ANSWERS: 1 Aphra Behn, 2 Battle of Actium, 3 Gene Hackman, 4 Zadie Smith, 5 Wisconsin, 6 Bicycle Thieves, 7 James, 8 Max Planck, 9 Honkytonk Man, 10 Sir Peter Pears, 11 Twenty, 12 Heel, 13 Paul Newman, 14 General Certificate of Secondary Education, 15 Bel canto.

GENERAL KNOWLEDGE

1. Which Belgian artist painted Golconda, in which bowler-hatted men fall like rain?

2. Who wrote the music for the hymn Onward Christian Soldiers?

3. Before Steven Soderbergh in 2001 who was the last director to get two Best Director Oscar nominations in the same year?

4. What is the capital of Belize?

5. Which bird of the crow family has the Latin name Pica pica?

6. To which family of plants does cyclamen belong?

7. In which country are the headquarters of the multinational company Nestlé?

8. Who wrote No Orchids for Miss Blandish?

9. By what first name is Alexandra Pettifer, nee Legge-Bourke, commonly known?

10. In which Shakespeare play do Elbow and Mistress Overdone appear?

11. Do male or female sea horses carry the eggs until they hatch?

12. Who wrote Doctor in the House?

13. Which Italian jockey became an honorary MBE in the 2001 New Year Honours List?

14. What name is given to an Hindu prince ranking above a rajah?

15. Which French-born poet wrote Cautionary Tales?

ANSWERS: 1 Rene Magritte, 2 Sir Arthur Sullivan, 3 Michael Curtiz, 4 Belmopan, 5 Magpie, 6 Primrose, 7 Switzerland, 8 James Hadley Chase, 9 Tiggy, 10 Measure for Measure, 11 Male, 12 Richard Gordon, 13 Frankie Dettori, 14 Maharajah, 15 Hilaire Belloc.

GENERAL KNOWLEDGE

1. What is the surname of Emma in the novel by Jane Austen?

2. In which Shakespeare play does Lancelot Gobbo appear?

3. By what name do we know the Bahia de los Cochinos on the Cuban coast?

4. Which horse became the first National Hunt horse to win £1 million in prize-money?

5. What was the real first name of jazz musician Bix Beiderbecke?

6. Which English poet wrote The Listeners?

7. Janeway and Chakotay are characters in which television sci-fi series?

8. With which sport is Lou Gehrig associated?

9. What name is given to the process of removing waste products from the blood?

10. Of which country is Geelong a major port?

11. Which American actress founded United Artists with Charlie Chaplin, Douglas Fairbanks and D. W. Griffith?

12. What is the capital of the Lebanon?

13. Where was the actor Joaquin Phoenix born?

14. What name was given to the settlers who established the first permanent colony in New England in 1620?

15. Which London theatre was formerly called the Royal Victoria Hall?

SPORT

1. Which classic horserace was won by Love Divine in June 2000?

2. How many dogs take part in a greyhound race in Britain?

3. Which team lost 5-1 to Rangers in the final of the Scottish Cup in 1996?

4. The marathon is how many miles and 385 yards long?

5. At which Olympics did Briton Matthew Pinsent win his first gold medal?

6. Which Australian athlete won the women's 400m in front of her home crowd at the Sydney Olympics?

7. Who did Pakistan beat in the final of the cricket World Cup in 1992?

8. Which horse won the Derby in 1971?

9. Naim Suleymanoglu from Turkey is a top name in which sport?

10. Which team beat Celtic 2-1 in the final of the 1970 European Cup?

11. Which county beat Glamorgan to win cricket's 2000 Benson and Hedges Cup final?

12. Which number lies between seven and eight on a dartboard?

13. Who beat Don Curry to become undisputed world welterweight boxing champion in 1986?

14. Which former middle-distance runner became a Tory MP in 1992?

15. What type of game is battledore?

ANSWERS: 1 The Oaks, 2 Six, 3 Hearts, 4 26, 5 Barcelona, 6 Cathy Freeman, 7 England, 8 Mill Reef, 9 Weightlifting, 10 Feyenoord, 11 Gloucestershire, 12 16, 13 Lloyd Honeyghan, 14 Sebastian Coe, 15 An ancient racket game.

GENERAL KNOWLEDGE

1. The film Dr Ehrlich's Magic Bullet is about the search for a cure for which disease?

2. Which American director made the films Carrie, Scarface and The Untouchables?

3. Who was the president of the Democratic Republic of Congo who was killed by a bodyguard in January 2001?

4. Which Irish author wrote Borstal Boy?

5. Against which disease can the BCG vaccine offer protection?

6. Who was U.S. secretary of state from 1949 to 1953?

7. How many Police Academy films have been made?

8. Which South African president shared the 1993 Nobel Peace prize with Nelson Mandela?

9. Who was the world No 1, knocked out of the 2001 Australian Open by Greg Rusedski?

10. In which English county is the market town of Thetford?

11. Which jockey won the Derby nine times between 1954 and 1983?

12. What is added to vodka to make a bloody Mary?

13. Who played Thora Blacklock in the sitcom Meet the Wife?

14. In which athletics event did Bob Beamon hold the world record for 23 years?

15. Which French singer is associated with the song Non, Je Ne Regrette Rien?

ANSWERS: 1 Syphilis, 2 Brian De Palma, 3 Laurent Kabila, 4 Brendan Behan, 5 Tuberculosis, 6 Dean Acheson, 7 7, 8 F W de Klerk, 9 Gustavo Kuerten, 10 Norfolk, 11 Lester Piggott, 12 Tomato juice, 13 Thora Hird, 14 Long jump, 15 Edith Piaf.

GENERAL KNOWLEDGE

1. Who played Peter in the film Peter's Friends?

2. Which American song is sung to the tune of God Save the Queen?

3. On which naval vessel did Charles Darwin serve as naturalist from 1831 to 1836?

4. Which Oscar-winning actor plays the Marquis de Sade in the film Quills?

5. What name is given to the series of chemical elements with atomic numbers 89 to 103?

6. Which Irish port was formerly called Queenstown?

7. After which author is the verse form the Clerihew named?

8. In the Old Testament, which powerful animal has 'limbs like bars of iron'?

9. Who directed the 1959 film À Bout de Souffle?

10. Which Apollo mission was manned by Charles Conrad, Alan Bean and Richard Gordon?

11. Which American talk show host received an Oscar nomination for The Color Purple?

12. Who wrote the television drama A Sense of Guilt?

13. Which veteran British actor renewed his marriage vows in a church service in 2001, at the age of 92?

14. How much is a 'double top' worth in darts?

15. Which Shakespeare play is set against the background of enmity between the Capulets and Montagues?

ANSWERS: 1 Stephen Fry, 2 My Country 'Tis of Thee, 3 The Beagle, 4 Geoffrey Rush, 5 Actinides, 6 Cobh, 7 E C Bentley, 8 Behemoth, 9 Jean-Luc Godard, 10 Apollo 12, 11 Oprah Winfrey, 12 Andrea Newman, 13 Sir John Mills, 14 Forty, 15 Romeo and Juliet.

GENERAL KNOWLEDGE

1. In which country did television presenter Phillip Schofield begin his TV career?

2. Which rock group recorded the song Smells Like Teen Spirit?

3. What became the new corporate name for organisations run by the Post Office in 2001?

4. Which Australian tennis player won the men's singles at Wimbledon in 1956 and 1957?

5. In which South American country is the Atacama Desert?

6. What sort of creature is a gelada?

7. The film Picnic at Hanging Rock begins on which day?

8. Which British actor became a Companion of Honour in the 2001 New Year Honours List?

9. Which well-known Oxford Street department store has been awarded its first royal warrant?

10. What name was given to the public market district of a Persian town?

11. Which comet is shown in the Bayeux Tapestry?

12. What name is given to a musical composition for six instruments?

13. Which team were 1991-92 Football League Champions?

14. Of which European country is Piedmont a region?

15. Which Spanish painter was noted for his 'blue period' in the early 20th century?

ANSWERS: 1 New Zealand, 2 Nirvana, 3 Consignia, 4 Lew Hoad, 5 Chile, 6 A monkey, 7 Valentines Day, 8 Paul Schofield, 9 Selfridges, 10 Bazaar, 11 Halley's Comet, 12 Sextet, 13 Leeds United, 14 Italy, 15 Pablo Picasso.

ENTERTAINMENT

1. Who played bar owner Sam Malone in the U.S. sitcom Cheers?

2. Which British band had a U.K. top ten hit in 1991 with No Son of Mine?

3. Which detective, created by Ruth Rendell, was played on TV by George Baker?

4. Which 2000 American Pie-esque film was co-produced by Ghostbusters' Ivan Reitman?

5. Which ITV drama series set in a slimming club was written by Kay Mellor?

6. What was the title of the Real McCoy's 1995 U.K. top ten hit?

7. Who directed and co-produced the 1988 film The Milagro Beanfield War?

8. Which US series starred James Gandolfini as a New Jersey gangster?

9. Which diva had a U.K. top five hit in 1989 with This Time I Know It's For Real?

10. Which star of The X-Files appeared in the 2000 film The House of Mirth?

11. Which actor played eight roles in the 2000 film sequel Nutty Professor II: The Klumps?

12. Which Australian entertainer was accompanied during his early 1960s TV appearances by Coojee Bear, a koala puppet?

13. Which Irish band returned to the U.K. charts with the number one single Beautiful Day in 2000?

14. What was the subtitle of the 1988 film Halloween 4?

15. Which actress played Dr Victoria Merrick in the BBC1 drama series Holby City?

ANSWERS: 1 Ted Danson, 2 Genesis, 3 (Detective Chief) Inspector Wexford, 4 Road Trip, 5 Fat Friends, 6 Run Away, 7 Robert Redford, 8 The Sopranos, 9 Donna Summer, 10 Gillian Anderson, 11 Eddie Murphy, 12 Rolf Harris, 13 U2, 14 The Return of Michael Myers, 15 Lisa Faulkner.

GENERAL KNOWLEDGE

1. Who wrote The Joy Luck Club?

2. Which American actress was the elder sister of Joan Fontaine?

3. What nickname was given to the M9A1 rocket launcher?

4. Which figure in the Profumo scandal has claimed that Sir Roger Hollis was the 'fifth man' in the 1960s spy ring?

5. What is the thickest and most powerful tendon in the human body?

6. Which device for detecting radiation was invented by Donald A Glaser?

7. Which American author wrote the Studs Lonigan trilogy?

8. To which continent is the bird called the cock-of-the-rock native?

9. Which singer and actor had hits with Banana Boat Song and Mary's Boy Child in 1957?

10. What is the highest-pitched woodwind instrument in an orchestra?

11. Which English poet wrote an Ode to a Nightingale?

12. Which star of It Aint Half Hot Mum was the voice of Sgt Major Zero in the children's television series Terrahawks?

13. Which Oscar-winning actor stars in the film Cast Away?

14. Who was the first professional England cricketer to be knighted?

15. What is the capital of Greece?

GENERAL KNOWLEDGE

1. In which novel by Charles Dickens does the character Bill Sikes appear?

2. Which constellation contains the Coalsack?

3. In which country is Lake Athabasca?

4. From which Italian football team did Sven-Goran Eriksson resign as manager in 2001?

5. Which English philosopher wrote Leviathan?

6. In the Old Testament, which Midianite priest became Moses' father-in-law?

7. Television series Diagnosis Murder features an amateur sleuth whose main job is what?

8. Which English novelist wrote Headlong Hall and Nightmare Abbey?

9. What surname did Turkish leader Mustafa Kemal receive in 1934?

10. Which West Saxon king was the grandson of Alfred the Great?

11. Which American actress became Princess Grace of Monaco?

12. Which Australian author wrote The Chant of Jimmy Blacksmith?

13. Which city hosted the 2001 F.A. Cup Final?

14. What was the former name of Ho Chi Minh City?

15. With which athletics event is Sergey Bubka associated?

ANSWERS: 1 Oliver Twist, 2 Crux, or Southern Cross, 3 Canada, 4 Lazio, 5 Thomas Hobbes, 6 Jethro, 7 Hospital doctor, 8 Thomas Love Peacock, 9 Atatürk, 10 Athelstan, 11 Grace Kelly, 12 Thomas Keneally, 13 Cardiff, 14 Saigon, 15 Pole vault.

GENERAL KNOWLEDGE

1. Which American writer claimed that men seldom make passes at girls who wear glasses?

2. Which Irish dancer and choreographer was born Edris Stannus?

3. Of which football team did David Jones become manager in January 2001?

4. Which Kenyan runner won the 1500m at the 1968 Olympics?

5. What was the apt middle name of union leader Jimmy Hoffa who mysteriously disappeared in 1975?

6. Which cat is also called a desert lynx?

7. How many Oscars were won by the 1994 film Forrest Gump?

8. Which American author wrote Saint Jack and The Mosquito Coast?

9. What is the oldest of the three classic races that constitute the American Triple Crown?

10. Which darts player was made an MBE in the 2001 New Year Honours List?

11. Which American actor won a Best Actor Oscar for To Kill a Mockingbird?

12. Which future novelist appeared in the 1965 film A High Wind in Jamaica?

13. Which Coronation Street actor is the only member of the original cast still in the show?

14. In Greek mythology, what name was given to a one-eyed giant?

15. Which U.S. government agency of volunteers was founded by John F Kennedy in 1961?

ANSWERS: 1 Dorothy Parker, 2 Dame Ninette de Valois, 3 Wolverhampton Wanderers, 4 Kip Keino, 5 Riddle, 6 Caracal, 7 Six, 8 Paul Theroux, 9 Belmont Stakes, 10 Phil Taylor, 11 Gregory Peck, 12 Martin Amis, 13 Bill Roache, 14 Cyclops, 15 Peace Corps.

ENTERTAINMENT

1. Which eighties comedy drama set in the world of snooker starred Robert Lindsay and Paul McGann?

2. Which 1990 film thriller starred Rob Lowe and James Spader?

3. In which English city was the Channel 4 drama series North Square set?

4. What was the title of the Hollies' 1965 U.K. number one single?

5. Which star of Jerry Maguire and Stuart Little appeared in the 2000 film The Little Vampire?

6. Which US vocalist had a U.K. top ten hit in 1989 with I Drove All Night?

7. In what type of car did Michael J. Fox travel through time in the Back to the Future movies?

8. Who played the title role in the BBC1 drama series The Scarlet Pimpernel?

9. Which female group had a U.K. top ten hit in 1981 with Attention to Me?

10. Which star of the U.S. sitcom Roseanne appeared in the 2000 film Coyote Ugly?

11. Which US soul singer released an album entitled Renaissance in 2000?

12. What were the first names of the Harts in the U.S. drama series Hart to Hart?

13. Which British band hit the UK number one spot with Stomp in 2000?

14. Which 1990 Coen Brothers film starred Gabriel Byrne and Albert Finney?

15. Where did the Coronation Street siege take place in 2000?

ANSWERS: 1 Give Us a Break, 2 Bad Influence, 3 Leeds, 4 I'm Alive, 5 Jonathan Lipnicki, 6 Cyndi Lauper, 7 A Delorean, 8 Richard E. Grant, 9 The Nolans, 10 John Goodman, 11 Lionel Richie, 12 Jonathan & Jennifer, 13 Steps, 14 Miller's Crossing, 15 Freshco's supermarket.

GENERAL KNOWLEDGE

1. Which British author wrote Ballet Shoes?

2. Which Russian impresario founded the Ballets Russes in 1909?

3. Who lost his world heavyweight boxing title in the first championship bout under the Queensberry rules?

4. With which musical instrument is Coleman Hawkins associated?

5. Who wrote The English Constitution in 1867?

6. Which Italian poet won the 1959 Nobel prize for literature?

7. Borat Karabzhanov is a character created by which televison comedian?

8. Which actor starred in Dr Zhivago and The Dresser?

9. In Chinese philosophy, what name is given to the ethereal substance of which everything is composed?

10. What sort of creature is a thickhead?

11. Which literary family is associated with Haworth Parsonage in West Yorkshire?

12. What was the affliction suffered by Jennifer Jones in the film Love Letters?

13. Which clarinettist had a hit with Stranger on the Shore in 1961?

14. What name is given to the apparent brightness of a celestial body in astronomy?

15. To which country do the Cyclades belong?

GENERAL KNOWLEDGE

1. What was the name of the city where television's The Jetsons lived?

2. Which novelist became the first Baron Tweedsmuir?

3. In Greek mythology, which swift-footed huntress lost a race when she stopped to pick up golden apples?

4. Which Somerset farmer runs the Glastonbury Festival?

5. What is the common name for the hallucinogenic drug Phencyclidine or PCP?

6. Which English artist painted Mr and Mrs Clark and Percy?

7. Which British author wrote the Mallen trilogy?

8. Which Austrian composer wrote the Resurrection Symphony and the Symphony of a Thousand?

9. In Greek mythology, who killed the Minotaur?

10. Which plant of the parsley family is also called Queen Anne's lace?

11. Which well-known British medical journal was established in 1823?

12. What is added to vodka to make a screwdriver?

13. What nationality was the poet Gabriela Mistral who won the 1945 Nobel Prize for literature?

14. Who was the third president of the United States?

15. Which poison is represented by the letters CN?

ANSWERS: 1 Orbit City, 2 John Buchan, 3 Atalanta, 4 Michael Eavis, 5 Angel dust, 6 David Hockney, 7 Catherine Cookson, 8 Gustav Mahler, 9 Theseus, 10 Wild carrot, 11 The Lancet, 12 Orange juice, 13 Chilean, 14 Thomas Jefferson, 15 Cyanide.

GENERAL KNOWLEDGE

1. Which film was advertised as having a cast of 125,000?

2. Which actress was the eldest child of Roger Kemble?

3. Who invented the vacuum flask?

4. Which composer became a Companion of Honour in the 2001 New Year Honours List?

5. What was the surname of the uncle and nephew who discovered the North Magnetic Pole?

6. Which member of the Royal Family has the title Baron Greenwich?

7. Who is the author of the River Cottage Cookbook?

8. In which Australian city is the newspaper The Age published?

9. Which Greek poet is said to have introduced actors into dramatic performances?

10. Which condiment has the chemical formula NaCl?

11. Which English poet wrote The Rime of the Ancient Mariner?

12. Where did Ivor the Engine live?

13. Which well-known cycle race was first held in 1903?

14. On which island was the BBC series Castaway 2000 set?

15. Which English fashion designer opened the boutique Bazaar on the King's Road in 1957?

ANSWERS: 1 Ben Hur, 2 Sarah Siddons, 3 Sir James Dewar, 4 Sir Harrison Birtwistle, 5 Ross, 6 Prince Philip, 7 Hugh Fearnley-Whittingstall, 8 Melbourne, 9 Thespis, 10 Salt, 11 Samuel Taylor Coleridge, 12 (In the top left-hand corner of) Wales, 13 Tour de France, 14 Taransay, 15 Mary Quant.

ENTERTAINMENT

1. What was the title of Billie Piper's second album?

2. Which actress starred as Buffy the Vampire Slayer in the BBC 2 series?

3. Which actor played an alcoholic Scottish poet in the 1983 film Reuben, Reuben?

4. What was the title of the Police's 1981 U.K. number one single?

5. In which 2000 Paul Verhoeven film did Kevin Bacon star as a scientist who makes himself invisible?

6. Whose Weird Weekends were the subject of a BBC2 documentary series?

7. In which year did Oasis celebrate their second number one hit single, Don't Look Back in Anger?

8. Which actor played The Spy Who Came in from the Cold in the 1966 film of that name?

9. What was the surname of the EastEnders sisters who performed at the Vic's karaoke night as the Nolans in 2000?

10. What was the Supremes' first UK number one, which hit the charts in 1964?

11. Who played Inspector Clouseau in the 1968 film of that name?

12. On which satirical Channel 4 programme did Ricky Gervais appear as a reporter before launching his own comedy chat show?

13. What was the title of Texas' first U.K. top ten hit?

14. In which 2000 film did Antonio Banderas and Woody Harrelson play two boxers?

15. Who was the original presenter of the British version of Family Fortunes?

ANSWERS: 1 Walk of Life, 2 Sarah Michelle Gellar, 3 Tom Conti, 4 Every Little Thing She Does is Magic, 5 Hollow Man, 6 Louis Theroux's, 7 1996, 8 Richard Burton, 9 Slater, 10 Baby Love, 11 Alan Arkin, 12 The 11 O'Clock Show, 13 I Don't Want a Lover, 14 Play it to the Bone, 15 Bob Monkhouse.

GENERAL KNOWLEDGE

1. Who wrote the novel All Quiet on the Western Front?

2. Which hymn is named from the first word of the Latin for "my soul magnifies the Lord"?

3. What was the pen name of authors Frederic Dannay and Manfred B. Lee?

4. Which character in The Archers is played by Trevor Harrison?

5. Who was principal conductor of the Bavarian Radio Symphony Orchestra from 1961 to 1979?

6. Which American TV show host was known as 'the Great Stone Face'?

7. Which TV series featured the characters Ludicrus and Nausius?

8. In which city is the former cathedral Hagia Sophia?

9. In which story by Nathaniel Hawthorne is Hester Prynne the main character?

10. What is the second most abundant mineral in the Earth's crust after feldspar?

11. Which Mediterranean island was invaded by Turkish troops in 1974?

12. Which author also writes under the name Barbara Vine?

13. Which TV character beat Westlife to the coveted Christmas number one spot in 2000?

14. Who wrote the novel Gormenghast?

15. Which town is the administrative centre of Kent?

ANSWERS: 1 Erich Maria Remarque, 2 Magnificat, 3 Ellery Queen, 4 Eddie Grundy, 5 Rafael Kubelik, 6 Ed Sullivan, 7 Up Pompeii, 8 Istanbul, 9 The Scarlet Letter, 10 Quartz, 11 Cyprus, 12 Ruth Rendell, 13 Bob the Builder, 14 Mervyn Peake, 15 Maidstone.

GENERAL KNOWLEDGE

1. Who wrote the sitcoms Beast and Men Behaving Badly?

2. Which pretender to the English crown worked in the royal kitchens after his capture at the Battle of Stoke?

3. What is the name of Patrick Stewart's character in Star Trek: The Next Generation?

4. Which Jerzy Kosinski novel was filmed in 1979 starring Peter Sellers?

5. What is the SI unit of radiation dose equivalent?

6. Which New Zealand rugby player was known as 'Pine Tree'?

7. Who wrote The Wonderful Wizard of Oz?

8. Which volcano between Java and Sumatra erupted catastrophically in 1883?

9. By what name was Polish-born ballet dancer and teacher Cyvia Rambam known?

10. Which musical composition takes its name from the French for 'study'?

11. Which American white supremacist organisation is represented by the initials KKK?

12. Who was kidnapped in the 1953 film The Kidnappers?

13. Which British rower was awarded a knighthood in the 2001 New Year Honours List?

14. Of which Italian island is Palermo the capital?

15. Which Australian tree is also called a gum tree?

ANSWERS: 1 Simon Nye, 2 Lambert Simnel, 3 Captain Jean-Luc Picard, 4 Being There, 5 Sievert, 6 Colin Meads, 7 L Frank Baum, 8 Krakatoa, 9 Dame Marie Rambert, 10 Etude, 11 Ku Klux Klan, 12 A baby, 13 Steve Redgrave, 14 Sicily, 15 Eucalyptus.

GENERAL KNOWLEDGE

1. What was Red Dwarf in the television comedy series of that name?

2. Which American retail chain was founded by Sam Walton in 1962?

3. What is the capital of Sierra Leone?

4. What name is given to the study of human improvement by genetic means?

5. By what name were supporters of the Youth International Party known?

6. Which American tennis player won the men's singles at Wimbledon in 1947?

7. Who wrote My Family and Other Animals?

8. Which Oscar-winning American actor died in December 2000 at the age of 78?

9. Which Italian composer was elected to the Central Committee of the Italian Communist Party in 1975?

10. What sort of creature is a krait?

11. Which Hampshire city is on a peninsula between the estuaries of the Rivers Test and Itchen?

12. Which science fiction author wrote the novel Hothouse?

13. Which pop star married Lisa Marie Presley in 1994?

14. Which Norwegian dramatist wrote A Doll's House?

15. Which Mongol emperor was the grandson of Genghis Khan?

ANSWERS: 1 A spaceship, 2 Wal-Mart, 3 Freetown, 4 Eugenics, 5 Yippies, 6 Jack Kramer, 7 Gerald Durrell, 8 Jason Robards, 9 Luigi Nono, 10 A snake, 11 Southampton, 12 Brian Aldiss, 13 Michael Jackson, 14 Henrik Ibsen, 15 Kublai Khan.

ENTERTAINMENT

1. Which British band released their seventh studio album, Painting It Red, in 2000?

2. Which 1972 film featured Yul Brynner playing a mysterious bomber?

3. Which former EastEnders actor starred as DC Jack Mowbray in the ITV drama series Without Motive?

4. Which U.S. group had a 1977 number one hit in the U.K. with Show You the Way to Go?

5. Which former newsreader presented the BBC1 series The Crime Squad?

6. What was the title of the Bond theme with which Wings had a UK top ten hit in 1973?

7. Which 1967 musical film starring Tommy Steele was based on H.G. Wells' novel Kipps?

8. Which BBC1 sitcom starred Rab C. Nesbitt's Gregor Fisher and The Vicar of Dibley actor James Fleet?

9. Which British group's first U.K. top ten hit was 1993's How Can I Love You More?

10. Which 2000 British film featured Tim Curry as a club-owning drugs dealer called Damian?

11. Which former Bond girl starred alongside Jon Favreau in the 2000 film Love & Sex?

12. What was Miss Piggy's surname in the TV show The Muppets?

13. Which British actress played a ballet teacher in the 2000 film Billy Elliot?

14. Which girl group had a 2000 U.K. number one hit with Black Coffee?

15. Which 1970 film set in World War II featured Michael Caine, Cliff Robertson and Henry Fonda?

ANSWERS: 1 The Beautiful South, 2 Fuzz, 3 Ross Kemp, 4 The Jacksons, 5 Sue Lawley, 6 Live and Let Die, 7 Half a Sixpence, 8 Brotherly Love, 9 M People, 10 Sorted, 11 Famke Janssen, 12 Lee, 13 Julie Walters, 14 All Saints, 15 Too Late the Hero.

GENERAL KNOWLEDGE

1. What is the sequel to the film 101 Dalamatians called?

2. Which U.S. president was known as 'Old Hickory'?

3. With which branch of mathematics is Euclid chiefly associated?

4. Which Danish comedian and pianist died in 2000 at the age of 91?

5. Who directed the films Invasion of the Body Snatchers, Dirty Harry and The Shootist?

6. Which rare gas has the chemical symbol Kr?

7. Who wrote How to Win Friends and Influence People?

8. Which American golfer won the British Open, U.S. Open and U.S. Masters in 1953?

9. What was the Greek name for Khufu, builder of the Great Pyramid at Giza?

10. In which U.S. state is Diamond Head?

11. Which Christian sacrament is also called Holy Communion and the Lord's Supper?

12. Which American comic actor wrote Don't Stand Too Close to a Naked Man?

13. Which American film director received an honorary knighthood in 2001?

14. What is the highest active volcano in Europe?

15. Which famous square is on the east side of the Kremlin in Moscow?

ANSWERS: 1 102 Dalmatians, 2 Andrew Jackson, 3 Geometry, 4 Victor Borge, 5 Don Siegel, 6 Krypton, 7 Dale Carnegie, 8 Ben Hogan, 9 Cheops, 10 Hawaii, 11 The Eucharist, 12 Tim Allen, 13 Steven Spielberg, 14 Mount Etna, 15 Red Square.

? **GENERAL KNOWLEDGE** ?

1. Which English author wrote Love in a Cold Climate?

2. In which 1969 television comedy series did Spike Milligan play an Asian with an Irish father?

3. Who was the skipper of the accident-prone catamaran Team Philips?

4. What nationality was the composer Carl Nielsen?

5. Which French tennis player won the first of her six Wimbledon singles titles in 1919?

6. What was the first name of the furniture designer Hepplewhite?

7. Which British boxer needed emergency surgery after a fight in December 2000?

8. What name is given to a monologue in which a character in a play speaks his thoughts aloud?

9. Who scored the winning goal of the 1979 European Cup final?

10. What was the title of the ruler of Egypt from 1867 to 1914?

11. Which sociologist, historian and economist co-wrote The Communist Manifesto with Friedrich Engels?

12. What name is given to the mature female of domesticated cattle?

13. What nationality is the novelist Chinua Achebe?

14. Who was the father of Queen Mary II, wife of King William III?

15. In which country is the port of Tangier located?

ANSWERS: 1 Nancy Mitford, 2 Curry and Chips, 3 Pete Goss, 4 Danish, 5 Suzanne Lenglen, 6 George, 7 Paul Ingle, 8 Soliloquy, 9 Trevor Francis, 10 Khedive, 11 Karl Marx, 12 Cow, 13 Nigerian, 14 James II, 15 Morocco.

? **GENERAL KNOWLEDGE** ?

1. Which French dramatist wrote the 1897 play Cyrano de Bergerac?

2. Who won the F.A. Cup in 1972?

3. Which great Czech distance runner died in 2000 at the age of 78?

4. What name is given to an aquatic mammal with four limbs modified into flippers?

5. Which American poet wrote The Bridge?

6. What nationality was the composer Paul Hindemith?

7. Which fictional character made his first appearance in the novel The Little White Bird?

8. What sort of plant is a lady's slipper?

9. Who designed the wedding dress worn by Catherine Zeta Jones when she married Michael Douglas?

10. At which public school are most of the boys known as Oppidans?

11. What form of exercise was popularised by Bill Bowerman in a 1967 book?

12. The film The Deep was about the search for what beneath the sea?

13. Which British actress starred in The Killing of Sister George and Entertaining Mr Sloane?

14. In which South American country did Prince William spend ten weeks as part of an Operation Raleigh expedition?

15. What sort of dog has Labrador and golden varieties?

ANSWERS: 1 Edmond Rostand, 2 Leeds United, 3 Emil Zatopek, 4 Pinniped, 5 Hart Crane, 6 German, 7 Peter Pan, 8 An orchid, 9 Christian Lacroix, 10 Eton College, 11 Jogging, 12 Treasure, 13 Beryl Reid, 14 Chile, 15 Retriever.

GENERAL KNOWLEDGE

1. What was the former name, until 1973, of the island Bioko?

2. Who was the author of the poem The Lady of Shalott?

3. In which year was British cartoonist Gerald Scarfe born?

4. What is the name of the fielding position in cricket between cover and mid-off ?

5. What Israeli monetary unit is worth one hundredth of a shekel?

6. Which jockey won the St. Leger in 1995 and 1996 on horses Classic Cliche and Shantou respectively?

7. Who wrote the 1963 novel The Unicorn?

8. What is the name given to the artistic distribution of light and dark masses in a painting?

9. Who wrote the 1988 novel The Satanic Verses?

10. What is the name given to the South African coin containing 1 troy ouce of gold?

11. What is the name given to the set of chalk stacks off the west coast of the Isle of Wight?

12. What is the chief port of Tanzania?

13. Which pop group's record albums include Black Celebration and Construction Time Again?

14. Who was the male star of the 1989 film How to Get Ahead in Advertising, directed by Bruce Robinson?

15. Who was the 1950-9 British Open women's squash champion?

ANSWERS 1. Fernando Po 2. Alfred Tennyson 3. 1936 4. Extra cover 5. Agora 6. Frankie Dettori 7. Iris Murdoch 8. Chiaroscuro 9. Salman Rushdie 10. Krugerrand 11. The Needles 12. Dar-es-Salaam 13. Depeche Mode 14. Richard E. Grant 15. Janet Morgan.

ENTERTAINMENT

1. Which actor directed his wife Joanne Woodward in the 1968 film Rachel Rachel?

2. Who composed the 1775 opera The Feigned Gardener?

3. Who plays Lilith in the TV sitcom Frasier?

4. Which actor directed the 1981 film Race to the Yankee Zephyr?

5. In which year did Bill Maynard make his stage debut, with comedian Terry Scott?

6. Which playwright was replaced by Stephen Zaillian as the writer of the film Hannibal, the follow-up to The Silence of the Lambs?

7. In which town was Larry Grayson born in 1923?

8. In which year was Scottish mezzo-soprano Linda Finnie born?

9. What was the real name of comedienne Joyce Grenfell?

10. Who played Mrs. Chapman in the 1978 sitcom Going Straight?

11. Who played Chuy Castillos in the 1990s sitcom The Golden Palace?

12. In which year did American actor-manager David Belasco die?

13. Who plays Jack in Radio Four's The Archers?

14. Which playwright's works include the 1986 play Kafka's Dick?

15. Which comic actress played Susie Deruzza in the 1990s sitcom Good Advice?

ANSWERS 1. Paul Newman 2. Mozart 3. Bebe Neuwirth 4. David Hemmings 5. 1951 6. David Mamet 7. Bolton 8. 1952 9. Joyce Phipps 10. Rowena Cooper 11. Cheech Marin 12. 1931 13. Arnold Peters 14. Alan Bennett 15. Shelley Long.

SPORT

1. How many players are there in a softball side?

2. In which year was runner Ato Boldon born?

3. How many minutes did Ravi Shastri take to hit 200 runs in Bombay's cricket game against Boroda in January 1985?

4. In which year was runner Linford Christie born?

5. Who was voted basketball's most valuable player in the NBA in 1992?

6. By what score did Brazil beat Morocco in their 1998 football World Cup Group A game?

7. Which Test cricket team has wicket-keeper Chris Nevin represented?

8. Who was 1978 women's 100m breaststroke swimming world champion?

9. Which U.S. golfer was leading money winner on the 1952 U.S. tour?

10. Who captained England's rugby union side in their 2000 Six Nations game against Wales?

11. At what sport does Troy Corser compete?

12. Which Briton was 1906-7 world figure skating champion?

13. In cricket, who scored 167 for Somerset against Glamorgan in the 2nd innings of their 1999 county championship game?

14. Which two teams met in the 1947 play-off for the NFL championship in American Football?

15. Who was the 1961 French Open women's singles tennis champion?

ANSWERS 1. Nine 2. 1973 3. 113 4. 1960 5. Michael Jordan 6. 3-0 7. New Zealand 8. Yulia Bogdanova 9. Julian Boros 10. Matt Dawson 11. Motorcycling 12. Madge Syers 13. Marcus Trescothick 14. Philadelphia Eagles and Chicago Cardinals 15. Ann Haydon.

POP MUSIC

1. Who was the female singer in the Leeds group Girls at Our Best?

2. Kenny Pickett was lead singer in which 1960s group?

3. Who is the lead singer in the group Hefner?

4. On which label did Melanie C record her debut solo album?

5. Who recorded the 1999 album In Reverse?

6. Lee Gorton and Ian Smith are members of which Salford group?

7. On which label did Steve Earle record his album Guitar Town?

8. Who had a 1966 hit with the song Sweet Talking Guy?

9. Blade, Chevette, Woodcock, Generate. Which punk group?

10. Who is the keyboard player with the group Embrace?

11. Which label did Leiber and Stoller launch in 1964?

12. Which Bob Dylan studio album features the song Gates of Eden?

13. Which 1990 Kylie Minogue hit does Nick Cave recite on the 2000 spoken-word C.D. release The Secret Life of the Love Song?

14. Which duo wrote the song Hit Me With Your Rhythm Stick?

15. What was the nickname of producer George Morton?

ART & LITERATURE

1. Who authored the children's book Pure Dead Magic?

2. Who wrote the 1705 story A True Relation of the Apparition of One Mrs. Veal?

3. What was Jeffrey Archer's first published novel?

4. Who wrote the 1921 narrative poem King Cole?

5. Who wrote the 1946 novel Chloe Marr?

6. Who wrote the 1983 novel The Philosopher's Pupil?

7. Who wrote the 1945 novel The English Teacher?

8. Whose poetry collections include 1956's One Foot in Eden?

9. Which novel by Stephen King features the character Paul Sheldon?

10. Who wrote the 1941 novel The Real Life of Sebastian Knight?

11. Which photographer did the artist Roland Penrose marry in 1947?

12. Who authored the children's book Artemis Fowl?

13. Who wrote the semi-autobiographical novel Eight Minutes Idle?

14. Which writer's debut was the book After You'd Gone?

15. Which architect designed the 1970 San Francisco cathedral and co-designed the 1958 Pirelli skyscraper in Milan?

? GENERAL KNOWLEDGE ?

1. In which year did the Welsh actor, songwriter and dramatist Ivor Novello die?

2. Who wrote the 1934 novel A Man Lay Dead?

3. In which year did David Koresh and the Branch Davidians Christian cult hold a siege in Waco, Texas?

4. Which New York-born actor-comedian played Nicely-Nicely Johnson in the film Guys and Dolls?

5. Which 1971 book by Hunter S. Thompson is subtitled A savage journey to the heart of the American Dream?

6. Who directed the 1995 film Heat which starred Al Pacino?

7. Who was the author of the 1945 poetry collection The North Ship?

8. Which comedy actor's television roles included Dennis Dunstable in Please Sir!?

9. Who were the four members of the pop group the Monkees?

10. Which Labour M.P. for Birmingham Ladywood did Tony Blair appoint as Secretary of State for International Development?

11. In which year did the saint known as 'the Venerable Bede' die?

12. Of which French overseas region in N.E. South America is Cayenne the capital?

13. Which trio of actors were cell-mates in the 1960 film comedy Two Way Stretch?

14. Which town in N.W. England is the administrative centre of Lancashire?

15. Which television talent show was hosted from 1956-78 by Hughie Green?

ANSWERS 1. 1951 2. Ngaio Marsh 3. 1993 4. Stubby Kaye 5. Fear and Loathing in Las Vegas 6. Michael Mann 7. Philip Larkin 8. Peter Denyer 9. Peter Tork, Davy Jones, Mike Nesmith and Micky Dolenz 10. Clare Short 11. 735 A.D. 12. French Guiana 13. Peter Sellers, David Lodge and Bernard Cribbins 14. Preston 15. Opportunity Knocks!

ENTERTAINMENT

1. Which duo wrote the 1974 sitcom Thick As Thieves?

2. In which year in the future is the 1982 film Blade Runner set?

3. Which actress played Ophelia in the 1996 film Hamlet?

4. Which actor voiced Sgt. Major Zero in the 1980s children's puppet show Terrahawks?

5. Which 1972 film by Ken Russell is about sculptor Henri Gaudier-Brzeska?

6. Which actor directed and starred in the 1973 film Antony and Cleopatra?

7. Who plays Ron in the soap Brookside?

8. Who played gangster John Dillinger in the 1979 film The Lady in Red?

9. Who directed the 1988 film Talk Radio?

10. Who directed the 1936 film musical Anything Goes?

11. Who was the first husband of actress Brigitte Bardot?

12. Who played Little Lord Fauntleroy in the 1936 film?

13. Who starred opposite Pierce Brosnan in the remake of The Thomas Crown Affair?

14. In which city was actor John Barrymore born?

15. Which actor stars opposite Jennifer Aniston in the film Metal God?

ANSWERS 1. Dick Clement and Ian La Frenais 2. 2019 3. Kate Winslet 4. Windsor Davies 5. Savage Messiah 6. Charlton Heston 7. Vince Earl 8. Robert Conrad 9. Oliver Stone 10. Lewis Milestone 11. Roger Vadim 12. Freddie Bartholomew 13. Rene Russo 14. Philadelphia 15. Mark Wahlberg.

SPORT

1. Which snooker player won the 2000 Benson & Hedges Masters?

2. Who was flat racing champion jockey from 1909-1912?

3. At what sport do Mark Covell and Ian Walker compete?

4. Which club won the first rugby league Challenge Cup Final?

5. In cricket, who took 14-169 against Somerset for Gloucestershire in 1993?

6. With what sport are Hans Nielsen and Erik Gundersen associated?

7. Who knocked Leigh Centurions out of the rugby league Challenge Cup in February 2000?

8. Colin Blythe took 17 wickets for Kent against Northants in June 1907. For how many runs?

9. What nationality is athlete Leonard Myles-Mills?

10. At what ball game was Willie Smith a 1923 world professional champion?

11. Which country won the 1956 Olympic football tournament?

12. How many horses have won Cheltenham's Champion Hurdle three years in a row?

13. Who did the Leeds Rhinos beat in the 2000 rugby league Challenge Cup quarter-finals?

14. By what score did the U.S.A. win the 1924 Walker Cup?

15. Which golfer won the Catalonia Open in 1994?

ANSWERS 1. Matthew Stevens 2. Frank Wootton 3. Sailing 4. Batley 5. Martyn Ball 6. Speedway 7. Wakefield Wildcats 8. 48 9. Ghanaian 10. Billiards 11. U.S.S.R. 12. Five 13. Dewsbury Rams 14. 9-3 15. Jose Coceres.

POP MUSIC

1. From which country do the girl group Ex-Girl hail?

2. Who recorded the song Mansion on the Hill on the 2000 album Badlands: A Tribute to Bruce Springsteen's "Nebraska"?

3. Which singer recorded the 2001 album Love and Theft?

4. In which year did Siouxsie and the Banshees release the single Hong Kong Garden?

5. Which singer recorded the 2001 single We Need A Resolution?

6. Which group recorded the 2001 single Digital Love?

7. Which member of the group The Stranglers recorded the 1979 album Nosferatu?

8. Which group recorded the 2001 single Mind Over Money?

9. Which group recorded the 1978 single Shot By Both Sides?

10. Which studio album by the Fall includes the song Pumpkin Soup and Mashed Potatoes?

11. Which singer recorded the 2000 album Lovers Rock?

12. Which member of the rock group The Who studied at the Ealing College of Art?

13. Which group recorded the 1983 Top 20 single Oblivious?

14. Which group recorded the 2001 single Hash Pipe?

15. Which blues singer was born Chester Burnett?

GEOGRAPHY

1. What is the highest point on Bodmin Moor?

2. How many islands comprise the Cayman Islands in the West Indies?

3. In which Asian country is the village of My Lai?

4. In which year did Burma become Myanmar?

5. Gerlachovka is the highest peak of which mountain system?

6. What is the name of the 19th century castle five miles N.W. of Cardiff?

7. The Rio Negro forms part of the border between which two countries?

8. Which canal in Venice does the Rialto Bridge cross?

9. Into which sea does the River Scheldt flow?

10. Into which river does the River Neckar flow at Mannheim?

11. Santa Fé is the capital of which U.S. state?

12. The Shiré Highlands is an upland area of which African country?

13. In which European country is the town of Schwyz?

14. What did the Netherlands East Indies become in 1945?

15. In which English county is the textile town of Nelson?

ANSWERS 1. Brown Willy 2. Three 3. Vietnam 4. 1989 5. Carpathian Mountains 6. Castle Coch 7. Colombia and Venezuela 8. Grand Canal 9. North Sea 10. Rhine 11. New Mexico 12. Malawi 13. Switzerland 14. Indonesia 15. Lancashire.

? GENERAL KNOWLEDGE ?

1. Which Old Testament brother of Moses was first high priest of the Israelites?

2. Which plant with pinkish-white flowers is a hybrid of Saxifraga umbrosa and Saxifraga spathularis?

3. Who is the cartoon adversary of Road Runner?

4. Leopold Bloom is the central character in which novel?

5. In which year was True Blue a No. 1 single for Madonna?

6. Who wrote the 1982 novel Light Thickens?

7. Which motor racing driver won the 1975 Spanish Grand Prix in Formula 1?

8. Who did Guillermo Vilas beat in the 1977 French Open men's singles tennis championship final?

9. Who was the 1946/7 National Hunt champion jockey?

10. Who was Labour Secretary of State for Trade from 1974-6?

11. Actor Nicholas Hannen was the second husband of which English comedy actress?

12. In which year did the U.S. painter Edward Hopper die?

13. Who was the author of the novel Lorna Doone?

14. Who was the archbishop of Canterbury from 1980-91?

15. In which year did Austrian psychiatrist Alfred Adler die?

ENTERTAINMENT

1. In which South American capital is the 1988 film Apartment Zero set?

2. What was the name of the guinea pig in the 1960s children's show Tales of the Riverbank?

3. In which year did Victor Borge make his British television debut?

4. Who played Jenny in the BBC TV drama Take Three Girls?

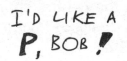

5. Who presented the 1960s gameshow Take A Letter?

6. Who directed the 1985 historical film Lady Jane?

7. Who played Latka Gravas in the sitcom Taxi?

8. Which actress provides the love interest in the 1955 film The Tall Men?

9. Who played author Knut Hamsun in the 1996 film Hamsun?

10. What is Coronation Street actor Bill Tarmey's real name?

11. Which actress played Blanche Simmons in the television drama Tenko?

12. Who directed the 1972 film Hammersmith is Out?

13. In which year did Telly Addicts begin on BBC TV?

14. Who directed the 1955 film Apache Woman?

15. Who created the sitcom Tell it to the Marines which began in 1959?

SPORT

1. Who was Wimbledon men's singles tennis champion in 1946?

2. In which year was wicket-keeper A.N. Aymes born?

3. Who won the 1995 League Cup in football?

4. Which players met in the 2000 Thailand Masters snooker final?

5. How long did Ann Jansson take to walk 15,000 metres on 25th October 1987?

6. In which year was athlete Gail Devers born?

7. In which month is the Prix de l'Arc de Triomph run?

8. In which year was athlete Sheila Echols born?

9. In which year was the Henley Royal Regatta inaugurated?

10. Who was named top female athlete of the 20th Century by the I.A.A.F. in November 1999?

11. Who was the 1980 individual world speedway champion?

12. Who was the Scotland rugby union coach for their 2000 Six Nations game against France?

13. In his 36,049 first-class runs total from 1957-83, how many centuries did Alan Jones make?

14. In which year was athlete Dawn Sowell born?

15. Who was the 1968 Olympic men's 20km biathlon champion?

ANSWERS 1. Yvon Petra 2. 1964 3. Liverpool 4. Mark Williams & Stephen Hendry 5. 1hr 15:37 6. 1966 7. October 8. 1964 9. 1839 10. Fanny Blankers-Koen 11. Michael Lee 12. Ian McGeechan 13. 56 14. 1966 15. Magnar Solberg.

POP MUSIC

1. Which U.S. group recorded the 1999 album Villa Elaine?

2. Who recorded the 1999 album Awake and Breathe?

3. What did the Four Tops change their name from?

4. Jackie Mittoo was a founder member of which reggae group?

5. In which year did the German group Nektar form?

6. Who produced B. Bumble and the Stingers' single Nut Rocker?

7. On which label did Lew Lewis record his 1978 single Lucky Seven?

8. Which group recorded the 1991 live album Raw Melody Men?

9. Who is the eldest of the four Neville Brothers?

10. Which guitarist recorded the album After the Satellite Sings?

11. Which rap group recorded the 1999 album There's a Poison Goin' On...?

12. What is the B-side of the 1974 John Lennon single Whatever Gets You Through the Night?

13. Which singer's early groups included Crepe Soul and Snakepit Banana Barn?

14. What is the B-side of Jona Lewie's single The Baby, She's on the Street?

15. Which group recorded the 1999 country album Fly?

ANSWERS 1. Remy Zero 2. B*witched 3. The Four Aims 4. The Ska-Talites 5. 1971 6. Kim Fowley 7. Stiff 8. New Model Army 9. Art 10. Bill Nelson 11. Public Enemy 12. Beef Jerky 13. John 'Cougar' Mellencamp 14. Denny Laine's Valet 15. Dixie Chicks

HISTORY

1. In which year did Khrushchev replace Bulganin as premier of the Soviet Union?

2. Which smuggler, captain of the brig Rebecca, reputedly had an ear cut off by Spanish coastguards in 1731?

3. In which month of 1949 was the Berlin Blockade lifted?

4. In November 1853 the Russians destroyed the Turkish fleet at which Black Sea port?

5. Which two South American countries fought the Chaco War from 1932-5?

6. In which battle was Richard Neville, Earl of Warwick, slain?

7. In which year did Edward III of England die?

8. Who was vice-president of the U.S. from 1905-9?

9. Who was president of South Korea during the Korean War?

10. In which year did Burma gain independence?

11. In which year did Ethelbert, Anglo-Saxon king of Kent die?

12. Which pope crowned Charlemagne Emperor of the Romans in 800?

13. The Onin War in 15th century Japan was fought in and around which city?

14. How did French minister Léon Gambetta escape Paris in 1870 during the Franco-Prussian War?

15. In which year did Elizabeth I succeed Mary as queen?

ANSWERS 1. 1958 2. Robert Jenkins 3. May 4. Sinope 5. Bolivia and Paraguay 6. Battle of Barnet 7. 1377 8. Charles Warren Fairbanks 9. Syngman Rhee 10. 1948 11. 616 12. Pope Leo III 13. Kyoto 14. By balloon 15. 1558.

GENERAL KNOWLEDGE

1. Which flower of Greek legend was said to cover the Elysian fields?

2. For which 1994 film did Jessica Lange win a Best Actress Oscar?

3. Which former Pakistan Test cricket captain scored 211 against Australia at Karachi in 1988-9?

4. Who directed the 1991 film Thelma & Louise?

5. Who was president of South Africa from 1984-9?

6. What was the name of the character played by Rodney Bewes in the sitcom The Likely Lads?

7. What was the first Top 10 single, in 1967, for the group the Jimi Hendrix Experience?

8. Who was the author of the 1934 novel Gaudy Night?

9. Which actor played Officer Francis Poncherello in the television police drama CHiPS?

10. Who was a Best Supporting Actress Oscar winner for her role as Mrs. Van Daan in The Diary of Anne Frank?

11. Which island in Indonesia is the largest of the Lesser Sunda Islands?

12. What is the name given to the study of the composition and formation of rocks?

13. Which 1990 film starring Jack Nicholson was a belated follow-up to Chinatown ?

14. For which 1995 film was Sharon Stone a Best Actress Oscar nominee?

15. In Hindu mythology, what is the food of the gods that bestows immortality?

ANSWERS 1. Asphodel 2. Blue Sky 3. Javed Miandad 4. Ridley Scott 5. P.W. Botha 6. Bob Ferris 7. Hey, Joe 8. Dorothy L. Sayers 9. Erik Estrada 10. Shelley Winters 11. Timor 12. Petrology 13. The Two Jakes 14. Casino 15. Amrita.

ENTERTAINMENT

1. Who directed the 2000 film The Million Dollar Hotel?

2. Who wrote the play Over the Moon which played in the West End of London in 2001?

3. What was Jerry Hardin's character name in the television series The X-Files?

4. What are the names of the rival gangs in the 1961 film West Side Story?

5. Who plays groupie Penny Lane in the 2000 film Almost Famous?

6. What was Derek Fowlds's character name in the comedy series Yes, Minister?

7. Who is the star of the television comedy show Trigger Happy TV?

8. Which rock star produced the 2001 film Enigma?

9. Who directed the 1998 film The Horse Whisperer?

10. What is the first name of Zoolander in a 2001 film?

11. Who played Nev in the 1994 television drama series Common as Muck?

12. Who played the Duke of Alençon in the television drama series Elizabeth R?

13. Which musician composed the soundtrack to the 2000 film American Psycho?

14. Who is the male lead in the 2001 film Vertical Limit?

15. Who directed the 1931 film The Champ?

ANSWERS 1. Wim Wenders 2. Ken Ludwig 3. Deep Throat 4. The Jets and the Sharks 5. Kate Hudson 6. Bernard Woolley 7. Dom Joly 8. Mick Jagger 9. Robert Redford 10. Derek 11. Edward Woodward 12. Michael Williams 13. John Cale 14. Chris O'Donnell 15. King Vidor.

SPORT

1. Which driver was a member of the R.A.C. Rally-winning team from 1960-2?

2. Which jockey was 1977 Sports Illustrated Sportsman of the Year?

3. At which Olympic sport have Louis Debray and Yevgeny Petrov been champions?

4. Who did rugby league side Wigan play on 5th September 1999 in the last game at Central Park?

5. Which Cuban was 1974 world amateur flyweight boxing champion?

6. Who did Peter Nicol beat in the quarter-finals of the Flanders Open squash tournament in 2000?

7. How many times did Eddy Merckx win the Liége-Bastogne-Liége cycle race?

8. How many cricket Tests did Dermot Reeve play for England?

9. Which horse was Jem Robinson's last winning mount in the 2000 Guineas?

10. How many times did Will Carling lead England in Tests at rugby union?

11. At what sport was Dave Thorpe a world champion in 1989?

12. What sport do Newcastle Riverkings play?

13. Which football club has won the Scottish First Division/Premier Division the most times?

14. What nationality was 1972 women's European water-skiing champion Willi Stahle?

15. Who won the 1996 London women's marathon?

ANSWERS 1. Erik Carlsson 2. Steve Cauthen 3. Shooting 4. St. Helens 5. Douglas Rodriguez 6. David Evans 7. Five 8. Three 9. Flatcatcher 10. 59 11. Moto-cross 12. Ice hockey 13. Rangers 14. Dutch 15. Liz McColgan.

POP MUSIC

1. Douglas Vipond was the drummer with which late 1980s Scottish band?

2. Which member of Morphine died in July 1999?

3. Which Tom Waits song features at the start of the film Down By Law?

4. Which rapper recorded the 1995 album Mr. Smith?

5. Which song by The Young Rascals did Birth cover on the E.P. Sweet Idol?

6. Which singer joined the group Living Colour in 1985?

7. How old was singer Doug Sahm when he died in 1999?

8. Which duo had a 2000 Top 10 single with You Only Tell Me You Love Me When...?

9. Who played electric organ on Bob Dylan's single Like A Rolling Stone?

10. Who had a Top 10 single in 1979 with Born to Be Alive?

11. Who had a Christmas 1999 hit with Say You'll Be Mine/Better the Devil...?

12. What was Transvision Vamp's last Top 20 hit, in August 1989?

13. What were Traffic's three Top 10 hit singles in 1967?

14. Which song made famous by Johnny Cash did Blondie perform in the film Roadie?

15. Which studio album by Warren Zeavon features Dirty Little Religion and Porcelain Monkey?

ANSWERS 1. Deacon Blue 2. Mark Sandman 3. Jockey Full of Bourbon 4. LL Cool J 5. Groovin' 6. Corey Glover 7. 58 8. Pet Shop Boys 9. Al Kooper 10. Patrick Hernandez 11. Steps 12. Landslide of Love 13. Paper Sun, Hole in My Shoe & Here We Go Round the Mulberry Bush 14. Ring of Fire 15. Life'll Kill Ya.

WORDS

1. The word honcho, meaning boss, derives from which language?

2. What is an opsimath?

3. What would you do in Papua New Guinea with a toea?

4. In which game would you employ a zwischenzug?

5. What does the phrase foie gras mean, as in pâté de foie gras?

6. What is the plural of monsieur?

7. What in film-making is a foley?

8. What in Ireland is a loy?

9. If you perform hongi in New Zealand, how do you greet someone?

10. For what sporting activity would you wear salopettes?

11. Where does an Orcadian live?

12. What would you keep in a frail?

13. What is the resin olibanum better known as?

14. Who might use a roband?

15. The branch of science called odontology refers to which part of the body?

GENERAL KNOWLEDGE

1. In which year was English guitarist and lutenist Julian Bream born?

2. What is the U.S. name for the card game patience?

3. Who was the 37th president of the U.S.?

4. Who is the American composer of the opera Akhnaten?

5. With which Olympic field event is Sergey Bubka associated?

6. Who wrote the 1983 novel Ancient Evenings?

7. Which 1876 novel by Mark Twain features the character Becky Thatcher?

8. Which actor's television roles included the lead in the 1979 series Charles Endell Esquire?

9. Which Indian Test cricketer scored 121 against England in Bombay in the 1972-73 season?

10. What is the third sign of the zodiac?

11. Who wrote the 1975 novel The Shepherd?

12. Which rider was the 1994 and 1996 winner of the Badminton Horse Trials?

13. Which American singer released the 1975 album Desire?

14. Who wrote the 1989 novel A Prayer for Owen Meany?

15. Which unit of weight is equal to 24 grains in the Troy system?

ENTERTAINMENT

1. Who directed the 1998 film American History X?

2. Who starred as Father Charlie in the 1982 sitcom?

3. Which pop star hosted the TV show Victoria's Secrets in 2000?

4. In which European capital city is the 1988 film American Roulette set?

5. Who plays Shula in Radio Four's The Archers?

6. Who created the 1970s science fiction show Survivors?

7. Which Oscar-winning actor starred in the 1980s U.S. sitcom Bosom Buddies?

8. In which year did Survival begin on British television?

9. Who played Cory Matthews in the U.S. sitcom Boy Meets World?

10. Who directed the 1989 comedy film The Tall Guy?

11. Who directed the 1988 film A Handful of Dust?

12. Who produced the 1993 fly-on-the-wall programme Sylvania Waters?

13. Who starred in, and directed, the 1974 film The Savage is Loose?

14. Which actress played Angelica in the ITV adventure series Sword of Freedom?

15. Who directed the 1995 film Apollo 13?

ANSWERS 1. Tony Kaye 2. Lionel Jeffries 3. Victoria Beckham 4. London 5. Judy Bennett 6. Terry Nation 7. Tom Hanks 8. 1961 9. Ben Savage 10. Mel Smith 11. Charles Sturridge 12. Paul Watson 13. George C. Scott 14. Adrienne Corri 15. Ron Howard.

THE PUB QUIZ BOOK

SPORT

1. Who was men's overall water-skiing world champion in 1957?

2. What nationality is cyclist Barbara Heeb?

3. In which year was sprinter Andre Cason born?

4. In which year was the jockey club formed in England?

5. For which Test cricket side have Damien Martyn and Matthew Hayden both played?

6. How many Grand Prix wins did motorcyclist Mike Hailwood achieve in total?

7. Who was named female athlete of 1999 by the I.A.A.F.?

8. Who scored West Bromwich Albion's goal in their 1970 League Cup Final defeat?

9. In which year was athlete Dennis Mitchell born?

10. What nationality is athlete Masako Chiba?

11. Which country does Obadele Thompson run for?

12. Which American rode Northern Trick to victory in the 1983 Prix de Diane Hermès?

13. In which year was athlete Bruny Surin born?

14. For which university did Boris Rankov row in the University Boat Race from 1978-83?

15. In cricket, who was Man of the Match in the 1998 NatWest Final for Lancashire?

ANSWERS 1. Joe Cash 2. Swiss 3. 1969 4. 1750 5. Australia 6. 76 7. Gabriela Szabo 8. Jeff Astle 9. 1966 10. Japanese 11. Barbados 12. Cash Asmussen 13. 1967 14. Oxford 15. Ian Austin.

POP MUSIC

1. On which label did Alanis Morissette record the 1995 album Jagged Little Pill?

2. Which of his own compositions was on the B-side of Bryan Ferry's single Let's Stick Together?

3. Which songwriter recorded the album Pink Moon?

4. Which pair wrote the Echo and the Bunnymen song Read it in Books?

5. Simon Mills and Nail comprise which duo?

6. Nick Hallam and Rob Birch comprise which rock/rap collective?

7. Who was the lead singer of the group The Left Banke?

8. Which comedian was responsible for the reformation of the group The Cult in 2000?

9. Who is the eldest member of the group Travis?

10. Which Rolling Stones song did Eddie and the Hot Rods cover on their Live at the Marquee E.P.?

11. On which label did the Eurythmics record their album Peace?

12. Which unlikely duo sang the song Where the Wild Roses Grow at Nick Cave's Meltdown Festival in 1999?

13. Who featured on the 1990 Top 10 single Got to Have Your Love by Mantronix?

14. Bid was a singer in which London-based group, formed in the late 1970s?

15. What were the forenames of the Louvin Brothers?

ANSWERS 1. Maverick 2. Sea Breezes 3. Nick Drake 4. Ian McCulloch and Julian Cope 5. Bent 6. Stereo MC's 7. Steve Martin 8. Vic Reeves 9. Neil Primrose 10. Satisfaction 11. RCA 12. Kylie Minogue and Sir Les Patterson 13. Wondress 14. The Monochrome Set 15. Ira and Charlie.

SCIENCE

1. Who won the 1970 Nobel prize in chemistry?

2. In which year did Pierre Curie die?

3. In which European country was the chemist George de Hevesy born?

4. Which chemist was Vice-Chancellor at Graz University from 1920-1?

5. Which of these is not a prime number - 11, 12 or 13?

6. Which American won the 1923 Nobel prize in physics?

7. Os is the symbol of which chemical element?

8. Who won the 1913 Nobel prize in chemistry?

9. Of what is rheology the scientific study?

10. Which Nobel prize-winning physicist was born in Tonbridge, Kent in 1903?

11. Who discovered carborundum in 1891?

12. At what temperature in degrees centigrade does tin boil?

13. Ronald Ross was awarded the 1902 Nobel prize in medicine for his work on which disease?

14. Which has the higher melting point - copper or iron?

15. Which scientist invented the word anaphylaxis to describe extreme sensitivity to the injection of a protein following a previous injection?

ANSWERS 1. Luis F. Leloir 2. 1906 3. Hungary 4. Fritz Pregl 5. 12 6. Robert Andrews Millikan 7. Osmium 8. Alfred Werner 9. The flow of matter 10. Cecil Frank Powell 11. Henri Moissan 12. 2690 13. Malaria 14. Iron 15. Charles Richet.

GENERAL KNOWLEDGE

1. Which actor's television roles included Chris Hawthorne in the comedy The Cuckoo Waltz?

2. Who won a Best Supporting Actor Oscar for the film The Fugitive?

3. Who wrote the 1981 novel A Good Man in Africa?

4. Which British aircraft designer was chairman of the Hawker Siddeley Group from 1935-63?

5. Who wrote the 1936 novel A Gun for Sale?

6. Who was the author of the 1904 volume Ghost Stories of an Antiquary?

7. Which politician was elected M.P. for Edinburgh East and Musselburgh in 1997?

8. Which poisonous marsh plant is also called water hemlock?

9. What is the name of the Polish river upon which Poznan stands?

10. Which English ballerina was born Lilian Alicia Marks?

11. Who was the 1988 U.S. Open men's singles tennis champion?

12. Which poet's works included 1889's Days and Nights?

13. Who was the 26th president of the U.S.?

14. Who wrote the 1894 play Little Eyolf?

15. Which England Test bowler took a hat-trick against the West Indies at Leeds in 1957?

ANSWERS 1. David Roper 2. Tommy Lee Jones 3. William Boyd 4. Sir Thomas Sopwith 5. Graham Greene 6. M.R. James 7. Gavin Strang 8. Cowbane 9. Warta 10. Alicia Markova 11. Mats Wilander 12. A.W. Symons 13. Theodore Roosevelt 14. Henrik Ibsen 15. P.J. Loader.

ENTERTAINMENT

1. The 1960 film All the Fine Young Cannibals was inspired by the life of which jazz musician?

2. Which Hollywood actress played Max in the 1990 sitcom Freddie and Max?

3. Which actor plays a sleazy tabloid publisher in the 1997 film L.A. Confidential?

4. Rowland Rivron and Simon Brint comprised which musical comedy act?

5. Who plays the vet James Herriot in the 1979 film All Things Bright and Beautiful?

6. Who starred as television show host Ben Black in the 1999 television drama Sex 'N' Death?

7. Who directed the 1981 film Excalibur?

8. Who appears as sports writer Ring Lardner in the 1988 film Eight Men Out?

9. Who directed the 1983 film Local Hero?

10. Who plays Roz Doyle in the sitcom Frasier?

11. Which comedy duo starred in the 1937 film All Over Town?

12. What is Dawn French's character's name in the sitcom The Vicar of Dibley?

13. What is Fred McMurray's profession in the 1947 film The Egg and I?

14. Which actor plays a Spanish police chief in the 1984 film Target Eagle?

15. What is Rock Hudson's job in the 1955 film All That Heaven Allows?

SPORT

1. In which sport do Simon Archer and Joanne Goode play as a doubles team?

2. Who was men's figure skating champion at the 1998 Olympics?

3. In which year did wicket-keeper Keith Brown make his county debut for Middlesex?

4. Who scored seven field goals for Minnesota against the Los Angeles Rams in their American football game in November 1989?

5. Who partnered Bob Hewitt to victory in the 1979 U.S. Open mixed doubles tennis championship?

6. Over what distance in yards is a drag race?

7. In which year did U.S. tennis player Hazel Hotchkiss die?

8. Which American won the 1980 single-handed transatlantic yacht race?

9. In which year did cricketer Jason Brown make his county debut for Northamptonshire?

10. Ulderico Sergo was the 1936 Olympic bantamweight champion. Which country did he represent?

11. In which year did cricketer Douglas Brown make his county debut for Warwickshire?

12. Which Italian won the 1925 Tour de France?

13. At what sport have Janelle Kirkley, Sylvie Hulsemann and Renate Hansluvka been world champions?

14. Tudor Minstrel won the 1947 2000 Guineas. Who was the rider?

15. What nationality is tennis player Francisco Clavet?

POP MUSIC

1. Which female singer was formerly a member of the bands Kukl and Tappi Tikarrass?

2. Which group recorded the 1982 album Destiny Street?

3. Which was the only No. 1 single by the pop group Madness?

4. In which year did De La Soul chart with the single Me, Myself and I?

5. What is the title of the debut album by the group The Strokes?

6. In which Scottish town did the group The Cocteau Twins originate?

7. Which group recorded the 2001 album Let It Come Down?a

8. Which group released the 1978 E.P. Damaged Goods?

9. Which Leeds-based group recorded the 2000 album Signal Hill?

10. Which group recorded the 2001 studio album Wonderland?

11. What was the title of Macy Gray's 2001 album release?

12. In which year did Japan release the single Ghosts?

13. Which singer-songwriter recorded the 2000 album Crossing Muddy Waters?

14. Which member of the Spice Girls recorded the 2000 album Hot?

15. Which group recorded the 2000 album Life in Transition?

PEOPLE

1. Which actress wrote the memoir White Cargo?

2. Which former politician wrote the autobiography Pride and Perjury?

3. What is the middle name of actress Joan Collins?

4. On what day of 1997 did the funeral of Diana, Princess of Wales, take place?

5. With which card game is Ely Culbertson associated?

6. Who was U.S. secretary of state from 1949-53?

7. Which writer was born Leslie Charles Bowyer Yin?

8. In which year was composer Richard Rodney Bennett born?

9. Little Girl Lost is a biography of which current Hollywood actress?

10. Which blues guitarist was born in Itta Bena, Mississippi in 1925?

11. In which year did Christopher Reeve become paralysed from the neck down following an accident?

12. Which singer has been given exclusive use of the island Ellidaey by the Iceland government?

13. Which actor appeared in TV's Ally McBeal as attorney Larry Paul after serving time in prison?

14. In which country was landscape painter John La Farge born in 1835?

15. How was actress Grace Kelly killed?

SPORT

1. Which snooker player was the World Championship runner-up from 1990-94?

2. Which West Indian scored centuries in both innings of his debut versus New Zealand in 1972?

3. Which country lost 29-9 to New Zealand in the final of the 1987 rugby union World Cup?

4. How many times did golfer Severiano Ballesteros win the British Open?

5. What is the meaning of the word karate?

6. Who won the all-Welsh final at snooker's 2000 World Championship?

7. In which year did Newcastle United sign Alan Shearer?

8. What is the nickname of the darts player Ted Hankey?

9. Who did Mohammed Ali beat in May 1975 to retain his world heavyweight crown?

10. Catch-as-catch-can is a style of which sport?

11. Which German footballer set a new world record when he won his 144th international cap in February 2000?

12. Which female tennis player was singles champion at the 1976 French Open?

13. Which bowler took most the wickets for England in the 2000 Test series against Pakistan?

14. From which club did Aston Villa sign Juan Pablo Angel?

15. Which country did Abdelatif Benazzi represent at the 1999 rugby union World Cup?

ANSWERS: 1 Jimmy White, 2 Lawrence Rowe, 3 France, 4 Three, 5 Empty hand, 6 Mark Williams, 7 1996, 8 The Count, 9 Ron Lyle, 10 Wrestling, 11 Lothar Matthäus, 12 Sue Barker, 13 Ashley Giles, 14 River Plate, 15 France.

? GENERAL KNOWLEDGE ?

1. What is Princess Anne's second name of four?

2. With which branch of biological science was Jules Bordet associated?

3. Who recorded the 2002 album Harry's Bar?

4. Who wrote the 1829 novel Frank Mildmay?

5. In which year in the 1st century did emperor Nero die?

6. Which American painter's works include the 1931 oil The Midnight Ride of Paul Revere?

7. Why is an American military policeman known as a snow-drop?

8. On which river is the Welsh town of St. Asaph?

9. What was the name of the supermarket in the 1980s sit-com Slinger's Day?

10. In which play by Shakespeare does the character Pandarus appear?

11. In which game might you use a bonce?

12. St. Boniface is a suburb of which Canadian city?

13. What is a bullace - a type of bird or tree?

14. Of what quantity is the ampere the SI unit?

15. Which is further east - Monte Carlo or St. Tropez?

ANSWERS: 1 Elizabeth, 2 Immunology, 3 Gordon Haskell, 4 Frederick Marryat, 5 68, 6 Grant Wood, 7 From the colour of their white helmets, 8 Clwyd, 9 Supafare, 10 Troilus and Cressida, 11 Marbles, 12 Winnipeg, 13 Tree, 14 Electric current, 15 Monte Carlo.

? **GENERAL KNOWLEDGE** ?

1. In which country was the chemist Robert Burns Woodward born?

2. What in British rhyming slang is a Peckham rye?

3. On which river is the French town of St. Amand?

4. In which year did Michael Jackson have a No. 1 hit with the single Billie Jean?

5. Who wrote the 1954 novel Sayonara?

6. What type of flower is a coquelicot?

7. In which European country is the town of Gelsenkirchen?

8. What was the nationality of scientist Schack August Steenberg Krogh?

9. In which Asian country is the city of Suwon?

10. Who presents the television quiz show They Think It's All Over?

11. In which novel by Charles Dickens does the character Steerforth appear?

12. What in the 1930s did the services' slang abbreviation OAO mean?

13. Which surrealist artist's works include 1941's Honey is Sweeter Than Blood?

14. What was the name of the wife of King Richard I of England?

15. Who was Queen of Scotland from 1286-1290?

ANSWERS: 1 United States, 2 Tie, 3 Cher, 4 1983, 5 James A. Michener, 6 Poppy, 7 Germany, 8 Danish, 9 South Korea, 10 Nick Hancock, 11 David Copperfield, 12 Sweetheart (one and only), 13 Salvador Dali, 14 Berengaria, 15 Margaret.

GENERAL KNOWLEDGE

1. Which painter and poet's watercolours include Job Confessing his Presumption to God who Answers from the Whirlwind?

2. Which country administers the Canary Islands?

3. What food in military slang is rooty?

4. Who did Richard Nixon defeat in the 1972 presidential election?

5. Which member of the Beach Boys recorded the 1977 solo album Going Public?

6. Who wrote the 1852 novel Henry Esmond?

7. Which musical instrument is known as a slush pump?

8. Which explorer won the 1922 Nobel peace prize?

9. Which Scot won the 1904 Nobel Prize in chemistry?

10. The island Davaar is in the mouth of which Scottish loch?

11. Who plays Dot in the drama series EastEnders?

12. Which physicist published the 1913 work Les Atomes?

13. Who wrote the 1832 novel Eugene Aram?

14. What are you in New Zealand if you are boohai?

15. In which English county is the village of Wymeswold?

ANSWRS: 1 William Blake, 2 Spain, 3 Bread, 4 George McGovern, 5 Bruce Johnston, 6 William Thackeray, 7 Trombone, 8 Fridtjof Nansen, 9 Sir William Ramsey, 10 Campbeltown Loch, 11 June Brown, 12 Jean Baptiste Perrin, 13 Edward Bulwer-Lytton, 14 Lost, 15 Leicestershire.

ENTERTAINMENT

1. Which cult 1987 film, set in the sixties and starring Richard E. Grant, was re-released in 1996?

2. Which pioneering singer/songwriter was backed by the Crickets?

3. What was the name of Dick Dastardly's canine companion in the cartoon series Wacky Races?

4. What was the title of the debut album by The Bluetones?

5. Which Monty Python star played Robin Hood in the 1981 film Time Bandits?

6. Which German model sang on the Velvet Underground's first album?

7. Who starred as the father/grandfather in the 1995 film Father of the Bride Part II?

8. Which actress appeared as a landlady both in the sitcom Goodnight Sweetheart and in the drama series Ballykissangel?

9. With which instrument was the jazz musician Buddy Rich associated?

10. Which Emmerdale character was played by Tonicha Jeronimo?

11. Which actress played Lizzie Kavanagh in Kavanagh QC?

12. Which Disney film won a special Academy Award in 1938 for significant screen innovation?

13. What was the title of Chris Evans's live Friday night TV show?

14. Who sang the lead vocal on the Crusaders' 1979 U.K. top ten hit single Streetlife?

15. Which Claude Lelouch cinematic epic won a Golden Globe award in 1996 for Best Foreign Film?

ANSWERS: 1 Withnail and I, 1 Buddy Holly, 3 Muttley, 4 Expecting to Fly, 5 John Cleese, 6 Nico, 7 Steve Martin, 8 Dervla Kirwan, 9 The drums, 10 Linda Glover, 11 Lisa Harrow, 12 Snow White and the Seven Dwarfs, 13 TFI Friday, 14 Randy Crawford, 15 Les Miserables.

GENERAL KNOWLEDGE

1. Of what is otorhinolaryngology the scientific study?

2. Which author penned the short story collection The Angel on the Roof?

3. In which year did Napoleon leave Elba?

4. In which country might you dance a czardas?

5. Which is further east - Cannes or Nice?

6. Which group recorded the 2001 album How I Long To Feel That Summer In My Heart?

7. In which novel by Thomas Hardy does the character Thomasin Yeobright appear?

8. Why might you avoid a euripus if you were a sailor?

9. On which river is the town of Saint-Hyacinthe in Canada?

10. Which Conservative politician was involved in a scandal with Monica Coghlan in 1986?

11. Which artist's works include 1920's The Skat Players?

12. At what temperature in degrees centigrade does nickel boil?

13. In which European country are the provinces of Evora and Beja?

14. Who directed the 2000 film Loser?

15. What is proustite - a type of mineral or a condition of unwillingness to change ones mind?

ANSWERS: 1 Diseases of the ear, nose and throat, 2 Russell Banks, 3 1815, 4 Hungary, 5 Nice, 6 Gorky's Zygotic Mynci, 7 The Return of the Native, 8 It's a strait with strong currents, 9 Yamaska, 10 Jeffrey Archer, 11 Otto Dix, 12 3110, 13 Portugal, 14 Amy Heckerling, 15 Mineral.

GENERAL KNOWLEDGE

1. In which Asian country is the city of Gwangju?

2. What type of creature might have a banged tail?

3. How did Louis XVI of France die in 1793?

4. Who penned the 2000 book Decisive Measures?

5. In which European country was the winner of the 1991 Nobel prize in physics P.G. de Gennes born?

6. What would you do with entremets?

7. In which European country is the Furka Pass?

8. Which guitarist recorded the album Money and Cigarettes?

9. Who wrote the 1967 novel No Laughing Matter?

10. In which country was the Nobel prize-winning scientist Georg von Bekesy born?

11. How did the boxer Rocky Marciano die?

12. Who directed the 1959 film Rio Bravo?

13. What does the Latin phrase ut supra mean?

14. In which county is Calke Abbey?

15. In which novel by Charles Dickens does the character Augustus Snodgrass appear?

ANSWERS: 1 South Korea, 2 A horse, 3 He was beheaded, 4 John Nichol, 5 France, 6 Eat it, it's a dessert, 7 Switzerland, 8 Eric Clapton, 9 Angus Wilson, 10 Hungary, 11 In an air crash, 12 Howard Hawks, 13 As above, 14 Derbyshire, 15 Pickwick Papers.

GENERAL KNOWLEDGE

1. Which part of the body is known in slang as a potato trap?

2. In which European country is the seaport of Falconara Marittima?

3. Who authored the memoir This Bloody Mary is the Last Thing I Own?

4. In which year was the Septennial Act?

5. Which has the higher melting point - tin or zinc?

6. On which Hawaiian island is Pearl Harbor?

7. Which male singer recorded the 1985 top 30 single Stories of Johnny?

8. Who wrote the 1970 novel A Fairly Honourable Defeat?

9. In which city was the mime Marcel Marceau born?

10. Mince pies is a slang term for which parts of the body?

11. In which English county is Rendlesham Forest?

12. Who wrote the 1819 novel The Bride of Lammermoor?

13. What is the cube root of the number 1?

14. For what is the word payt an abbreviation?

15. Who was the male presenter on the final series of the game show You Bet! in 1996?

ENTERTAINMENT

1. Which 2000 film starred Clint Eastwood, Tommy Lee Jones, James Garner and Donald Sutherland as former airmen pulled out of retirement by NASA?

2. Which eighties TV programme was the first British police series to have an ethnic hero, played by David Yip?

3. Which Spice Girl had a 2000 U.K. top five hit with Tell Me?

4. Which actor starred as Sylvester Stallone's prison warden in the 1989 film Lock Up?

5. Who wrote the novel upon which the BBC1 drama Other People's Children was based?

6. Which group had a 1968 U.K. number one with Blackberry Way?

7. Which film-making brothers were behind the 2000 movie Me, Myself & Irene?

8. Which BBC1 fly-on-the-wall series following environmental health officers was narrated by John Peel?

9. Who had a U.K. number one hit in 1979 with We Don't Talk Anymore?

10. Which sex symbol actress of the fifties and sixties was born Vera Jayne Palmer in 1933?

11. Which actress played an orphaned teenage horse rider in the 1978 film International Velvet?

12. Which ITV show exposed real-life cowboy builders by using hidden cameras?

13. Which U.S. vocalist duetted with Joe Cocker on the 1983 U.K. top ten single Up Where We Belong?

14. Which 2000 film starred Edward Norton as a priest and Ben Stiller as a rabbi?

15. Who was Gary's original flatmate, played by Harry Enfield, in the sitcom Men Behaving Badly?

ANSWERS: 1 Space Cowboys, 2 The Chinese Detective, 3 Melanie B, 4 Donald Sutherland, 5 Joanna Trollope, 6 Move, 7 The Farrelly Brothers, 8 A Life of Grime, 9 Cliff Richard, 10 Jayne Mansfield, 11 Tatum O'Neal, 12 House of Horrors, 13 Jennifer Warnes, 14 Keeping the Faith, 15 Dermot.

GENERAL KNOWLEDGE

1. What was the name by which Harold I of Denmark was known?

2. What is the capital of France?

3. In which discipline did the scientist Earl W. Sutherland, Jr. receive a Nobel prize in 1971?

4. On which river is the French town of St. Die?

5. Who authored the 2001 novel The Same Sea?

6. If something is belemnoid, what is it shaped like?

7. Which female singer had a 1999 Top Twenty single with the song Turn It Around?

8. On which river is the Norfolk market town of Diss?

9. Who was Israeli minister for Foreign Affairs from 1956-66?

10. Which painter's works include the 1939 oil painting Mandragora?

11. Po is the symbol of which chemical element?

12. Which country administers the Galapagos Islands?

13. Who directed the 1992 film Singles?

14. What nationality was the painter José Clemente Orozco?

15. The adjective haptic refers to which of the five senses?

ANSWERS: 1 Harold Bluetooth, 2 Paris, 3 Medicine, 4 Meurthe, 5 Amos Oz, 6 A dart, 7 Alena, 8 Waveney, 9 Golda Meir, 10 Diego Rivera, 11 Polonium, 12 Ecuador, 13 Cameron Crowe, 14 Mexican, 15 Touch.

GENERAL KNOWLEDGE

1. In which Asian country is the city of Niigata?

2. What animal is also known as a foumart?

3. Who was King of Scotland from 1292-1296?

4. Who played Colonel Krieger in the 1980s drama series Wish Me Luck?

5. Who wrote the 1929 play Symphony in Two Flats?

6. What type of performer is an ecdysiast?

7. Who became Secretary of State for Scotland in May 1997?

8. Which group recorded the 2000 album Howdy!?

9. Which African country lies immediately west of Botswana?

10. In which novel by Charles Dickens does the character Walter Gay appear?

11. What quality do cattle which are muley have?

12. Who won the 1984 Nobel prize in chemistry?

13. Which island is larger - Java or Hispaniola?

14. Who wrote the children's book For Maritsa, with Love?

15. In which country was the Nobel prize-winning chemist Dorothy Crowfoot born?

GENERAL KNOWLEDGE

1. Which drug is known in the U.S. as duji?

2. On which Hawaiian island is Mount Tantalus?

3. Which American artist's works include 1904's Portrait of J. Carroll Beckwith?

4. Which Bee Gees song do Chumbawamba cover on the 2000 album WYSIWYG?

5. In which year was the first Bishops' War?

6. Of what is neurology the scientific study?

7. Who wrote the 1822 novel Maid Marian?

8. In which African country is the seaport of Gabès?

9. Who was the Princess Royal before the current holder of the title, Anne?

10. Jimmy is nautical slang for which crew member?

11. Who starred as the boxer Salamo in the 1989 film Triumph of the Spirit?

12. Moheli and Mayotte belong to which island group?

13. What are the constituent elements of the alloy solder?

14. In which sport might you perform a septime?

15. Who authored the 1981 novella July's People?

SPORT

1. Which team won the Premiership title in May 2000 with a victory over Tottenham Hotspur?

2. Who scored 174 against Australia in the Centenary Test in 1977?

3. In which city will the 2004 Olympic Games be staged?

4. Which team lost to Celtic in the final of the 1967 European Cup?

5. Which horse did Bob Champion ride to win the Grand National in 1981?

6. Who scored the winning goal for Arsenal in the 1979 F.A. Cup Final?

7. Which team lost to Aston Villa in the final of the European Cup in 1982?

8. Which cyclist won the Tour de France from 1991-1995?

9. With which sport are Sean Long and Chris Joynt associated?

10. In which country was tennis star Monica Seles born?

11. Which qualifier reached the men's singles semi-finals at Wimbledon in 2000?

12. Which horse won the Grand National in 1975?

13. In which event did Daley Thompson win two Olympic gold medals?

14. What is the value of the black ball in snooker?

15. In which three events did U.S. athlete Marion Jones strike gold at the Sydney Olympics?

ANSWERS: 1 Manchester United, 2 Derek Randall, 3 Athens, 4 Inter Milan, 5 Aldaniti, 6 Alan Sunderland, 7 Bayern Munich, 8 Miguel Indurain, 9 Rugby league, 10 Yugoslavia, 11 Vladimir Voltchkov, 12 L'Escargot, 13 Decathlon, 14 7, 15 100m, 200m & 4 x 400m relay.

GENERAL KNOWLEDGE

1. Who wrote the 1875 novel The Way We Live Now?

2. Which actor played the male lead in the 1949 film They Live By Night?

3. In which European country was the Nobel prize-winning chemist Wilhelm Ostwald born?

4. In which Australian state is Lake Disappointment?

5. Which of the Beatles is following the other three across a zebra crossing on the album cover for Abbey Road?

6. In which English county is the seaside resort of Budleigh Salterton?

7. What in Australian slang is a jonnop?

8. Which novel won the 1994 Whitbread Book of the Year award?

9. Which countries fought in the Battle of Rocroi in 1643?

10. For what is stbd an abbreviation?

11. Approximately how long is the Hadrian's Wall Path - 21 miles, 51 miles or 81 miles?

12. Which portrait painter's works included The Lomellini Family of the 1620s?

13. Which creature's name derives from the Greek phrase 'fearful lizard'?

14. Which soldier wrote the 1961 book The Path to Leadership?

15. Who discovered heavy hydrogen?

GENERAL KNOWLEDGE

1. To what former British coin does the slang term tanner refer?

2. Who wrote the novel Henry and Cato?

3. Which major English city houses the Church of St. Martin-in-the-Bull-Ring?

4. Which group's second album is entitled La Peste?

5. Who won the 1904 Nobel prize in medicine?

6. In which city was the American artist Jasper Johns born?

7. The town of Cuttack is in which Asian country?

8. What was the third and last film made by the director Michael Reeves?

9. If you were echinate what would you be covered with?

10. In which year did Newcastle upon Tyne become a city?

11. Which poet's works include 1667's Annus Mirabilis?

12. Who became assistant to Max Planck at the Institute for Theoretical Physics at Berlin in 1905?

13. In which city was the publisher Rupert Murdoch born?

14. In which country is the Ormeli waterfall?

15. What is a lea a poetic term for?

ANSWERS: 1 Sixpence, 2 Iris Murdoch, 3 Birmingham, 4 Alabama 3, 5 Ivan Pavlov, 6 Augusta, Georgia, 7 India, 8 Witchfinder General, 9 Bristles or spines, 10 1882, 11 John Dryden, 12 Max von Laue, 13 Melbourne, Australia, 14 Norway, 15 Meadow or field.

GENERAL KNOWLEDGE

1. Who plays comic-book expert Elijah Price in the 2000 film Unbreakable?

2. Is a brach a male or female hunting hound?

3. On which island was the scientist Willem Einthoven born?

4. Who authored the 2001 novel Outlaws?

5. In which South American country is the port of Encarnacion?

6. From what phrase was the 1980s term yuppie originally derived?

7. In which year was James Callaghan made a life peer?

8. Which group recorded the 2000 album Painting It Red?

9. Which American artist's works include the 1931 oil Red, White, and Blue?

10. In which African country is the town of Nelspruit?

11. At what temperature in degrees centigrade does magnesium boil?

12. In which year did William of Orange land in England?

13. Who authored the novel The Girl at the Lion d'Or?

14. What type of dancer is a figurant?

15. In which Asian country is the city of Jeonju?

ENTERTAINMENT

1. Who played Nurse Betty in the 2000 film of that name?

2. Which former Chancellor of the Exchequer's daughter launched her own cookery series on Channel 4 in 2000?

3. Which girl group's 2000 debut album was entitled The Way It Is?

4. What was the name of David Hasselhoff's character in the TV series Baywatch?

5. Which actress played Jane Eyre in the 1971 film version of the story?

6. Which sitcom duo embarked on a tour of Australia in the 2000 series Men Down Under?

7. Which flamboyant singer reached the UK number one spot posthumously in 1993 with Living on My Own?

8. Who directed the 2000 film Snatch?

9. Which actor played Jim in the comedy series The Royle Family?

10. Who wrote the novels upon which the seventies films The Stud and The Bitch were based?

11. What was the title of the 1995 UK top five hit by the Nightcrawlers featuring John Reid?

12. Which actor played the title role in the 1973 film Hitler - The Last Ten Days?

13. Which US vocalist had a 1966 UK number one hit with These Boots Are Made For Walking?

14. Which 2000 film about a set of Siamese twins was written by and starred real-life twins Michael and Mark Polish?

15. In which eighties sitcom did Geoffrey Palmer star as Major Harry Kitchener Wellington Truscott?

GENERAL KNOWLEDGE

1. Who narrated the TV series The World At War?

2. Which countries are connected by the Khyber Pass?

3. Who plays the father in the film Meet The Parents?

4. Which communist movement ruled Cambodia from 1975 to 1979?

5. In which country is the port of Mocha, which gives its name to a type of coffee?

6. Which German composer wrote the opera König Hirsch?

7. Who was Sorry on TV for 43 episodes?

8. Which American puppeteer created The Muppets?

9. Which island of the Netherlands Antilles gives its name to a liqueur flavoured with orange peel?

10. In which film did Katharine Hepburn first co-star with Spencer Tracy?

11. Which English monarch was known as the Virgin Queen?

12. Who created The Saint?

13. Which country was the first visiting cricket side to beat Pakistan in a Test match in Karachi?

14. What nationality was former world heavyweight boxing champion Ingemar Johansson?

15. Which detective died in Agatha Christie's 1975 novel Curtain?

GENERAL KNOWLEDGE

1. In which sport was the father of Grace Kelly an Olympic gold medallist?

2. Which jazz group was formed by Milt Jackson, John Lewis, Kenny Clarke and Percy Heath in 1952?

3. Who was the first American racing driver to win the Formula 1 world championship?

4. Which American pair won golf's World Cup in 2000?

5. What is the smaller of the two main islands of New Zealand?

6. Which English-born writer wrote The American Way of Death?

7. In which film was the main character Benjamin Braddock?

8. By what name was Joseph Merrick known when he appeared in freak shows?

9. Which English prince was the father of Henry IV?

10. Which breed of dog is noted for its blue-black tongue?

11. Which English novelist wrote Goodbye Mr Chips and Random Harvest?

12. Which Irish author wrote The Ballroom of Romance?

13. Which U.S. actress starred in Anatomy of a Murder, Days of Wine and Roses and The Omen?

14. Who was voted BBC Sports Personality of the Year in 2000?

15. Which British administrator originated the penny postage system?

GENERAL KNOWLEDGE

1. In which film did Humphrey Bogart play Charlie Allnut?

2. In literature and drama, what name is given to an extended speech by one person?

3. By what name is Mendelssohn's Fourth Symphony known?

4. Which American rapper reached Number 1 in the singles charts with Stan?

5. Of which former Soviet state is Bishkek the capital?

6. Which Canadian novelist wrote What's Bred in the Bone?

7. Who was The Girl Who Can't Help It?

8. By what name is 16th-century astrologer Michel de Notredame better known?

9. By what name was jazz composer and pianist Ferdinand Joseph La Menthe known?

10. Which English poet wrote The Task and the hymn God Moves in a Mysterious Way?

11. Which Swiss tennis player is the daughter of former Czech tennis star Melanie Molitor?

12. Who wrote The Old Men at the Zoo and Anglo-Saxon Attitudes?

13. Which strait separates Anglesey from the Welsh mainland?

14. How many dalmatians are there in Disney's sequel to 101 Dalmatians?

15. What is the name of the alphabet used for writing Russian?

ANSWERS: 1 The African Queen, 2 Monologue, 3 Italian Symphony, 4 Eminem, 5 Kyrgyzstan, 6 Robertson Davies, 7 Jayne Mansfield, 8 Nostradamus, 9 Jelly Roll Morton, 10 William Cowper, 11 Martina Hingis, 12 Angus Wilson, 13 Menai Strait, 14 102, 15 Cyrillic alphabet.

ENTERTAINMENT

1. Which 2000 spoof horror film was directed and co-written by Keenan Ivory Wayans?

2. Which early nineties sitcom starred Penelope Keith as MP Jean Price?

3. What were the names of The Blues Brothers played by John Belushi and Dan Ackroyd in the 1980 film?

4. From which country are the guitar band Barenaked Ladies?

5. Which 1975 film starred James Caan and Robert Duvall as mercenaries who end up stalking each other?

6. Which ITV game show, presented by Cilla Black, challenged family members to complete certain tasks to win prizes?

7. Which Swedish duo had The Look in the UK top ten in 1989?

8. Which English actress starred opposite John Turturro in the 2000 film The Luzhin Defence?

9. Which 2000 BBC1 drama featured Judi Dench as a saxophone-playing pensioner?

10. What was the Who's first UK top ten hit, which entered the chart in 1965?

11. Which US boy band had a UK number one hit in 1989 with You Got It (The Right Stuff)?

12. Which was the first film of the National Lampoon's series to star Chevy Chase?

13. Which UK band had a 1967 UK top five hit with Itchycoo Park?

14. Which Oscar-winning actor played the title role in the 2000 film Titus?

15. Which comic actor's TV roles have included Trigger in Only Fools and Horses and Owen Newitt in The Vicar of Dibley?

GENERAL KNOWLEDGE

1. Which fictional diarist was created by Helen Fielding?

2. Which actor, whose films included The Sting and Jaws, wrote The Man in the Glass Booth?

3. What was the title of the BBC's controversial four-part drama about the 1916 Easter Rising?

4. Which American jazz pianist was known as Fatha?

5. What is the largest lake in Europe?

6. Which fish is also called a suckerfish?

7. What was the first name of Crocodile Dundee?

8. In which London borough is Heathrow Airport?

9. Which South African province was formerly known as Natal?

10. Which Nazi politician led the SS from 1929 and the Gestapo from 1936?

11. Which novel by Mary Norton first featured the Clock family?

12. Who played the lead in the film Life of Brian?

13. Which former England cricket captain died in 2000 at the age of 67?

14. What were Marilyn Monroe's real first names?

15. Which British racing driver won the Formula 1 world championship in 1962 and 1968?

ANSWERS: 1 Bridget Jones, 2 Robert Shaw, 3 Rebel Heart, 4 Earl Hines, 5 Lake Ladoga, 6 Remora, 7 Michael, 8 Hillingdon, 9 KwaZulu/Natal, 10 Heinrich Himmler, 11 The Borrowers, 12 Graham Chapman, 13 Lord (Colin) Cowdrey of Tonbridge, 14 Norma Jean, 15 Graham Hill.

? GENERAL KNOWLEDGE ?

1. Which musical has won the most Oscars?

2. Which English actress starred in film versions of Pygmalion and Major Barbara?

3. In Greek mythology, who was the husband of Helen of Troy?

4. Which country beat Australia to win the Davis Cup for the first time?

5. Of which U.S. state is Bismarck the capital?

6. Which American soul singer founded the Blue Notes?

7. Who wrote the novel The Magic Toyshop?

8. Which British dramatist wrote The Caretaker and The Birthday Party?

9. What is the brightest star in the constellation Leo?

10. Which Pakistan cricketer made his 100th Test appearance in 2000?

11. Which American actor starred in Cape Fear, Thunder Road and The Winds of War?

12. What is the first name of the fictional detective Miss Marple?

13. Which former England manager joined Middlesbrough as first-team coach in 2000?

14. In which country did reggae music originate?

15. Which holiday is observed on the first Monday in September in the U.S.?

GENERAL KNOWLEDGE

1. On which river does Chepstow stand?

2. Which member of the dog family is also called a prairie wolf?

3. Which American jazz trumpeter died in Spain in 1995?

4. In which city was the film Bullitt set?

5. What is the capital of Tanzania?

6. Which hand tool was used for threshing grain until the mid-19th century?

7. Which French revolutionary leader was murdered by Charlotte Corday?

8. Of what would a person suffering from hypertrichosis have an abnormal amount?

9. Which director made eight films based on the works of Edgar Allan Poe in the 1960s?

10. Which member of the Royal Family was elevated to the Order of the Thistle in 2000?

11. Which English novelist wrote Brave New World and Eyeless in Gaza?

12. Which film star was born Charles Carter?

13. Which dramatist wrote Major Barbara and Pygmalion?

14. In which building was the 2000 Miss World contest held?

15. Which town is West Bengal gives its name to a high-quality tea?

ANSWERS: 1 River Wye, 2 Coyote, 3 Don Cherry, 4 San Francisco, 5 Dodoma, 6 Flail, 7 Jean-Paul Marat, 8 Hair, 9 Roger Corman, 10 The Princess Royal, 11 Aldous Huxley, 12 Charlton Heston, 13 George Bernard Shaw, 14 The Millennium Dome, 15 Darjeeling.

SPORT

1. Which American tennis player won the men's singles title at the 2000 Australian Open?

2. Who beat the Brisbane Broncos 20-18 to win the rugby league World Club Challenge in January 2001?

3. Which British swimmer won the 200m breaststroke gold medal at the 1976 Olympics?

4. Which British boxer lost a world title fight to Roberto Duran in June 1972?

5. Which country won the cricket World Cup in 1987?

6. At which racecourse did jockeys Frankie Dettori and Ray Cochrane survive a plane crash in June 2000?

7. Mick the Miller is a famous name from which sport?

8. Which team lost in the final of the FA Cup in 1992?

9. Which golfer won the US Masters in 1995?

10. In which weight division did Robin Reid win bronze at the 1992 Olympics?

11. Which university won the 2000 Boat Race?

12. How many players make up a cricket team?

13. In which year was British showjumper Harvey Smith born?

14. What nationality is swimming sensation Ian Thorpe, who won three gold medals and one silver at the Sydney Olympics?

15. At which Olympics did Allan Wells win Olympic gold in the 100m?

ANSWERS: 1 Andre Agassi, 2 St Helens, 3 David Wilkie, 4 Ken Buchanan, 5 Australia, 6 Newmarket, 7 Greyhound racing, 8 Sunderland, 9 Ben Crenshaw, 10 Light-middleweight, 11 Oxford, 12 11, 13 1938, 14 Australian, 15 Moscow (1980).

GENERAL KNOWLEDGE

1. Which best-selling novelist wrote Going Home and Mixed Blessings?

2. Which courtier of Dionysius the Elder had to sit beneath a sword hanging by a single thread?

3. Who wrote and directed the film Boogie Nights?

4. Which European country was the first to legalise euthanasia?

5. For what form of fuel is LPG an abbreviation?

6. Which English poet wrote The Village and The Borough?

7. How many Rocky films have there been?

8. Which former Sunderland and England forward was known as the 'Clown Prince of Soccer'?

9. Who succeeded Yuri Andropov as leader of the Soviet Union in 1984?

10. Which award-winning French actress made her Hollywood debut in Heaven's Gate?

11. Which novel by Michael Ondaatje was adapted into an Oscar-winning film?

12. What was the name of the submarine in Voyage to the Bottom of the Sea?

13. Which pop superstar played a one-off concert at the Brixton Academy which was broadcast on the Internet in 2000?

14. What sort of puzzles originated as educational devices to teach geography?

15. Which actor first played James Bond in GoldenEye?

ANSWERS: 1 Danielle Steel, 2 Damocles, 3 Paul Thomas Anderson, 4 The Netherlands, 5 Liquefied petroleum gas, 6 George Crabbe, 7 Five, 8 Len Shackleton, 9 Konstantin Chernenko, 10 Isabelle Huppert, 11 The English Patient, 12 Seaview, 13 Madonna, 14 Jigsaw puzzles, 15 Pierce Brosnan.

GENERAL KNOWLEDGE

1. Which film star was known as Duke?

2. Which Anglo-Irish novelist wrote Good Behaviour and Time After Time?

3. Of which planet is Hyperion a satellite?

4. Which arts prize was won by German photographer Wolfgang Tillmans in 2000?

5. What were the first names of author GK Chesterton?

6. Which long-necked wading bird has crowned, whooping and sandhill varieties?

7. What was the first film to be directed by Danny DeVito?

8. Which country won the 2000 Rugby League World Cup?

9. Which Canadian-born actress and dancer married Al Jolson in 1928?

10. Which Italian poet wrote The Divine Comedy?

11. Which organisation controls horse racing and racehorse breeding in Great Britain?

12. Who provided the voices for the TV cartoon characters Roobarb and Custard?

13. Which French entertainer starred in the films Love in the Afternoon and Gigi?

14. Who became the world's most expensive defender when he joined Leeds United from West Ham United?

15. Which insect is commonly called a daddy longlegs?

ANSWERS: 1 John Wayne, 2 Molly Keane, 3 Saturn, 4 Turner Prize, 5 Gilbert Keith, 6 Crane, 7 Throw Momma From the Train, 8 Australia, 9 Ruby Keeler, 10 Dante Alighieri, 11 The Jockey Club, 12 Richard Briers, 13 Maurice Chevalier, 14 Rio Ferdinand, 15 Crane fly.

GENERAL KNOWLEDGE

1. Which TV family had a maid called Alice?

2. Who was head of Fighter Command during the Battle of Britain?

3. What is the second brightest star in the night sky?

4. Who scored the try that gave England victory over Australia at Twickenham in November 2000?

5. With which Italian motor company is the Agnelli family associated?

6. Which English poet was born in Cockermouth in 1770?

7. Which of the Monty Python team wrote Rutland Weekend Television?

8. Of which Canadian province is St John's the capital?

9. Which was the first of the Great Lakes to be seen by Europeans?

10. Which American actor starred in The Third Man and Under Capricorn?

11. Which English adventurer and courtier to Elizabeth I was executed in 1618?

12. Which British poet wrote Waving at Trains and The Stowaway?

13. Which actress starred in Dangerous Liaisons and Fatal Attraction?

14. Judith Keppel was the first person to win £1 million on which TV quiz show?

15. In which country did the rottweiler originate?

ENTERTAINMENT

1. Which Coen brothers film starred George Clooney as a thirties conman?

2. Which former Doctor Who played Professor Geoffrey Hoyt in the nineties drama series Medics?

3. Which legendary comic duo first appeared on screen together in a scene in the short film A Lucky Dog?

4. With which US singer did Westlife collaborate with on their UK number one hit, Against All Odds?

5. Which 1974 film set in South Africa starred Roger Moore as a mine foreman?

6. Which Channel 5 gameshow challenged ten contestants to escape from a prison in order to win a cash prize?

7. Which US vocalist had a 1959 UK number one hit with Dream Lover?

8. Which Pulp Fiction actor starred in the remake of the movie Shaft?

9. Who emerged as the winner of the first series of the Channel 4 gameshow phenomenon Big Brother?

10. Which British group had a 1984 UK top ten hit with Heaven Knows I'm Miserable Now?

11. Which Fatal Attraction actress starred in the 1991 film Meeting Venus as a lead soprano in the fictional Opera Europa?

12. Which former Casualty star played DC Mel Silver in the BBC1 thriller Waking the Dead?

13. Which eighties group had a 1984 UK top five hit with Doctor Doctor?

14. Who directed the 2000 rites-of-passage drama Liberty Heights?

15. Which sixties sitcom featured Carry On stars such as Hattie Jacques, Charles Hawtrey and Joan Sims?

ANSWERS: 1 O Brother, Where Art Thou?, 2 Tom Baker, 3 Laurel & Hardy, 4 Mariah Carey, 5 Gold, 6 Jailbreak, 7 Bobby Darin, 8 Samuel L. Jackson, 9 Craig Phillips, 10 The Smiths, 11 Glenn Close, 12 Claire Goose, 13 Thompson Twins, 14 Barry Levinson, 15 Our House.

GENERAL KNOWLEDGE

1. Who wrote the novel Roots: The Saga of an American Family?

2. By what collective name were tennis players Jean Borotra, Jacques Brugnon, Henri Cochet and René Lacoste known?

3. Which Turkish dish comprises thin layers of filo pastry containing nuts and honey?

4. In what year was there an unofficial truce on Christmas Day during World War I?

5. Which chemical element has the symbol B?

6. Who directed the films The Graduate and Who's Afraid of Virginia Woolf?

7. What was the name of the lion in the Chronicles of Narnia?

8. Which English novelist wrote The Middle Ground and The Needle's Eye?

9. How much did John Duthie win in the world's most lucrative poker tournament in 2000?

10. Which former Soviet leader was head of the KGB from 1967 to 1982?

11. Kurt Cobain was the lead singer with which grunge rock group?

12. Who was born William Jefferson Blythe III in 1946?

13. What was the name of the character played by Richard Wilson in One Foot in the Grave?

14. Who was the first man to run a mile in less than four minutes?

15. Which oriental eating utensils originated in China?

ANSWERS: 1 Alex Haley, 2 The Four Musketeers, 3 Baklava, 4 1914, 5 Boron, 6 Mike Nichols, 7 Aslan, 8 Margaret Drabble, 9 £1 million, 10 Yuri Andropov, 11 Nirvana, 12 Bill Clinton, 13 Victor Meldrew, 14 Sir Roger Bannister, 15 Chopsticks.

GENERAL KNOWLEDGE

1. What was the first name of novelist D H Lawrence?

2. Which female American sprinter won Olympic gold medals in 1984, 1988 and 1992?

3. Who plays the third son of the devil in the film Little Nicky?

4. Cinnabar is the chief ore of which metallic element?

5. Whom did Neil Kinnock succeed as leader of the Labour Party?

6. Which American jockey inspired the phrase 'on one's tod' in rhyming slang?

7. Which Charlie Chaplin film was banned in America?

8. Which English physicist and mathematician was born on Christmas Day in 1642?

9. In which Welsh town is the National Library of Wales?

10. Who was the first chancellor of West Germany?

11. Which English novelist wrote The Ipcress File?

12. In which city was the TV series Quincy set?

13. Which member of the Royal Family was photographed wringing a pheasant's neck in November 2000?

14. Of which organisation was John Reith director general from 1927 to 1938?

15. Which Russian city was formerly called Leningrad?

ANSWERS: 1 David, 2 Evelyn Ashford, 3 Adam Sandler, 4 Mercury, 5 Michael Foot, 6 Tod Sloan, 7 Limelight, 8 Sir Isaac Newton, 9 Aberystwyth, 10 Konrad Adenauer, 11 Len Deighton, 12 Los Angeles, 13 The Queen, 14 BBC, 15 St Petersburg.

GENERAL KNOWLEDGE

1. What was the name of Dick Dastardly's car in the cartoon Wacky Races?

2. After which Roman god is January named?

3. Which Spanish composer, best known for his Concierto de Aranjuez, was born in 1901?

4. Under what name was Michael Caine knighted?

5. Which bone is also called the talus?

6. What name is given to the night of anti-Jewish rioting on the night of November 9 1938?

7. In which series of films did the maniac Michael Myers appear?

8. Which Spanish surrealist artist painted The Persistence of Memory?

9. What is the fifth book of the Old Testament?

10. Which English novelist wrote Eating People is Wrong and The History Man?

11. Which British monarch died in January 1901?

12. What is the first name of the South African author J M Coetzee?

13. Which pop star famously ran up a £293,000 bill for flowers?

14. Coronas, cheroots and panatelas are types of what?

15. Which American actor starred in the films Cool Hand Luke and The Hustler?

ANSWERS: 1 The Mean Machine, 2 Janus, 3 Joaquin Rodrigo, 4 Sir Maurice Micklewhite, 5 Ankle bone, 6 Kristallnacht, 7 Halloween, 8 Salvador Dali, 9 Deuteronomy, 10 Malcolm Bradbury, 11 Queen Victoria, 12 John, 13 Sir Elton John, 14 Cigars, 15 Paul Newman.

GENERAL KNOWLEDGE

1. In which U.S. state is Mount Elbert, the highest peak in the Rocky Mountains?

2. Which English conductor founded the Promenade Concerts in London?

3. Which American actor was known as The Great Profile?

4. Who wrote the 1976 science fiction novel Children of Dune?

5. What is a fly agaric?

6. What was the food of the gods in classical mythology?

7. Who wrote the 1979 novel Office Life?

8. Who wrote the 1889 operetta The Gondoliers?

9. In which novel by Charles Dickens does the character Uriah Heep appear?

10. What is the name of the British unit of measurement equal to one-eighth of a fluid ounce?

11. Which type of writing paper, measuring 13 and a half inches by 17 inches, is named after the watermark which was formerly used on it?

12. Which opera by Ponchielli contains the ballet Dance of the Hours?

13. What was the name of the actor who played Grandpa in the television series The Waltons?

14. Which comic book character's alter ego is Dr. Banner?

15. Who was the director of the 1980 comedy film The Blues Brothers?

ANSWERS 1. Colorado 2. Henry Wood 3. John Barrymore 4. Frank Herbert 5. A fungus 6. Ambrosia 7. Keith Waterhouse 8. Gilbert and Sullivan 9. David Copperfield 10. Drachm (or fluid dram) 11. Foolscap 12. La Gioconda 13. Will Geer 14. The Incredible Hulk 15. John Landis.

ENTERTAINMENT

1. Actor Matthew James Almond is the son of which actress?

2. What was Sharon's surname in the sitcom The Fenn Street Gang?

3. The 1969 Disney film Rascal centres around a boy and his pet. What type of animal is his pet?

4. Who played Jack Mowbray in the 1980s sitcom Ffizz?

5. Who wrote and appeared in the 1972 sitcom A Class By Himself?

6. Who directed the 1943 film musical I Dood It?

7. Who composed the 1838 opera Benvenuto Cellini?

8. Gillian Pieface was formerly a stage name of which alternative comedian?

9. What nationality was soprano Erna Berger, who died in 1990?

10. Who played Jerry Leadbetter in the sitcom The Good Life?

11. In which year did the R.S.C. move to the Barbican Theatre in London?

12. What was the name of Frank Spencer's wife in the sitcom Some Mothers Do 'Ave 'Em?

13. The 1962 film Damn the Defiant! is set during which series of wars?

14. What was the middle name of showman Phineas T. Barnum?

15. Which U.S. actress appeared as Madame Trentoni in the play Captain Jinks of the Horse Marines in New York in 1901?

ANSWERS 1. Genevieve Bujold 2. Eversleigh 3. A raccoon 4. Richard Griffiths 5. Richard Stilgoe 6. Vincente Minnelli 7. Berlioz 8. Julian Clary 9. German 10. Paul Eddington 11. 1982 12. Betty 13. Napoleonic Wars 14. Taylor 15. Ethel Barrymore.

SPORT

1. How many Tests did cricketer Derek Pringle play for England?

2. Which horse won the 1981 Dewhurst Stakes?

3. What is the nickname of cricketer Mark Broadhurst?

4. Of what sport have Penny Fellows and Charlotte Cornwallis been British Open Champions?

5. How many gold medals did the U.S. win at the 1999 World Athletics Championships?

6. With what winter sport would you associate Fabrice Becker and Nikki Stone?

7. Which team won the Wadworth 6X National Village Cricket Championship final in 1999?

8. At which ground did cricketer Victor Richardson of Australia take five field catches against South Africa in March 1936?

9. Who did Wasps play in the quarter-finals of rugby union's Heineken Cup in 2000?

10. Who did the Baseball Writers' Association make Most Valuable Player of the Year in the National League in 1958?

11. In which fencing event was Laura Flessel the 1996 Olympic champion?

12. Who scored Ireland's winning try in their 1988 victory over Scotland in the Five Nations?

13. Who was the 1996 Olympic women's springboard diving champion?

14. Which American golfer won the 1979 World Matchplay Championship?

15. In which year did Sergio Garcia first play in the Ryder Cup?

ANSWERS 1. 30 2. Wind and Wuthering 3. Broady 4. Real tennis 5. Eleven 6. Freestyle skiing 7. Linton Park 8. Durban 9. Northampton 10. Ernest Banks 11. Epée 12. Michael Bradley 13. Fu Mingxia 14. Bill Rogers 15. 1999.

POP MUSIC

1. What name does Conrad Lambert record under?

2. Who had a 2000 Top 10 hit with Move Your Body?

3. On which 1971 studio album by King Crimson does the song Sailor's Tale appear?

4. Which solo artist had a 1984 Top 10 single with Self Control?

5. Which member of Pink Fairies died in 1994?

6. From which country do the group Don Air originate?

7. Which solo artist recorded the 1984 hit single Never Ending Story?

8. Who composed the soundtrack to the Bond film Thunderball?

9. What was Jimmy Young's follow-up to his two No. 1 hits in 1955?

10. Yes had a U.S. No. 1 single with Owner of a Lonely Heart. What was the song's highest chart placing in the U.K.?

11. On which studio album by Creedence Clearwater Revival does the song Bad Moon Rising appear?

12. Who recorded the 1999 dance track Destination Sunshine?

13. Which singer released the soundtrack album Pola X in 2000?

14. Which group recorded the 1990 double album i?

15. Which male singer's Top 20 hits include Tomb of Memories and Now I Know What Made Otis Blue?

ART & LITERATURE

1. Who authored the book (Un)Arranged Marriage?

2. In which U.S. city is the Whitney Museum of American Art?

3. Whose short story collections include 1967's A Flag on the Island?

4. Which former politician wrote the novel The Prodigal Daughter?

5. Which artist's works include 1954's Hilda and I at Pond Street?

6. In which decade did the artist J.M.W. Turner first visit Venice?

7. Which Scottish artist's works include the 1913 painting Saint Bride?

8. Who wrote the 1996 novel Executive Orders?

9. Who wrote the 2001 novel The Bulgari Connection?

10. Which Iris Murdoch work won the 1974 Whitbread Book of the Year award?

11. Who wrote the 1933 book Down and Out in Paris and London?

12. Which artist's works include 1944's Pelvis with Blue?

13. Whose paintings include 1918's The Mule Track?

14. Which German expressionist painter's works include 1920's The Dancers?

15. Who wrote the 1926 volume of verse Enough Rope?

ANSWERS 1. Bali Rai 2. New York 3. V.S. Naipaul 4. Jeffrey Archer 5. Stanley Spencer 6. 1810s 7. John Duncan 8. Tom Clancy 9. Fay Weldon 10. The Scared and Profane Love Machine 11. George Orwell 12. Georgia O'Keeffe 13. Paul Nash 14. Emil Nolde 15. Dorothy Parker.

GENERAL KNOWLEDGE

1. What was the name of the character played by Ursula Andress in the Bond film Dr. No?

2. In which year was the Verdi opera Aida first performed?

3. What was the name of the Turkish city Ankara until 1930?

4. In which African country do the Ibibio people live?

5. Who was the lover of Leander in Greek mythology?

6. In which country does the River Siret rise before flowing through Romania to the Danube?

7. Who authored the 1976 novel The Family Arsenal?

8. Which inland port in Argentina is the second-largest city in the country?

9. Who composed the ballet Agon, first performed in 1957?

10. The 1951 film Ten Tall Men starring Burt Lancaster, is about which organisation?

11. Who was a Best Actress Oscar nominee for the 1961 film The Hustler?

12. Carthaginian general Hasdrubal was the brother of which famous historical character?

13. Who wrote the book Cakes and Ale?

14. Who directed the 1974 film Bring Me the Head of Alfredo Garcia?

15. Who composed the 1733 oratorio Athalia?

ENTERTAINMENT

1. Who is the female star of the 1987 film Adventures in Babysitting?

2. Who did Peter Vaughan play in a 1962 television adaptation of Oliver Twist?

3. Who co-directed and starred in the 1944 film Tawny Pipit?

4. Who directed the 1927 film Easy Virtue?

5. What does VHS stand for?

6. Who was the female presenter of the late-night TV show Something for the Weekend?

7. The 1964 film Advance to the Rear is set during which war?

8. Who composed the 1942 opera Capriccio?

9. Who directed and starred in the 1988 film spoof I'm Gonna Git You Sucka?

10. Who played Lyn Turtle in the 1980s drama series A Very Peculiar Practice?

11. On which W. Somerset Maugham story is the 1962 film Adorable Julia based?

12. Which film director's daughter-in-law scripted the 1981 film Tattoo?

13. In which year did Lucille Ball marry Desi Arnaz?

14. Which comedian starred in the 1983 film Easy Money?

15. What nationality is mezzo-soprano Grace Bumbry?

ANSWERS 1. Elisabeth Shue 2. Bill Sikes 3. Bernard Miles 4. Alfred Hitchcock 5. Video Home System 6. Denise Van Outen 7. American Civil War 8. Richard Strauss 9. Keenen Ivory Wayans 10. Amanda Hillwood 11. W. Somerset Maugham's Theatre 12. Luis Buñuel 3. 1940 14. Rodney Dangerfield 15. American.

SPORT

1. Who was the 1956 world 500cc motor cycling champion?

2. Which Olympic event did the Osborne Swimming Club, Manchester win in 1900?

3. In which month was the 1903 F.A. Cup Final between Bury and Derby County played?

4. What sport have Andrew Baggaley and Juan Yong Yun both played at international level?

5. How long did Petrus Silkinas take to run 1,000 miles in March 1998?

6. In which year was the first limited-overs international played in cricket?

7. What nationality is boxer Erik Morales?

8. Three Troikas won the 1979 Prix de l'Arc de Triomphe. Which other French classic did it win that year?

9. Which country were the men's coxless fours Olympic rowing champions from 1924-32?

10. What country does boxer Dodie Penalosa represent?

11. With which ball game are Karen Corr and Tessa Davidson associated?

12. Which horse won the 1972 Irish 1000 Guineas?

13. Which wicket-keeper made five dismissals for India against Zimbabwe in the 1983 cricket World Cup?

14. Who won the 1987 European Champion Clubs' Cup in football?

15. With which sport are Wilt Chamberlain and Scottie Pippen associated?

ANSWERS 1. John Surtees 2. Water polo 3. April 4. Table tennis 5. 11 days, 13 hours, 54 minutes and 58 seconds 6. 1971 7. Mexican 8. Poule d'Essai des Pouliches 9. Great Britain 10. Philippines 11. Snooker 12. Pidget 13. Syed Kirmani 14. FC Porto 15. Basketball.

POP MUSIC

1. Which U.S. rap group had a 1994 hit single with Tap the Bottle?

2. Dan Crouch and Adrian Stephens record under what name?

3. Which guitarist co-wrote the song Split Decision with Steve Winwood?

4. Who recorded the 1993 album Surfing on Sine Waves?

5. Which U.S. group's singles include They Cleaned My Cut With a Wire Brush?

6. Which Irish group had a hit single in 1998 with That's Why We Lose Control?

7. Who is the leader of the group My Life Story?

8. What did the Cranberries change their name from in 1990?

9. Which Rolling Stones studio album features the song Fool to Cry?

10. Nasty Suicide was guitarist in which Finnish punk band?

11. Which author guests on the 1983 Hawkwind album Zones?

12. What was the B-side of the Cream single Wrapping Paper?

13. Who recorded the 1995 hit single No More I Love Yous?

14. Which singer-songwriter recorded the 1978 album The Future Now?

15. Animal, P.J., Magoo and Winston comprised which punk group?

ANSWERS 1. Young Black Teenagers 2. Bell 3. Joe Walsh 4. Aphex Twin 5. Happy Flowers 6. Young Offenders 7. Jake Shillingford 8. The Cranberry-Saw-Us 9. Black and Blue 10. Hanoi Rocks 11. Michael Moorcock 12. Cat's Squirrel 13. Annie Lennox 14. Peter Hammill 15. Anti-Nowhere League.

GEOGRAPHY

1. On which island is the Sinharaja Forest Reserve?

2. On which Greek island is the resort of Nidri?

3. Which National Trail runs from Edale to Kirk Yetholm?

4. On which island is the Indonesian port of Rembang?

5. In which Asian country is the town of Ar-Rutbah?

6. In which U.S. state is the Redoubt volcano?

7. Of which country is Tashkent the capital?

8. Which African capital has the larger population - Harare or Accra?

9. In which European country is the resort of Le Touquet?

10. On which Aegean island is the beach resort of Myrties?

11. In which European country is the city of Pori?

12. On which lake does the Italian village of Bellagio lie?

13. In which English county is the coastal village of Staithes?

14. In which English county is the fishing port of Padstow?

15. In which country is the Tongariro National Park?

ANSWERS 1. Sri Lanka 2. Lefkas 3. Pennine Way National Trail 4. Java 5. Iraq 6. Alaska 7. Uzbekistan 8. Harare 9. France 10. Kalymnos 11. Finland 12. Lake Como 13. North Yorkshire 14. Cornwall 15. New Zealand.

GENERAL KNOWLEDGE

1. Off which U.S. state does the island of Nantucket, a former centre of the whaling industry, lie?

2. To which genus does the climbing plant the hop belong?

3. Which city and spa in Germany was the northern capital of Charlemagne's empire?

4. Who is the author of the Booker Prize-winning novel In a Free State?

5. Which island in N.E. Indonesia is the largest of the Moluccas?

6. Which bone of the body is also called the innominate bone?

7. Which town in central Scotland is the administrative centre of Clackmannanshire?

8. Who was the French designer of the modern two-piece swimsuit?

9. Who was a Best Actor Oscar winner for the film Goodbye, Mr. Chips?

10. Who was the 1981 world rallying champion?

11. Who was the female lead in the 1964 film Woman of Straw?

12. Of which U.S. state is Augusta the capital?

13. Who wrote the novel Salar the Salmon?

14. Lake Champlain in the northeastern U.S. lies between which two mountain ranges?

15. Who composed the music for the ballet Appalachian Spring?

ANSWERS 1. Massachusetts 2. Humulus 3. Aachen 4. V.S. Naipaul 5. Halmahera 6. Hipbone 7. Alloa 8. Louis Réard 9. Robert Donat 10. Ari Vatanen 11. Gina Lollobrigida 12. Maine 13. Henry Williamson 14. The Green Mountains and the Adirondack Mountains 15. Aaron Copland.

ENTERTAINMENT

1. Who directed the 1976 film The Killing of a Chinese Bookie?

2. Which duo star in the BBC drama series In Deep?

3. How did Lady Marjorie Bellamy perish in the drama series Upstairs, Downstairs?

4. Who played Anne Hathaway in the 1978 television drama series Will Shakespeare?

5. Which composer became artistic director of the Vienna State Opera House in 1897?

6. What is the real name of 'Handy Andy' of TV's Changing Rooms?

7. Who directed the 1967 film The Sorcerers which starred Boris Karloff?

8. In which year did The Two Ronnies begin on television?

9. Who played Dolly Rawlins in the 1983 television drama series Widows?

10. Who directed the 1988 film The Milagro Beanfield War?

11. Who plays the title role in the 2001 film Amelie?

12. Who played the title role in the 1937 film Kid Galahad?

13. Who directed the 2000 film Erin Brockovich?

14. In which radio programme did the character Lucas Madakane appear in 2001?

15. Who plays Karen in the television drama Cold Feet?

SPORT

1. In the first Test between the West Indies and Zimbabwe in March 2000, which over of the Zimbabwe innings saw their first run?

2. How many wins did jockey Fred Archer have in 1878?

3. Who was captain of Scotland's 1990 rugby union grand slam side?

4. In which year was netball invented?

5. For which country did former England rugby union player Martin Donnelly play cricket?

6. In which year was the Squash Rackets Association formed?

7. Which club won the 1948 rugby league Challenge Cup Final?

8. How many times did Mike Procter take five wickets in an innings in his First-Class career?

9. Whose cap for the England rugby union team in March 2000 against Italy was his 81st?

10. Raymond Ceulemans of Belgium was a 1983 world champion. At which ball game?

11. Who became the first full time professional coach to the England rugby union squad in 1997?

12. What major contribution did Gabriel Hanot, soccer editor of newspaper L'Equipe, make in 1955?

13. What nationality is canoe racer Nikolai Boukhalov?

14. At what Olympic sport have Hubert Hammerer and Gary Anderson been champions?

15. Which country won the 1958 Eisenhower Trophy in golf?

POP MUSIC

1. In which year did Duran Duran have the hit single Wild Boys?

2. Which band covered the song God Save the Queen by the Sex Pistols on the 1985 mini-LP Armed and Dangerous?

3. Which German singer recorded the 1982 album Nun Sex Monk Rock?

4. Which group recorded the song How Does a Duck Know? on the album God Shuffled His Feet?

5. In which year was Blur's single End of a Century released?

6. Who recorded the 1978 single Murder of Liddle Towers?

7. What is the real name of Guns N' Roses guitarist Izzy Stradlin?

8. Which female singer's albums include Welcome to the Cruise?

9. Who did Barry Jenkins replace as drummer in The Animals?

10. Which solo singer had a 1999 Top 10 single with (You Drive Me) Crazy?

11. Which jazz band backed Bob Wallis on his 1961 hit I'm Shy Mary Ellen I'm Shy?

12. In which city did the Legendary Pink Dots form in 1980?

13. In which year did the Walker Brothers have a Top 10 single with My Ship Is Coming In?

14. In which year did Blondie have a Top 10 single with Dreaming?

15. Which Suzanne Vega song did The Lemonheads cover on the album Lick?

ANSWERS 1. 1984 2. Anthrax 3. Nina Hagen 4. Crash Test Dummies 5. 1994 6. Angelic Upstarts 7. Jeff Isabelle 8. Judie Tzuke 9. John Steel 10. Britney Spears 11. Storyville Jazz Band 12. London 13. 1965 14. 1979 15. Luka.

HISTORY

1. In which ship did John Cabot set sail from Bristol in May 1497?

2. Who succeeded Anthony Crosland in 1977 as Foreign Secretary?

3. Who was appointed Youth Leader of the Reich in June 1933?

4. The War of the Pacific from 1879-83 was between Chile and which two other countries?

5. From 1880-81, James Longstreet was U.S. minister to which country?

6. In which year did Minister of Defence Hafez al-Assad seize control of the Syrian government?

7. Marcus Junius Brutus, an assassin of Julius Caesar, was the nephew of which Roman philosopher?

8. Who was shadow Chancellor of the Exchequer from 1955-61?

9. What age was Konrad Adenauer when he resigned as West German Chancellor in 1963?

10. In which year did Daniel Arap Moi become president of Kenya?

11. Which Israeli prime minister was born in Brest Litovsk in 1913?

12. In which year did Julio Maria Sanguinetti first take office as Uruguayan president?

13. In which city was Lambert Simnel crowned on Whit Sunday in 1487?

14. In which year did Malta become independent?

15. Who became prime minister of New Zealand in 1990?

GENERAL KNOWLEDGE

1. Who was the author of The Canterbury Tales?

2. What is the name given to the liquorice-flavoured seeds of the anise plant?

3. Which sport is played by the Toronto Blue Jays and Boston Red Sox?

4. Who wrote the 1986 novel The Bridge?

5. The 1989 Ken Russell film The Lair of the White Worm was based on a tale by which writer?

6. In which European country is the market town of Eger?

7. What was the Indian Mutiny of 1857-8 also known as?

8. Which European freshwater fish is also called a pope?

9. Who was Roman emperor from 54-68 A.D.?

10. What is the name given to either of the two large flat triangular bones on each side of the back part of the shoulder?

11. In which year did British field marshal Douglas Haig die?

12. Who was the German composer of 1717's Water Music?

13. Who wrote the 1600 play Hamlet?

14. What is the 20th letter in the Greek alphabet?

15. In which year did German Green Party activist Petra Kelly die?

ANSWERS 1. Geoffrey Chaucer 2. Aniseed 3. Baseball 4. Iain Banks 5. Bram Stoker 6. Hungary 7. The Sepoy Rebellion (or Sepoy Mutiny) 8. Ruffe 9. Nero 10. Scapula 11. 1928 12. George Frederick Handel 13. Shakespeare 14. Upsilon 5. 1992.

ENTERTAINMENT

1. Which Oscar-winning song was the theme song of the 1965 film The Sandpiper?

2. What was Georgina Moon's character's name in the sitcom Up Pompeii?

3. What was the name of the Glaswegian crook in the 1996 sitcom Bad Boys?

4. In which opera do the characters Canio and Nedda appear?

5. Who played Laurence Kirbridge in the television drama Upstairs Downstairs?

6. Who composed the 1836 opera The Night Bell?

7. In which city was the 1994 film Immortal Beloved, about the composer Beethoven, filmed?

8. What was Reg Varney's character's name in the sitcom On the Buses?

9. Which stand-up comedian starred in the 1990 film The Adventures of Ford Fairlane?

10. Who played Major Mohn in the television drama series Colditz?

11. In which year was Welsh tenor Stuart Burrows born?

12. What is Roddy McDowall's profession in the 1967 Disney film The Adventures of Bullwhip Griffin?

13. Who played Al Capone in the television show The Untouchables?

14. Which model was the original female presenter of Channel 5's Fort Boyard?

15. Which creature does the eating in Tobe Hooper's film Eaten Alive?

SPORT

1. In which year did tennis player Pancho Gonzales die?

2. In which year was the National Hockey League founded in Montreal?

3. Who won the 1974 Tournament Players' Championship in golf?

4. Who scored 18 points in the 1985 Super Bowl for the San Francisco 49ers?

5. Who was the 1997 U.S. Open women's singles tennis champion?

6. Where were the 1994 Asian Games held?

7. In which year did the Curtis Cup finish in a draw for the first time?

8. What was the name of the winning craft in the 1885 America's Cup?

9. What nationality is boxer Jorge Paez?

10. Which Japanese boxer was a 1996 WBA light-flyweight boxing champion?

11. Which New Zealand golfer won the 2000 Australian Masters in Melbourne?

12. Which country were team pursuit champions at the 1990 world championships in cycling?

13. Where were the 1970 World Student games held?

14. In which year was the Le Mans 24-hour race inaugurated?

15. Which women's team won the FIH World Cup in hockey in 1994 and 1998?

POP MUSIC

1. Which female duo had a 1989 hit with Lolly Lolly?

2. In which year did Kool and the Gang have a Top 10 single with Ladies Night?

3. Whose Top 20 hits in 1993 included Sunflower and Wildwood?

4. Whose singles include MTV Makes Me Want to Smoke Crack?

5. Which group had a hit in 1992 with The Queen of Outer Space?

6. On which label was Wet Wet Wet's 1994 No. 1 single Love Is All Around?

7. Who was the original female singer in the group The Beautiful South?

8. Which male vocalist had a 1967 Top 40 single with the song Sam?

9. What band was Robert Plant singing with immediately prior to joining Led Zeppelin?

10. Who recorded the 1999 Top 10 hit Straight From the Heart?

11. Which member of The Housemartins was also known as D.J. Ox?

12. Which ex-member of the group Kraftwerk penned the autobiography Ich War Ein Roboter?

13. Which Leicester group recorded the 1989 album Shakespeare, Alabama?

14. Which UK garage act recorded the 2000 Top 10 single Movin' Too Fast?

15. Which U.S. female singer fronted the 1970s rock band Blue Angel?

WORDS

1. What type of creature is a galah - a cockatoo or kangaroo?

2. What would you do with a casaba - eat it or wear it?

3. For which part of the body are the pearlies a slang word?

4. What is farina?

5. What in military slang is a Roman Candle?

6. If a tree is balaniferous, what does it bear?

7. For what type of space is a barton an archaic word?

8. A blocker is a British slang term for which item of headgear?

9. What was a cicisbeo in 18th century Italy?

10. Which war did recipients of the trio of commemorative medals known as Pip, Squeak and Wilfred serve in?

11. What is chiminage?

12. If something is dendriform what is it shaped like?

13. Tom Thumb is Australian rhyming slang for which alcoholic drink?

14. On what part of the body would you wear a blucher?

15. Which musical instrument is known as a gob-stick?

ANSWERS 1. Cockatoo 2. Eat it, it's a melon 3. Teeth 4. A type of meal or flour 5. A parachute jump in which the parachute fails to open 6. Acorns 7. Farmyard 8. A bowler hat 9. Male escort of a married woman 10. The Great War (World War I) 11. A toll for passing through a forest 12. A tree 13. Rum 14. The foot, it's a shoe or half-boot 15. Clarinet.

GENERAL KNOWLEDGE

1. Which 18th century politician was caricatured as Scragg in the novel The Adventures of Peregrine Pickle by Tobias Smollett?

2. Which theatre in the Waterloo Road, London, was managed by Lilian Baylis from 1912?

3. Who wrote the play The Corn is Green?

4. Who penned the 1984 novel The Angels Weep?

5. Which England Test cricket captain was known as 'The Champion'?

6. Which U.S. president was known as Ike?

7. Who wrote the 1939 novel Happy Valley?

8. The 1951 film The Magic Box was about the life of which film pioneer?

9. Which former England Test cricket captain was India's representative at the League of Nations?

10. Who was the director of the 1964 film The Pink Panther?

11. What is a bobwhite?

12. Which chesspiece can only move diagonally?

13. Which pop singer was born Marvin Lee Aday?

14. Which German was the composer of the choral work A German Requiem?

15. Who wrote the 1960 book Born Free?

ENTERTAINMENT

1. Who plays a con-man in the 1945 film Yolanda and the Thief?

2. Which comic duo played Randall and Hopkirk (Deceased) in the BBC1 comedy drama series remake?

3. Which cast member of Friends plays The Pallbearer in the 1996 film?

4. What nationality is bass baritone Simon Estes?

5. Who choreographed the 1957 film The Pajama Game?

6. What nationality is counter-tenor Paul Esswood?

7. What is William B. Davis's character name in the television show The X-Files?

8. Who is the star of the 1961 film Yojimbo?

9. Who composed the 1854 opera The Northern Star?

10. In which country is the 1969 film Valley of Gwangi set?

11. Which comedy actress appeared as Kate Bancroft in the 1992 sitcom Don't Tell Father?

12. The 1997 biopic Private Parts is about which disc jockey?

13. Which actor plays Deborah Foreman's father in the 1983 film Valley Girl?

14. Who composed the 1844 opera Ernani?

15. Who plays the title role in the 2000 film Ordinary Decent Criminal?

ANSWERS 1. Fred Astaire 2. Vic Reeves and Bob Mortimer 3. David Schwimmer 4. American 5. Bob Fosse 6. English 7. Cigarette Smoking Man 8. Toshiro Mifune 9. Meyerbeer 10. Mexico 11. Caroline Quentin 12. Howard Stern 13. Frederick Forrest 14. Verdi 15. Kevin Spacey.

SPORT

1. Who lost 13-0 to New Zealand in a 1981 football World Cup qualifying game?

2. Where were the 1967 World Student Games held?

3. Who was the 1973 women's 400m freestyle swimming world champion?

4. Which country won the 1997 Alfred Dunhill Cup in golf?

5. Where were the 1999 Pan-American Games held?

6. With which sport are Julia King and Kertsen Kielgass associated?

7. How many times did cyclist Eddy Merckx win the Milan-San Remo race?

8. At which sport was Clas Thunberg an Olympic champion in 1924 and 1928?

9. In which year did Gladiateur win the Epsom Derby?

10. Which women's event did Sarka Kasparkova win at the 1997 world championships in athletics?

11. What nationality is former moto-cross world champion Alessandro Chiodi?

12. What sport do Manchester Giants and London Towers play?

13. What was the attendance at the 1886 Scottish F.A. Cup Final?

14. Who partnered Anne Smith to victory in the 1982 French Open women's doubles tennis championship?

15. Who won the 1995 New York women's marathon?

ANSWERS 1. Fiji 2. Tokyo 3. Heather Greenwood 4. South Africa 5. Winnipeg 6. Swimming 7. Seven 8. Speed skating 9. 1865 10. Triple jump 11. Italian 12. Basketball 13. 7,000 14. Martina Navratilova 15. Tegla Loroupe.

POP MUSIC

1. Which singer-songwriter recorded the 2000 album You're the One?

2. Which group recorded the albums Kilimanjaro and Wilder?

3. In which year did Kate Bush have a hit with the single Running Up That Hill?

4. Which group recorded the 2001 album If You've Never Been?

5. In which year did The Who make their U.S. television debut?

6. From which city do the group JJ72 hail?

7. Which Scottish band recorded the 2000 album Understanding Music?

8. Which group had a 1990 Top 20 single with the song Chime?

9. Which group recorded the 2001 album Sound-Dust?

10. Which group recorded the 2000 album Black Market Culture?

11. In which year did Paul McCartney release the album McCartney?

12. Who left the group Hüsker Dü to form Nova Mob?

13. Which two Americans comprise the duo Suicide?

14. Which rapper recorded the 1997 album Infinite?

15. Which group recorded the 1986 album Liberty Belle and the Black Diamond Express?

ANSWERS 1. Paul Simon 2. The Teardrop Explodes 3. 1985 4. Embrace 5. 1965 6. Dublin 7. AC Acoustics 8. Orbital 9. Stereolab 10. Placebo 11. 1970 12. Grant Hart 13. Martin Rev and Alan Vega 14. Eminem 15. The Go-Betweens.

SCIENCE

1. In which U.S. state is the Woods Hole Oceanographic Institution?

2. What is the approximate temperature of the surface of Neptune in degrees Celsius?

3. In which year did botanist Andrea Cesalpino die?

4. In which European capital was biochemist Max F. Perutz born?

5. Which Yorkshire-born biologist named the field of genetics?

6. What nationality was psychologist Jean Piaget?

7. In which year did electronic digital computer Colossus first become operational?

8. What period of time is defined as the duration of 9,192,631,770 periods of radiation corresponding to the transition between two hyperfine levels of the ground state of caesium-133?

9. In which year was British physicist Sir James Chadwick knighted?

10. In which year was Saturn's moon Hyperion discovered?

11. Approximately how many miles in diameter is Uranus's moon Cordelia?

12. What is seismology?

13. In which year did Max Planck die?

14. What nationality is astronaut Wubbo Ockels?

15. In computing, what did the initials of military computer ENIAC represent?

GENERAL KNOWLEDGE

1. From which poem by Shelley did Mick Jagger quote in tribute to the late Brian Jones at a 1969 Hyde Park concert by The Rolling Stones?

2. On which island did the writer Mervyn Peake live from 1946-9?

3. In which country is the Islamic sacred city of Mecca?

4. What is Almas Diamond?

5. What happened to St. Benet Sherehog in 1666?

6. Who scripted the 1993 film Sliver, which starred Sharon Stone?

7. In which English county is the village of Thursford, famous for its annual Christmas show?

8. In which country was the BBC news reporter Lyse Doucet born?

9. Which famous London record shop celebrated its 25th anniversary in February 2001?

10. How did the Rylstone & District W.I. hit the headlines in 1999?

11. What nationality is the cyclist Eddy Merckx?

12. With which instrument is the performer Yaltah Menuhin associated?

13. Which sociologist wrote the 1968 book War and Peace in the Global Village?

14. Which U.S. city is nicknamed Bean Town?

15. In which European country is the ski resort of Serre-Chevalier?

ANSWERS 1. Adonais 2. Sark 3. Saudi Arabia 4. A type of caviar 5. A church, it was destroyed in the Great Fire of London 6. Joe Eszterhas 7. Norfolk 8. Canada 9. Rough Trade 10. By producing a calendar featuring their members naked 11. Belgian 12. Piano 13. Marshall McLuhan 14. Boston 15. France.

ENTERTAINMENT

1. What pseudonym did Ronnie Barker use to write the 1988 sitcom Clarence?

2. In which year did American music-hall artist Josephine Baker die?

3. Who plays demonic child Damien in the 1978 film Damien – Omen II?

4. In which year did U.S. actress Tallulah Bankhead die?

5. Which actress played the lead in the children's show Clarissa Explains It All?

6. Who directed the 1954 film The Dam Busters?

7. What was Michael Caine's character's name in the 1967 movie Billion Dollar Brain?

8. Which actress plays Jack Palance's girlfriend in the 1955 film I Died a Thousand Times?

9. Who directed the 1999 film The Hurricane?

10. Which actor's son plays the kidnapped child in the 1996 film Ransom?

11. Who played the title role in the 1993 film The Adventures of Huck Finn?

12. What was Robert Vaughn's character called in the television series The Protectors?

13. What nationality is opera singer Sally Burgess?

14. Which English comedian starred in the 1960 film Sands of the Desert?

15. Which comedian played the manager of Ballyskillen Opera House in a 1981 sitcom?

SPORT

1. Which Briton became world undisputed welterweight boxing champion in 1986?

2. Which Irish jockey won the 1991 Breeders' Cup Sprint?

3. Who beat Biarritz in the 1999/00 European Shield quarter-finals in rugby union?

4. What nationality is Olympic archer Darrell Pace?

5. At what sport were Judy Wills and Nancy Smith world champions in 1967?

6. Which New Zealander won the 1973 Swedish Grand Prix in F1?

7. Who was the 1994 Commonwealth men's 200m champion?

8. Which university has won the rugby union varsity match most times - Oxford or Cambridge?

9. What sport do Stephen Cooper and Rick Brebant play for Britain?

10. In which year did cricketer Christopher Batt make his county debut for Middlesex?

11. Who set a world record of 26:38.08 for the 10,000m on 23th August, 1996?

12. In which year was the Grand Caledonian Curling Club formed in Edinburgh?

13. In which year did Lew Hoad & Ken Rosewall win the Wimbledon men's doubles tennis title for the second time?

14. What nationality is rhythmic sportive gymnast Bianka Panova?

15. In which year did French tennis player Jean Cochet die?

POP MUSIC

1. Which group had a 1990 hit with Papa Was a Rolling Stone?

2. On which label did Will Smith record the album Willennium?

3. In which year was Dionne Warwick born?

4. In which year did Sheryl Crow have a Top 10 single with All I Wanna Do?

5. In which year did Madness have a hit single with One Step Beyond?

6. With whom did Mark Knopfler record the 1990 album of guitar duets Neck and Neck?

7. Which group recorded the 1999 Top 10 hit Boom, Boom, Boom, Boom!!!?

8. Which label did Leftfield sign for in 1992?

9. Which female singer had a 1993 hit with Careless Whisper?

10. Who had a 1999 Top 10 single with Back In My Life?

11. Which group had a 1999 Top 10 single with Every Day I Love You?

12. Which orchestra featured on Marti Webb's 1986 hit Always There?

13. Which 1950s singer released the 1989 album Yo Frankie?

14. Which group had a 1993 hit single with Glastonbury Song?

15. In which year did Jimmy Nail chart with the single Crocodile Shoes?

PEOPLE

1. What was the nickname of the painter Joseph Crawhall, who died in 1913?

2. In which year did the rock guitarist Johnny Thunders die?

3. At which registry office did Paul McCartney marry Linda Eastman in 1969?

4. Who won the 1992 Nobel prize for literature?

5. Who wrote the 2001 self-help-cum-autobiographical book Take It From Me: Life's a Struggle But You Can Win?

6. In which year was the former prime minister Edward Heath first elected to Paliament?

7. In which year did Charles Kennedy become leader of the Liberal Democrats?

8. In which country was the actor Robert Donat born?

9. Which actor played in a Z.Z. Top tribute band called Tres Hombres in the late 1970s?

10. In which year did the television presenter and producer Muriel Young die?

11. Which poet wrote the novella Michaelmas Term at St. Bride's under the pseudonym Brunette Coleman?

12. Which singer was born Louisa Gabrielle Bobb?

13. In which year did the artist Jean Dubuffet die?

14. In which year was the playwright Trevor Griffiths born?

15. Which actress was married to Ronald Reagan from 1940-8?

ANSWERS 1. Creeps 2. 1991 3. Marylebone Registry Office 4. Derek Walcott 5. Erin Brockovich 6. 1950 7. 1999 8. England 9. Billy Bob Thornton 10. 2001 11. Philip Larkin 12. Gabrielle 13. 1985 14. 1935 15. Jane Wyman.

ENTERTAINMENT

1. Which star of The Full Monty played Fred in the 2000 movie, The Flintstones in Viva Rock Vegas?

2. Which Eighties series, starring Tony Haygarth and Patsy Rowlands, featured a repairman who dreamed of visiting another planet?

3. Which British singer hit the top of the U.K. charts with Rock DJ?

4. Which 1982 film about a search for gold featured Charlton Heston and Kim Basinger?

5. Which Coronation Street character left Weatherfield and his girlfriend Toyah to 'find himself' in India?

6. Which British singer/songwriter scored a top five album with White Ladder, featuring his hit song Babylon?

7. Which chat show host became a National Lottery presenter in 2000, fronting the travelling quiz show On the Spot?

8. Which former footballer featured alongside Nicolas Cage and Robert Duvall in the film Gone in 60 Seconds?

9. Who was the commander of the spacecraft in Gerry Anderson's Sixties puppet series Fireball XL5?

10. Which former Spice Girl had a U.K. number one hit with I Turn to You?

11. Which actor was the fifth Doctor Who in the TV sci-fi series?

12. What was the title of Louise's third solo album, released in 2000?

13. Which 1973 film starred Rod Steiger and Robert Ryan as the heads of two feuding families?

14. What was Moby's first top ten hit, which entered the charts in 1991?

15. Which animated movie, set after the destruction of Earth, featured the voices of Matt Damon and Drew Barrymore?

ANSWERS: 1 Mark Addy, 2 Kinvig, 3 Robbie Williams, 4 Mother Lode, 5 Spider Nugent, 6 David Gray, 7 Des O'Connor, 8 Vinnie Jones, 9 Colonel Steve Zodiac, 10 Melanie C, 11 Peter Davison, 12 Elbow Beach, 13 The Lolly-Madonna War, 14 Go, 15 Titan AE.

GENERAL KNOWLEDGE

1. With which sport was Geoff Capes most famously associated?

2. What was the name of Othello's wife in Shakespeare's play?

3. In the Old Testament, what was the birthplace of King David?

4. Which Bedfordshire town has the lowest rates of divorce and separation?

5. With which sport is Reggie Jackson associated?

6. Which English film studio was associated with comedies such as Passport to Pimlico?

7. What is Salman Rushdie's real first name?

8. Which river did George Washington cross on Christmas night in 1776?

9. For which month is emerald the traditional birthstone?

10. Which actor played Julian to Kenneth Williams's Sandy on Round the Horne?

11. Which marine creature has hermit, spider and king varieties?

12. Who wrote the novel Sophie's Choice?

13. Which former country was also known as the GDR?

14. The Remorseful Day was the last episode of which TV drama series starring John Thaw?

15. Which Texas city has an American football team called the Cowboys?

GENERAL KNOWLEDGE

1. How many countries changed their currencies to the Euro in January 2002?

2. Which figure of speech is an intentional extravagant exaggeration?

3. From which English Premiership team was Chris Hutchings dismissed as manager in 2000?

4. Which Hungarian-born actress provided the voice of Bianca in the Disney Rescuers films?

5. What name is given to the use of obstructive delaying tactics in parliaments?

6. In which English county is the Vale of Eden?

7. What was artist John Callcott Horsley the first to design?

8. How many players make up an American football team?

9. What nationality was the singer and political activist Fela Kuti?

10. Which American author of 'hard-boiled' fiction had the middle name Mallahan?

11. Which archangel announced the birth of Jesus to the Virgin Mary?

12. What is a two-man bobsleigh called?

13. Which beauty contest was invented by Eric Morley who died in 2000?

14. In which German city is the Brandenburg Gate?

15. Which British actress won an Oscar for Howards End?

ANSWERS: 1 Twelve, 2 Hyperbole, 3 Bradford City, 4 Eva Gabor, 5 Filibustering, 6 Cumbria, 7 A Christmas card, 8 11, 9 Nigerian, 10 James M Cain, 11 Gabriel, 12 Boblet, 13 Miss World, 14 Berlin, 15 Emma Thompson.

GENERAL KNOWLEDGE

1. Who was the Formula One world champion in 1976?

2. Which German poet and dramatist wrote Mother Courage and Her Children?

3. Who painted Woman with Crossed Arms, which has sold for more than £38 million at auction?

4. In computing, what does HTML stand for?

5. What sort of creature is a looper?

6. Which Italian poet wrote the libretti for Mozart's Don Giovanni and Cosi Fan Tutte?

7. In which imaginary country was The Prisoner of Zenda set?

8. Which state underwent several recounts to decide the outcome of the 2000 U.S. presidential election?

9. What nationality was the 8th century poet Tu Fu?

10. Which Bavarian town was the site of the first concentration camp set up by the Nazis?

11. Which American singer-songwriter wrote Blowin' in the Wind?

12. What is the capital of Colombia?

13. Which boxer won heavyweight gold at the 1968 Olympics?

14. Who was the British prime minister at the start of World War II?

15. Which American author wrote The Fall of the House of Usher?

ENTERTAINMENT

1. Which actor starred as a theatrical entrepreneur and serial killer in the 1968 film No Way to Treat a Lady?

2. Which EastEnders family with an Italian background left the Square for a life in Leicester?

3. Which U.K. garage artist released the debut album Born to Do It?

4. In which Scottish city was the BBC2 drama series Tinsel Town set?

5. Which film memoir about a young boy and his dog featured Kevin Bacon and Diane Lane as the boy's parents?

6. Which British sporting team's progress over a four-year period was depicted in the video diary series Gold Fever?

7. With which song did Spiller beat Victoria Beckham to the number one spot in 2000?

8. Who narrated the former children's series Roobarb and Custard?

9. On whose novel was the 1979 Otto Preminger film The Human Factor based?

10. Which BBC1 fly-on-the-wall documentary series focused on the lives of people in an area of West London?

11. Which actor directed and starred in the 1992 film Mac?

12. What was Mike and the Mechanics' 1995 U.K. Top 20 hit?

13. Which 2000 animated film featured the voices of Kevin Kline and Kenneth Branagh?

14. Which 2002 film starring Hugh Grant was based on a Nick Horby novel?

15. Who had a U.K. number one hit in 1983 with Baby Jane?

GENERAL KNOWLEDGE

1. Who captained the 1995 rugby union World Cup winners?

2. Which London theatre was rebuilt by a trust set up by the American actor Sam Wanamaker?

3. Of which country is Bratislava the capital?

4. Which French composer wrote España and Le Roi malgé lui?

5. What is the French name for the German city of Aachen?

6. Which British novelist wrote The Alexandria Quartet?

7. Where did Paula Radcliffe finish in the 10,000 metres final at the Sydney Olympics?

8. Which Stone Age village in the Orkneys was exposed by a storm in 1850?

9. Who was appointed as the England football team's first foreign coach?

10. Which English novelist wrote Joseph Andrews?

11. Which form of recreation originated on paved areas along California beaches in the 1960s?

12. What is the name of The Barber of Seville in the play by Beaumarchais?

13. Who wrote Tarzan of the Apes?

14. In which Spanish city is the Prado Museum?

15. Which nut is also called a filbert?

ANSWERS: 1 Francois Pienaar, 1 The Globe, 3 Slovakia, 4 Emmanuel Chabrier, 5 Aix-la-Chapelle, 6 Lawrence Durrell, 7 4th, 8 Skara Brae, 9 Sven Goran Eriksson, 10 Henry Fielding, 11 Skateboarding, 12 Figaro, 31 Edgar Rice Burroughs, 14 Madrid, 15 Hazelnut.

GENERAL KNOWLEDGE

1. Who was born Michael Dumble-Smith?

2. Which American dancer died when her scarf caught in the wheel of a car?

3. What were the first names of the poet W.B. Yeats?

4. Which Canadian author won the 2000 Booker Prize for her novel The Blind Assassin?

5. What nationality was the golfer Bobby Locke?

6. In which English county is the new town of Skelmersdale?

7. What was the second Walt Disney film?

8. Who wrote the songs for the musicals Guys and Dolls and Hans Christian Andersen?

9. Of which country is Suva the capital?

10. The Faroe Islands is a self-governing region of which European country?

11. Which music-hall comedienne and singer was born Grace Stansfield?

12. Who was the leader of the mutiny on HMS Bounty?

13. What nationality is tennis player Gustavo Kuerten?

14. What was the tallest building in the world before the Chrysler Building in New York was completed in 1930?

15. Which actor starred in the Death Wish series of films?

ANSWERS: 1 Michael Crawford, 2 Isadora Duncan, 3 William Butler, 4 Margaret Atwood, 5 South African, 6 Lancashire, 7 Pinocchio, 8 Frank Loesser, 9 Fiji, 10 Denmark, 11 Dame Gracie Fields, 12 Fletcher Christian, 13 Brazilian, 14 Eiffel Tower, 15 Charles Bronson.

GENERAL KNOWLEDGE

? ?

1. Which country hosted the football World Cup in 1982?

2. Which French composer wrote The Sorcerer's Apprentice?

3. Who was the Green Party candidate in the 2000 U.S. presidential election?

4. Which African-American Muslim organisation is led by Louis Farrakhan?

5. In which country was John Prescott born?

6. Which American author wrote The Foxes of Harrow?

7. Which Irish singer was voted the world's most beautiful woman in a poll in 2000?

8. Who was the famous ice dancing partner of Jayne Torvill?

9. What sort of creature is a prairie dog?

10. In which U.S. state is Dodge City?

11. Which tubes between the ovary and uterus are also called oviducts?

12. How many legs does a lobster have?

13. Which American golfer won the British Open in 1996?

14. In which country is the city of Eindhoven?

15. In which country was Albert Einstein born?

ANSWERS: 1 Spain, 2 Paul Dukas, 3 Ralph Nader, 4 The Nation of Islam, 5 Wales, 6 Frank Yerby, 7 Andrea Corr, 8 Christopher Dean, 9 A rodent, 10 Kansas, 11 Fallopian tubes, 12 Ten, 13 Tom Lehman, 14 The Netherlands, 15 Germany.

SPORT

1. Which snooker player won the 2002 World Championships with a last frame victory?

2. Which section of the World Championship Triathlon is 10km long?

3. In which sport was Greg Louganis the first person to exceed 700 points?

4. Which American Football team did quarterback John Elway lead to victory in the 1998 Super Bowl?

5. Which British athlete successfully defended her Commonwealth Games 10,000m title in 1990?

6. Which rugby union club side play at Stoop Memorial Ground?

7. Which famous basketball team was founded in 1927?

8. From which club did Kenny Dalglish join Liverpool in 1977?

9. In which year were the Winter Olympics held in Grenoble, France?

10. Who succeeded Ron Saunders as manager of Aston Villa?

11. Which English football team won the 1998 Coca Cola Cup?

12. Which players wear red caps in the sport of water polo?

13. Which event first appeared at the 1964 Winter Olympics?

14. Which British boxer lost two world title fights to Steve Collins in 1995?

15. Which French footballer scored 13 goals in the 1958 World Cup finals?

GENERAL KNOWLEDGE

1. Which film actor died on 2 February 1996?

2. Which American poet wrote the verse collection Leaves of Grass?

3. What name is given to the fatty substance released by sebaceous glands?

4. Which team did England beat in Sven-Göran Eriksson's first game as England coach?

5. What is a jingling Johnny?

6. Which American football legend was called the 'Gipper'?

7. What sort of creature is Akela in Rudyard Kipling's The Jungle Book?

8. Which star of the film Billy Elliot won the Best Actor award at the 2001 BAFTAs?

9. Which group picked up the 2001 Brit Awards for Best British Group and Best British Album?

10. What sort of creature is a whydah?

11. Which screen legend played Bottom in a 1935 film version of A Midsummer Night's Dream?

12. In which English city is the National Railway Museum?

13. Which Charles Dickens novel is dedicated to Thomas Carlyle?

14. How many feet are there in a yard?

15. Which winter sports event combines cross-country skiing and rifle shooting?

GENERAL KNOWLEDGE

1. What was the top grossing film in 1998 in America?

2. Which port is the capital of Spain's Biscay (or Vizcaya) province?

3. Who led a rebellion against Henry VI in 1450?

4. Which actor received an Academy Fellowship at the 2001 BAFTAs?

5. What does someone suffering from dysphagia have difficulty doing?

6. Which cartoon character created by Chic Young married Dagwood Bumstead?

7. Who is the native referred to in the title of Thomas Hardy's The Return of the Native?

8. Who was the first athlete to win two Olympic marathons?

9. Which boxer became the oldest-ever world heavyweight champion in 1994?

10. Who wrote the lyrics of the song Three Coins in a Fountain?

11. Which English composer wrote five Pomp and Circumstance marches?

12. What was the name of the pet space monkey in Lost In Space?

13. Which football team beat Birmingham City on penalties to win the 2001 Worthington Cup?

14. After whom is the month July named?

15. Which Irish poet wrote The Lake Isle of Innisfree?

GENERAL KNOWLEDGE

1. Where was the television series The Lotus Eaters set?

2. Which king led England into the Hundred Years' War with France?

3. What was Ronnie Hilton's only number one hit in Britain?

4. Which South African political activist died from head injuries suffered in police custody in 1977?

5. An Angel at My Table is an autobiographical work by which New Zealand author?

6. What name is given to the first part of the small intestine?

7. Which was allegedly the favourite film of Joseph Stalin?

8. Who sculpted the statue of Peter Pan in Kensington Gardens?

9. Which U.S. author wrote An Occurrence at Owl Creek Bridge?

10. Which rare-earth metal has the chemical symbol Dy?

11. Which queen was the daughter of Henry VIII and Anne Boleyn?

12. Who played a nun in the film All About My Mother?

13. Which British singer duetted with Eminem at the 2001 Grammy Awards?

14. Who became the youngest winner of a world-ranking snooker tournament when he won the 1993 U.K. championship?

15. By what first name was Emad Mohamed al-Fayed known?

ANSWERS: 1 Crete, 2 Edward III, 3 No Other Love, 4 Stephen Biko, 5 Janet Frame, 6 Duodenum, 7 Volga Volga, 8 Sir George Frampton, 9 Ambrose Bierce, 10 Dysprosium, 11 Elizabeth I, 12 Penelope Cruz, 13 Sir Elton John, 14 Ronnie O'Sullivan, 15 Dodi.

ENTERTAINMENT

1. Which U.S. band asked What's the Frequency, Kenneth in the U.K. top ten in 1994?

2. Which rapper starred as a Cincinatti arch-criminal nicknamed 'God' in the film In Too Deep?

3. What was the name of the Orkans' leader who Mork reported back to at the end of every episode of the sitcom Mork and Mindy?

4. Which girl group had a U.K. top five hit with Jumpin' Jumpin'?

5. Which Western star appeared in the films Rio Grande, Rio Bravo and Rio Lobo?

6. Who persuaded EastEnders' Ian Beale to sign papers beginning his divorce from Melanie?

7. Which former member of Boyzone released a self-titled debut solo album in 2000?

8. Who succeeded Nick Hancock as host of Room 101?

9. In which film does George Clooney star as the skipper of the Andrea Gail, a swordfishing-boat?

10. Which Oscar-winning actress played Susan Traherne in Plenty, a 1985 film set just after the Second World War?

11. Which DJ and pianist released his debut album Sincere, featuring the U.K. top ten single Crazy Love?

12. Which 2000 sci-fi sequel starring Christopher Lambert followed his escape from a futuristic prison?

13. What was Hong Kong Phooey's everyday alias in the Seventies cartoon series?

14. Which 2000 album release was a collaboration between Jimmy Page and the Black Crowes?

15. Who played The Man With the Golden Gun in the 1974 Bond film?

ANSWERS: 1 R.E.M., 2 LL Cool J, 3 Orson, 4 Destiny's Child, 5 John Wayne, 6 Steve Owen, 7 Ronan Keating (Ronan), 8 Paul Merton, 9 The Perfect Storm, 10 Meryl Streep, 11 M.J. Cole, 12 Fortress 2, 13 Penrod 'Penry' Pooch, 14 Live at the Greek, 15 Christopher Lee.

GENERAL KNOWLEDGE

1. In which golf competition did Europe beat the United States at Loch Lomond in October 2000?

2. Which Oscar-winning actor was born Muni Weisenfreund in 1895?

3. Whose first novel was called Kate Hannigan?

4. Which Scottish racing driver was the world champion in 1963 and 1965?

5. Who directed The Dirty Dozen and The Killing of Sister George?

6. With which instrument is jazz musician Jack Teagarden associated?

7. Who made his directorial debut with Star Trek III: The Search For Spock?

8. Which soft white clay is also known as china clay?

9. Of which American orchestra was Sir Georg Solti the music director from 1969 to 1991?

10. Which English novelist wrote A Kind of Loving?

11. Which actor starred in Yes, Minister and The Good Life?

12. By what first name was world heavyweight boxing champion Charles Liston known?

13. Which major conflict was also called the War Between the States?

14. Roald Dahl wrote the script for which Bond film?

15. Which English poet wrote A Shropshire Lad?

GENERAL KNOWLEDGE

1. What is the value of the pink ball in snooker?

2. Which English surgeon was the founder of antiseptic medicine?

3. What name is given to the seafood picnic traditional in the New England region of the United States?

4. Which child actor appeared in the films The Little Vampire, Stuart Little and Jerry Maguire?

5. From which two places did the Bren gun get its name?

6. Which Indian novelist wrote A Suitable Boy?

7. Which horse won the Derby in 1981?

8. Which 19th-century Irish nationalist MP's career was ended by proof of his affair with Katherine O'Shea?

9. What name is given to the natural painkillers secreted by the brain that resemble opiates?

10. Who directed the 1960 film La Dolce Vita?

11. Which American composer wrote An American in Paris and Porgy and Bess?

12. What were the first names of aviation pioneers the Wright brothers?

13. What is the surname of the little people in the Mary Norton book The Borrowers?

14. Who resigned as England football manager in October 2000?

15. Which Walt Disney film is based on a story by Carlo Collodi?

ANSWERS: 1 Six, 2 Joseph Lister, 3 Clambake, 4 Jonathan Lipnicki, 5 Brno and Enfield, 6 Vikram Seth, 7 Shergar, 8 Charles Stewart Parnell, 9 Endorphins, 10 Federico Fellini, 11 George Gershwin, 12 Orville and Wilbur, 13 Clock, 14 Kevin Keegan, 15 Pinocchio.

GENERAL KNOWLEDGE

1. Who wrote The Ordeal of Richard Feverel?

2. Which American silent film star was known as 'The Man of a Thousand Faces'?

3. From which British port did John Cabot set sail on the Matthew in 1497?

4. Which nonsense poem by Lewis Carroll is subtitled An Agony in Eight Fits?

5. Who won Best Score Oscars for Out of Africa and Dances With Wolves?

6. What name is given to the two dots placed above a vowel in German?

7. What nationality is the gymnast Andreea Raducan who was stripped of an Olympic gold medal after failing a drugs test?

8. Which zodiac sign governs the period from February 19 to March 20?

9. What sort of creature is a moccasin?

10. Which American author wrote The Case of Charles Dexter Ward?

11. Which child star sang On the Good Ship Lollipop in the 1934 film Bright Eyes?

12. On whose book was the film Fahrenheit 451 based?

13. Which Australian singer sang Dancing Queen at the Olympic Games closing ceremony after entering the stadium on a giant flip-flop?

14. In which country did the dance the Turkey Trot originate?

15. Which narcotic was removed from Coca-Cola's formula in 1905?

ENTERTAINMENT

1. What was the name of Noel Edmonds's nostalgic quiz show of the mid-Nineties?

2. Which soul singer had a U.K. number one hit in 1974 with You're the First, the Last, My Everything?

3. Which Monty Python star provided the voice of a frog in the 1994 film The Swan Princess?

4. What does ER stand for in the title of the U.S. drama series?

5. Leather trousers belonging to which rock star were sold for £28,000 at Sotheby's in 1996?

6. Which British actor played General Douglas MacArthur in the 1981 film Inchon?

7. What was Angus Loughran's alter-ego in the cult series Fantasy Football League?

8. Who had a U.K. top ten hit single in 1972 with You're So Vain?

9. Which 1995 thriller starred Brad Pitt as a cop on the trail of a serial killer?

10. Unemployed Robert Hoskins received a ten-year jail sentence in 1996 after being found guilty of stalking which pop star?

11. Which Supremes song did Phil Collins take to the U.K. number one spot in 1982?

12. Who starred as the athlete fighting for his free will in the 1975 film Rollerball?

13. Which ethereal singer released an album in 1996 entitled The Memory of Trees?

14. What sort of animal was the star of the 1995 film Babe?

15. Which police drama series starred Reece Dinsdale as Detective Inspector Charlie Scott?

? GENERAL KNOWLEDGE ?

1. In which European country are the provinces of Fyn and Ribe?

2. Who authored the play The Quare Fellow?

3. In which country is a grosz a monetary unit?

4. Which country in Africa is immediately west of western Zambia?

5. Who plays Polonius in the 2000 film Hamlet which starred Ethan Hawke?

6. What in Australia is a skirter?

7. Who wrote the 1960 novel The Ballad of Peckham Rye?

8. Where are the ashes of scientist Ernest Rutherford buried?

9. In which African country is the airport town of Gondar?

10. Which group's second album is entitled Whatever and Ever Amen?

11. What won the 1977 Whitbread Book of the Year award?

12. Where would you find echard - in a boil or in the soil?

13. In which year did Innocent III become pope?

14. Which has the lower melting point - cobalt or nickel?

15. Which Japanese author had a private army called the Shield Society?

ANSWERS: 1 Denmark, 2 Brendan Behan, 3 Poland, 4 Angola, 5 Bill Murray, 6 A type of sheep shearer, 7 Muriel Spark, 8 Westminster Abbey, 9 Ethiopia, 10 Ben Folds Five, 11 Injury Time by Beryl Bainbridge, 12 The soil, 13 1198, 14 Nickel, 15 Yukio Mishima.

GENERAL KNOWLEDGE

1. Which Spanish painter collaborated with the director Luis Buñuel on the film Un chien andalou?

2. What in the U.S. is a flack?

3. The Musgrave Ranges straddle which two Australian states?

4. Where was William Rufus killed by an arrow in 1100?

5. Who succeeded Jomo Kenyatta as president of Kenya in 1978?

6. Which European country houses the river Ythan?

7. Who drove the Ring-a-Ding Convert-a-Car in the cartoon series Wacky Races?

8. What is the English equivalent of a dome fastener?

9. Who won the 1982 Nobel prize in physics?

10. Which writer's debut novel was entitled Carole King is an Alien?

11. In Australian slang, what is a drummer?

12. Into which body of water does the Fitzroy River in Western Australia flow?

13. Which female singer had a 1992 Top 20 single with the song Crucify?

14. Whose Treatise on the Motion of Vortex Rings won him the Adams Prize in 1884?

15. Who wrote the 2001 novel The Falls?

ANSWERS: 1 Salvador Dali, 2 A press or publicity agent, 3 South Australia and Northern Territory, 4 New Forest, 5 Daniel arap Moi, 6 Scotland, 7 Prof. Pat Pending, 8 Press stud, 9 Kenneth G. Wilson, 10 Yasmin Boland, 11 The slowest shearer in a team, 12 King Sound, 13 Tori Amos, 14 Sir Joseph John Thompson, 15 Ian Rankin.

GENERAL KNOWLEDGE

1. What is adularia - a disease or a gemstone?

2. Which U.S. state is further south - Missouri or Nebraska?

3. What did physicist Ernest Orlando Lawrence invent in 1929?

4. Who wrote the 1829 novel The Misfortunes of Elphin?

5. Which actress played Lady Angela Forbes in the television drama series The Monocled Mutineer?

6. Where would you find a crumple zone?

7. In which year did the arranger and songwriter Jack Nitzsche die?

8. Which French city is further north - Bordeaux or Marseilles?

9. Which American artist's works include 1905's Stone Bridge, Old Lyme, Connecticut?

10. Whose books include The Quark and the Jaguar: Adventures in the Simple and the Complex?

11. Who was prime minister of Russia from 1953-5?

12. Which Roman emperor was killed by the Goths in 251?

13. In which sea is Tiran island?

14. Which American artist painted the 1911 oil The Masquerade Dress?

15. In what establishment might you find a liberty horse?

ANSWERS: 1 Gemstone, 2 Missouri, 3 The cyclotron, 4 Thomas Love Peacock, 5 Penelope Wilton, 6 On a motor vehicle, 7 2000, 8 Bordeaux, 9 Childe Hassam, 10 Murray Gell-Mann, 11 Georgi Malenkov, 12 Decius, 13 Red Sea, 14 Robert Henri, 15 A circus. It is a riderless performing horse.

SPORT

1. Who scored Chelsea's winning goal in the 2000 FA Cup Final?

2. How many golf majors has Jack Nicklaus won?

3. Which Test cricket team has the cricketer Wavell Hinds played for?

4. Which team won the FA Cup in 1973?

5. Which darts player is nicknamed The Power?

6. Which British Formula 1 racing driver survived a Learjet crash in May 2000?

7. Who won the U.S. Masters in golf in 2002?

8. In which sport did Felix Savon win gold at the Sydney Olympics?

9. Which number lies between 19 and 17 on a dartboard?

10. What position did Manchester United finish in the 2001/2002 Premier league?

11. Who won the women's singles title at the 2000 French Open?

12. Which golfer won the U.S. PGA in 1995?

13. Which Argentinian scored two goals in the final of the 1978 World Cup?

14. Who was the world snooker champion in 1986?

15. Which city hosted the 1980 Olympic Games?

ANSWERS: 1 Roberto Di Matteo, 2 18, 3 West Indies, 4 Sunderland, 5 Phil Taylor, 6 David Coulthard, 7 Tiger Woods, 8 Boxing, 9 3, 10 Third, 11 Mary Pierce, 12 Steve Elkington, 13 Mario Kempes, 14 Joe Johnson, 15 Moscow.

? GENERAL KNOWLEDGE ?

1. What is jaconet - a type of fabric or a kind of soldier?

2. Which sculptress was the second wife of the painter Ben Nicholson?

3. In which year did Admiral Rooke take Gibraltar?

4. For his research into which disease was J.A.G. Fibiger awarded the 1926 Nobel prize in medicine?

5. In which novel by Thomas Hardy does the character John Loveday appear?

6. What might you do with kulfi?

7. In which English county is the town of Louth?

8. In which play by Shakespeare does the character Feste appear?

9. Which has the lower melting point - magnesium or strontium?

10. In which year did the punk singer Wendy O. Williams commit suicide?

11. In which English county is the town of Great Harwood?

12. What is a briolette?

13. Which French painter's works include the 1939 oil The Terrace at Vernonnet?

14. Which U.S. city is further east - Chicago or New Orleans?

15. Who played the baseball player 'Nuke' LaLoosh in the 1988 film Bull Durham?

ANSWERS: 1 Fabric, 2 Barbara Hepworth, 3 1704, 4 Cancer, 5 The Trumpet Major, 6 Eat it, it's an Indian sweet, 7 Lincolnshire, 8 Twelfth Night, 9 Magnesium, 10 1998, 11 Lancashire, 12 A pear-shaped gem, 13 Pierre Bonnard, 14 Chicago, 15 Tim Robbins.

GENERAL KNOWLEDGE

1. What is spinifex?

2. Of which king was King George V the second son?

3. Who wrote the children's book The Other Side of Truth?

4. In which year did physicist Otto Stern move from Germany to the U.S.?

5. In which Australian state is the town of Dubbo?

6. Who wrote the 1964 novel Late Call?

7. If an animal is fluvioterrestrial, where does it live?

8. On which sea is the English resort of Withersea?

9. Which female singer had a Top Five single with the song What A Girl Wants?

10. Which English actress stars in the film Up At The Villa?

11. Of what quantity is the kilogram the SI unit?

12. Who wrote the 1830 novel Paul Clifford?

13. How is the river Granta, which flows through Cambridge, otherwise known?

14. What in Scotland is hodden?

15. Which continent is the larger land mass - Antarctica or South America?

ANSWERS: 1 A type of grass, 2 Edward VII, 3 Beverley Naidoo, 4 1933, 5 New South Wales, 6 Angus Wilson, 7 In rivers and on land, 8 North Sea, 9 Christina Aguilera, 10 Kristin Scott Thomas, 11 Mass, 12 Edward Bulwer-Lytton, 13 The Cam, 14 Type of coarse cloth, 15 South America.

GENERAL KNOWLEDGE

1. Which cult author collaborated on The Unspeakable Mr. Hart with artist Malcolm McNeil?

2. In which European country are the provinces of Olt and Cluj?

3. What is the middle name of the American Football player Joe Montana?

4. What in India was a mohur?

5. In which African country is the city of Ekiti?

6. In which year was the second Bishops' War?

7. Which American artist, born in 1870, painted the watercolour Brooklyn Bridge?

8. If something is dentoid, what does it resemble?

9. Who directed the 1957 film Wild Strawberries?

10. S.A. Waksman received a Nobel prize in medicine for his discovery of which antibiotic?

11. From which creatures, other than bees, would you get beestings?

12. In which novel by Charles Dickens does the character Madame Mantalini appear?

13. Which was the first Top 20 single for the group ABC?

14. Of what is malocology the scientific study?

15. In Scotland, is Motherwell north or south of Falkirk?

ANSWERS: 1 William Burroughs, 2 Romania, 3 Clifford, 4 A gold coin, 5 Nigeria, 6 1640, 7 John Marin, 8 A tooth, 9 Ingmar Bergman, 10 Streptomycin, 11 Cows, 12 Nicholas Nickleby, 13 Tears Are Not Enough, 14 Molluscs, 15 South.

ENTERTAINMENT

1. Which Emmerdale character was played by Sandra Gough during her first stint with the soap?

2. Who starred as Doctor Dolittle in the 1967 film?

3. Who had a U.K. top ten hit in 1977 with 2-4-6-8 Motorway?

4. Who played Stephen Biko in the 1987 film Cry Freedom?

5. Who sang the title track for the 1995 Bond film GoldenEye?

6. Which 1995 film starred Demi Moore and Gary Oldman?

7. Which veteran comedienne played Aunt Florence in the Nineties TV adaptation of Just William?

8. Which animated film featuring Wallace and Gromit won Nick Park his third Oscar?

9. Which former cult soccer show featured 'Phoenix from the Flames'?

10. Which 1995 film starred Leonardo DiCaprio as a sportsman turned performance poet?

11. Which actress played Hannah in the sitcom Faith in the Future?

12. Which Geordie singer and actor released an album entitled Big River in 1995?

13. Which comic actor was married to Tuesday Weld and Suzy Kendall?

14. Paul and Pauline Calf were creations of which British comic actor?

15. Which U.K. vocal trio released an album entitled Power of a Woman in 1995?

ANSWERS: 1 Doreen Shuttleworth, 2 Rex Harrison, 3 The Tom Robinson Band, 4 Denzel Washington, 5 Tina Turner, 6 The Scarlet Letter, 7 Mollie Sugden, 8 A Close Shave, 9 Fantasy Football League, 10 The Basketball Diaries, 11 Julia Sawalha, 12 Jimmy Nail, 13 Dudley Moore, 14 Steve Coogan, 15 Eternal.

GENERAL KNOWLEDGE

1. In which African National Park is the tourist camp of Skukuza?

2. What form of transport is a travois?

3. Who authored the 1990 play The Piano Lesson?

4. Which female singer had a 1995 Top 30 single with the song Never Knew Love?

5. Who was the Home Secretary and Minister of Home Security from 1940-45?

6. What is another word for an alligator pear?

7. Which country in Africa is immediately west of Egypt?

8. In which year was the naval Battle of Sluys?

9. Which Frenchman designed and developed the electric-arc furnace?

10. Who wrote the 1951 play The Rose Tattoo?

11. In which English county is the market town of Great Dunmow?

12. Who penned the stage play Boy Gets Girl which was performed at the Royal Court in London in 2001?

13. In which game is a caman used?

14. Who wrote the 1866 novel Hereward the Wake?

15. Who was awarded the 1983 Nobel prize in medicine?

ANSWERS: 1 Kruger National Park, 2 A sled, 3 August Wilson, 4 Oleta Adams, 5 Herbert Morrison, 6 Avocado, 7 Libya, 8 1340, 9 Henri Moissan, 10 Tennessee Williams, 11 Essex, 12 Rebecca Gilman, 13 Shinty, 14 Charles Kingsley, 15 Barbara McClintock.

? **GENERAL KNOWLEDGE** **?**

1. Which singer-songwriter recorded the 2000 album Ghost of David?

2. In which country would you find a shanty or shantytown called a favela?

3. Which U.S. state is further north - Alabama or Utah?

4. La is the symbol of which chemical element?

5. In which play by Shakespeare does the character Polonius appear?

6. What is Tshiluba - an African language or the holy name of the highest ranking official in Brunei?

7. Which leader of Mercian died on 26th July, 796?

8. Which Spanish artist's paintings included 1934's Girl Reading at a Table?

9. On which body of water does the Devon resort Ilfracombe lie?

10. In which city was the jazz composer Jelly Roll Morton born?

11. In which year did Philipp von Lenard first work with cathode rays?

12. On which river is the town of Guelph, Ontario?

13. Who played DI Alan Witty in the long-running television cop show Z Cars?

14. If an actor dries what do they do?

15. In which U.S. state was the artist Jackson Pollock born?

ANSWERS: 1 Damien Jurado, 2 Brazil, 3 Utah, 4 Lanthanum, 5 Hamlet, 6 A language, 7 Offa, 8 Pablo Picasso, 9 Bristol Channel, 10 New Orleans, 11 1888, 12 Speed, 13 John Woodvine, 14 Forget their lines, 15 Wyoming.

? **GENERAL KNOWLEDGE** ?

1. What in poetry is a hemistich?

2. Who wrote the short story Super-Toys Last All Summer Long on which the film AI is based?

3. Who was awarded the 1907 Nobel prize in chemistry for his discovery of non-cellular fermentation?

4. The town of Ince-in-Makerfield forms part of which northern Metropolitan District?

5. What was the first Top 30 single by the singer Shakin' Stevens?

6. Who played Sue Ann Nivens in the television show The Mary Tyler Moore Show?

7. In which industry would you use neroli oil?

8. In which Asian country is the city of Luang Prabang?

9. Who wrote the 1947 stage play A Moon for the Misbegotten?

10. What is the square root of the number 16?

11. Who wrote the 1847 novel The Children of the New Forest?

12. In which year did the golfer Jack Nicklaus turn professional?

13. What in U.S. military slang is a cigarette roll?

14. In which European country is Biesbosch?

15. In which year was Queen Victoria's Diamond Jubilee?

ANSWERS: 1 A half line of verse, 2 Brian Aldiss, 3 Eduard Buchner, 4 Wigan, 5 Hot Dog, 6 Betty White, 7 Perfumery, 8 Laos, 9 Eugene O'Neill, 10 4, 11 Frederick Marryat, 12 1962, 13 A parachute jump in which the parachute fails to open, 14 Netherlands, 15 1897.

ENTERTAINMENT

1. Who directed the 1978 classic punk movie Jubilee?

2. Who played Neil in the eighties comedy series The Young Ones?

3. Which legendary singer/songwriter was killed on December 8th, 1980?

4. Who directed the 1962 film Lolita?

5. Which Irish singer reinterpreted his own material backed by an orchestra on the album Beautiful Dreams?

6. Which sitcom was set in Bayview Retirement Home?

7. Who played bass for Joy Division and New Order?

8. Who played Dr Paul Dangerfield in the drama series Dangerfield?

9. Which 1995 Jean Becker film starred Gerard Depardieu and Vanessa Paradis?

10. Which barefoot sixties singer was born Sandra Goodrich?

11. Which Brookside character was played by Paul Usher?

12. The Ghost of Tom Joad was a 1995 album release by which rock star?

13. In which country is the soap opera Shortland Street set?

14. How many U.K. number one singles did the Rolling Stones have in the sixties?

15. Who played Billie Holiday in the 1972 film Lady Sings the Blues?

GENERAL KNOWLEDGE

1. What craftsman in Ireland might use a scollop?

2. Which Scottish island is further north - Colonsay or Rhum?

3. In which decade did gangster Al Capone die?

4. Who wrote the 1858 novel The Three Clerks?

5. Which playwright is married to the actor Sir John Mills?

6. Which sculptor's works include the 1923 marble Bird in Space?

7. How many pounds are there in the unit of weight a cental?

8. In which year did Texas gain independence from Mexico?

9. In which country was the Nobel prize-winning physicist Isidor Isaac Rabi born?

10. Which English resort is further south - Bridlington or Fleetwood?

11. Miquette Giraudy is the partner and collaborator of which former member of the group Gong?

12. What shape is a clevis?

13. Who wrote the 1968 novel The Nice and the Good?

14. What was Simon Williams's character name in the sitcom Agony?

15. Which forest lies north-west of Auchtermuchty, Scotland?

ANSWERS: 1 A thatcher, 2 Rhum, 3 1940s, 4 Anthony Trollope, 5 Mary Hayley Bell, 6 Constantin Brancusi, 7 A hundred, 8 1836, 9 Austria, 10 Fleetwood, 11 Steve Hillage, 12 U-shaped, 13 Iris Murdoch, 14 Laurence Lucas, 15 Pitmedden Forest.

GENERAL KNOWLEDGE

1. Which U.S. playwright wrote the Pulitzer prize-winning drama Angels in America?

2. In which year was the Battle of Neville's Cross?

3. Who directed the film The Legend of Bagger Vance?

4. What are you in Australia if you are on one's pat?

5. In which English county is the seaside resort of Sidmouth?

6. Scientist Max Theiler received a Nobel prize for his work on combatting which disease?

7. Which Russia-born painter's works include 1931's South of Scranton?

8. Which duo recorded the album Loveboat?

9. What might you do with petit pois?

10. Which has the lower melting point - chromium or vanadium?

11. In which U.S. state is Fort Knox?

12. Which Italian sculptor's works include 1913's Antigraceful?

13. Of which country did Wolfgang Schüssel become Chancellor in 2000?

14. What type of creature is an ariel - a gazelle or a goat?

15. In which European country is the ski resort of La Clusaz?

ANSWERS: 1 Tony Kushner, 2 1346, 3 Robert Redford, 4 On your own, 5 Devon, 6 . Yellow fever, 7 Peter Blume, 8 Erasure, 9 Eat them they're peas, 10 Chromium, 11 Kentucky, 12 Umberto Boccioni, 13 Austria, 14 Gazelle, 15 France.

GENERAL KNOWLEDGE

1. On which river is the town of Wisbech?

2. In which city was the art historian Ernst Gombrich born?

3. What is a balata - a type of bird or tree?

4. Who sang lead vocals on the 1999 hit Walk Like A Panther by the group The All Seeing I?

5. In which year was the U.S.S. Maine blown up in Havana harbour?

6. Who wrote the 1963 novel One Fat Englishman?

7. Rathlin Island lies between which two parts of the British Isles?

8. Of what is limnology the scientific study?

9. Who played Michelle Fowler in the soap opera EastEnders from 1985-95?

10. What does the Scottish adjective forfochen mean?

11. In which play by Shakespeare does the character Jaques appear?

12. Who succeeded Rutherford Hayes in 1881 as U.S. president?

13. In which African country is the oasis town of Bilma?

14. If you have hypermnesia, what are you good at?

15. In which year did the Nobel prize-winning chemist Irving Langmuir die?

GENERAL KNOWLEDGE

1. Who is the author of the novel The Famished Road?

2. Which name was adopted by comedian Julius Marx?

3. Who was the female star of the 1997 film G.I. Jane?

4. The name of which god of the Philistines in the Old Testament meant lord of flies?

5. What was the name given to the journey of about 6,000 miles undertaken by around 100,000 Chinese Communists between 1934-5?

6. Who wrote the novel Tarzan of the Apes?

7. Who authored the 1962 novel King Rat?

8. Who was the male star of the 1964 comedy film A Shot in the Dark?

9. Who wrote the poem Ode on a Grecian Urn?

10. What is the smallest unit of weight in the avoirdupois system?

11. What is the name of the marshy area of S.E. England which includes Dungeness?

12. Who became Labour's Chancellor of the Exchequer in 1997?

13. In the sitcom Are You Being Served?, which actor played Mr. Humphries?

14. Who was the author of the play The Glass Menagerie?

15. In which U.S. state was tennis player Pancho Gonzales born?

ANSWERS 1. Ben Okri 2. Groucho 3. Demi Moore 4. Beelzebub 5. The Long March 6. Edgar Rice Burroughs 7. James Clavell 8. Peter Sellers 9. John Keats 10. Grain 11. Romney Marsh 12. Gordon Brown 13. John Inman 14. Tennessee Williams 15. California.

ENTERTAINMENT

1. Who won a Best Supporting Actress Oscar for the 1944 film National Velvet?

2. Who won Best Actor in a Comedy/Musical at the 2000 Golden Globes?

3. Who did Gregory Peck play in the 1978 film The Boys From Brazil?

4. In which Verdi opera does Princess Eboli appear?

5. Who directed the 1994 film Underneath?

6. Who plays a pursued murder witness in the 1990 film Narrow Margin?

7. The 1983 film Under Fire is set in which country?

8. Who played Morticia in the sitcom The Addams Family on television?

9. Who composed the 1882 opera The Devil's Wall?

10. Who directed the 1958 film The Big Country?

11. Which Perrier Award-winning comic starred in the 1999 sitcom Small Potatoes?

12. Who played Carolyn in the film American Beauty?

13. In which Mozart opera does the aria Dove sono appear?

14. Who played Monsignor Renard in the 2000 ITV drama series?

15. What illness does Glenn Ford contract in the 1966 film Rage?

SPORT

1. Which rugby league club released Brett Green in February 2000?

2. Who rode Alydaress to victory in the 1989 Irish Oaks?

3. At what sport do James Cracknell, Tim Foster and Ed Coode compete?

4. At what sport were Boris Dubrovsky and Oleg Tyurin Olympic champions in 1964?

5. What sport has Ahmed Barada played at international level?

6. Which snooker player won the 1997 Scottish Masters?

7. By what score did England win in Italy in the 2000 Six Nations tournament in rugby union?

8. For which country did cricketer Ian Healy keep wicket?

9. At what sport do Ian Schuback and David Gourlay compete?

10. In basketball, in which year were the Chicago Bulls first crowned NBA champions in the U.S.?

11. What is the main difference between a Rugby Fives court and an Eton Fives court?

12. What game do Bracknell Bees and Sheffield Steelers play?

13. Who was the 1973 men's 200m breaststroke swimming world champion?

14. Which U.S. pair won the 1994 World Cup in golf?

15. What is the nickname of Test bowler Shoaib Akhtar?

ANSWERS 1. Hull 2. Michael Kinane 3. Rowing 4. Rowing 5. Squash 6. Nigel Bond 7. 59-12 8. Australia 9. Bowls 10. 1991 11. There is no buttress 12. Ice hockey 13. David Wilkie 14. Fred Couples and Davis Love III 15. The Rawalpindi Express.

POP MUSIC

1. Which group had a 1980 Top 10 single with the song Young Parisians?

2. Which group's second album was entitled Flying Low?

3. Which punk singer was formerly an art student in Hull and a worker in a lemonade factory?

4. Which group recorded the 2000 album Songs of Strength and Heartbreak?

5. Which group had a 1980 Top 20 single with the song Rock 'n' Roll Ain't Noise Pollution?

6. Which studio album by Dexy's Midnight Runners includes the track Old?

7. Which female singer-songwriter recorded the debut album Shine Like It Does?

8. Which French musician recorded the 2000 album Metamorphoses?

9. Which singer-songwriter fronted the band LAX when he toured Britain in 2001?

10. Which female singer duetted with Bryan Adams on the 1985 Top 30 single It's Only Love?

11. Which female singer recorded a 2000 covers album entitled It's Like This?

12. Which Australian group recorded the 1976 single I'm Stranded?

13. Which singer-songwriter recorded the 2001 album Say It Is So?

14. From which U.S. city does hip-hop star Nelly hail?

15. Which group recorded the 1977 album L.A.M.F.?

ANSWERS 1. Adam and the Ants 2. Willard Grant Conspiracy 3. Wreckless Eric 4. The Mighty Wah! 5. AC/DC 6. Too-Rye-Ay 7. Eileen Rose 8. Jean Michel Jarre 9. Ryan Adams 10. Tina Turner 11. Rickie Lee Jones 12. The Saints 13. Tim Finn 14. St. Louis 15. Johnny Thunders and the Heartbreakers.

ART & LITERATURE

1. Who is the author of the thriller Southern Cross?

2. In which century did Italian sculptor Nicola Pisano live?

3. Which thriller writer authored The White House Connection?

4. In which country was artist Edvard Munch born?

5. Who is the author of the 2000 crime novel Set in Darkness?

6. Who painted the 1850 work Burial at Ornans?

7. In which city was artist Sir Sidney Nolan born?

8. In which century did artist Honoré Daumier live?

9. Who painted 1829's Ulysses Mocking Polyphemus?

10. Simon Tappertit appears in which novel by Charles Dickens?

11. Which painter's works include 1903's Girl in a Straw Hat and 1925's The Table?

12. In which century did French painter Jean-François Millet live?

13. Who wrote the novel Enduring Love?

14. In which year did artist Paul Cézanne die?

15. Who is the author of the murder mystery The Drowning People?

ANSWERS 1. Patricia Cornwell 2. 13th 3. Jack Higgins 4. Norway 5. Ian Rankin 6. Gustave Courbet 7. Melbourne, Australia 8. 19th century 9. J.M.W. Turner 10. Barnaby Rudge 11. Pierre Bonnard 12. 19th century 13. Ian McEwan 14. 1906 15. Richard Mason.

GENERAL KNOWLEDGE

1. Which actor played an assassin in the 1973 film The Day of the Jackal?

2. Which of The Marx Brothers was born Leonard Marx?

3. In which year did Italian composer Luigi Nono die?

4. Which comedian starred with Richard Burton in the 1981 film Absolution?

5. Who was the director of the 1945 film Blithe Spirit?

6. What is the name given to the back part of a golf club head where it bends to join the shaft?

7. In which year did British conductor Sir Georg Solti die?

8. Who did actress Mary Tamm play in the television series Doctor Who?

9. Who were the male and female leads in the 1997 film A Life Less Ordinary?

10. Which river in eastern France joins the Rhône at Lyon?

11. Anchorage is the largest city in which U.S. state?

12. In which play by Shakespeare does the characer Iras appear?

13. Which cult television series featured Kyle MacLachan as Agent Dale Cooper?

14. In which year was dancer and choreographer Robert Cohan born?

15. Who wrote the 1969 novel The Estate?

ANSWERS 1. Edward Fox 2. Chico 3. 1990 4. Billy Connolly 5. Sir David Lean 6. Heel 7. 1997 8. Romana 9. Ewan McGregor and Cameron Diaz 10. Saône 11. Alaska 12. Antony and Cleopatra 13. Twin Peaks 14. 1925 15. Isaac Bashevis Singer

ENTERTAINMENT

1. Who played the lead in the 1970 film Captain Nemo and the Underwater City?

2. Who is 'entertainer' John Shuttleworth's agent?

3. Who plays a truck driver and singer in the 1959 film Daddy-o?

4. Which comedy duo's revues included 1957's At the Drop of a Hat?

5. The 1997 film The Ice Storm is an adaptation of whose novel?

6. Which sitcom arose from the 1962 Comedy Playhouse show The Offer?

7. Who played Leanne Battersby in Coronation Street?

8. Who played Captain Dobey in Starsky and Hutch?

9. Who composed the 1957 opera Dialogues of the Carmelites?

10. Who composed the 1889 opera Edgar?

11. Who originally produced the ITV game show The Price is Right in the UK?

12. Who directed the 1995 film Strange Days?

13. Who played The Invisible Man's boss, Walter Carlson, in the sci-fi TV show?

14. Who plays a seedy private eye in the 1992 film Under Suspicion?

15. In which year did the comedy actress Joan Sanderson die?

ANSWERS 1. Robert Ryan 2. Ken Worthington 3. Dick Contino 4. Flanders and Swann 5. Rick Moody 6. Steptoe and Son 7. Jane Danson 8. Bernie Hamilton 9. Poulenc 10. Puccini 11. William G. Stewart 12. Kathryn Bigelow 13. Craig Stevens 14. Liam Neeson 15. 1992.

SPORT

1. What nationality is former moto-cross world champion Eric Geboers?

2. With which sport would you associate Alex Zülle?

3. Which club won the 1885 Scottish F.A. Cup Final?

4. For which UK ice hockey team did Shawn Wansborough play during the 1999/2000 season?

5. Who won the 1994 New York women's marathon?

6. What nationality is cricketer Usman Afzaal?

7. Who was champion flat racing jockey from 1964-71?

8. Who was Yorkshire's Young Player of the Year in cricket in 1989?

9. Which club won the 1947 rugby league Challenge Cup?

10. Who beat Featherstone in rugby league's 2000 Silk Cut Challenge Cup 4th Round?

11. With what sport are Sam Ermolenko and Joe Screen associated?

12. What nationality is judo's Heidi Rakels?

13. Which cricketer took four wickets in consecutive balls twice, in the 1931-2 and 1934 seasons?

14. At which sport did Barry Dancer coach Great Britain?

15. Who was the 1979 U.K. professional billiards champion?

ANSWERS 1. Belgian 2. Cycling 3. Renton 4. London Knights 5. Tegla Loroupe 6. Pakistani 7. Lester Piggott 8. Richard Blakey 9. Bradford Northern 10. Leeds Rhinos 11. Speedway 12. Belgian 13. Bob Crisp 14. Hockey 15. Rex Williams.

POP MUSIC

1. From which UK city do drum and bass outfit Kosheen hail?

2. Who featured on Eminem's 1999 hit single Guilty Conscience?

3. In which year did the Boo Radleys form?

4. Which U.S. country group's albums include Odessa and Milk and Scissors?

5. Who had a Top 10 single in 1999 with 2 Times?

6. Who, under the pseudonym of Apollo C. Vermouth, produced the single I'm the Urban Spaceman by The Bonzo Dog Doo-Dah Band?

7. Which guitarist guested on Love's 1970 track The Everlasting First?

8. Which group recorded the live album Music For Hangovers?

9. Which group's singles include 2000's The F-Word?

10. Are You Receiving Me is the second album by which group?

11. Which former member of The Cult formed a band called the Holy Barbarians?

12. Who had a 2000 Top 10 single with Stand Tough?

13. Which member of The Kinks wrote two tracks on Big Country's album Driving to Damascus?

14. Who wrote the song The Band Played Waltzing Matilda which features on the album Rum Sodomy & the Lash by The Pogues?

15. What is the title of Fun Lovin' Criminals' Barry White tribute single?

ANSWERS 1. Bristol 2. Dr. Dre 3. 1988 4. The Handsome Family 5. Ann Lee 6. Paul McCartney 7. Jimi Hendrix 8. Cheap Trick 9. Babybird 10. Subcircus 11. Ian Astbury 12. Point Break 13. Ray Davies 14. Eric Bogle 15. Love Unlimited.

GEOGRAPHY

1. Karl Johans Gate is the main thoroughfare of which European capital city?

2. Which country is larger in area - Iceland or Hungary?

3. In which country is the Turrialba volcano?

4. On which river is the French town of Vierzon?

5. On which river is Tonbridge in Kent?

6. In which Asian country is the Sambhar salt lake?

7. On which island is the Canadian seaport of Sydney?

8. On which Greek island is the port of Patitiri?

9. Which Bavarian town lies at the confluence of the Rivers Ilz, Danube and Inn?

10. Is the Coromandel Peninsula on the North or South Island of New Zealand?

11. On which island is the Samaria Gorge, the longest in Europe?

12. In which European country is the Lemmenjoki National Park?

13. Which river lies immediately south-west of Southwold, Suffolk?

14. In which sea is the mountain island of Telendos?

15. On which European island is the town of Erice which houses Pepoli Castle?

ANSWERS 1. Oslo 2. Iceland 3. Costa Rica 4. Cher 5. Medway 6. India 7. Cape Breton Island 8. Alonissos 9. Passau 10. North 11. Crete 12. Finland 13. Blythe 14. Aegean Sea 15. Sicily.

GENERAL KNOWLEDGE

1. Who was the author of the classic novel The Three Musketeers?

2. Who was the author of the novel The Red Badge of Courage?

3. Who wrote the 1976 play American Buffalo?

4. The 1989 film Scandal was about which political controversy?

5. Which novel by Nick Hornby features the characters Will and Marcus?

6. What is the name given to any one of the four officers who command the Yeomen of the Guard?

7. Elba is a mountainous island off the west coast of which country?

8. Who authored the 1971 play Butley?

9. In which year did English actor and clown Joseph Grimaldi die?

10. What was the 1998 venue of the winter Olympic Games?

11. Which western author's works include Trail Boss?

12. With which music hall performer would you associate the song Any Old Iron?

13. Which large wolf-like breed of dog is also called a German shepherd?

14. Who wrote the 1920 novel This Side of Paradise?

15. Which maiden in Greek mythology agreed to marry any man who could defeat her in a running race?

ANSWERS 1. Alexandre Dumas 2. Stephen Crane 3. David Mamet 4. The 1963 Profumo affair 5. About A Boy 6. Exon 7. Italy 8. Simon Gray 9. 1837 10. Nagano 11. J.T. Edson 12. Harry Champion 13. Alsatian 14. F. Scott Fitzgerald 15. Atalanta.

ENTERTAINMENT

1. Who directed the 1961 film Viridiana?

2. Which father and daughter team appeared in the television series Remington Steele?

3. Who directed the 1950 film Night and the City which starred Richard Widmark?

4. Who directed the 1992 film Night and the City which starred Robert De Niro?

5. Who played television's Doctor Who from 1966-9?

6. Who did Neville Brand play in the television series The Untouchables which began in 1959?

7. On which quiz show would you hear the phrase 'a starter for ten'?

8. Which director's film debut was 1991's Boyz N the Hood?

9. In which year did Michael Parkinson return as a BBC chat show host after a 16 year absence?

10. What is the name of the character played by Robson Green in the television series Touching Evil?

11. Which actor played Jeb Gaine in the U.S. television series Wells Fargo?

12. What are the three lifelines on the quiz show Who Wants To Be A Millionaire?

13. In which year did the play Comedians by Trevor Griffiths first appear, at the Nottingham Playhouse?

14. Which trio starred in the 1967 television series Three of a Kind?

15. In which opera does the character Cavaradossi appear?

ANSWERS 1. Luis Buñuel 2. Efrem Zimbalist Jr. and Stephanie Zimbalist 3. Jules Dassin 4. Irwin Winkler 5. Patrick Troughton 6. Al Capone 7. University Challenge 8. John Singleton 9. 1998 10. Dave Creegan 11. William Demarest 12. 50/50, Phone a Friend and Ask the Audience 13. 1975 14. Lulu, Mike Yarwood and Ray Fell 15. Tosca by Puccini.

SPORT

1. Which team appeared in the 1992 and 1996 European Championship Finals in football?

2. What nationality is golfer Mathias Gronberg?

3. With which sport are Tamas Darnyi and Luca Sacchi associated?

4. In which year was the Eisenhower Trophy first competed for in golf?

5. Which horse was the dam of Istabraq?

6. Which veteran golfer won the Energis Senior Masters in August 1999?

7. Which horse won the Melbourne Cup in 1974 & 1975?

8. Who won the 2000 London men's marathon?

9. Which Canadian Football team won the Grey Cup in 1939 for the first time?

10. In which year did Gerald Patterson and Suzanne Lenglen win the Wimbledon mixed doubles tennis title?

11. How many Formula 1 Grand Prix wins did Carlos Reutemann have in his career from 1972-82?

12. In which city were the 1951 Pan-American Games held?

13. In which year was the Scottish Club Championship in rugby union inaugurated?

14. In cricket, who scored 111 n.o. for Hampshire against Somerset in the 1st innings of their 1999 county championship game?

15. Which Frenchman was a 1928 undisputed featherweight boxing world champion?

ANSWERS 1. Germany 2. Swedish 3. Swimming 4. 1958 5. Betty's Secret 6. Neil Coles 7. Think Big 8. Antonio Pinto 9. Winnipeg Blue Bombers 10. 1920 11. Twelve 12. Buenos Aires 13. 1974 14. Adrian Aymes 15. Andre Routis.

POP MUSIC

1. Which country artist recorded the album Love Will Always Win?

2. Which group released the 1983 mini-L.P. The Splendour of Fear?

3. Who features on Chicane's 2000 No. 1 single Don't Give Up?

4. Who recorded the 1994 Top 10 single Oh Baby I ...?

5. Which singer released the 1973 album Heart Food?

6. Which group recorded the 1999 single I Wouldn't Believe Your Radio?

7. Which member of R.E.M. produced the 1986 album The Good Earth by The Feelies?

8. Which U.S. singer fronted a band called Popcorn Blizzard?

9. Which group had a 1999 No. 1 single with We're Going To Ibiza?

10. Who had a Top 10 hit in February 2000 with Sweet Love 2K?

11. Who was lead singer of the group Black Grape?

12. Which punk group had a 1980 hit single with Party in Paris?

13. With what song did the Ramones have a 1980 Top 10 hit?

14. Who had a 1999 Christmas hit with Two in a Million/You're My Number One?

15. In which year did the Crusaders have a Top 10 single with Street Life?

ANSWERS 1. Faith Hill 2. Felt 3. Bryan Adams 4. Eternal 5. Judee Sill 6. Stereophonics 7. Peter Buck 8. Meat Loaf 9. Vengaboys 10. Fierce 11. Shaun Ryder 12. UK Subs 13. Baby I Love You 14. S Club 7 15. 1979.

HISTORY

1. In which year was the ANZUS Pact signed between Australia, New Zealand and the U.S.?

2. In which year did Edward VI succeed to the throne?

3. In which year did James Cook first sight the east coast of Australia?

4. Who became chaplain to Henry VIII in 1541?

5. In which year did Paddy Ashdown become a member of the Liberal Party?

6. Gabriel Bethlen was king of which country from 1620-1?

7. Who became king and queen of England following the 'Glorious Revolution'?

8. In which year did William Hague become the leader of the Conservative Party?

9. Who in 1387 became Queen of Denmark, Norway and Sweden?

10. In which year was the Rye House Plot?

11. In which year did the Japanese statesman Tokugawa Ieyasu die?

12. In which year did Erwin Rommel join the German Army?

13. In which year was the Battle of Worcester?

14. In which year did Catherine the Great of Russia die?

15. In which year was the Boston Port Act passed?

ANSWERS 1. 1951 2. 1547 3. 1770 4. Nicholas Ridley 5. 1976 6. Hungary 7. William and Mary 8. 1997 9. Margaret 10. 1683 11. 1616 12. 1910 13. 1651 14. 1796 15. 1774.

GENERAL KNOWLEDGE

1. Which U.S. chemist created, with Edwin McMillan, the element neptunium?

2. What is the name given to the scale of temperature in which 0° represents the melting point of ice?

3. Who was the author of the autobiographical novel A Death in the Family?

4. Which actor's television roles include Thomas Magnum in Magnum PI?

5. Rothesay is a town on the east coast of which Scottish island?

6. In which year was U.S. car manufacturer Ransom Eli Olds born?

7. Who authored the 1848 novel Mary Barton?

8. Who was the male star of the 1955 Alfred Hitchcock film To Catch A Thief?

9. Which river forms the boundary between Montenegro and Bosnia-Herzegovina?

10. Which German playwright wrote the 1964 work Marat/Sade?

11. In which European capital city was cellist Yo-Yo Ma born in 1955?

12. Who wrote the 1947 play A Streetcar Named Desire?

13. In which year did German engineer and car manufacturer Gottlieb Daimler die?

14. Who was the author of the 1955 novel The Angry Hills?

15. Which is the smaller of the two satellites of Mars?

ANSWERS 1. Philip Abelson 2. Celsius 3. James Agee 4. Tom Selleck 5. Bute 1 6. 1864 7. Elizabeth Gaskell 8. Cary Grant 9. Drina 10. Peter Weiss 11. Paris 12. Tennessee Williams 13. 1900 14. Leon Uris 15. Deimos.

ENTERTAINMENT

1. In which year did the BBC first broadcast opera on the radio?

2. In which country is the 1959 war film Yesterday's Enemy set?

3. Who plays cop Della Pesca in the 1999 biopic The Hurricane?

4. On whose novella is the 1998 film Apt Pupil based?

5. Who won Best Pop Act at the 2000 Brit Awards?

6. Who played The Last Musketeer on television in the 2000 ITV drama?

7. Who created the role of Swallow in the opera Peter Grimes?

8. Which film won the Best Visual Effects Oscar in 2000?

9. Who played the title role in the 1999 television show Lucy Sullivan is Getting Married?

10. Who directed the 1968 film Yellow Submarine?

11. Which football club's hooligan element did Donal MacIntyre travel to Denmark with in the 1999 series MacIntyre Undercover?

12. Who won Best International Male at the 2000 Brit Awards?

13. Which French actress stars in the 1969 comedy film The April Fools with Jack Lemmon?

14. Who plays Dr. John Becker in the U.S. sitcom Becker?

15. What nationality was the soprano Julie Dorus-Gras?

ANSWERS 1. 1923 2. Burma 3. Dan Hedaya 4. Stephen King 5. Five 6. Robson Green 7. Owen Brannigan 8. The Matrix 9. Sam Loggin 10. George Dunning 11. Chelsea 12. Beck 13. Catherine Deneuve 14. Ted Danson 15. Belgian.

SPORT

1. In cricket, who scored 153 for Yorkshire against Kent in the 1st innings of their 1999 county championship game?

2. Which female skater was the 1925 world figure skating champion?

3. By what score did Ireland beat France in Paris in the 2000 Six Nations rugby tournament?

4. Which two teams met in the 1946 play-off for the NFL championship in American Football?

5. Who partnered Anders Järryd to victory in the 1983 French Open men's doubles tennis title?

6. Who was the 1988 and 1989 world rally driving champion?

7. How many golds did Cuba win at the 1999 World Athletic Championships?

8. At which Olympic sport have Russell Mark and Vasiliy Borissov been champions?

9. Which cyclist was the 1989 Sports Illustrated Sportsman of the Year?

10. At what Olympic sport have Rolf Peterson and Mihaly Hesz been champions?

11. Who coached Surrey cricket club in the 1999 season?

12. Which Swiss cyclist won the 1992 Tour of Lombardy?

13. By how many runs did New Zealand beat England in the 1999 4th Test at the Oval?

14. In which year did Election win the Epsom Derby?

15. Which year saw Colin Montgomerie's first Ryder Cup appearance?

ANSWERS 1. Michael Vaughn 2. Herma Jaross 3. 27-25 4. New York Giants and Chicago Bears 5. Hans Simonsson 6. Mikki Biasion 7. Two 8. Shooting 9. Greg LeMond 10. Canoe racing 11. Keith Medlycott 12. Tony Rominger 13. 83 runs 14. 1807 15. 1991.

POP MUSIC

1. Which duo recorded the 1999 hit single Feel Good?

2. Which group recorded the 1982 album Pornography?

3. Which female singer recorded the 1999 album Electric Chair?

4. Who had a hit single in 1980 with And the Beat Goes On?

5. Which Tammy Wynette song did Lyle Lovett cover on album Lyle Lovett and his Large Band?

6. Which member of The Band died in December 1999?

7. Which reggae artist was born Roy Reid in 1950?

8. Who replaced bassist Louis Steinberg in Booker T and the MGs?

9. Which group recorded the 1999 mini-album Stranger Blues?

10. Which reggae artist recorded the 1977 album Police and Thieves?

11. In which year was Culture Club's first Top of the Pops appearance on television?

12. Which studio album by Sly and the Family Stone features the song Spaced Cowboy?

13. Who recorded the 2000 album 2001?

14. Who was the Swedish-American singer with Curved Air?

15. Which Temptations song did Love and Rockets cover as their first single?

ANSWERS 1. Phats and Small 2. The Cure 3. Sandy Dillon 4. The Whispers 5. Stand By Your Man 6. Rick Danko 7. I-Roy 8. Donald 'Duck' Dunn 9. Dream City Film Club 10. Junior Murvin 11. 1982 12. There's A Riot Goin' On 13. Dr. Dre 14. Sonja Kristina 15. Ball of Confusion.

WORDS

1. If something is bacciform, what is it shaped like?

2. Which U.S. city is nicknamed Big D?

3. What animal is affected by the disease braxy?

4. Of which metal is galena a major source?

5. What sort of animal is a macaque?

6. If an actor corpses what do they do?

7. What is a carioca - a Brazilian tree or a Brazilian dance?

8. Which drug is known in the U.S. as happy dust?

9. What type of entertainer is an engastrimyth?

10. What is a shim to a thief in the U.S.?

11. What on a plane is a dustbin according to British military slang?

12. In western Australia, which object might be known as a kylie?

13. What might you do in Australia with a durry?

14. To which period of time did the word sennight refer?

15. What item of clothing is also known as a filibeg?

GENERAL KNOWLEDGE

1. Who was the 1997 world professional snooker champion?

2. Which diminutive pop singer had a 1977 No. 1 single with When I Need You?

3. What is the capital and chief port of Papua New Guinea?

4. Which golfer won the 1976 Volvo PGA Championship?

5. Who was the comedy partner of Lou Costello?

6. What place near Lewes in Sussex was the site of a famous scientific forgery of 1912?

7. What is the name of the city in S. France whose Roman antiquities include the Maison Carrée?

8. Who wrote the 1965 play A Patriot For Me?

9. In which year did Scottish explorer Mungo Park die?

10. In which African country is the Atlantic port of Tema?

11. Paramaribo is the capital of which republic in South America?

12. Who was the 11th president of the U.S.?

13. What was the legendary birthplace of Romulus and Remus?

14. Who was the author of the novel Kim published in 1901?

15. What is the brightest star in the constellation Virgo?

ANSWERS 1. Ken Doherty 2. Leo Sayer 3. Port Moresby 4. Neil Coles 5. Bud Abbott 6. Piltdown 7. Nimes 8. John Osborne 9. 1806 10. Ghana 11. Surinam 12. James K. Polk 13. Alba Longa 14. Rudyard Kipling 15. Spica.

ENTERTAINMENT

1. In which year did Yes, Minister first appear on television?

2. Which presenter of Stars on Sunday was known as 'The Bishop'?

3. Which actresses played the two wives of Alec Guinness in the 1953 film The Captain's Paradise?

4. What is the name of the French housemaid in The Wombles?

5. Which politician did Eric Porter play in the 1981 television drama Winston Churchill - The Wilderness Years?

6. What was the name of Sir Arthur Bliss's 1949 opera?

7. Who starred as The Clairvoyant in a 1986 sitcom?

8. Who played Zorro in a 1958 television series?

9. In which city was Alfred Hitchcock's I Confess made?

10. What was the name of the ranger in the cartoon series Yogi Bear?

11. Who played Russian diplomat Grischa Petrovitch in the 1960s sitcom Foreign Affairs?

12. Akira Kurosawa's film Ran is an adaptation of which Shakespeare play?

13. Which actor played patriarch Samuel Foster in the 1970s sitcom The Fosters?

14. What nationality was tenor Jussi Björling?

15. Who played Captain Sindbad in a 1963 film?

ANSWERS 1. 1980 2. Jess Yates 3. Celia Johnson and Yvonne De Carlo 4. Mme Cholet 5. Neville Chamberlain 6. The Olympians 7. Roy Kinnear 8. Guy Williams 9. Quebec 10. John Smith 11. Ronnie Barker 12. King Lear 13. Norman Beaton 14. Swedish 15. Guy Williams.

SPORT

1. At what sport was Nikolay Bayukov a 1976 Olympic champion?

2. What nationality is alpine skier Spela Pretnar?

3. How many times did Allan Border captain the Australian Test cricket team from 1984-94?

4. At what sport has Julia Mann been England's No. 1?

5. Valeriy Maslov of the U.S.S.R. won eight gold medals from 1961-77 at the world championships of which team game?

6. Who was the 1986 individual Three-Day Eventing champion at the world championships?

7. In which sport might one perform a Danish swipe?

8. Who was the 1988 Olympic men's 100m butterfly swimming champion?

9. At what sport was George Lee of the U.K. an Open world champion in 1978?

10. What nationality is golfer Rachel Hetherington?

11. Whose goal for Sheffield Wednesday beat Chelsea 1-0 in April 2000?

12. In which year were the women's world championships in ice hockey first held?

13. In which city were the 1965 World Student Games held?

14. Who were voted outstanding college American Football team in 1986 by United Press?

15. Who was the 1965 U.S. men's singles tennis champion?

ANSWERS 1. Nordic skiing 2. Slovenian 3. 93 4. Badminton 5. Bandy 6. Virginia Leng 7. Badminton 8. Anthony Nesty 9. Gliding 10. Australian 11. Wim Jonk 12. 1990 13. Budapest 14. Penn State 15. Manuel Santana.

POP MUSIC

1. Which Belgian group recorded the 1982 album Swimming?

2. On which studio album by Lou Reed does the song Like A Possum appear?

3. Which group's albums included the live recording Bless Its Pointed Little Head?

4. Which group had a 1998 Christmas Top 20 single with the song Always Have, Always Will?

5. Which group's first album, in 1982, was called Garlands?

6. Ari Up and Palmolive were members of which female punk group?

7. Which singer-songwriter recorded the 2001 album The Tiki Bar Is Open?

8. Which singer recorded the 2001 album Invincible?

9. Which group recorded the 2000 album Buzzle Bee?

10. Which group had a 1991 Top 20 single with the song Unfinished Sympathy?

11. On which John Lennon studio album does the song How Do You Sleep? appear?

12. Which singer recorded the 2001 album Songs From the West Coast?

13. To what did the group The Detours change their name in 1964?

14. Which U.S. singer's only U.K. Top 10 single was 1985's Trapped?

15. Which British album went straight to No. 1 in the U.S. charts in 2000?

ANSWERS 1. The Names 2. Ecstasy 3. Jefferson Airplane 4. Ace of Base 5. The Cocteau Twins 6. The Slits 7. John Hiatt 8. Michael Jackson 9. The High Llamas 10. Massive Attack 11. Imagine 12. Elton John 13. The Who 14. Colonel Abrams 15. Kid A by Radiohead.

SCIENCE

1. Which chemical element has the symbol V?

2. Approximately how many days does the moon Enceladus take to orbit Saturn?

3. In which year did Edison invent the kinetoscope?

4. Which chemical element has the symbol Ce?

5. Who was appointed director of the Kaiser Wilhelm Institute for Physics in Berlin in 1913?

6. Approximately how many miles in diameter is Uranus's satellite Cressida?

7. In which year was the Royal Society founded?

8. What is the atomic number of Rutherfordium?

9. Which liquid's formula is C6H6?

10. What does a bolometer measure?

11. In which year did Atari introduce the video game 'Pong'?

12. The largest of the seas on the Moon is the Mare Imbrium. What does it translate as?

13. What is the atomic number of Scandium?

14. In the hexadecimal system, what letter represents the number 15?

15. In which country was British biologist Sir Peter Brian Medawar born?

ANSWERS 1. Vanadium 2. 1.37 days 3. 1888 4. Cerium 5. Albert Einstein 6. 40 miles 7. 1660 8. 104 9. Benzene 10. Radiant energy 11. 1972 12. Sea of Rains 13. 21 14. F 15. Brazil

? **GENERAL KNOWLEDGE** **?**

1. Which channel of the Irish Sea separates the Welsh mainland from Anglesey?

2. What is the capital of South Korea?

3. Who wrote the 1975 novel Blott on the Landscape?

4. What is the name of the great plain of central South America between the Andes and the Paraguay River?

5. Debbie Harry is the lead singer of which pop group?

6. The throstle is a poetic name for which bird?

7. Who was a Best Actor Oscar nominee for his role in the 1951 film Bright Victory?

8. Who choreographed the one-act ballet The Firebird which was composed by Stravinsky?

9. Lake Iliamna is the largest lake in which U.S. state?

10. What is the acknowledgement in fencing that a scoring hit has been made?

11. Who was the 1972 Olympic men's high jump bronze medal winner?

12. Who directed and starred in the 1973 film High Plains Drifter?

13. Who was the first Protestant Archbishop of Canterbury?

14. In which county is the ancient town of Winchelsea?

15. Which poet's volumes include The Less Deceived?

ANSWERS 1. Menai Strait 2. Seoul 3. Tom Sharpe 4. Gran Chaco 5. Blondie 6. Thrush 7. Arthur Kennedy 8. Fokine 9. Alaska 10. Touché 11. Dwight Stones 12. Clint Eastwood 13. Thomas Cranmer 14. East Sussex 15. Philip Larkin.

ENTERTAINMENT

1. Who played the lead in the 1996 film Sgt. Bilko?

2. What was the name of Marina's pet seal in the puppet show Stingray?

3. Who hosts the comedy quiz show Never Mind the Buzzcocks?

4. Who directed the 1970 film Ned Kelly?

5. Which actor wrote the 1985 sitcom Affairs of the Heart?

6. Which actress stars in the sitcom Gimme Gimme Gimme?

7. In which year was television presenter Michaela Strachan born?

8. Who plays a cook in the 1992 film Under Siege?

9. Who plays twin brothers in the 1942 film Nazi Agent?

10. Which female doctor was a host on the television science show Don't Ask Me?

11. What nationality is the opera singer Otto Edelmann?

12. Who played Loana in the 1966 film One Million Years B.C.?

13. Which musician scored the 1984 film The Natural?

14. Who played Jane Wellington-Bull in the 1959 sitcom The Adventures of Wellington-Bull?

15. Who played Det. Chief Supt. Jack Lambie in the television show Strangers?

ANSWERS 1. Steve Martin 2. Oink 3. Mark Lamarr 4. Tony Richardson 5. Paul Daneman 6. Kathy Burke 7. 1966 8. Steven Seagal 9. Conrad Veidt 10. Miriam Stoppard 11. Austrian 12. Raquel Welch 13. Randy Newman 14. Valerie Singleton 15. Mark McManus.

SPORT

1. How many races did Jochen Rindt win in the European Formula Two Championship?

2. In which city were the 1975 Pan-American Games held?

3. In which country is the Ranfurly Shield contested in rugby union?

4. Who scored two goals for Aston Villa in their 4-2 win at Tottenham in April 2000?

5. At what weight was Dado Marino 1950-2 world boxing champion?

6. Who was voted England's Player of the Series against the West Indies in cricket in 1995?

7. Which Japanese cyclist was men's world sprint champion from 1977-86?

8. In which city were the 1951 Asian Games held?

9. Which two men's teams won every Olympic hockey gold from 1928-68?

10. In which year did tennis player Lew Hoad die?

11. Who was the 1953 and 1954 world 250cc motorcycling champion?

12. In which Brazilian port were the 1963 World Student games held?

13. Who did Newcastle United beat 1-0 in the 1952 F.A. Cup Final?

14. At which sport did Inna Ryskal of the U.S.S.R. win four Olympic medals from 1964-76?

15. In which year did Iolanda Balas set a world record of 1.86m for the women's high jump?

POP MUSIC

1. Which U.S. author wrote the sleeve notes for Lotion's 1995 album Nothing's Cool?

2. Who recorded the 1999 dance hit Rendez-Vu?

3. Which U.S. rock 'n' roll singer recorded the 1961 hit Quarter to Three?

4. Who had a 1999 No. 1 single with Genie in a Bottle?

5. Which singer recorded the 1999 album Staying Power?

6. Which singer produced the 1971 album Heavy on the Drum by Medicine Head?

7. Which Joni Mitchell song is covered by Travis on the B-side of single Why Does It Always Rain On Me??

8. Which group recorded the 2000 album Sleeve with Hearts?

9. Which group recorded the 1993 album Give a Monkey a Brain & He'll Swear He's the Centre of the Universe?

10. The 1999 No. 1 single Lift Me Up was by which female singer?

11. What was Tiffany's only U.K. and U.S. No. 1?

12. Who joined Mott the Hoople on keyboards in 1973?

13. Who had a 1999 Top 10 single with their song Mickey

14. In which year did Johnny Tillotson have a U.K. No. 1 single with Poetry in Motion?

15. Which group recorded the 1989 single Under the God?

PEOPLE

1. Which Oscar nominee once worked as a doorman at the Manhattan Plaza apartment block?

2. Born in India, in which English city was the singer Englebert Humperdinck raised?

3. Which Hollywood actress owns a dog called Woof?

4. How old was Jeanne Calment when she died in August 1997?

5. What is the profession of the Briton Maria Grachvogel?

6. Serena Rees and Joe Corré own which London clothes shop?

7. What is crossword compiler John Graham's pseudonym?

8. Which pop music producer ran a Coventry record shop called the Soul Hole?

9. In which country did the author D.H. Lawrence die in 1930?

10. Which comedian's catchphrase was 'You lucky people'?

11. What is the real name of the comedienne Ruby Wax?

12. Who was the first winner in 1999 of the $1m prize on the U.S. edition of the television quiz show Who Wants To Be A Millionaire?

13. In which year did the artist Peter Paul Rubens die?

14. Who is the mother of the actress Liv Tyler?

15. Who designed the Seagram Building on New York's Park Avenue?

ANSWERS 1. Samuel L. Jackson 2. Leicester 3. Renée Zellweger 4. 122 5. Fashion designer 6. Agent Provocateur 7. Araucaria 8. Pete Waterman 9. Italy 10. Tommy Trinder 11. Ruby Wachs 12. John Carpenter 13. 1640 14. Bebe Buell 15. Mies van der Rohe.

SPORT

1. Which sport's matches are divided into chukkas?

2. Who did George Foreman beat to win the world heavyweight boxing title in January 1973?

3. Which football team won the League Cup in 1988?

4. Which driver was on pole position 65 times in his 161 Grand Prix starts?

5. In which Olympic event did Ed Moses win gold and set a new world record in 1976?

6. Which tennis player won the men's singles at the 1998 Australian Open?

7. Which rugby union club side play at the Recreation Ground?

8. In which sport is the Swaythling Cup contested?

9. Which side did France beat 36-3 in the 1991 rugby union Five Nations championships?

10. Which two titles did Lasse Viren successfully defend at the 1976 Olympics?

11. Which British swimmer retained his Commonwealth 50m freestyle title in 1998 in a new Games record time?

12. In which event did Sally Gunnell win her 1992 Olympic gold medal?

13. Which football team was coached by Carlos Alberto Parreira at the 1994 World Cup?

14. Which Russian tennis player was knocked out of Wimbledon by Venus Williams in 1999?

15. Which international rugby union competition was first staged in 1987?

ANSWERS: 1 Polo, 2 Joe Frazier, 3 Luton Town, 4 Ayrton Senna, 5 400m hurdles, 6 Petr Korda, 7 Bath, 8 Table tennis, 9 Wales, 10 5,000m & 10,000m, 11 Mark Foster, 12 400m hurdles, 13 Brazil, 14 Anna Kournikova, 15 The World Cup.

GENERAL KNOWLEDGE

1. In what year did This is Your Life begin in Britain?

2. Which North African dish is made of semolina and is often served with meat, vegetables and spices?

3. To which English monarch was Mary of Teck consort?

4. Which Mexican volcano erupted at the end of 2000?

5. What name was given to Church of England priests who refused to take oaths of allegiance to William and Mary?

6. What was the first name of West Indian cultural historian C. L. R. James?

7. Which British novelist wrote The Citadel?

8. Which actor won a Best Supporting Actor Oscar for The Treasure of the Sierra Madre?

9. The hypothalamus is part of which organ of the body?

10. Which former world heavyweight boxing champion was born Arnold Cream?

11. Which American city hosted its first marathon in 1897?

12. Which film director produced the 1999 hit song Everybody's Free (To Wear Sunscreen)?

13. Which 70s TV series was made into a film starring Cameron Diaz, Drew Barrymore and Lucy Liu?

14. What is the longest river in Spain?

15. In which European country is Katowice?

ANSWERS: 1 1955, 2 Couscous, 3 George V, 4 Popocatepetl, 5 Nonjurors, 6 Cyril, 7 A J Cronin, 8 Walter Huston, 9 The brain, 10 Jersey Joe Walcott, 11 Boston, 12 Baz Luhrmann, 13 Charlie's Angels, 14 Ebro River, 15 Poland.

GENERAL KNOWLEDGE

1. In which novel by Tolstoy does Konstantin Levin appear?

2. Which English Metaphysical poet wrote To His Coy Mistress?

3. Electronics entrepreneur Sir Alan Sugar sold his controlling interest in which football club in 2000?

4. Who translated the first printed English Bible?

5. In what organ of the body is the pons?

6. Which country hosted the football World Cup in 1966?

7. In which English county are the Potteries?

8. Which U.S. president was associated with the Square Deal?

9. Which music hall star wrote the song My Old Dutch?

10. What sort of creature is a jacana?

11. Which French oceanographer and filmmaker invented the aqualung?

12. What was the title of actor David Niven's first autobiography?

13. Which model turned actress played Leeloo in The Fifth Element?

14. What was the pen name of mathematician and author Charles Lutwidge Dodgson?

15. In which European country is the town of Genk?

ANSWERS: 1 Anna Karenina, 2 Andrew Marvell, 3 Tottenham Hotspur, 4 Miles Coverdale, 5 Brain, 6 England, 7 Staffordshire, 8 Theodore Roosevelt, 9 Albert Chevalier, 10 A bird, 11 Jacques Cousteau, 12 The Moon's a Balloon, 13 Milla Jovovich, 14 Lewis Carroll, 15 Belgium.

GENERAL KNOWLEDGE

1. Which ex-Neighbours star had a hit single entitled Mona in 1990?

2. Which Australian tennis player is the only woman to have achieved the grand slam in both doubles and singles?

3. Which barrister and author wrote the play A Voyage Round My Father?

4. Of which African country was Kwame Nkrumah the first president?

5. In what year did the Siege of Leningrad begin?

6. Which English novelist wrote The Pumpkin Eater and Long Distance?

7. Which actor made his film debut in the 1958 movie The Cry Baby Killer?

8. Yves Saint Laurent was ordered to take down posters featuring which British model in 2000?

9. By what nickname was James Edward Stuart known?

10. What sort of creature is a noctule?

11. Which member of the Marx Brothers adopted an Italian accent?

12. Who beat Southampton 4-3 in the F.A. Cup in February 2001?

13. Which Scottish town became a city in 2000?

14. Who is the hero of John Buchan's novel The Thirty-Nine Steps?

15. Which code used in telegraphy uses dots and dashes?

ENTERTAINMENT

1. In which 1999 Woody Allen movie did Sean Penn play fictitious Thirties jazz guitarist Emmet Ray?

2. What was the title of the Jewish comedy series which was Sid James' first solo vehicle?

3. Who released the solo debut album, Hear My Cry?

4. Which 1967 film set in America's deep South starred Sidney Poitier and Rod Steiger?

5. What was Frankie Goes to Hollywood's second U.K. number one hit?

6. Which 1999 U.S. teen film starred Sabrina, the Teenage Witch actress Melissa Joan Hart?

7. Who originally had a U.K. hit with the track Mambo Italiano, in 1954?

8. Which veteran Irish actress played John Candy's mother in the 1991 film Only the Lonely?

9. Which Coronation Street character tragically lost both his wife and new-born son in 2000?

10. Which actor played Rose's fiancé Cal Hockley in the 1997 film Titanic?

11. Which Top Gun star played a political activist in the 1988 film The House on Carroll Street?

12. Which British group had a 1968 U.K. number one hit with Lily the Pink?

13. Which British comedian wrote and directed the film Maybe Baby?

14. Which Nineties drama series set in the Twenties starred Stella Gonet and Louise Lombard as sisters Beatrice and Evangeline?

15. Which former docu-soap star released a second album called Inspiration?

GENERAL KNOWLEDGE

1. What is another name for the gumshield of a boxer?

2. Which U.S. guitarist and composer was the leader of the Mothers of Invention?

3. In which Scottish town were the poems of Robert Burns first published?

4. To which continent is the chickadee native?

5. What name is given to a verbal device for aiding the memory, such as 'i before e, except after c'?

6. Which art critic wrote Ways of Seeing?

7. Which Italian conductor became the music director of Milan's La Scala in 1986?

8. What name is given to a marriage in which the wife and children do not succeed to the titles or property of the husband?

9. Who led the Labour Party from 1955 to 1963?

10. Which species of red algae is also called Irish moss?

11. Which billionaire stood as a candidate in the U.S. presidential elections in 1992 and 1996?

12. Which American author wrote The Sound and the Fury?

13. Which political party's name means 'Party of Wales'?

14. Who claimed Britain's first Olympic boxing gold medal for 32 years at the Sydney Olympics?

15. Which Asian country changed its name to Myanmar in 1989?

ANSWERS: 1 Mouthpiece, 2 Frank Zappa, 3 Kilmarnock, 4 North America, 5 Mnemonic, 6 John Berger, 7 Riccardo Muti, 8 Morganatic marriage, 9 Hugh Gaitskell, 10 Carrageen, 11 Ross Perot, 12 William Faulkner, 13 Plaid Cymru, 14 Audley Harrison, 15 Burma.

GENERAL KNOWLEDGE

1. What is the first name of the fictional detective Maigret?

2. Which boxer, born Archibald Lee Wright, held the world light-heavyweight title from 1952 to 1962?

3. What was the number on Sir Geoff Hurst's shirt that sold for £91,750 at Christie's?

4. Which fishing port is the most easterly town in Scotland?

5. What sort of creature is a mud puppy?

6. Which French cake was immortalised by Marcel Proust in his novel Swann's Way?

7. Who did Pat Cash beat in the final of Wimbledon in 1987?

8. What name is given to the outermost region of the sun's atmosphere?

9. To which English monarch was Sir Francis Walsingham principal secretary?

10. Which African country was represented by the swimmer Eric Moussambani at the Sydney Olympics?

11. Which character in Greek mythology fell in love with his reflection?

12. Who wrote On the Origin of Species by Means of Natural Selection?

13. Who scored the winning goal of the 1996 FA Cup final?

14. What type of school is named from the German for 'children's garden'?

15. Which town is the administrative centre of Suffolk?

ANSWERS: 1 Jules, 2 Archie Moore, 3 Ten, 4 Peterhead, 5 A salamander, 6 Madeleine, 7 Ivan Lendl, 8 Corona, 9 Elizabeth I, 10 Equatorial Guinea, 11 Narcissus, 12 Charles Darwin, 13 Eric Cantona, 14 Kindergarten, 15 Ipswich.

GENERAL KNOWLEDGE

1. Which golfer captained the European Ryder Cup team in 1999?

2. Which novel by Elizabeth Gaskell was left unfinished at her death?

3. What do the initials stand for in the name of the American guitarist B.B. King?

4. Which former prime minister of Canada died in 2000 at the age of 80?

5. In algebraic chess notation, which figure begins the game on square e1?

6. Which prolific American author wrote Riders of the Purple Sage?

7. Who played Edna the Inebriate Woman on TV in 1971?

8. By what name is the perennial plant Nigella damascena better known?

9. Which U.S. lawman killed Billy the Kid?

10. What is the sixth book of the Old Testament?

11. Which young Jewish girl is famous for the diary she kept while her family hid from the Nazis in Amsterdam?

12. Who was the first Hanoverian king of Great Britain?

13. Bob Dylan won an Oscar for Best Song for which film?

14. Who was the director of the FBI from 1924 to 1972?

15. Which Russian leader was associated with the policies of glasnost and perestroika?

ANSWERS: 1 Mark James, 2 Wives and Daughters, 3 Blues Boy, 4 Pierre Trudeau, 5 White's king, 6 Zane Grey, 7 Patricia Hayes, 8 Love-in-a-mist, 9 Pat Garrett, 10 Book of Joshua, 11 Anne Frank, 12 George I, 13 Wonder Boys, 14 J Edgar Hoover, 15 Mikhail Gorbachev.

ENTERTAINMENT

1. Which 1990 film set in Fifties Cuba starred Robert Redford as Jack Weil?

2. Which newsreader presented the emergency rescue show 999?

3. What was MN8's biggest hit, which reached number two in 1995?

4. Which Hollywood actor starred as an aging baseball star in the film For the Love of the Game?

5. Which Italian singer had a 1988 top five hit with Boys (Summertime Love)?

6. In which 1990 film did Joan Plowright play Tracey Ullman's mother?

7. Which BBC1 comedy series set in the world of barristers starred John Bird and Sarah Lancashire?

8. Which horror actor's performances included the Monster in 1935's Bride of Frankenstein and 1939's Son of Frankenstein?

9. What was the title of Thin Lizzy's first U.K. top ten hit, in 1973?

10. Which film starred Sandra Bullock as a would-be writer who goes through rehab?

11. Which British actress starred alongside David Duchovny in the film Return to Me?

12. Which comedian's Video Show on TV featured a dance troupe called Hot Gossip?

13. What was the title of Babybird's 2000 album release?

14. Who directed and starred in the 1986 film sequel Psycho III?

15. Which Australian soap was axed by ITV after more than 10 years?

GENERAL KNOWLEDGE

1. Which well-known novel by Graham Greene is set in Sierra Leone?

2. Of which river is the Aare River a tributary?

3. Which county did Ian Botham play cricket for from 1987-91?

4. By what name is the vitamin B1 also known?

5. Which American comedy duo performed the routine Who's On First?

6. What name is given to trees of the genus Platanus?

7. In which previously dry Essex resort did the Lock and Barrel pub open in September 2000?

8. Who was the first footballer to be sent off in an FA Cup final at Wembley?

9. Which famous Dublin theatre was established in 1904?

10. What name is given to the full moon nearest the autumn equinox?

11. Which former American football star was acquitted of murder in October 1995?

12. Who was the manager of the Manchester United team that won the European Cup in 1968?

13. Which poet wrote Songs of Innocence?

14. What sort of animal is a Clydesdale?

15. Which French leader called the English a 'nation of shopkeepers"?

ANSWERS: 1 The Heart of the Matter, 2 Rhine, 3 Worcestershire, 4 Thiamine, 5 Abbott and Costello, 6 Plane trees, 7 Frinton, 8 Kevin Moran, 9 Abbey Theatre, 10 Harvest moon, 11 O J Simpson, 12 Matt Busby, 31 William Blake, 14 A horse, 15 Napoleon.

GENERAL KNOWLEDGE

1. Which U.S. social scientist coined the term 'conspicuous consumption' in The Theory of the Leisure Class?

2. In Greek mythology, who was the daughter of Cassiopeia and Cepheus?

3. In what year was the original version of the film The Fly made?

4. Of which country did Bhumibol Adulyadej become king in 1946?

5. Which American author wrote the novels Exodus and QB VII?

6. What name is given to the tiles used in a mosaic?

7. Which country hosted the football World Cup in 1990?

8. What is the administrative centre of Hampshire?

9. Which Indian religion and philosophy was founded by Vardhamana?

10. What is the birthstone of people born in July?

11. What is the name given to the common foot infection caused by fungi?

12. What is the second largest city in the Republic of Ireland?

13. Who was the female member of the Not The Nine O'Clock News team?

14. What animal has a name which means 'river horse'?

15. Which former coin was worth a quarter of an old penny?

ANSWERS: 1 Thorstein Veblen, 2 Andromeda, 3 1958, 4 Thailand, 5 Leon Uris, 6 Tesserae, 7 Italy, 8 Winchester, 9 Jainism, 10 Ruby, 11 Athlete's foot, 12 Cork, 13 Pamela Stephenson, 14 Hippopotamus, 15 Farthing..

GENERAL KNOWLEDGE

1. Which Austrian composer wrote The Creation and The Seasons?

2. In which U.S. state is the town of Tombstone, famous in Westerns?

3. Who created the detective Jemima Shore?

4. At which ground did England secure their fastest Test victory since 1912 when they beat the West Indies in the 4th Test in 2000?

5. Which British author wrote Lavengro and The Romany Rye?

6. In computing, what does the abbreviation OCR stand for?

7. Which drug used in premedication is derived from deadly nightshade?

8. The Blaydon Races song is associated with which football club?

9. Who wrote the lyrics for Andrew Lloyd Webber's musical The Beautiful Game?

10. Which marksman won Great Britain's second gold medal at the Sydney Olympics?

11. Which former prime minister became the Earl of Stockton?

12. What is the second largest country in the world?

13. What number wood in golf is a driver?

14. What was the name of the ship that carried the Pilgrim Fathers to America in 1620?

15. Which black American singer and actor had his passport withdrawn by the U.S. government in 1950?

ANSWERS: 1 Joseph Haydn, 2 Arizona, 3 Antonia Fraser, 4 Headingley, 5 George Borrow, 6 Optical character recognition, 7 Atropine, 8 Newcastle United, 9 Ben Elton, 10 Richard Faulds, 11 Harold Macmillan, 12 Canada, 13 One, 14 The Mayflower, 15 Paul Robeson.

SPORT

1. To whom did Michael Bentt lose a WBO world heavyweight title fight in 1994?

2. Which nation competes with England for the rugby union Calcutta Cup?

3. In which year did England win the football World Cup?

4. From which track event was Ben Johnson disqualified after winning at the 1988 Olympics?

5. In 1980, Nadyezda Tkatchenko become the first athlete to exceed 5,000 points in which event?

6. Which British racing driver was World Championship runner-up from 1955 to 1958?

7. Which Scottish golfer won $1 million in 1998 as the Andersen Consulting World Champion?

8. For which event did Trevor Bickle win the gold medal at the 1962 Commonwealth Games?

9. What is the Argentinian rugby union side's nickname?

10 Which Canadian was the 1997 Formula 1 World Motor Racing Champion?

11. Which horse won the 1998 Cheltenham Gold Cup?

12. Which American sport do the New York Yankees and the Atlanta Braves compete in?

13. For which German football team did Kevin Keegan play?

14. In which year did Salt Lake City, USA, host the Winter Olympics?

15. Which side did England knock out of the 1995 rugby union World Cup with a late Rob Andrew drop goal?

ANSWERS: 1 Herbie Hide, 2 Scotland, 3 1966, 4 100m, 5 Pentathlon, 6 Stirling Moss, 7 Colin Montgomerie, 8 Pole vault, 9 The Pumas, 10 Jacques Villeneuve, 11 Cool Dawn, 12 Baseball, 13 Hamburg, 14 2002, 15 Australia.

GENERAL KNOWLEDGE

1. Which 1986 film features the Queen song Who Wants to Live Forever?

2. Which American football team did Chuck Noll lead to four Super Bowl victories?

3. What was the name of the ship in which Captain Cook discovered Australia?

4. Which British singer/songwriter was killed in a speedboat accident in 2000?

5. Who wrote Le Morte d'Arthur?

6. Which post was held by William Courtenay from 1381 to 1396?

7. In which year was the first Cannes Film Festival held?

8. Which English seaside resort became a city in 2000?

9. What type of musical composition was invented by Irish composer John Field?

10. Which musical comedy star was married to Jack Hulbert?

11. Which port on the Isle of Wight is famous for its annual sailing regatta?

12. By what name is the I Ching also known?

13. Which film director married Madonna at Skibo Castle?

14. Of which country is Colombo the capital?

15. Which American jazz singer was known as 'Lady Day'?

ANSWERS: 1 Highlander, 2 Pittsburgh Steelers, 3 Endeavour, 4 Kirsty MacColl, 5 Sir Thomas Malory, 6 Archbishop of Canterbury, 7 1946, 8 Brighton and Hove, 9 Nocturne, 10 Dame Cicely Courtneidge, 11 Cowes, 12 Book of Changes, 13 Guy Ritchie, 14 Sri Lanka, 15 Billie Holiday.

GENERAL KNOWLEDGE

1. Who wrote My Brilliant Career?

2. Which Welsh artist painted portraits of George Bernard Shaw, Dylan Thomas and James Joyce?

3. Who was European Footballer of the Year in 1973 and 1974?

4. Which English county contained Parts of Holland?

5. Of which country did Jean Chrétien become prime minister in 1993?

6. What sort of creature is a curassow?

7. Which is the longest-running police series in American TV history?

8. Which English artist is best known for A Rake's Progress?

9. In the Old Testament, which prophet was carried up to heaven in a fiery chariot?

10. In which U.S. state is the city of Nome?

11. Which god of love is the Roman counterpart of Eros?

12. What was the name of the character played by John Malkovich in the film Dangerous Liaisons?

13. Which English king was known as Lackland?

14. Ethan Hawke played the title role in a 2000 film version of which Shakespeare play?

15. Which examination was used after 1944 to select children for grammar schools?

ANSWERS: 1 Miles Franklin, 2 Augustus John, 3 Johan Cruyff, 4 Lincolnshire, 5 Canada, 6 A bird, 7 Hawaii Five-O, 8 William Hogarth, 9 Elijah, 10 Alaska, 11 Cupid, 12 Valmont, 13 King John, 14 Hamlet, 15 Eleven Plus.

GENERAL KNOWLEDGE

1. In which country was movie actor Andy Garcia born?

2. What is the capital of Senegal?

3. What name is given to members of a Christian sect founded by John Thomas in New York in 1848?

4. Which publication launched in 1926 has merged with the NME?

5. What is the khamsin?

6. In what year did U.S. sprinter Bobby Morrow win the Olympic 100m and 200m?

7. For her performance in which film did Grace Kelly receive an Oscar in 1954?

8. What is the northernmost point of the British Isles?

9. Which suburb of Amsterdam is the centre of the Dutch broadcasting industry?

10. To which organ does the adjective hepatic relate?

11. Which poet and dramatist wrote The Waste Land and The Cocktail Party?

12. What are the chapters of A Christmas Carol by Charles Dickens called?

13. Which figure personifying Englishness was created by Scottish physician John Arbuthnot?

14. Who has become the 43rd President of the United States?

15. Which alloy of copper and nickel is used for coins?

ANSWERS: 1 Cuba, 2 Dakar, 3 Christadelphians, 4 Melody Maker, 5 A wind, 6 1956, 7 Country Girl, 8 Muckle Flugga, 9 Hilversum, 10 Liver, 11 T S Eliot, 12 Staves, 13 John Bull, 14 George W Bush, 15 Cupronickel.

ENTERTAINMENT

1. Who presented us with The Awful Truth about Americans on Channel 4?

2. Three members of which girl group appeared as sisters in the film Honest?

3. Which actor and writer hosted the 2002 BAFTA Film Awards?

4. Which British R&B singer/songwriter released a second album, called The Other Side?

5. Which Seventies comedy series starred Michael Crawford and Michael Gambon as warring neighbours?

6. In which country is Elvis Presley's character stationed in the 1960 film G.I. Blues?

7. Who represented the U.K. in the 2000 Eurovision Song Contest, with an entry entitled Don't Play That Song Again?

8. Which boy band collaborated with Queen on the 2000 number one hit We Will Rock You?

9. Which film starred Kevin Bacon as a reluctant psychic?

10. Which EastEnders character informed the police about the bent cars being sold on the Square's car lot?

11. Who had a Top 20 hit single in 1984 with Get Out Of Your Lazy Bed?

12. Which 1977 film set in the world of car racing starred Richard Pryor and Beau Bridges?

13. Which actress played the title role in the Channel 4 adaptation of Tolstoy's Anna Karenina?

14. What was Debbie Reynolds' only U.K. top five hit?

15. Which actress played Grace in the British film Saving Grace?

ANSWERS: 1 Michael Moore, 2 Stephen Fry, 3 Des Lynam, 4 Lynden David Hall, 5 Chalk and Cheese, 6 Germany, 7 Nicki French, 8 Five, 9 Stir of Echoes, 10 Dan Sullivan, 11 Matt Bianco, 12 Greased Lightning, 13 Helen McCrory, 14 Tammy, 15 Brenda Blethyn.

GENERAL KNOWLEDGE

1. Which member of the Royal Family joined Cheltenham Ladies' Hockey Club in 2000?

2. Which former silent film star is best known for her portrayal of Norma Desmond in the 1950 film Sunset Boulevard?

3. Of which constellation is Deneb the brightest star?

4. What is the minimum number of points needed to win a tie-break in tennis?

5. What sort of creature is a bichon frise?

6. Which English novelist wrote The Cruel Sea?

7. Which unconventional director made the films M*A*S*H, Nashville, and The Player?

8. To which novel by Anthony Hope is Rupert of Hentzau a sequel?

9. When was the London Marathon first held?

10. Which British actor who died in 1995 starred in the Halloween series of films?

11. Which Venetian merchant is famous for his accounts of his travels to Asia in the late 13th century?

12. Who played the title role in the 1952 film Hans Christian Andersen?

13. Which race was won by Golden Fleece in 1982 and Teenoso in 1983?

14. By what first name was Nelson Mandela's second wife known?

15. Which English poet wrote Paradise Lost?

ANSWERS: 1 Zara Phillips, 2 Gloria Swanson, 3 Cygnus, 4 7, 5 A dog, 6 Nicholas Monsarrat, 7 Robert Altman, 8 The Prisoner of Zenda, 9 1981, 10 Donald Pleasence, 11 Marco Polo, 12 Danny Kaye, 13 The Derby, 14 Winnie, 15 John Milton.

GENERAL KNOWLEDGE

1. Who connects TV dramas Blott on the Landscape and Poirot?

2. Which U.S. novelist wrote The Ballad of the Sad Cafe and The Heart is a Lonely Hunter?

3. What was the name of the only horse ever to beat Brigadier Gerard in his three-year racing career?

4. Which chemical element is represented by the symbol Sr?

5. Of which planet is Phobos a satellite?

6. Which country lost in the final of the rugby union World Cup in 1999?

7. What was the title of A A Milne's second collection of stories about Winnie-the-Pooh?

8. What name is given to the dried excrement of fish-eating birds used as a fertiliser?

9. Which American actress starred in You Can't Take It With You and Shane?

10. Of which Shakespeare play is Imogen the heroine?

11. Which Dutch Post-Impressionist painter cut off part of his left ear?

12. To which king is the Book of Proverbs in the Old Testament traditionally ascribed?

13. Which 2000 British film was about an 11-year-old boy who takes up ballet?

14. What nationality was the actress Sarah Bernhardt?

15. Which sign of the zodiac governs the period from July 23 to August 22?

ANSWERS: 1 David Suchet, 2 Carson McCullers, 3 Roberto, 4 Strontium, 5 Mars, 6 France, 7 The House at Pooh Corner, 8 Guano, 9 Jean Arthur, 10 Cymbeline, 11 Vincent van Gogh, 12 Solomon, 13 Billy Elliot, 14 French, 15 Leo.

GENERAL KNOWLEDGE

1. How many squares does a chessboard have?

2. What name was adopted by Goldie Myerson when she became Israel's foreign minister in 1956?

3. In which African country was cricket's ICC Knockout Trophy held in 2000?

4. Which British dramatist wrote Entertaining Mr Sloane and Loot?

5. Who created the voices of Porky Pig, Daffy Duck, Sylvester, Tweety Pie and Bugs Bunny?

6. Which feature of chronic alcoholism is known as the DTs?

7. What is the points value of a drop goal in rugby union?

8. Which author wrote the screenplays for Chitty Chitty Bang Bang and You Only Live Twice?

9. Who might be given an Apgar score?

10. By what name was the U.S.-sponsored postwar European Recovery Program known?

11. Which U.S. novelist wrote The Sun Also Rises and A Farewell to Arms?

12. What was the name of the character played by Gene Hackman in The French Connection?

13. Which French actress and animal rights activist starred in the film And God Created Woman?

14. Who won the gold medal in the men's triple jump at the Sydney Olympics?

15. Which horror film actor was born William Henry Pratt?

ANSWERS: 1 64, 2 Golda Meir, 3 Kenya, 4 Joe Orton, 5 Mel Blanc, 6 Delirium tremens, 7 3, 8 Roald Dahl, 9 A newborn baby, 10 Marshall Plan, 11 Ernest Hemingway, 12 Popeye Doyle, 13 Brigitte Bardot, 14 Jonathan Edwards, 15 Boris Karloff.

ENTERTAINMENT

1. In which sci-fi film did John Travolta star as the head of security of a race called Psychlos?

2. Which Welsh actress played Sandra Hutchinson in The Liver Birds and Megan Roberts in The District Nurse?

3. What was the title of the fourth album by the Glasgow group Belle & Sebastian?

4. Which hit British film, directed by Guy Ritchie, was adapted for a Channel 4 series?

5. Which 1969 film set in the Philippines starred David Niven, Faye Dunaway and Alan Alda?

6. Who presented his view of Car Years on BBC2?

7. What was the title of Billy Ray Cyrus' 1992 top five hit?

8. Which film set in a World War II submarine starred Matthew McConaughey and Harvey Keitel?

9. Which former This Life actress starred as Lieutenant Eve Turner in the ITV drama Rough Treatment?

10. What was the title of Whitney Houston's first U.K. number one hit?

11. Which U.S. group had a 1977 U.K. top five smash with Native New Yorker?

12. Which 1966 film starred Warren Beatty and Susannah York?

13. Which former children's presenter played vet Adam Forrester in ITV's Emmerdale?

14. What was the title of the song that was a U.K. top ten hit for both Stacy Lattisaw in 1980, and Dannii Minogue in 1991?

15. Which actor starred as Deuce Bigalow: Male Gigolo in the 1999 film?

ANSWERS: 1 Battlefield Earth, 2 Nerys Hughes, 3 Fold Your Hands Child, You Walk Like a Peasant, 4 Lock, Stock and Two Smoking Barrels, 5 The Extraordinary Seaman, 6 Jeremy Clarkson, 7 Achy Breaky Heart, 8 U-571, 9 Daniela Nardini, 10 Saving All My Love For You, 11 Odyssey, 12 Kaleidoscope, 13 Tim Vincent, 14 Jump to the Beat, 15 Rob Schneider.

GENERAL KNOWLEDGE

1. Who wrote The Good Soldier?

2. Which former Olympic swimming champion played Flash Gordon and Buck Rogers in films?

3. What is the name of Olivia's ambitious steward in Shakespeare's Twelfth Night?

4. Which four-time world superbike champion announced his retirement in 2000?

5. In what year was the Great Train Robbery in Britain?

6. What is basketball player Magic Johnson's real first name?

7. Against which country did David Beckham score his first senior international goal for England?

8. By what name were the Nazi police force the Geheime Staatspolizei known?

9. Which common childhood illness related to shingles is also called varicella?

10. In Christianity, what name is given to the cup used in the celebration of the Eucharist?

11. In which European country did the dish goulash originate?

12. A luge is a type of what?

13. Which British physicist wrote A Brief History of Time?

14. In which event did Denis Lewis win a gold medal at the Sydney Olympics?

15. Which sign of the zodiac is also called the Water Bearer?

GENERAL KNOWLEDGE

1. Which rock star was born Marvin Lee Aday?

2. Which book by Gavin Maxwell describes his life with two pet otters in the Scottish Highlands?

3. What does the legal term 'caveat emptor' mean?

4. Which 2000 film starred veteran actors Clint Eastwood, Tommy Lee Jones, Donald Sutherland and James Garner?

5. Of which planet is Phoebe a satellite?

6. Which public school was founded by Bishop William of Wykeham in 1382?

7. Who wrote The Thorn Birds?

8. Which film actress and wartime pin-up girl married bandleader Harry James in 1943?

9. How many counters does each player have in a game of backgammon?

10. Which group won the 1994 Mercury Music Prize for their album Elegant Slumming?

11. Which food item takes its name from the French for 'twice cooked'?

12. In what year was The Magic Roundabout first shown on television?

13. Which singer and actress starred in the films The Wizard of Oz and Meet Me in St Louis?

14. How many rowing gold medals did Great Britain win at the Sydney Olympics?

15. Who wrote The Call of the Wild and White Fang?

GENERAL KNOWLEDGE

1. Whose comedy sketch show was entitled Attention Scum?

2. Which American singer had hits with Papa's Got a Brand New Bag and It's a Man's, Man's World?

3. Who won Britain's only medal for judo at the Sydney Olympics?

4. Which Yiddish word, meaning fit or proper, is applied to food that meets the requirements of Jewish dietary laws?

5. What were the first names of the pioneer film director D W Griffith?

6. Raging Bull was the autobiography of which American boxer?

7. Who wrote the books on which the TV series Follyfoot Farm was based?

8. Which comic actor starred in the film Me, Myself and Irene?

9. In which sport is Doggett's Coat and Badge contested?

10. Who directed the films To Have and Have Not, The Big Sleep and Rio Bravo?

11. What is the English name for what the French call La Manche?

12. Which Indian novelist wrote Journey to Ithaca and Village by the Sea?

13. What was the first of C.S. Lewis's books about the kingdom of Narnia?

14. In which event did Steve Backley win a silver medal at the Sydney Olympics?

15. How many lines are there in a limerick?

ANSWERS: 1 Simon Munnery, 2 James Brown, 3 Kate Howey, 4 Kosher, 5 David Ward, 6 Jake La Motta, 7 Monica Dickens, 8 Jim Carrey, 9 Rowing, 10 Howard Hawks, 11 The English Channel, 12 Anita Desai, 13 The Lion, the Witch and the Wardrobe, 14 Javelin, 15 Five.

SPORT

1. What colour ball is worth three points in snooker?

2. At which Olympics did gymnast Ecaterina Szabo's four golds and a silver make her the most successful competitor?

3. Which country knocked Germany out of the 1998 World Cup finals?

4. In which sport did Raymond Barneveld successfully defend his World Professional title in 1999?

5. Which nation won its first Olympic skiing medal in 1948, courtesy of Gretchen Fraser?

6. Who managed Leeds United for only 44 days?

7. How many points are awarded for a touchdown in American football?

8. In which city was Rory Underwood born?

9. Which British amateur golfer finished joint fourth in the Open at Royal Birkdale in 1998?

10. In which year did Donovan Bailey win the Olympic men's 100m event?

11. In 1998, which Premiership football team signed the defender Jaap Stam, for £10.5 million?

12. Which country's rugby union side is known as the All Blacks?

13. How old was Cassius Clay when he became the 1960 Olympic light-heavyweight boxing champion?

14. For which two events did Merlene Ottey win gold medals at the 1990 Commonwealth Games?

15. For which club did Ronaldo leave Barcelona?

ANSWERS: 1 Green, 2 1984, 3 Croatia, 4 Darts, 5 USA, 6 Brian Clough, 7 Six, 8 Middlesbrough, 9 Justin Rose, 10 1996, 11 Manchester United, 12 New Zealand's, 13 19, 14 100m and 200m, 15 Inter Milan.

GENERAL KNOWLEDGE

1. Which former British intelligence officer wrote the controversial book Spycatcher?

2. Of which country did Jean-Bédel Bokassa proclaim himself emperor in 1977?

3. What was the first name of Ironside?

4. How many players are there in a Gaelic football team?

5. What name is given to the Japanese art of flower arranging?

6. Of which Italian island is Cagliari the capital?

7. Which American novelist wrote Goodbye Columbus?

8. By what name is the plant Helleborus niger better known?

9. Which British contralto died in 1953 at the age of 41?

10. A daguerreotype was an early form of what?

11. Which member of the Royal Family popularised the Christmas tree in the mid-19th century?

12. Which product did soap salesman William Wrigley Jr begin distributing in 1892?

13. On which river does Glasgow stand?

14. Which country won the cricket World Cup in 1975?

15. Which title was first granted to John Dryden?

ANSWERS: 1 Peter Wright, 2 Central African Republic, 3 Robert, 4 Fifteen, 5 Ikebana, 6 Sardinia, 7 Philip Roth, 8 Christmas rose, 9 Kathleen Ferrier, 10 Photograph, 11 Prince Albert, 12 Chewing gum, 13 River Clyde, 14 West Indies, 15 Poet laureate.

GENERAL KNOWLEDGE

1. Which English team won football's U.E.F.A. Cup in 2001?

2. What is the literal meaning of the word cenotaph?

3. The Wish Tower and the Redoubt are features of which East Sussex seaside resort?

4. What is the name of the 203-carat diamond that thieves tried to steal from the Dome in 2000?

5. In which English county is The Wrekin?

6. Which American football team won the Super Bowl in 1997?

7. Which dog takes its name from the German for 'badger dog'?

8. In broadcasting, for which channel is CNN an abbreviation?

9. Which joint is also known as the carpus?

10. Christmas Island in the Indian Ocean is a territory of which country?

11. Which newspaper was founded by Alfred Harmsworth in 1896?

12. What country has cricketer Lance Klusener represented?

13. Which English novelist wrote Moll Flanders?

14. In which European country is the ski resort of Kaprun?

15. Who is the patron saint of music?

GENERAL KNOWLEDGE

1. Which city is West Sussex was called Noviomagus Regnensium by the Romans?

2. Who wrote Rebecca of Sunnybrook Farm?

3. Which British sprinter won the 100m at the world junior championships after passing up the chance to go to the Olympics?

4. By what name was Sir Henry Percy, who died in 1403, known?

5. Which blacklisted U.S. director made the films The Servant and The Go-Between?

6. What was the first name of the composer Mussorgsky?

7. Of which ocean is the Kara Sea an arm?

8. How many players make up a rugby union team?

9. What is the title of the Clement Moore poem that begins "Twas the night before Christmas"?

10. What nationality is the soprano Montserrat Caballe?

11. What part of the body is affected by glaucoma?

12. In which year was the Grand National race declared void?

13. Which British actress starred in the 2000 remake of the 1967 film Bedazzled?

14. By what name was American lyricist Samuel Cohen known?

15. Which actor appeared in Superman and Apocalypse Now?

ANSWERS: 1 Chichester, 2 Kate Wiggin, 3 Mark Lewis-Francis, 4 Hotspur, 5 Joseph Losey, 6 Modest, 7 Arctic Ocean, 8 Fifteen, 9 A Visit from St Nicholas, 10 Spanish, 11 The eye, 12 1993, 13 Liz Hurley, 14 Sammy Cahn, 15 Marlon Brando.

ENTERTAINMENT

1. Which historian presented the Channel 4 documentary series Elizabeth?

2. Which Swindon teenager had a number one hit with Day & Night?

3. Which showbiz stalwart became the first celebrity to be inducted into the BBC's Hall of Fame?

4. Which Friends actor starred as a dentist in the film comedy The Whole Nine Yards?

5. Which actor played Vince Pinner in the Eighties sitcom Just Good Friends?

6. Which pop group told us to Reach in the top five in 2000?

7. Who played Marcus in the 1971 film Jennifer on My Mind?

8. Which former BBC foreign correspondent introduced us to his Forgotten Britain on BBC1?

19. Which U.S. vocalist had a 1976 U.K. top ten hit with This is It?

10. In which film did Ewan McGregor star as the writer James Joyce?

11. In which film did Meg Ryan, Diane Keaton and Lisa Kudrow star as the daughters of a dying father, played by Walter Matthau?

12. Who were the two contestants on the first celebrity edition of the quiz show Who Wants to Be a Millionaire?

13. Which U.K. group had a 1973 top ten hit with Pyjamarama?

14. Which actor directed the 1987 version of the film The Glass Menagerie?

15. Which McGann played Jonathan Vishnevski in the BBC1 drama series Fish?

GENERAL KNOWLEDGE

1. Which country hosted the rugby union World Cup in 1995?

2. Which British actress starred in The Lady Vanishes and The Wicked Lady?

3. Who won the 200m freestyle at the Sydney Olympics to become the first Dutchman to win an Olympic swimming gold medal?

4. Which Italian dramatist wrote Accidental Death of an Anarchist?

5. By what name is Beethoven's Sixth Symphony known?

6. Who is generally regarded as the first British prime minister?

7. What number wood in golf was formerly known as a spoon?

8. What name is given to the deliberate and systematic destruction of a racial, religious or ethnic group?

9. What is the title of the novel Jane Austen left unfinished at her death?

10. How is the material polyvinyl chloride commonly known?

11. Which American actor starred in Twelve Angry Men and On Golden Pond?

12. How many goals were scored in the first international football match between England and Scotland?

13. Which Australian runner lit the Olympic cauldron in the opening ceremony of the Sydney Olympics?

14. By what name was singer and comedian Asa Yoelson better known?

15. Which large cat is also called a cougar?

ANSWERS: 1 South Africa, 2 Margaret Lockwood, 3 Pieter van den Hoogenband, 4 Dario Fo, 5 Pastoral Symphony, 6 Robert Walpole, 7 3, 8 Genocide, 9 Sanditon, 10 Pakistan, 11 Henry Fonda, 12 0, 13 PVC, 14 Al Jolson, 15 Puma.

GENERAL KNOWLEDGE

1. By how many shots did Tiger Woods win the U.S. Masters in 1997?

2. Which U.S. comedian and pianist was known as Schnozzola or The Schnoz?

3. Who was the first British woman to win an Olympic cycling medal?

4. Which Australian marsupial is also called a banded anteater?

5. With which branch of the arts was Robert Mapplethorpe chiefly associated?

6. Which U.S. rapper and actor was murdered in a drive-by shooting in 1996?

7. The 11th hole on which golf course is called White Dogwood?

8. By what name was the American striptease artiste Rose Louise Hovick better known?

9. Which Canadian singer recorded the album Jagged Little Pill?

10. Which three sports are included in the Triathlon?

11. Which branch of mathematics takes its name from the Greek for 'earth measurement'?

12. Who wrote The Adventures of Tom Sawyer and The Adventures of Huckleberry Finn?

13. Where is the Sabina Park cricket ground?

14. In which film did Pierce Brosnan first play James Bond?

15. Which horse won the Grand National in 1973, 1974 and 1977?

GENERAL KNOWLEDGE

1. In which sport is the term hookcheck often used?

2. The Man of Property is the first book in which sequence of novels by John Galsworthy?

3. Cardinal Richelieu was the chief minister of which French monarch?

4. Which cyclist won Great Britain's first gold medal at the Sydney Olympics?

5. In the Old Testament, who was the mother of Ishmael?

6. Which U.S. rock band features Bob Dylan's son Jakob?

7. Who won the 2000 Mercury Music Prize for his album The Hour of the Bewilderbeast?

8. What is the middle name of basketball legend Michael Jordan?

9. Which French artist painted Olympia and Le Déjeuner sur l'herbe?

10. What sort of creatures transmit Lyme disease?

11. Which English artist was famous for his bleak industrial landscapes featuring matchstick figures?

12. In Indian philosophy, what term is used for the sum of a person's actions, carried forward into his next life?

13. Which flamboyant Russian-born ballet dancer died in Paris in 1993?

14. Who scored a world record 26 runs from a single Test match over in March 2001?

15. The Hindenburg Line was a defensive barrier built by the Germans in which war?

ANSWERS: 1 Ice hockey, 2 The Forsyte Saga, 3 Louis XIII, 4 Jason Queally, 5 Hagar, 6 The Wallflowers, 7 Badly Drawn Boy, 8 Jeffrey, 9 Edouard Manet, 10 Ticks, 11 L S Lowry, 12 Karma, 13 Rudolf Nureyev, 14 Craig MacMillan, 15 World War I.

GENERAL KNOWLEDGE

1. To which genus of trees does the larch belong?

2. What is the capital of Botswana?

3. In which year did British contralto Kathleen Ferrier die?

4. Which bandleader, born in 1891, was known in his early days as 'the King of Jazz'?

5. Which 1970s television drama starred Julie Covington as singer Dee Rhoades?

6. What was the name of the imperial dynasty of China from 1279-1368?

7. In which year did William Bligh, former commander of the H.M.S. Bounty, die?

8. Who was the England cricket captain from 1993-8?

9. What is the colour of the ball worth six points in snooker?

10. Which Hebrew prophet led the Israelites out of Egypt into the Promised Land?

11. Which genus of trees and shrubs includes the holly?

12. What is the sixth letter in the Greek alphabet?

13. In which European country is the formerly important gold-mining town of Tomsk?

14. What is the state capital of Pennsylvania?

15. Who was the 1988 world professional darts champion?

ANSWERS 1. Larix 2. Gaborone 3. 1953 4. Paul Whiteman 5. Rock Follies 6. Yuan dynasty 7. 1817 8. Michael Atherton 9. Pink 10. Moses 11. Ilex 12. Zeta 13. Russia 14. Harrisburg 15. Bob Anderson.

ENTERTAINMENT

1. Which Friends actress appeared in the 1998 film The Opposite of Sex?

2. What was the name of David Hasselhoff's character in the television series Knight Rider?

3. Who plays Buffy the Vampire Slayer on television?

4. Which Hollywood actress played Audrey Griswold in the 1989 film National Lampoon's Christmas Vacation?

5. Who directed the 1999 film Runaway Bride?

6. Who plays Rigsby in the sitcom Rising Damp?

7. Who plays Frank Pierce in the 1999 film Bringing Out the Dead?

8. Who directed the 1946 film The Dark Mirror?

9. Who played Kramer in the sitcom Seinfeld?

10. Which comedy actor played Sgt. Sam Short in the 1970s sitcom Coppers End?

11. Which singer played Renfield in the 1992 film Bram Stoker's Dracula?

12. Which comedian directed and starred in the 1960 film Mr. Topaze?

13. Who played playwright Eugene O'Neill in the 1981 film Reds?

14. Which 1989 British film was released in the U.S. in 1991 as Dark Obsession?

15. The 1993 film Sommersby is a remake of which earlier film?

ANSWERS 1. Lisa Kudrow 2. Michael Knight 3. Sarah Michelle Gellar 4. Juliette Lewis 5. Garry Marshall 6. Leonard Rossiter 7. Nicolas Cage 8. Robert Siodmak 9. Michael Richards 10. Bill Owen 11. Tom Waits 12. Peter Sellers 13. Jack Nicholson 14. Diamond Skulls 15. The Return of Martin Guerre.

SPORT

1. Irina Kiselyeva was 1986 and 1987 world champion at what sport?

2. What nationality is the former European triathlon champion Gregor Stam?

3. What was the attendance at the 1891 F.A. Cup Final?

4. What nationality is runner Derartu Tulu?

5. Jarmila Kratochvilova set a women's world record for the 800m on 26th July 1983. What time did she run?

6. By what score did Scotland beat Romania at rugby union in August 1999?

7. Which horse won the 1976 Irish 2000 Guineas?

8. In which year did Australian tennis player Norman Brookes die?

9. What sport is governed by the Fédération Internationale des Sociétés d'Aviron?

10. How many golds did Denmark win in the 1999 World Athletics Championships?

11. Who won the 1980 British Open in snooker?

12. Who won the 1999 German Grand Prix in Formula 1?

13. Who took 7-37 for Pakistan against India in a Limited-Overs International on 25th October 1991?

14. What nationality is swimmer Pieter van den Hoogenband?

15. In which city is the U.S. governing body of basketball, the NBA, based?

ANSWERS 1. Modern Pentathlon 2. Dutch 3. 23,000 4. Ethiopian 5. 1:53.28 6. 60-19 7. Northern Treasure 8. 1968 9. Rowing 10. One 11. Alex Higgins 12. Eddie Irvine 13. Aaqib Javed 14. Dutch 15. New York.

POP MUSIC

1. What is the B-side of David Gamson's Rough Trade single Sugar Sugar?

2. Who is lead singer with the Scottish group The Blue Nile?

3. On which label did the Flying Lizards release the 1979 single Money?

4. Who was the singer with the band Gaye Bykers on Acid?

5. Who had a 1999 Top 10 single with Bailamos?

6. After which songwriter was guitarist Jerry Garcia named?

7. In which year did Abba have a Top 10 single with Gimme Gimme Gimme (A Man After Midnight)?

8. What was the second single by Leeds group The Mission?

9. Which studio album by the Gang of Four features I Love a Man in a Uniform?

10. Who sang lead vocal on the Moonglows song Mama Loocie?

11. Which group's second single was called Subhuman?

12. On what are the baby birds riding on the cover of Gallon Drunk's single Some Fool's Mess?

13. Who produced The Glitter Band's 1974 single Goodbye My Love?

14. Which girl group recorded the 1969 album Philosophy of the World?

15. Who wrote Gloria Gaynor's hit Never Can Say Goodbye?

ART & LITERATURE

1. Who wrote the children's book Stuart Little?

2. Which French artist's works include 1873's Trouville Harbour?

3. Who wrote the 2001 children's book Secret Heart?

4. Who wrote the 1987 stage play Serious Money?

5. What nationality was the 17th century painter Aelbert Cuyp?

6. Where did the artist Max Weber study from 1898-1900?

7. Who wrote the 1948 novel The Heart of the Matter?

8. Which pop art painter's works include 1978's Stepping Out?

9. Who wrote the 1831 novel Castle Dangerous?

10. Which artist's works include 1922's At the Mirror?

11. Which modern artist's works include the 1899 painting Three Tahitians?

12. Who wrote the stage play Cat on a Hot Tin Roof?

13. Who sculpted the bronze statue of the dog Greyfriars Bobby which stands on the junction of Candlemaker Row and the George IV bridge in Edinburgh?

14. In which year did the artist Jean-Antoine Watteau die?

15. Which 18th century artist's works include Achilles Lamenting the Death of Patroclus?

ANSWERS 1. E.B. White 2. Eugène Boudin 3. David Almond 4. Caryl Churchill 5. Dutch 6. The Pratt Institute in Brooklyn 7. Graham Greene 8. Roy Lichtenstein 9. Walter Scott 10. Otto Dix 11. Paul Gauguin 12. Tennessee Williams 13. William Brodie 14. 1721 15. Gavin Hamilton.

GENERAL KNOWLEDGE

1. In which novel does Rawdon Crawley marry Becky Sharp?

2. What is the colour of the ball worth one point in snooker?

3. Which character in the film Star Wars was played by Mark Hammill?

4. Who were the mother and father of Galahad in Arthurian legend?

5. Who created the fictional district attorney Perry Mason?

6. What type of creature is an australorp?

7. What is the name given to the strap which runs between the reins and the girth of a horse and prevents it from carrying its head too high?x

8. What is the real name of writer Barbara Vine, a.k.a. Ruth Rendell?

9. Which stand-up comic and actor starred in the 1986 film The Golden Child?

10. What is the former name of Kennedy airport, New York?

11. What is the derived SI unit of electric capacitance?

12. Who was the French composer of the ballet Daphnis et Chloé?

13. Which 1996 film directed by Roland Emmerich featured Bill Paxton as the U.S. President?

14. What is the other name used for cocuswood, which is used for inlaying?

15. Which Dublin-born actress's films included 1943's Jane Eyre?

ANSWERS 1. Vanity Fair 2. Red 3. Luke Skywalker 4. Elaine and Lancelot 5. Erle Stanley Gardner 6. A heavy black breed of domestic fowl 7. (Running) Martingale 8. Ruth Barbara Grasemann 9. Eddie Murphy 10. Idlewild 11. Farad 12. Maurice Ravel 13. Independence Day 14. Jamaican ebony (or West Indian ebony) 15. Sara Allgood.

ENTERTAINMENT

1. Who composed the opera Les Danaïdes?

2. Who played Jim Phelps in the 1996 film Mission: Impossible?

3. Who plays Darby Snow in the 1993 film The Pelican Brief?

4. Who plays Dr. Fu Manchu in the 1931 film Daughter of the Dragon?

5. Who does Jim Carrey play in the 1994 film The Mask?

6. Who directed and starred in the 1996 film Matilda?

7. Who played Flay in the 2000 BBC TV production of Gormenghast?

8. During which war was the 1970 film Darling Lili set?

9. Who directed the 1971 film The French Connection?

10. What was Arthur Bostrom's character name in the sitcom 'Allo 'Allo!?

11. Who plays brain surgeon George Brent's wife in the 1939 film Dark Victory?

12. In which U.S. state was the television drama Whirlybirds set?

13. Who directed the 1991 film New Jack City?

14. Who directed the 1995 film Waiting to Exhale?

15. Which actress played the manager of an amateur rugby league side in the 1973 sitcom All Our Saturdays?

ANSWERS 1. Salieri 2. Jon Voight 3. Julia Roberts 4. Warner Oland 5. Stanley Ipkiss 6. Danny DeVito 7. Christopher Lee 8. World War I 9. William Friedkin 10. Crabtree 11. Bette Davis 12. California 13. Mario Van Peebles 14. Forest Whitaker 15. Diana Dors.

SPORT

1. In which year was the athlete Carl Lewis born?

2. Who rode Victory Note to victory in the 1998 Poule d'Essai des Poulains?

3. What is the nickname of cricketer Kim Barnett?

4. Which country were coxless four rowing champions in the 1997 world championships?

5. How many golds did Greece win in the 1999 World Athletics Championships?

6. In which year was the Amateur Softball Association of America formed?

7. In which year did Darren Clarke first take part in the Ryder Cup?

8. Which cricket team scored 1107 runs in their game with New South Wales in December 1926?

9. In cricket, who scored 150 for Worcestershire against Essex in the 2nd innings of their 1999 county championship game?

10. David Robinson was NBA's leading scorer in 1994. What was his average per game?

11. Who scored Scotland's goal in their 1998 Group A football World Cup finals game against Norway?

12. Which former American football player is uncle of Leicester Riders' basketball star Purnell Perry?

13. Who was the 1975 women's 100m breaststroke swimming world champion?

14. Which U.S. golfer was the leading money winner in 1953 on the US tour?

15. For which rugby league team did Martin Offiah make his debut in February 2000?

ANSWERS 1. 1961 2. John Reid 3. Barn 4. Britain 5. Two 6. 1933 7. 1997 8. Victoria 9. Graeme Hick 10. 29.8 points 11. Craig Burley 12. William 'The Refrigerator' Perry 13. Hannelore Anke 14. Lew Worsham 15. Salford City Reds.

POP MUSIC

1. What was the final single made by the original line-up of the group Gang of Four?

2. Which duo had a 1981 hit with Wedding Bells?

3. Which U.S. group recorded the album Double Nickels on the Dime?

4. Which 1960s model was the subject of a 1979 single by Glaxo Babies?

5. Aston, Aston, Rizzo, Stevenson, Gilvear. Which 1980s group?

6. Which group's first single, in 1989, was Retard Girl?

7. Who had a 1999 Top 10 single with The Launch?

8. Who had a 1990 Top 10 single with Tears on My Pillow?

9. Which 1970s singer featured on the song Walk Like A Panther by the All Seeing I?

10. In which year did singer David McComb die?

11. In which year was Bobby Vinton's Blue Velvet a U.K. Top 10 single?

12. Who had a 1999 Top 10 hit with Right Now?

13. Who had a 1980 Top 10 single with So Good To Be Back Home Again?

14. Who had a 1979 top 10 with Strut Your Funky Stuff?

15. In which year did Bo Diddley tour Britain for the first time?

ANSWERS 1. To Hell With Poverty 2. Godley and Creme 3. The Minutemen 4. Christine Keeler 5. Gene Loves Jezebel 6. Hole 7. DJ Jean 8. Kylie Minogue 9. Tony Christie 10. 1999 11. 1990 12. Atomic Kitten 13. The Tourists 14. Frantique 15. 1963.

GEOGRAPHY

1. In which county is the carpet manufacturing town of Wilton?

2. On which sea coast is Scotland's St. Andrews?

3. Which river flows through the Sea of Galilee?

4. What is the name of the channel between the mainland of N. Scotland and the Orkney Islands?

5. St. Cloud is a suburb of which French city?

6. The port of Galata is a suburb of which city in Turkey?

7. Which country claimed Queen Maud Land, Antarctica, in 1939?

8. In which country has the most southern point in South America?

9. The island of Quemoy, off the coast of China, lies in which strait?

10. Gatun Lake is part of which canal?

11. Which is larger - El Salvador or Guatemala?

12. On which river does Bedford stand?

13. Which has the greater population - Norfolk or Suffolk?

14. In which ocean are the volcanic D'Entrecasteaux Islands?

15. In which country is Mount Sir Sandford in the Selkirk Mountains?

ANSWERS 1. Wiltshire 2. North Sea 3. River Jordan 4. Pentland Firth 5. Paris 6. Istanbul 7. Norway 8. Chile 9. Formosa Strait 10. Panama Canal 11. Guatemala 12. Ouse 13. Norfolk 14. Pacific 15. Canada.

GENERAL KNOWLEDGE

1. How many pennies was the English silver coin a groat worth?

2. Who were the two male leads in the 1997 film Blood and Wine?

3. Who was the designer of the British aircraft the Spitfire which was used in the Battle of Britain?

4. Who became president of Gabon in 1967?

5. What is the standard monetary unit of Botswana?

6. In which year did the long-running BBC current affairs TV programme Panorama begin?

7. Who wrote the 1973 play Equus?

8. In which year was BBC news reporter Kate Adie born?

9. Which Roman road runs from London to Wroxeter near Shrewsbury?

10. Which ancient Greek city was site of the most famous oracle of Apollo?

11. Who wrote the one-act play Salomé, which was produced in Paris in 1896?

12. What was the signature tune of violinist and bandleader Joe Loss?

13. Which creature of Australia and New Guinea is also called a spiny anteater?

14. What is the name given to the first period of the Mesozoic era during which reptiles flourished?

15. Who authored the 1879 novel Daisy Miller?

ANSWERS 1. Four 2. Jack Nicholson and Michael Caine 3. Reginald Mitchell 4. Omar Bongo 5. Pula 6. 1953 7. Peter Shaffer 8. 1945 9. Watling Street 10. Delphi 11. Oscar Wilde 12. In the Mood 13. Echidna 14. Triassic period 15. Henry James.

ENTERTAINMENT

1. Who is the female star of the 2000 film The Next Best Thing?

2. Which English actor played photographer Brian in the 1996 film The Truth About Cats and Dogs?

3. In which year did The Wheeltappers' and Shunters' Social Club first appear on television?

4. Who directed and starred in the 1997 comedy film Waiting for Guffman?

5. The stories of which three historical figures is told in the 1954 film Daughters of Destiny?

6. Which Oscar-winning actress played Pearl Slaghoople in the 1994 film The Flintstones?

7. Which author does Chris O'Donnell play in the 1997 film In Love and War?

8. Who played the title role in the 1951 western film Sugarfoot?

9. What nationality was soprano Suzanne Danco?

10. Who played Mr. Step in the 1997 film Spice World?

11. Which comedienne played music hall singer Millie Goswick in the sitcom The Fossett Saga?

12. Who directed and starred in the 1971 film comedy A New Leaf with Walter Matthau?

13. Who starred as Wild Bill in a 1995 western film of the same name?

14. In which year was comedian Allan Sherman born?

15. Who plays a small town barber in the 1952 film Wait till the Sun Shines, Nellie?

ANSWERS 1. Madonna 2. Ben Chaplin 3. 1974 4. Christopher Guest 5. Elizabeth I, Joan of Arc and Lysistrata 6. Elizabeth Taylor 7. Ernest Hemingway 8. Randolph Scott 9. Belgian 10. Michael Barrymore 11. June Whitfield 12. Elaine May 13. Jeff Bridges 14. 1924 15. David Wayne.

SPORT

1. Which female swimmer held the UK shortcourse 100m and 200m breaststroke records in 2001-2002?

2. Which Indian cricketer scored 1604 runs in the 1964/5 season?

3. Who won the 1998 World Championhsip snooker title?

4. How many Olympic gold medals did gymnast Vera Caslavska win from 1964-8?

5. What nationality is golfer Eric Carlberg?

6. Who was the 1987-91 men's open world judo champion?

7. Which Ethiopian runner broke the world two mile record in February 2000?

8. The European Super Cup in football was first played in 1972, at the suggestion of which Dutch newspaper?

9. What nationality is hurdler Anier Garcia?

10. Who was the men's 100m winner at the 1982 European Championships?

11. Which golfer won the 2001 Qatar Masters?

12. Who rode the 1993 July Cup-winning horse Hamas?

13. For which rugby union club side did Mark Mapletoft play before his move to Harlequins?

14. At what sport have Britain's Bob Spalding and Jonathan Jones been world champions?

15. How long did the 19-frame qualifying match between Garry Wilkinson and Jason Ferguson in the 2000 World Championships in snooker take to complete?

ANSWERS 1. Heidi Earp 2. Chandu Borde 3. John Higgins 4. Seven 5. Swedish 6. Naoya Ogawa 7. Hailu Mekkonen 8. De Telegraaf 9. Cuban 10. Frank Emmelmann 11. Tony Johnstone 12. Willie Carson 13. Saracens 14. Powerboating 15. 11 hours and 38 minutes.

POP MUSIC

1. Which band recorded the 1999 single No Distance Left To Run?

2. In which year did Kiss drummer Eric Carr die?

3. Which solo singer had a 1999 No. 1 with When You Say Nothing At All?

4. Which studio album by Queen features the song We Will Rock You?

5. Which solo artist had a 1984 Top 10 single with Too Late For Goodbyes?

6. In which year did John Foxx have a hit single with Underpass?

7. Which John Lennon song did Generation X cover on the B-side of the single King Rocker?

8. Jerry Rosalie was the lead singer of which 1960s group?

9. In which year did Marianne Faithful have a Top 10 hit with As Tears Go By?

10. In which city did the Raspberries form in 1970?

11. On which label did Fun Boy Three record the single The Lunatics have Taken Over the Asylum?

12. Who was the composer and lead vocalist with group Fischer Z?

13. Who recorded the 1992 album The Happy Club?

14. Which singer-songwriter released the 1979 single All Sewn Up?

15. Who recorded the 1977 album Don Juan's Reckless Daughter?

ANSWERS 1. Blur 2. 1991 3. Ronan Keating 4. News of the World 5. Julian Lennon 6. 1980 7. Gimme Some Truth 8. The Sonics 9. 1964 10. Cleveland 11. Chrysalis 12. John Watts 13. Bob Geldof 14. Patrik Fitzgerald 15. Joni Mitchel.

HISTORY

1. In which year was Pompeii destroyed by Vesuvius?

2. In which year did Anne of Cleves die?

3. Who replaced James A. Garfield as U.S. president in 1881?

4. In which year did the Praetorian Guard assassinate Emperor Pertinax?

5. Which U.S. battleship was blown up on February 15th, 1898 in Havana?

6. Who stood as Socialist Labour candidate at Newport East in May 1997?

7. Who was Chancellor of the Exchequer from 1964-67?

8. Where was Mary, Queen of Scots born in 1542?

9. In which year did Charles Howard, 1st Earl of Nottingham, die?

10. Who became dictator of Venezuela in July, 1811?

11. How many days did Hannibal take to cross the Alps during the Second Punic War?

12. Which treaty, signed in 1648, established Switzerland as an independent state?

13. In which year did Athelstan, King of Wessex, die?

14. Who succeeded Charles IV as Holy Roman Emperor in 1378?

15. In which year was the Battle of Dunbar?

ANSWERS 1. 79 A.D. 2. 1557 3. Chester A. Arthur 4. 193 5. Maine 6. Arthur Scargill 7. James Callaghan 8. Linlithgow 9. 1624 10. Francisco de Miranda 11. Fifteen 12. Peace of Westphalia 13. 939 14. Wenceslas 15. 1650.

GENERAL KNOWLEDGE

1. Of which republic in the Caribbean is Port-au-Prince the capital?

2. Who directed the 1998 film Godzilla starring Matthew Broderick?

3. Lake Taupo is the largest lake in which country?

4. Who was a Best Actor Oscar nominee for the 1948 film Sitting Pretty?

5. What was the debut novel by writer Nick Hornby?

6. What is the capital of the Ukraine?

7. Who is the author of the novel Schindler's Ark?

8. What is teosinte?

9. In which year did U.S. jazz pianist and composer Thelonious Monk die?

10. Which operetta by Gilbert and Sullivan is subtitled Bunthorne's Bride?

11. Between which two constellations in the southern hemisphere does the small constellation of Reticulum lie?

12. Who authored the 1869 novel Good Wives?

13. Who was the director and star of the 1995 film Braveheart?

14. Who wrote the novel Cry, the Beloved Country?

15. Who composed the one-act opera Suor Angelica?

ENTERTAINMENT

1. Who played the title role in the 1930 film Abraham Lincoln?

2. What are the surnames of television's Ant and Dec?

3. What was the Elizabethan name for a prompter in the theatre?

4. Who played the title role in the 1940 film The Earl of Chicago?

5. In which country was the stage actress Agnes Booth born in 1846?

6. Which landmark is featured in the finale of the 1942 Alfred Hitchcock film Saboteur?

7. Which former soap actress starred as Anna in the 1999 Broadway production of the play Closer?

8. Which Fast Show cast member played Annie in the 1987 sitcom The Corner House?

9. Who played Jenny in the television drama series Cold Feet?

10. In the animated television series Bob and Margaret, what is Bob's profession?

11. Who directed the 1999 film Felicia's Journey?

12. What is Brian Aherne's profession in the 1935 film I Live My Life?

13. Who directed, and is one of the stars of, the 1994 film Reality Bites?

14. Which comedian's alter egos include Tommy Cockles?

15. Who played television's Columbo?

ANSWERS 1. Walter Huston 2. Anthony McPartlin and Declan Donnelly 3. Bookholder 4. Robert Montgomery 5. Australia 6. Statue of Liberty 7. Anna Friel 8. Arabella Weir 9. Fay Ripley 10. Dentist 11. Atom Egoyan 12. Archaeologist 13. Ben Stiller 14. Simon Day 15. Peter Falk.

SPORT

1. Edouard Artigas was the 1947 sabre world champion. Which country did he represent?

2. What is the nickname of cricketer Mark Wayne Alleyne?

3. How old was Hjalmar Johansson when he won the 1908 Olympic highboard diving title?

4. Which U.S. golfer won the 1998 Tournament Players' Championship?

5. Which rider won the Badminton Horse Trials in 2000?

6. Who did Russia play in the quarter-finals of the 2000 Davis Cup?

7. Which horse won the 1996 Whitbread Gold Cup?

8. Which tennis player won the 1992 ATP Tour Championship Final?

9. In what time did Allen Johnson win the 1996 Olympic 110m hurdles title?

10. What was the married name of tennis player Kerry Melville?

11. Which Briton won the 1967 Italian Grand Prix in Formula 1?

12. For which team did cricketer J.E. Benjamin make his county debut in 1988?

13. By what score did England beat Wales at rugby union on 20th February 1998?

14. For which rugby league club side did Kris Radlinski play in the 2001/2202 season?

15. Who won the men's singles title in the 2002 world indoor bowls championships?

POP MUSIC

1. Which group recorded the 1992 single The Drowners?

2. Which electronic group recorded the 2000 album Add Insult to Injury?

3. Which singer was born Vera Margaret Welch in 1917?

4. Which legendary English drummer once played in a group called The Beachcombers?

5. Which singer-songwriter recorded the 2001 album The Convincer?

6. What was the song on the reverse of the 1977 single Jamming by Bob Marley and the Wailers?

7. In which year did Talking Heads have a Top 20 single with the song Once In A Lifetime?

8. Which group recorded the album Polyester Embassy?

9. Who produced the first two record albums by the group Buffalo Tom?

10. Which female singer created the 2000 album Light Years?

11. In which year did the Doors release the album Morrison Hotel?

12. Which female singer had a 1991 Top 10 single with Rush Rush?

13. Which group recorded the album A Different Lifetime?

14. In which year did The Associates have a Top 10 single with the song Party Fears Two?

15. Which girl group recorded the album One Touch?

ANSWERS 1. Suede 2. Add N To (X) 3. Vera Lynn 4. Keith Moon 5. Nick Lowe 6. Punky Reggae Party 7. 1981 8. Madison Avenue 9. J. Mascis 10. Kylie Minogue 11. 1970 12. Paula Abdul 13. Spearmint 14. 1982 15. Sugarbabes.

WORDS

1. In fencing, what is a Balestra?

2. What type of creature is a jumping mouse - a bird or a rodent?

3. What is the French term for a secondary school?

4. What call in solo whist declares that a hand will win no tricks?

5. What in ancient Greece was a peltast?

6. What in Greece is a flokati?

7. If an artist were an animalier what would they specialize in painting?

8. What is the name given to the end of a hammer head opposite the striking face?

9. If you suffered from apnoea, what would you be unable to do?

10. Where would you find a nobiliary particle?

11. The Italian sweet Tiramisu derives its name from which phrase?

12. What, on a bishop's mitre, are the infulae?

13. If you performed an escalade to attack a fort, what would you use?

14. What does the French phrase amour-propre mean?

15. In biology, what does the phrase ananthous mean?

ANSWERS 1. A short jump forward 2. Rodent 3. A lycée 4. Misère 5. A lightly-armed foot soldier 6. Rug 7. Animals 8. Peen 9. Breathe 10. In a title or surname 11. Pull me up 12. The ribbons hanging from the back 13. Ladders 14. Self-respect 15. Having no flowers.

GENERAL KNOWLEDGE

1. What is the name given to a young salmon that returns to fresh water after one winter in the sea?

2. Who is the author of the novel In the Land of Israel?

3. What is the name of the knife with a curved blade used by the Gurkhas?

4. Who was the 1939 U.S. Open golf champion?

5. Which actor played Barton Fink in a 1991 film of the same name?

6. What is the symbol of the silvery-grey element Technetium?

7. In which year did French sculptor Auguste Rodin die?

8. Who wrote the 1943 novel The Ship?

9. What is the 17th letter in the Greek alphabet?

10. What, in Australia, is a tammar?

11. Who wrote the 1977 novel Bloodline?

12. Which Phrygian goddess of nature was often called the 'Mother of the Gods'?

13. Which comic actor played the title role in the film Uncle Buck?

14. Which unit of fluid measure is equal to one sixtieth of a drachm?

15. What, in New Zealand, is a tawa?

ANSWERS 1. Grilse 2. Amos Oz 3. Kukri 4. Byron Nelson 5. John Turturro 6. Tc 7. 1917 8. C.S. Forester 9. Rho 10. Small wallaby 11. Sidney Sheldon 12. Cybele 13. John Candy 14. Minim 15. A tall timber tree.

ENTERTAINMENT

1. Who directed the 1935 film A Night at the Opera?

2. What was Ben's sister called in the sitcom 2point4 children?

3. What was June Whitfield's character name in the television sitcom Happy Ever After?

4. Which duo presented the BBC children's television programme The Saturday Show in 2001?

5. In which 1970's television series was the central character called William 'Spider' Scott?

6. Who directed the 1932 film The Bitter Tea of General Yen?

7. Who voices the children's television character Bob the Builder?

8. Who played Ethel in the television drama series EastEnders?

9. Who directed the 1959 film Eyes Without a Face?

10. Who directed the 1995 film The Underneath?

11. In which 1960's television series were the central characters called Tony Newman and Doug Phillips?

12. Who created the BBC television sitcom Up Pompeii!?

13. Who played Mr. Boffin in a 1998 television adaptation of Charles Dickens's Our Mutual Friend?

14. Who played Mr. Boffin in a 1976 television adaptation of Charles Dickens's Our Mutual Friend?

15. What was Brian Wilde's character name in the sitcom Last of the Summer Wine?

ANSWERS 1. Sam Wood 2. Tina 3. June Fletcher 4. Joe Mace and Dani Behr 5. The XYY Man 6. Frank Capra 7. Neil Morrissey 8. Gretchen Franklin 9. Georges Franju 10. Steven Soderbergh 11. The Time Tunnel 12. Talbot Rothwell 13. Peter Vaughan 14. Leo McKern 15. Foggy Dewhurst.

SPORT

1. What nationality is cyclist Paolo Bettini?

2. Who rode Pilsudski to victory in the 1997 Japan Cup in Tokyo?

3. In which event did Kate Allenby win a bronze medal for Britain at the 2000 Olympics?

4. Which Canadian Football team won the Grey Cup from 1978-82?

5. In which year did Randolph Lycett and Elizabeth Ryan win the Wimbledon mixed doubles tennis title for the second time?

6. How many Formula 1 Grand Prix wins did Alan Jones have in his career from 1975-86?

7. Which Argentinian tennis player won the Estoril Open men's singles title in April 2002?

8. How many times in the 1940s did St. Mary's Hospital win the Middlesex Sevens competition in rugby union?

9. Which golfer won the MCI Heritage Classic in April 2000?

10. Lupe Pintor was WBC super-bantamweight world boxing champion from 1985-6. Which was his nationality?

11. In cricket, who scored 117 for Warwickshire against Durham in the 1st innings of their 1999 county championship game?

12. What nation did Olympic cyclist Arie van Vliet represent?

13. Who beat Stephen Hendry in the first round of the 2000 World Professional Snooker Championships?

14. In which year were trotting races first held in the Netherlands?

15. Which women's golfer won the Du Maurier Classic in August 1999?

POP MUSIC

1. Which studio album by The Beloved features singles The Sun Rising and Hello?

2. Which institution did Annie Lennox quit in 1971 before sitting her final exams?

3. Which two 1950s hits for Malcolm Vaughan feature the word 'Roses'?

4. In which year did Soul II Soul have a Top 10 single with Get A Life?

5. Which group presented the 'Protected Passion Tour' in 1981?

6. Who had a 1999 Top 10 hit with Re-Rewind the Crowd Say Bo Selecta?

7. In which year did Visage have a Top 20 hit with Night Train?

8. Who had a 1989 No. 1 single with You Got It (The Right Stuff)?

9. What was Randy Vanwarmer's U.K. hit single called?

10. In which year did Frankie Vaughan have his last chart hit single with Nevertheless?

11. Which guitarist's early groups included Nightshift and The Tridents?

12. Which couple released the 1968 album Two Virgins?

13. Which U.S. group recorded 1990's Smooth Noodle Maps?

14. Who had a No. 1 album in 1999 with By Request?

15. Which country did The Waikikis, who had a 1965 hit with Hawaii Tattoo, come from?

SCIENCE

1. Thalassa is a small satellite of which planet?

2. In which English city was Nobel prize winner Sir Edward Victor Appleton born?

3. Who succeeded Sir Humphry Davy as Professor of Chemistry at the Royal Institution?

4. In which year did the comet Shoemaker-Levy 9 collide with Jupiter?

5. In which year did Hans Christian Oersted isolate aluminium?

6. In aeronautics, which organization is represented by the acronym ESA?

7. In which year did John Logie Baird first transmit pictures between London and Glasgow using telephone lines?

8. Who was named Professor of Chemistry at Lille University in 1854?

9. What is the approximate diameter in miles of Uranus's moon Miranda?

10. In which year did chemist Robert Wilhelm Bunsen die?

11. In which year did Charles Darwin graduate from Cambridge University?

12. Of what is thanatology the science?

13. In which century did scientist Daniel Bernoulli live?

14. Who won the 1905 Nobel prize for medicine?

15. Symbolic, connectionist and evolutionary are the three types of what?

THANATOLOGY DEPARTMENT

ANSWERS 1. Neptune 2. Bradford 3. Michael Faraday 4. 1994 5. 1825 6. European Space Agency 7. 1927 8. Louis Pasteur 9. 290 miles 10. 1899 11. 1831 12. Death and dying 13. 18th Century 14. Robert Koch 15. Artificial Intelligence.

GENERAL KNOWLEDGE

1. Which number is represented by the letters XIV in Roman numerals?

2. What is the cgs unit of force?

3. Who was South African prime minister from 1939-48?

4. Which U.S. stand-up comedian and film actor appeared as a con man in the 1997 film The Spanish Prisoner?

5. The 1997 film Starship Troopers by Paul Verhoeven was based on a novel by which author?

6. Who was the Best Supporting Actress Oscar winner for the film In Old Chicago?

7. Who wrote the 1973 novel The Onion Field?

8. In which BBC sitcom did Penelope Keith feature as Margo Leadbetter?

9. Tobermory is the chief town on which island in the Inner Hebrides?

10. In which year did Toronto-born jazz pianist and composer Gil Evans die?

11. Who authored the 1883 novel Under Drake's Flag?

12. Which 1996 film comedy starred Jack Nicholson as the U.S. president?

13. Who wrote the 1971 novel The Onion Eaters?

14. What is the name given to the national assembly of Spain?

15. Which Mexico-born film star played Rupert of Hentzau in 1922's The Prisoner of Zenda?

ENTERTAINMENT

1. Which actress does a striptease in the 1994 film Prêt-à-Porter?

2. Which stand-up comic's alter egos include Alan Parker: Urban Warrior?

3. Which comic magician starred in the 1952 BBC TV series It's Magic?

4. Which Live and Kicking presenter formerly worked on the Irish show The Den?

5. Who starred as Fagin in Alan Bleasdale's 1999 television adaptation of Oliver Twist?

6. Who directed the 1987 film Dark Tower under the pseudonym Ken Barnett?

7. What is the character name of Derek Fowlds in the drama series Heartbeat?

8. Who directed the 1993 film Shadowlands?

9. Who is the female lead in the 1945 film I Know Where I'm Going?

10. Which comedian starred in the 1999 film Big Daddy?

11. Who is the female star of the 2000 film Stigmata?

12. Who played Long John Silver in the 1996 film Muppet Treasure Island?

13. Which two actors co-star in the 2000 boxing film Play it to the Bone?

14. Who plays Grouty in the sitcom Porridge?

15. Which female novelist authored the television plays Splinter of Ice and Poor Cherry?

SPORT

1. How many times did Jacky Ickx win the Le Mans 24-hour race?

2. In cricket, who scored 164 for Glamorgan vs. Nottinghamshire in the 1st innings of their 1999 county championship game?

3. In sailing, in which year did Italy first win the Admiral's Cup?

4. In which year did French tennis player Marcel Bernard die?

5. At which Olympic Games was boxing first included in the programme?

6. How many Tests has cricketer Chris Lewis played for England?

7. What nationality was cyclist Georges Ronsse?

8. In which year was runner Maurice Greene born?

9. Which hockey team won the National Women's League in 1997 & 1998?

10. At what sport were Alfredo Mendoza and Willa McGuire world champions in 1955?

11. How many Grand Prix wins did motorcyclist Giacomo Agostini achieve in total?

12. Which Test cricket side has bowler Nicky Boje played for?

13. Who scored Arsenal's goal in their 1969 League Cup Final defeat?

14. In which year was runner Frank Fredericks born?

15. What nationality is athlete Ingrid Kristiansen?

ANSWERS 1. Six 2. Mike Powell 3. 1995 4. 1994 5. 1904 6. 32 7. Belgian 8. 1974 9. Slough 10. Water-skiing 11. 122 12. South Africa 13. Bobby Gould 1. 1967 15. Norwegian.

POP MUSIC

1. Which group had a 1985 hit with Sex Over the Phone?

2. Which duo charted in 1989 with the song Don't Know Much?

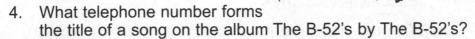

3. In which year did Gene Vincent have a U.K. Top 20 with Blue Jean Bop?

4. What telephone number forms the title of a song on the album The B-52's by The B-52's?

5. Which group released the 1994 album Meanwhile Gardens?

6. Which French group had a 1989 hit single with Lambada?

7. What was the Verve's first chart single, in 1992?

8. Which group charted in 1989 with Homely Girl?

9. Which punk group had a 1978 Top 40 single with Automatic Lover?

10. Which Dutch rock group recorded the 1995 album Lamprey?

11. In which year did Suzanne Vega have a hit single with Luka?

12. On which label did The Levellers record the 1995 album Zeitgeist?

13. For what was Chuck Berry imprisoned in 1979?

14. On which label did Ricky Martin record his eponymous 1999 album?

15. Which U.K. vocal group had a 1963 hit single with Do the Bird?

PEOPLE

1. What nationality is the baritone Bo Skovhus?

2. In which year did the artist Camille Pissarro die?

3. Which pair created the cartoon character Asterix?

4. In which year was the fashion designer Vivienne Westwood born?

5. Who was the first woman to obtain membership of the Royal Scottish Academy?

6. The 2001 television drama Anybody's Nightmare was a dramatization of whose wrongful imprisonment in 1993?

7. What was the surname of the three brothers who were in the original line-up of the Beach Boys?

8. Which comedian's catchphrases included 'Roses Grow on You'?

9. In which country was Olivia Newton-John born?

10. In which year did the comedian Bernie Winters die?

11. In which year did the artist Jean-Victor Bertin die?

12. In which year was Captain Timothy Laurence, husband of the Princess Royal, born?

13. In which year did the singer and dancer Josephine Baker move to Paris?

14. Who wrote the 2000 stage play Ancient Lights?

15. In which year was the U.S. actor Dennis Weaver born?

ANSWERS 1. Danish 2. 1903 3. René Goscinny & Albert Uderzo 4. 1941 5. Phoebe Anna Traquair 6. Sheila Bowler 7. Wilson 8. Norman Vaughan 9. UK 10. 1991 11. 1842 12. 1955 13. 1925 14. Shelagh Stephenson 15. 1924.

ENTERTAINMENT

1. Who had a U.K. number one hit single in 1983 with Wherever I Lay My Hat (That's My Home)?

2. Which Four Weddings and a Funeral actress starred in the 1995 film Unstrung Heroes?

3. Which arch-villain was played by John Shea in the TV series The New Adventures of Superman?

4. What was the name of Audrey Hepburn's character in the 1961 film Breakfast at Tiffany's?

5. Who played Richie Cunningham in the sitcom Happy Days?

6. Who had a U.K. number one hit in 1972 with You Wear It Well?

7. Which controversial former American football star played Nordberg in The Naked Gun movies?

8. Which multi-instrumentalist released a single entitled Pumpkin in 1995?

9. Which low-budget film about three Catholic brothers won the top prize at America's Sundance Film Festival in 1995?

10. Which comedy series written by Jimmy Perry and David Croft was set in Walmington-on-Sea?

11. At the 1995 Smash Hits Poll Winners' Party, who was voted Best Dressed Person, Best Haircut and Most Fanciable Male Star?

12. Which Brookside character was played by Andrew Fillis?

13. Which 1995 political comedy film was directed by When Harry Met Sally director Rob Reiner?

14. Which cult Sixties TV series starred David Janssen as Dr Richard Kimble?

15. Who had a U.K. top ten hit single in 1977 with No More Heroes?

ANSWERS: 1 Paul Young, 2 Andie MacDowell, 3 Lex Luthor, 4 Holly Golightly, 5 Ron Howard, 6 Rod Stewart, 7 OJ Simpson, 8 Tricky, 9 The Brothers McMullen, 10 Dad's Army, 11 Mark Owen of Take That, 12 Gary Stanlow, 13 The American President, 14 The Fugitive, 15 The Stranglers.

GENERAL KNOWLEDGE

1. What job would be performed by a fossarian?

2. In which European country is the seaport of Haparanda?

3. In which U.S. city did the Guggenheim open a museum in October 2001?

4. In which country was chemist Henry Taube born?

5. Which zoologist wrote the 1977 book Manwatching?

6. What was singer Jewel Akens's only Top 30 U.K. hit, in 1965?

7. What is a belah - a mammal or a tree?

8. Who wrote the 1831 novel Crotchet Castle?

9. In which Asian country is the port of Incheon?

10. Who won the 1961 Nobel prize in chemistry?

11. Who directed the 2000 film The Contender?

12. Of which country was U Nu the prime minister from 1948-56?

13. Which two bays does Baggy Point, North Devon overlook?

14. If something is strobic, what is it doing?

15. Which French painter's works include 1939's The Studio?

ANSWERS: 1 Gravedigging, 2 Sweden, 3 Las Vegas, 4 Canada, 5 Desmond Morris, 6 The Birds and the Bees, 7 Tree, 8 Thomas Love Peacock, 9 South Korea, 10 Melvin Calvin, 11 Rod Lurie, 12 Burma, 13 Morte Bay and Croyde Bay, 14 Spinning, 15 George Braque.

GENERAL KNOWLEDGE

1. Who plays the hoodlum John Baron in the 1954 film Suddenly?

2. Pig's ear is rhyming slang for which beverage?

3. Which U.S. city is further north - Charleston or San Francisco?

4. Who painted the 1867 landscape Niagara Falls, from the American Side?

5. What is carbon-14 dating also called?

6. Into which lake does the Hay River of Alberta, Canada flow?

7. Which reggae artist recorded the 2000 album Unchained Spirit?

8. What in Judaism is a luach?

9. Which American artist's works include 1922's A Storm?

10. Which European city is further north - Moscow or Newcastle?

11. In which year was the economist J.K. Galbraith awarded the Presidential Medal of Freedom?

12. As what is the Exclusion Principle also known?

13. In which year did Francis Drake begin the journey which ended as a round-the-world voyage?

14. Who wrote the 1905 novel A Modern Utopia?

15. From which fruit in Uganda would you derive the foodstuff matoke?

ANSWERS: 1 Frank Sinatra, 2 Beer, 3 San Francisco, 4 Frederic Edwin Church, 5 Radiocarbon dating, 6 Great Slave Lake, 7 Buju Banton, 8 Calendar, a9 Georgia O'Keeffe, 10 Moscow, 11 2000, 12 The Pauli Principle, 13 1577, 14 H.G. Wells, 15 Bananas.

GENERAL KNOWLEDGE

1. Why might a beaver have protected you in medieval times?

2. Who plays the character Judah Rosenthal in the 1989 Woody Allen film Crimes and Misdemeanors?

3. Which Briton won the 1917 Nobel prize in physics?

4. In which European country is the province of Cuenca?

5. Which gallery houses the painting The Honourable Mrs. Graham by Thomas Gainsborough?

6. What is the five letter abbreviation for the military rank of commander?

7. Who was the Archbishop of Canterbury from 1747-57?

8. On which bay is the English seaside resort of Hornsea?

9. In which European city was the scientist Charles Louis Alphonse Laveran born?

10. Who wrote the 1834 novel The Last Days of Pompeii?

11. In which year was the White Ship disaster in which William, son of Henry I, perished?

12. On which river does the town of Biggleswade stand?

13. Who wrote the 1975 novel The Eagle Has Landed?

14. What is episcopacy?

15. Which music journalist took over as manager of the Clash from Bernie Rhodes in 1978?

ANSWERS: 1 It was a hinged face guard on a helmet, 2 Martin Landau, 3 Charles Glover Barkla, 4 Spain, 5 National Gallery of Scotland, 6 Comdr, 7 Thomas Herring, 8 Bridlington Bay, 9 Paris, 10 Edward Bulwer-Lytton, 11 1120, 12 River Ivel, 13 Jack Higgins, 14 Government of a Church by bishops, 15 Caroline Coon.

SPORT

1. Which golf course hosted the Open Championship in 2000?

2. Who beat Stephen Hendry to win the snooker world championship in 1997?

3. What nationality is 1991 Wimbledon champion Michael Stich?

4. Which country won the cricket World Cup in 1992?

5. Which England player scored five goals against Cyprus in 1975?

6. Which Portuguese footballer became the world's most expensive player when he joined Real Madrid from Barcelona in 2000?

7. Who was the first boxer to beat Thomas Hearns in a professional bout?

8. How many gold medals did Jesse Owens win at the Berlin Olympics in 1936?

9. In which year was Mike Tyson born?

10. Which female tennis player won the Toyota Princess Cup in Tokyo in September 1999?

11. Which Arsenal player was sent off twice in three days at the start of the 2000/01 Premiership season?

12. How many balls are used in a game of snooker?

13. In which sport did Australia's Ian Baker-Finch make his name?

14. Who won the women's singles at Wimbledon in 1977?

15. What was the name of the dog that found the missing World Cup trophy in 1966?

GENERAL KNOWLEDGE

1. Who wrote the 2001 children's book Horrid Henry's Revenge?

2. What is a cotta?

3. In which African country is the Bwindi Impenetrable National Park?

4. Who became king of Norway in 872?

5. Which U.K. group had a minor chart hit in 1987 with the single Who's Afraid of the Big Bad Noise?

6. Where would you find an empennage - on a ship or an aircraft?

7. In which Asian country is the city of Ulsan?

8. Who composed the 1835 opera Lucia di Lammermoor?

9. Which Nobel prize-winning physicist was responsible for the microwave early warning radar system?

10. For which part of the body is boke a slang word?

11. Which Paris-born sculptor's works include the 1982 marble Eyes?

12. Who won the 1927 Nobel prize in medicine for his work on malaria inoculation?

13. Which body of water separates Madagascar from the African mainland?

14. In which year was the Battle of Evesham?

15. Who wrote the 1984 novel Stanley and the Women?

ANSWERS: 1 Francesca Simon, 2 A surplice in the Roman Catholic Church, 3 Uganda, 4 Harold I (Harold Fairhair), 5 Age of Chance, 6 Aircraft, it is the rear section comprising the rudder, fin and tailplane, 7 South Korea, 8 Donizetti, 9 Luis Walter Alvarez, 10 Nose, 11 Louise Bourgeois, 12 Julius Wagner-Jauregg, 13 Mozambique Channel, 14 1265, 15 Kingsley Amis.

GENERAL KNOWLEDGE

1. In which English county is the seaside resort of Bridport?

2. Who wrote the children's book The If Game?

3. What type of creature is a taipan?

4. On what bay does Pendine in South Wales lie?

5. Who was appointed chairman of the Conservative Party in September 2001?

6. Whose collections of short stories include 1931's Guests of the Nation?

7. Who became vice-president of Egypt in 1975?

8. The sausage dog is an informal name for which animal?

9. Who recorded the 1992 album Your Arsenal?

10. In 1896 Robert Kock went to South Africa to study the origin of which disease?

11. In which European country is the ski resort of Les Arcs?

12. Who wrote the 1853 novel Peg Woffington?

13. In which sport might you hit a home run?

14. At what temperature in degrees centigrade does iron boil?

15. Who presented the children's television programme We Are the Champions?

ANSWERS: 1 Dorset, 2 Catherine Storr, 3 Snake, 4 Carmarthen Bay, 5 David Davis, 6 Frank O'Connor, 7 Hosni Mubarak, 8 Dachshund, 9 Morrissey, 10 Rinderpest, 11 France, 12 Charles Reade, 13 Baseball, 14 3160, 15 Ron Pickering.

GENERAL KNOWLEDGE

1. Whose first published work, which appeared in 1870, dealt with the specific heats of gases?

2. On which Japanese island is Oita a prefecture?

3. What nationality was the poet Gabriela Mistral, winner of the 1945 Nobel prize for literature?

4. Which illustrator's books include Mister Magnolia?

5. What creature would the word whittret describe - a male wasp or a male weasel?

6. What was the name of the rock and roll group in the 1980s BBC comedy series Tutti Frutti?

7. Whose paintings include The Martyrdom of St. Philip, which hangs in the Prado?

8. On which British island would you find the villages of Totland Bay and Freshwater?

9. What is corium?

10. On which river does the town of Honiton, Devon lie?

11. As what is the female vocalist Patricia Daniels better known?

12. For his work on which disease did Charles Jules Henry Nicolle win the 1928 Nobel prize in medicine?

13. Which German painter's works include the 1949 triptych Beginning?

14. If you are performing oscitancy what are you doing?

15. Who was the Duke of Burgundy from 1467-77?

ANSWERS: 1 Wilhelm Röntgen, 2 Kyushu, 3 Chilean, 4 Quentin Blake, 5 Weasel, 6 The Majestics, 7 José de Ribera, 8 Isle of Wight, 9 The deep inner layer of the skin, 10 Otter, 11 Adeva, 12 Typhus, 13 Max Beckmann, 14 Yawning, 15 Charles the Bold.

ENTERTAINMENT

1. What was the title of Kylie Minogue's first U.K. number one single?

2. Which Stanley Kubrick film was based on a Stephen King novel and starred Jack Nicholson?

3. Who played Vince Pinner in the Eighties sitcom Just Good Friends?

4. Who duetted with Shakin' Stevens on the 1984 hit A Rockin' Good Way?

5. Which Frances Hodgson Burnett story was adapted into a 1995 Hollywood film?

6. Which British cop show starring Jack Warner ran from 1955 to 1976?

7. Which U.S. rock group was fronted by sisters Ann and Nancy Wilson?

8. Who played movie queen Joan Crawford in the 1981 film Mommie Dearest?

9. Which U.S. boy band released their second album, This Time Around, in 2000?

10. Which 1999 Star Trek send-up starred Sigourney Weaver as blonde communications officer Lieutenant Tawny Madison?

11. Who hosted the long-running TV quiz show Double Your Money?

12. Who starred as the American monster-hunter Dempsey in the 1995 film Loch Ness?

13. Which saucy late night quiz was presented by Maria McErlane and Graham Norton?

14. Which veteran rock group released an album in 1996 entitled Don't Stop?

15. Who directed the 1986 movie She's Gotta Have It?

GENERAL KNOWLEDGE

1. Which Canadian group recorded the 2000 album Maroon?

2. Indices is the plural of which word?

3. Approximately how many islands make up the Cyclades group - 220, 320 or 420?

4. Who was the president of the European Union Commission from 1967-70?

5. Who wrote the 2001 novel The Blue Nowhere?

6. Zr is the symbol of which chemical element?

7. Which former star of The Man from U.N.C.L.E. featured in the 1990s television series Trainer?

8. Which drug is known in Australia as twang?

9. In which U.S. state was the artist Charles Demuth born?

10. In which year did George III die?

11. Which physician became Permanent Secretary of the Prussian Academy of Sciences in 1912?

12. In which English county is the town of Runcorn?

13. If a candle relumes what does it do?

14. In which city was the artist Willem de Kooning born?

15. In which English county is the town of Melton Mowbray?

GENERAL KNOWLEDGE

1. To which part of the body does the adjective rhinal refer?

2. Simon Jeffes was the leader of which primarily instrumental group?

3. Which playwright wrote the 1995 work Knives in Hens?

4. Which has the lower melting point - potassium or sodium?

5. What was Tracey Ullman's character's name in the television drama series Ally McBeal?

6. On which river is the city of Lincoln?

7. Who was Shadow Foreign Secretary from 1987-92?

8. Who wrote the 1998 novel Master Georgie?

9. Which gulf separates the island of Hainan from mainland Vietnam?

10. In New Zealand, what might you put in a chilly bin?

11. In which year was the naval Battle of Navarino?

12. At what temperature in degrees centigrade does copper boil?

13. In which play by Shakespeare does the character Beatrice appear?

14. Which U.S. state is further east - Ohio or Wyoming?

15. Is the word 'consequently' an adjective or adverb?

ANSWERS: 1 Nose, 2 Penguin Cafe Orchestra, 3 David Harrower, 4 Potassium, 5 Dr. Tracey Clark, 6 Witham, 7 Gerald Kaufman, 8 Beryl Bainbridge, 9 Gulf of Tongking, 10 Food and drink - it's a cooler, 11 1827, 12 2855, 13 Much Ado About Nothing, 14 Ohio, 15 Adverb.

GENERAL KNOWLEDGE

1. Which dramatist's plays include The Late Henry Moss?

2. In which bay is Worms Head, Wales?

3. To which part of the body does the adjective malar apply?

4. Who played Petula in the sitcom Dinnerladies?

5. In the Bible, who was the ninth son of Jacob?

6. In which city was the physicist Hans Albrecht Bethe born?

7. Which American sculptor's works include the 1965 stainless steel piece Becca?

8. Which political party did Oswald Mosley represent as an M.P. from 1918-22?

9. In which European country is the village of Hallstatt?

10. Bitser is an Australian word for which animal?

11. Which Nick Cave song does Johnny Cash cover on the 2000 album Solitary Man?

12. Which Mexican painter's works include the 1932 lithograph Sueno?

13. Of what is the metre the basic SI unit?

14. Who in U.S. politics is the veep?

15. On which bay does Aldeburgh, Suffolk lie?

ANSWERS: 1 Sam Shepard, 2 Rhossili Bay, 3 Cheek or cheekbone, 4 Julie Walters, 5 Issachar, 6 Strasbourg, 7 David Smith, 8 Conservative Party, 9 Austria, 10 A mongrel dog, 11 The Mercy Seat, 12 Diego Rivera, 13 Length, 14 Vice-president, 15 Aldeburgh Bay.

ENTERTAINMENT

1. What was the title of the 1977 U.K. top five hit for the Tom Robinson Band?

2. Which actor played an FBI agent investigating a death in a rundown LA hotel in the 2000 film The Million Dollar Hotel?

3. Which Eighties sitcom starred William Gaunt and Patricia Garwood as Arthur and Beryl Crabtree?

4. Which U.S. singer just couldn't help having a U.K. number one single with Oops! I Did It Again! in 2000?

5. Which 1977 film starred Henry Winkler and Sally Field as a young couple dealing with the aftermath of the Vietnam War?

6. Which celebrity imitator has made a Big Impression with his BBC1 series?

7. Which singer/songwriter released his second album, entitled Living in the Present Future, in 2000?

8. Which actor played blacksmith Quint Asper in the classic western series Gunsmoke?

9. What was the title of Tom Jones' 2000 top five collaboration with Mousse T?

10. Which 1970 film starred Elliott Gould and Candice Bergen as college sweethearts?

11. What was the name of Stephen Tompkinson's reporter character in the topical comedy series Drop the Dead Donkey?

12. Which U.S. punk/ska band released their sixth studio album, Pay Attention, in 2000?

13. Which legendary actress played a school teacher in a Welsh mining community in the 1945 film The Corn is Green?

14. Which comedy panel game show hosted by Nick Hancock embarked on its ninth series on BBC1 in 2000?

15. Which 2000 British film starred the likes of John Hannah, Brian Conley and Eddie Izzard?

ANSWERS: 1 2-4-6-8 Motorway, 2 Mel Gibson, 3 No Place Like Home, 4 Britney Spears, 5 Heroes, 6 Alistair McGowan, 7 Eagle-Eye Cherry, 8 Burt Reynolds, 9 Sex Bomb, 10 Getting Straight, 11 Damien Day, 12 The Mighty Mighty Bosstones, 13 Bette Davis, 14 They Think It's All Over, 15 Circus.

GENERAL KNOWLEDGE

1. For what is the word rozzer slang?

2. What was the title of Martin Creed's 2001 Turner prize-winning entry?

3. Who became Pope in 590?

4. In which European country is the town of Gouda?

5. Who painted the portrait Lady Agnew of Lochnaw, which is housed in the National Gallery of Scotland?

6. What is samekh - an Arabian encampment or a letter of the Hebrew alphabet?

7. Which English resort is further west - Eastbourne or Hastings?

8. Of what is ethology the scientific study?

9. Which constituency does Conservative M.P. Liam Fox represent?

10. Who starred as Harry Lime in the television series version of The Third Man?

11. Which Scottish chemist won a Nobel prize for his work on nucleotides?

12. In which English county is the market town of Saxmundham?

13. Who had a 1968 U.S. number one single with the song This Guy's in Love With You?

14. Whose paintings include Saturn Devouring one of his Sons which hangs in the Prado?

15. To which former British coin does the slang term kick refer?

ANSWERS: 1 Policeman, 2 Lights Going On and Off, 3 Gregory I (Gregory the Great), 4 Netherlands, 5 John Singer Sargent, 6 A Hebrew letter, 7 Eastbourne, 8 Animal behaviour, 9 Woodspring, 10 Michael Rennie, 11 Sir A.R. Todd, 12 Suffolk, 13 Herb Alpert, 14 Francisco de Goya, 15 Sixpence.

GENERAL KNOWLEDGE

1. Which U.S. city is further west - Albuquerque or Phoenix?

2. What is an elf-cup?

3. Who won the 1955 Nobel prize in chemistry?

4. What were the forenames of the three Faed brothers, who were 19th century Scottish painters?

5. Which American did Marina Prusakova marry in 1961?

6. In which African country is the seaport of Bingerville?

7. What is a fundi in East Africa - a fish dish or a mechanic?

8. Who became the English monarch in 1558?

9. Who wrote the 1863 novel Hard Cash?

10. Who recorded the 2001 album One Nil?

11. Who was awarded the 1987 Nobel prize in medicine?

12. What was the name of the central character in the television comedy series The Wonder Years?

13. In which U.S. state is the city of Lynn?

14. What is a caparison?

15. Which artist's works include 1917's Artillery Duel?

ANSWRS: 1 Phoenix, 2 A type of fungi, 3 Vincent du Vigneaud, 4 Thomas, James and John, 5 Lee Harvey Oswald, 6 Côte d'Ivoire, 7 Mechanic, 8 Elizabeth I, 9 Charles Reade, 10 Neil Finn, 11 Susumu Tonegawa, 12 Kevin Arnold, 13 Massachusetts, 14 An ornamental covering for a horse, 15 Otto Dix.

GENERAL KNOWLEDGE

1. Who was Holy Roman emperor from 1410-37?

2. What is a polygala - a type of plant, or a festival at an educational institution?

3. Whose landscapes include The Vale of Dedham?

4. In which year was Anne Boleyn executed?

5. The Italian town of Faenza is at the foot of which mountain group?

6. Who was Professor of Organic Chemistry at the Technical University in Munich from 1921-45?

7. Which body of water in Scotland does the Kincardine Bridge span?

8. Who recorded the 2001 album Hot Shot?

9. Of what is stroud a type?

10. In which novel by Charles Dickens does the character James Harthouse appear?

11. In which African country is the city of Sharm El Sheikh?

12. For his work on the structure of which protein did chemist Frederick Sanger win a Nobel prize?

13. Which American artist painted the 1929 oil The Lighthouse at Two Lights?

14. Who created and produced the 1970s variety show The Wheeltappers' and Shunters' Social Club?

15. For what is the word china rhyming slang?

ANSWERS: 1 Sigismund, 2 A type of plant, 3 John Constable, 4 1536, 5 Apennines, 6 Hans Fischer, 7 Firth of Forth, 8 Shaggy, 9 Fabric, 10 Hard Times, 11 Egypt, 12 Insulin, 13 Edward Hopper, 14 John Hamp, 15 Mate.

SPORT

1. Who outpointed Oliver McCall in 1995 to win the WBC world heavyweight title?

2. Who won the F.A. Cup in 1969?

3. In which sport has David Bryant been both indoor and outdoor world champion?

4. What was the venue for the 1998 Winter Olympics?

5. In 1998, which Dutch footballer equalled his country's all-time scoring record of 35 goals?

6. Which Olympic double did Ethiopian Miruts Yifter achieve in 1980?

7. Holland lost to Scotland at the 1978 World Cup in Argentina - true or false?

8. Which British sprinter won gold in the 100m at the 1982 Commonwealth Games?

9. Which former British Lions captain became a team captain on the TV show A Question of Sport?

10. Which German football team lost the 1977 European Cup Final?

11. Which popular grey steeplechaser died at Aintree on the eve of the 1998 Grand National?

12. Between 1986 and 1995, which Scottish rugby union player scored 140 penalty goals for his country?

13. What is the name of the Paris-based controlling body of world motor racing?

14. In which year did Ronnie O'Sullivan win his first U.K. Open snooker championship?

15. Which team were knocked out of the 1998 World Cup despite winning their final group game 6-1?

GENERAL KNOWLEDGE

1. Which star of The X Files played Lily Bart in the film The House of Mirth?

2. Which British runner refused to compete in the 100m at the 1924 Olympics because it was held on a Sunday?

3. What was the first name of the poet W.H. Auden?

4. Which American fighter aircraft is also called the Fighting Falcon?

5. Who was the French signatory to the Munich Agreement of 1938?

6. Which Christmas decoration grows as a parasite on trees?

7. What is another name for the hop step and jump?

8. Which actress and singer had a hit with the single Cry Me a River in the 1950s?

9. What name is given to the fruits of plants of the genus Ficus?

10. Which much-married former child star was born Joe Yule?

11. Which American author wrote The Big Sleep and The Long Goodbye?

12. What is the state capital of Utah?

13. Which of the Brontes wrote The Tenant of Wildfell Hall?

14. By what first name was Gabrielle Chanel known?

15. Which Hollywood great was the subject of the book Mommie Dearest?

ANSWERS: 1 Gillian Anderson, 2 Eric Liddell, 3 Wystan, 4 F-16, 5 Edouard Daladier, 6 Mistletoe, 7 Triple jump, 8 Julie London, 9 Figs, 10 Mickey Rooney, 11 Raymond Chandler, 12 Salt Lake City, 13 Anne, 14 Coco, 15 Joan Crawford.

GENERAL KNOWLEDGE

1. Which Swedish tennis player won the Australian Open in 1983?

2. On which American city was the first Monopoly game based?

3. Which glamorous string quartet saw their album Born removed from the classical music charts after it reached number two in 2000?

4. In what year was the Channel Tunnel officially opened?

5. How many yards are there in a furlong?

6. With what style of music is Blind Lemon Jefferson associated?

7. What is the name of the home stadium of Leeds United?

8. Which British actor married the daughter of the playwright Eugene O'Neill in 1943?

9. Which scientific organisation is famous for its Christmas lectures?

10. Who wrote Confessions of an English Opium-Eater?

11. How many months of the year have 31 days?

12. What was the pen name of Charles Lutwidge Dodgson?

13. What was the former name for the temperature scale now called Celsius?

14. 1 is the title of a greatest hits album by which influential group?

15. Who was the first woman to make a solo flight across the Atlantic Ocean?

ANSWERS: 1 Mats Wilander, 2 Atlantic City, 3 Bond, 4 1994, 5 220, 6 Blues, 7 Elland Road, 8 Charlie Chaplin, 9 The Royal Institution, 10 Thomas de Quincy, 11 Seven, 12 Lewis Carroll, 13 Centigrade, 14 The Beatles, 15 Amelia Earhart.

GENERAL KNOWLEDGE

1. Which novel by Sir Laurens van der Post was filmed as Merry Christmas Mr Lawrence?

2. Which actor won an Oscar in 1950 for his performance in Cyrano de Bergerac?

3. Who was the unsuccessful Democrat candidate in the 1988 U.S. presidential election?

4. Who wrote the novel Princess Daisy?

5. In which country are the Plains of Abraham?

6. Which American composer wrote the opera Einstein on the Beach?

7. Which weather phenomenon takes its name from the Spanish for 'the child'?

8. In which British city is the TV detective series Taggart primarily set?

9. Which French New Wave director made the films Les Cousins and Les Biches?

10. Which English poet wrote Christmas Eve and Easter Day?

11. Who wrote the children's story James and the Giant Peach?

12. What sort of puzzle first appeared in the New York World in December 1913?

13. Which mythical monster is also called a yeti?

14. How many times did Oxford win the Boat Race during the 1980s?

15. Which country is known as Suomi in its native language?

ENTERTAINMENT

1. Which 1995 Forest Whitaker film starred Whitney Houston and Angela Bassett?

2. In which year did the reggae artist Bob Marley die?

3. In which 1995 film did Cindy Crawford star as Kate McQueen?

4. Who played the formidable Ena Sharples in Coronation Street?

5. Which Haircut 100 singer released an album entitled Tangled in 1996?

6. Who directed the 1948 film Key Largo?

7. Which Men Behaving Badly star could be heard on TV's The Morph Files in the Nineties?

8. Which singer had a hit in 1979 with Is She Really Going Out With Him??

9. Which fomer Hamish Macbeth star played the crazed skinhead Albie in a memorable episode of Cracker?

10. Which Hollywood heart-throb was the guitarist of the rock group P?

11. What was the nickname of Melvyn Hayes' character in the sitcom It Ain't Half Hot Mum?

12. Which Mike and the Mechanics singer released an album entitled Blue Views in 1996?

13. Which 1970 Ken Loach film starred David Bradley as a boy who becomes obsessed with a bird of prey?

14. Which Birmingham comedian was born Robert Davies?

15. Which singer/songwriter won an Oscar for his score for the 1971 film Shaft?

ANSWERS: 1 Waiting to Exhale, 2 1981, 3 Fair Game, 4 Violet Carson, 5 Nick Heyward, 6 John Huston, 7 Neil Morrissey, 8 Joe Jackson, 9 Robert Carlyle, 10 Johnny Depp, 11 Gloria, 12 Paul Carrack, 13 Kes, 14 Jasper Carrott, 15 Isaac Hayes.

GENERAL KNOWLEDGE

1. Who was the BBC Sports Personality of the Year 2000?

2. Which American union leader disappeared in 1975?

3. Who was elected MP for Ynys Mon in 1987?

4. Which controversial British artist is best known for works such as Mother and Child, Divided?

5. What is the highest navigable lake in the world?

6. Who was the first director to refuse an Oscar?

7. Which World War II battle is also known as the Ardennes Offensive?

8. What is the largest city in New Mexico?

9. Of which country is New Britain a part?

10. Which Latin legal term means 'you should have the body'?

11. Which sport involves the snatch and the clean and jerk?

12. What name is given to radioactive material that settles on the earth's surface following a nuclear explosion?

13. Who wrote the horror novel Dracula?

14. Staten Island is a borough of which U.S. city?

15. Which member of Whistler's family features in his most famous painting?

? **GENERAL KNOWLEDGE** ?

1. Whose was the first Royal wedding to be televised in colour?

2. In what year did beach volleyball become an Olympic sport?

3. What were the surnames of the animators who created Tom and Jerry, The Flintstones and Scooby-Doo?

4. In which country is the city of Abadan?

5. Who was the 15th U.S. president and the only one who never married?

6. Which Australian author wrote My Brilliant Career?

7. Which jazz pianist and composer won an Oscar for his score for the film Round Midnight?

8. In which sport is the Caulfield Cup contested?

9. Which former world footballer of the year joined Manchester City on a free transfer in 2000?

10. What was Mickey Mouse's original name?

11. Which former England cricket captain played for Somerset, Worcestershire and Durham?

12. Along with Holland, which country played host to football's Euro 2000 championships?

13. Which French footballer joined Aston Villa from Tottenham Hotspur in 2000?

14. What does AC stand for in physics?

15. Which English Romantic poet wrote Tintern Abbey and The Prelude?

GENERAL KNOWLEDGE

1. What was Rick's surname in the film Casablanca?

2. What is the capital of Azerbaijan?

3. Which South African boxer did Lennox Lewis defeat at the London Arena in 2000?

4. Of which country was Milton Obote the president from 1966 to 1971 and from 1980 to 1985?

5. Which English conspirator fabricated the Popish Plot?

6. What sort of bird is a lammergeier?

7. Which German author wrote the short novel Death in Venice?

8. What was the official newspaper of the Communist Party of the Soviet Union called?

9. Who was the archbishop of Canterbury at the time of Edward VIII's abdication?

10. Which Spanish cubist artist was born José Victoriano Gonzalez?

11. Which English actor starred in A Kind of Loving, Far from the Madding Crowd and Women in Love?

12. What name was given to the bubonic plague epidemic that ravaged Europe in the 14th century?

13. What is the name of Don Quixote's squire in Cervantes' novel?

14. What is the first name of Agatha Christie's Miss Marple?

15. Which Test cricket side was captained by Clive Lloyd?

ANSWERS: 1 Blaine, 2 Baku, 3 Francois Botha, 4 Uganda, 5 Titus Oates, 6 A vulture, 7 Thomas Mann, 8 Pravda, 9 Cosmo Gordon Lang, 10 Juan Gris, 11 Alan Bates, 12 Black Death, 13 Sancho Panza, 14 Jane, 15 West Indies.

ENTERTAINMENT

1. Which U.S. singer/songwriter released an album in 1996 entitled Tennessee Moon?

2. Who played Bill Sikes in the 1968 film version of Oliver!?

3. What are the surnames of The Two Ronnies?

4. What was the first U.K. number one single for the Kinks?

5. Who starred as an ex-Marine teacher in the 1995 film Dangerous Minds?

6. Which wartime entertainer was portrayed in the sitcom Goodnight Sweetheart by Phil Nice?

7. Who played Sid Vicious in the 1986 film Sid and Nancy?

8. Who presented the series on moral and ethical issues Heart of the Matter?

9. Which director made a cameo appearance in every one of his films from 1926's The Lodger onwards?

10. Which young pop/rock band released an album entitled This World and Body in 1996?

11. Who played Neville Hope in the comedy drama series Auf Wiedersehen, Pet?

12. Which 1995 film starred Al Pacino as a cop in pursuit of a criminal played by Robert De Niro?

13. Who starred as Kavanagh QC in the drama series of that name?

14. Of which Britpop band was Alex James the bass guitarist?

15. Who played Gordon Brittas in the sitcom The Brittas Empire?

GENERAL KNOWLEDGE

1. Which West Indian-born poet and playwright won the 1992 Nobel Prize for literature?

2. Who sang Stormy Weather in the 1943 film of the same name?

3. Which British novelist wrote Changing Places, Small World and Nice Work?

4. Who directed the film Mission: Impossible 2?

5. Which country takes its name from the Latin word for southern?

6. What is the general name for any hoofed mammal?

7. Which Roman highway was named after Appius Claudius Caecus?

8. Who directed the films Double Indemnity, The Lost Weekend and The Apartment?

9. Which feature of the Spencer coat of arms has been incorporated into Prince William's coat of arms?

10. For which old Spanish coin was a piece of eight another name?

11. Which form of partly dehydrated gypsum is used for making casts and moulds?

12. Of which country is the shekel the basic monetary unit?

13. Which Australian tennis player won the men's singles title at Wimbledon in 1987?

14. What is the first name of Tony Blair's eldest son?

15. Which Canadian city is the capital of Ontario?

GENERAL KNOWLEDGE

1. Which Canadian novelist wrote The Apprenticeship of Duddy Kravitz?

2. Who became emperor of Japan in 1989?

3. Which Australian tennis player knocked Tim Henman out of the Wimbledon championships in 2000?

4. What does the 'G' stand for in the name of the film company MGM?

5. Which British poet wrote The Whitsun Weddings and High Windows?

6. What sort of creature is a kuvasz?

7. What does 'A.E.' stand for in the title of the sci-fi film Titan A.E.?

8. Which British dramatist wrote The Churchill Play and The Romans in Britain?

9. How many ounces are there in an apothecary's pound?

10. Which country's deputy prime minister is known as the tanaiste?

11. Which waterway linking the Atlantic and Pacific oceans was completed in 1914?

12. What name is given to a score of one over par for a hole in golf?

13. Which country knocked the Netherlands out of Euro 2000 on penalties?

14. What name is given to a space devoid of matter?

15. Which British author wrote Three Men in a Boat?

GENERAL KNOWLEDGE

1. Who is the youngest man to have won all four of golf's major championships?

2. Which Roman historian wrote a history of Rome in 142 volumes?

3. What name is given to members of the United Society of Believers in Christ's Second Appearing?

4. Which former Defence Secretary did George W. Bush choose as his running-mate?

5. In computing, what does GUI stand for?

6. Which English novelist wrote The Four Feathers?

7. Of which French king was Madame Du Barry a mistress?

8. In which country was football's World Cup held in 1998?

9. What is the second-largest mountain system in North America?

10. Which singer was born Annie Mae Bullock in 1939?

11. Which British naval officer was the captain of the Bounty when the crew mutinied in 1789?

12. What was the popular name for the gallows which stood close to the present-day site of Marble Arch?

13. Which former star of ER appeared in the film The Perfect Storm?

14. Who does Hiawatha marry in Longfellow's famous poem?

15. Which U.S. president was known as Ike?

SPORT

1. Which European city hosted the 1997 World Athletics Championships?

2. Which England player scored after 27 seconds against France at the 1982 World Cup?

3. Which county cricket side play at Headingley?

4. In which year did Debbie Meyer become the first swimmer to win three Olympic gold medals in individual events?

5. Which U.S. tennis player won the women's singles title at Wimbledon in 2001?

6. In which year was football's World Cup held in Sweden?

7. Who was Willie Thorne beaten by in the final of the 1985 U.K. Open in snooker?

8. Which London Scottish rugby player suffered a serious ear injury in a match against Bath in 1998?

9. In which year were the summer Olympic Games held in Montreal, Canada?

10. Who won England's football League Cup in 1990?

11. Who knocked Stephen Hendry out of the 1998 world professional snooker championship at The Crucible?

12. Which British driver won the 1958 Argentine Grand Prix?

13. Which former England international became manager of Middlesbrough in 1973?

14. In which sport do teams play on a diamond?

15. In which specific rowing event did Steve Redgrave win three consecutive Olympic gold medals?

? GENERAL KNOWLEDGE ?

1. Who was the first actress to receive two Oscars before the age of thirty?

2. Which Belgian city was the site of the first battle between British and German forces in World War I?

3. The actor Ivan Owen was the voice of which popular TV glove puppet?

4. Which large triangular muscle covering the shoulder serves to raise the arm laterally?

5. What was Cecil B. DeMille's middle name?

6. Which part of a church contains the choir?

7. What was the pen name of Samuel Langhorne Clemens?

8. Which hoisting device used on ships is named after a 17th-century English hangman?

9. Who was the fifth wife of Henry VIII?

10. Which actress starred opposite Harrison Ford in the film thriller What Lies Beneath?

11. Which novel by Thomas Hardy tells the story of Michael Henchard?

12. Which actor's childhood nickname was Tootsie?

13. Which boy band became the first act to have seven U.K. number one singles in a row?

14. What name is given to July 15, which is supposed to set the weather for 40 days thereafter?

15. To what sort of cleric does the adjective episcopal relate?

ANSWERS: 1 Jodie Foster, 2 Mons, 3 Basil Brush, 4 Deltoid (deltoideus), 5 Blount, 6 Chancel, 7 Mark Twain, 8 Derrick, 9 Catherine Howard, 10 Michelle Pfeiffer, 11 The Mayor of Casterbridge, 12 Dustin Hoffman, 13 Westlife, 14 St Swithin's Day, 15 Bishop.

GENERAL KNOWLEDGE

1. Which French fashion designer launched the first ready-to-wear collection for men in 1960?

2. Who was the first black officer to hold the highest military post in the United States?

3. Which novel by Jeffrey Archer describes the competition between four men to become prime minister?

4. By what name was the powerful defoliant sprayed by U.S. forces in Vietnam known?

5. Which animal is also called a honey badger?

6. For what is epistaxis the medical term?

7. Which pop star bought a piano that belonged to John Lennon for more than £1 million at auction in October 2000?

8. Who won the 1985 Whitbread Award for fiction for his novel Hawksmoor?

19. Who was the Greek goddess of agriculture?

10. Which food additive is also known as MSG?

11. Which English admiral circumnavigated the globe from 1577 to 1580?

12. Of which U.S. state is Dover the capital?

13. What was Flipper in the 1960s TV series of that name?

14. What is removed from seawater in a desalination plant?

15. Which American novelist wrote Gentlemen Prefer Blondes?

GENERAL KNOWLEDGE

1. Who played Detective Inspector Maggie Forbes in The Gentle Touch on television?

2. Which American author wrote The Catcher in the Rye?

3. Who was the first woman to scale Mount Everest alone and without bottled oxygen?

4. Which country beat South Africa in the final of the Alfred Dunhill Cup at St Andrews in 2000?

5. What is the state capital of Iowa?

6. Which British dramatist wrote Trelawny of the 'Wells'?

7. At which film festival are the Golden Lions awarded?

8. Which ship, launched in 1906, became the basis of battleship design for more than 50 years?

9. Who was the first leader of the Labour Party in the House of Commons?

10. Who wrote the music for the ballet Coppélia?

11. Who was the first gymnast to score a perfect 10 in Olympic competition?

12. Which actor made his final film appearance as Proximo in Gladiator?

13. Who created Rumpole of the Bailey?

14. Qui Veut Gagner des Millions is a French version of which British TV quiz show?

15. From which country does the white wine Tokay come?

ANSWERS: 1 Jill Gascoigne, 2 J D Salinger, 3 Alison Hargreaves, 4 Spain, 5 Des Moines, 6 Sir Arthur Wing Pinero, 7 Venice, 8 Dreadnought, 9 Keir Hardie, 10 Leo Delibes, 11 Nadia Comaneci, 12 Oliver Reed, 13 John Mortimer, 14 Who Wants to Be a Millionaire, 15 Hungary.

GENERAL KNOWLEDGE

1. Which South African Zulu organization was founded by Chief Buthelezi in 1975?

2. Which off-Broadway play of 1971 reworked the Gospel according to St. Matthew?

3. Who was the author of the play The Government Inspector?

4. Which tennis player was runner-up in the 1993 U.S. Open ladies singles championship?

5. Which Italian poet is famous for his epic Orlando Furioso?

6. Which Dutch tennis player was the 1973 French men's doubles champion with John Newcombe?

7. Which Scottish psychiatrist's books include The Divided Self?

8. Which colourless acid found in sour milk is used in the preservative E270?

9. In which European country is the town of Ascoli Piceno?

10. Who was Best Actress Oscar winner for the film Coquette?

11. Which golf course hosted the 1989 British Open tournament?

12. Who was the 1968 Olympic men's 400m hurdles champion?

13. Who directed the 1979 film Mad Max starring Mel Gibson?

14. What is the common name of the poisonous Mediterranean plant, Hyoscyamus niger, which yields the drug hyoscyamine?

15. Who authored the 1937 novel The Citadel?

ANSWERS 1. Inkatha 2. Godspell 3. Nikolai Gogol 4. Helena Sukova 5. Ludovico Ariosto 6. Tom Okker 7. R.D. Laing 8. Lactic acid 9. Italy 10. Mary Pickford 11. Royal Troon 12. David Hemery 13. George Miller 14. Henbane 15. A.J. Cronin.

ENTERTAINMENT

1. Which former Coronation Street actress played Stella in the 1990s sitcom The Gingerbread Girl?

2. Which comedy actor played Richard Gander in the 1972 sitcom Alcock and Gander?

3. What was Tracey Ullman's character name in the sitcom Girls on Top?

4. Who composed the 1899 opera The Devil and Kate?

5. Which footballer appeared as Sacha Distel in a 1999 Stars In Their Eyes celebrity special?

6. Who played The Skipper in the U.S. sitcom Gilligan's Island?

7. Who is Tony Soprano's psychiatrist in The Sopranos?

8. Who voices Hamm in the film Toy Story 2?

9. Which comedian plays a sadistic gangster in the 1960 British film Never Let Go?

10. Which actor plays thug Muerte in the 1993 film Undercover Blues?

11. Who replaced Robert Lindsay as Jakie Smith in the sitcom Get Some In!?

12. In which opera does the maid Despina appear?

13. Who co-produced and starred in the 1999 film Never Been Kissed?

14. Who wrote 1970s children's sitcom The Ghosts Of Motley Hall?

15. In which year was U.S. comedian Alan King born?

SPORT

1. Which country were men's world team champions in short-track speed skating in 1992, 1994 and 1997?

2. What sport is played by Rowan Brassey and Richard Corsie?

3. Which Spanish team won the 1985 U.E.F.A. Cup?

4. Which four teams played in Pool 1 of the 1999/00 Heineken Cup in rugby union?

5. How many Commonwealth Games gold medals did Debbie Flintoff win from 1982-90?

6. What nationality is boxer Acelino Freitas?

7. Which peer owned horses that won 20 Classic races?

8. Who beat David Telesco on points in January 2000 to retain his three world light-heavyweight boxing titles?

9. How many a side play in a polo game?

10. What is the nickname of darts player Ted Hankey?

11. With what sport are Britt Laforgue and Patricia Emonet associated?

12. What nationality is tennis player Nicolas Lapentti?

13. With which sport are Stephen Train and Andrew Train associated?

14. In which year was the former England Test batsman Maurice Leyland born?

15. Tonny Olsen-Ahm and Aase Jacobsen were women's doubles winners at badminton at the 1952 All-England Championships. Which country did they represent?

ANSWERS 1. South Korea 2. Bowls 3. Real Madrid 4. Leicester, Leinster, Glasgow Caledonians and Stade Français 5. Three 6. Brazilian 7. 4th Duke of Grafton 8. Roy Jones Jr. 9. Four 10. The Count 11. Skiing 12. Ecuadorian 13. Canoeing 14. 1900 15. Denmark.

POP MUSIC

1. Which rock band originally formed in Wales, before including bassist Taka Hirose in its line-up?

2. Which song by the Beatles did Joe Cocker cover on the 1989 album Night Calls?

3. Which railway station features on the cover of Oasis' single Some Might Say?

4. Which duo's compilation hits album Tales From New York charted in 2000?

5. Which group released the single I Never Want An Easy Life If Me And He Were Ever To Get There?

6. D'Arcy Wretzky left which band in 1999?

7. Who had a 2000 Top 10 single with Ooh Stick You?

8. Which female singer formed the band Mice in 1995?

9. Which member of Crosby, Stills, Nash and Young broke both legs in a boating accident in 1999?

10. Oasis guitarist Jem was formerly in which band?

11. In which year did the band The James Gang form?

12. Which two musicians played piano and organ on the album Aftermath by the Rolling Stones?

13. Which former member of Pulp now plays with the group Venini?

14. Which singer gigged in 1999 under the name The Priory Of Brion?

15. Johnny Ha-Ha was the drummer with which London-based Goth band?

ART & LITERATURE

1. What did artist Max Ernst begin studying at the University of Bonn in 1909?

2. Whose stories include The Legend of Sleepy Hollow?

3. Which French artist born in 1881 painted 1954's The Great Parade?

4. Who wrote the 1956 novel A Walk on the Wild Side?

5. In which year was artist Bridget Riley made a Companion of Honour?

6. Who wrote the 1999 autobiography 'Tis?

7. Which French painter's works include The Belfry Of Douai and Bridge Of Narni?

8. Who wrote the novel Atlantis Found?

9. In which city was the painter Jacques-Louis David born?

10. Who wrote the novel Clayhanger?

11. In which year did the painter Otto Dix die?

12. Our House in the Last World was the first novel by which Pulitzer Prize-winning author?

13. Which French painter's works include 1906's The Three Umbrellas?

14. Which U.S. born Dadaist published the 1963 autobiography Self Portrait?

15. In which year was Jane Austen's Pride And Prejudice first published?

? GENERAL KNOWLEDGE ?

1. Who scripted the 1965 film What's New, Pussycat??

2. Who was a Best Supporting Actress Oscar winner for film Sayonara?

3. Who wrote the 1937 book Of Mice and Men?

4. Which republic occupies the western part of the island of Hispaniola?

5. Who was the 1952 Wimbledon men's singles tennis champion?

6. Which Ireland rugby union international was captain of the 1974 Lions tour of South Africa?

7. Who is wife of Antipholus of Ephesus in the play The Comedy Of Errors?

8. Who is the American author of the novel The Wapshot Chronicle?

9. What is the second sign of the zodiac?

10. Who was the director of the 1988 film Tequila Sunrise?

11. In which European country is the industrial city of Bytom?

12. Which bone of the human skeleton is also called the thighbone?

13. On which river is the German industrial city Cologne?

14. Which bowed stringed instrument is the alto of the violin family?

15. What is the derived S.I. unit of electrical resistance?

ANSWERS 1. Woody Allen 2. Miyoshi Umeki 3. John Steinbeck 4. Haiti 5. Frank Sedgman 6. Willie John McBride 7. Adriana 8. John Cheever 9. Taurus 10. Robert Towne 11. Poland 12. Femur 13. Rhine 14. Viola 15. Ohm.

ENTERTAINMENT

1. Which wrestler starred in the 1991 film Suburban Commando?

2. Who played the title role in the 1955 film Davy Crockett, King of the Wild Frontier?

3. Who is the documentary maker in the spoof television series People Like Us?

4. Which comedian stars in the 1923 silent comedy Safety Last?

5. Which duo created, wrote, and performed in the 1999 sitcom Spaced?

6. Who directed the video for Björk's single It's Oh So Quiet?

7. Who directed the 1975 film The Day of the Locust?

8. Which Walt Disney film was recreated as a stage musical in London in 1999?

9. The 1953 film Sabre Jet has which war as its backdrop?

10. Who played Tina in the television drama Casualty?

11. In the 1955 biopic I'll Cry Tomorrow who plays singer Lillian Roth?

12. Who played Major Otto Hecht in the 1979 film Escape to Athena?

13. Who plays a female cat-burglar in the 1993 film The Real McCoy?

14. Which British actress plays Marla Singer in the 1999 film Fight Club?

15. The 1936 Alfred Hitchcock film Sabotage was based on which novel by Joseph Conrad?

ANSWERS 1. Hulk Hogan 2. Fess Parker 3. Roy Mallard 4. Harold Lloyd 5. Simon Pegg and Jessica Stevenson 6. Spike Jonze 7. John Schlesinger 8. The Lion King 9. Korean War 10. Claire Goose 11. Susan Hayward 12. Roger Moore 13. Kim Basinger 14. Helena Bonham Carter 15. The Secret Agent.

SPORT

1. At what sport was Bjarte-Engen Vik a 1998 Olympic champion?

2. Who did Yevgeny Kafelnikov beat in the semi-finals of the 2000 Australian Open tennis singles championship?

3. How many centuries did David Gower make in his 117 Tests from 1978-92?

4. What is cricketer David Boon's middle name?

5. Which team lost the 1932 World Series in baseball?

6. Who rode Emily Little to victory in the 1952 Badminton Horse Trials in Three-Day Eventing?

7. What nationality is rugby union player Agustin Pichot?

8. Who was the 1968 Olympic men's highboard platform diving champion?

9. What nationality was golfer Bobby Locke?

10. For which Minor Counties side has Surrey cricketer J.N. Batty played?

11. Who was the women's individual world trampolining champion from 1964-8?

12. Which jockey was leading money-winner in the U.S. in 1951?

13. In cricket, who scored 259 n.o. for Glamorgan against Notts in the 1st innings of their 1999 county championship game?

14. Who were the men's team winners in archery at the 1996 Olympic Games?

15. Which U.S. pair won the 1957 Wimbledon men's doubles tennis title?

ANSWERS 1. Nordic skiing 2. Magnus Norman 3. 18 4. Clarence 5. Chicago Cubs 6. Mark Darley 7. Argentinian 8. Klaus Dibiasi 9. South African 10. Oxfordshire 11. Judy Wills 12. Bill Shoemaker 13. Steve James 14. U.S.A. 15. Gardnar Mulloy & Budge Patty.

POP MUSIC

1. Which country artists albums include Roses in the Snow and Angel Band?

2. In which year was Johnny Cash discharged from the U.S.A.F.?

3. Who records under the name Juryman?

4. Which former member of Gong recorded the 1975 album Fish Rising?

5. Who produced the Wannadies album Yeah?

6. Which duo's songs include Bloodsport for All and The Only Living Boy in New Cross?

7. In which year did Phil Collins have a Top 10 single with Another Day in Paradise?

8. Which Irish singer recorded the 2000 album Black River Falls?

9. Which group recorded the 1994 album Gideon Gaye?

10. Which group recorded the 2000 album Every Six Seconds?

11. Who recorded a solo album in 1991 entitled Fireball Zone?

12. In which year did Kirsty MacColl have a Top 10 single with A New England?

13. Which singer-songwriter recorded the 1993 album Perfectly Good Guitar?

14. Who released the 2000 album Waterfall Cities?

15. Who had a 1999 Top 10 single with Get Get Down?

ANSWERS 1. Emmylou Harris 2. 1954 3. Ian Simmonds 4. Steve Hillage 5. Ric Ocasek 6. Carter the Unstoppable Sex Machine 7. 1989 8. Cathal Coughlan 9. The High Llamas 10. Groop Dogdrill 11. Ric Ocasek 12. 1985 1. John Hiatt 14. Ozric Tentacles 15. Paul Johnson.

GEOGRAPHY

1. In which European country is the seaside resort of St. Jean de Luz?

2. In which county is Powderham Castle?

3. In which country is Lake Wakatipu?

4. In which county are the Quantock Hills, an area of outstanding natural beauty?

5. In which country in Britain is Pluscarden Abbey?

6. Carlisle lies near the confluence of which three rivers?

7. Which English city houses Kirkstall Abbey and Temple Newsam?

8. In which European country is the town of Sibiu?

9. In which African country is the port of Quelimane?

10. In which harbour is Brownsea Island?

11. The town of Street in Somerset lies at the foot of which hills?

12. In which European country is the mountain Santis?

13. In which English county is the resort of Thornton Cleveleys?

14. On which Asian island is the town of Galle?

15. The ski resort of Chamonix is at the base of which mountain?

ANSWERS 1. France 2. Devon 3. New Zealand 4. Somerset 5. Scotland 6. Eden, Petteril and Caldew 7. Leeds 8. Romania 9. Mozambique 10. Poole Harbour 11. Polden Hills 12. Switzerland 13. Lancashire 14. Sri Lanka 15. Mont Blanc.

GENERAL KNOWLEDGE

1. In which constellation is the group of stars known as The Plough?

2. Who was the wife of King Ahab in the Old Testament?

3. Who was the author of the 1939 novel The Grapes of Wrath?

4. In which century did the English composer and organist Thomas Tallis live?

5. Which actress' film roles include Diana in 1987's White Mischief?

6. Who wrote the 1664 play Tartuffe?

7. Who was Chancellor of the Exchequer from 1993-7?

8. Who wrote the 1911 story collection In a German Pension?

9. In Greek mythology, which king of Thessaly was married to Alcestis?

10. Ungava is a sparsely inhabited region of which country?

11. Liz Edgar is the sister of which Cardiff-born show jumper?

12. What is the brightest star in the constellation Cygnus?

13. Who wrote the 1961 novel The Old Men at the Zoo?

14. Which city in S.E. France was seat of the papacy from 1309-77?

15. What is the capital of the United Arab Emirates?

ANSWERS 1. Ursa Major 2. Jezebel 3. John Steinbeck 4. 16th Century 5. Greta Scacchi 6. Molière 7. Kenneth Clarke 8. Katherine Mansfield 9. Admetus 10. Canada 11. David Broome 12. Deneb 13. Angus Wilson 14. Avignon 15. Abu Dhabi.

ENTERTAINMENT

1. Which actor played Boris in the 1959 sitcom Gert and Daisy?

2. Which writing team created the 1992 sitcom Get Back?

3. Which actor plays the lead in the 1944 cowboy film Nevada?

4. What is the nickname of Peter Langford in the comedy group The Barron Knights?

5. In which country is the 1949 Alfred Hitchcock film Under Capricorn set?

6. Who won the award for Best Actress in a Drama at the 2000 Golden Globes?

7. Who directed the 1987 film Wall Street?

8. What does Esther Williams play in the 1949 film Neptune's Daughter?

9. Who played Ann Fourmile in the sitcom George and Mildred?

10. What was Richard Gere's character name in 1990 film Pretty Woman?

11. Who played Raquel in Coronation Street?

12. Who does Christopher Chittell play in the soap opera Emmerdale?

13. Who is the lover of Manon in an opera by Massenet?

14. Who voices Jessie in the film Toy Story 2?

15. Who plays a Houston dance instructor in the 1998 film Dance With Me?

ANSWERS 1. Hugh Paddick 2. Laurence Marks and Maurice Gran 3. Robert Mitchum 4. Peanut 5. Australia 6. Hilary Swank 7. Oliver Stone 8. A bathing-suit designer 9. Sheila Fearn 10. Edward Lewis 11. Sarah Lancashire 12. Eric Pollard 13. Des Grieux 14. Joan Cusack 15. Vanessa L. Williams.

SPORT

1. Which county does motor racing driver Jenson Button hail from?

2. Which horse won the Champion Hurdle at Cheltenham from 1949-51?

3. What nationality is boxer Wilson Palacios?

4. Who was Olympic men's discus champion from 1904-8?

5. How many nations contested the women's events at the 1993 Taekwondo world championships?

6. Which New Zealander won the 1967 German Grand Prix in F1?

7. Who won gold in the three-metre springboard for Britain in the 1999 European Championships?

8. In which year did a penalty kick in rugby union become worth three points?

9. In cricket, who scored 112 for Gloucestershire against Yorkshire in the 1999 Super Cup Final?

10. Who won the Professional Bowlers' Association's Tournament of Champions in ten-pin bowling in 1988?

11. Which golfer won the Alfred Dunhill Championship in Johannesburg in January 2000?

12. In which year did Leicestershire first take part in the cricket county championship?

13. In cricket, who scored 101 for Leicestershire against New Zealand XI in the 2nd innings of their 1999 game?

14. Zoltan Magyar was 1976 and 1980 Olympic men's pommel horse winner. Which country did he represent?

15. What nationality is skier Kjetil Andre Aamodt?

ANSWERS 1. Somerset 2. Hatton's Grace 3. Colombian 4. Martin Sheridan 5. 54 6. Denny Hulme 7. Tony Ali 8. 1892 9. Mark Alleyne 10. Mark Williams 11. Anthony Wall 12. 1895 13. Vincent Wells 14. Hungary 15. Norwegian.

POP MUSIC

1. Which songwriter's albums include Born Again and 12 Songs?

2. Who wrote Buddy Holly's hit It Doesn't Matter Anymore?

3. On which label was Embrace's Drawn From Memory released?

4. On which label did the Fall record the single Fiery Jack?

5. Which two of her own songs does Joni Mitchell sing on the 2000 standards album Both Sides Now?

6. Which female singer recorded the soundtrack to the 1999 movie Magnolia?

7. In which year did Hole bass player Kristen Pfaff die of an overdose?

8. Who recorded the 2000 album Welcome to the Palindrome?

9. From which West Yorkshire city do the group Orange Can hail?

10. Which Manchester group recorded the 1983 album Script of the Bridge?

11. What was the title of Erasure's debut album, released in 1985?

12. Which female singer recorded the 2000 album Tropical Brainstorm?

13. Which singer-songwriter recorded the 1981 album Black Snake Diamond Role?

14. On which label did Ocean Colour Scene record the album One From the Modern?

15. Which Bob Dylan song was covered by Nick Cave and the Bad Seeds on the album The First Born is Dead?

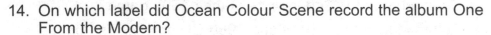

ANSWERS 1. Randy Newman 2. Paul Anka 3. Hut 4. Step Forward 5. Both Sides Now and A Case of You 6. Aimee Mann 7. 1994 8. Osmyyso 9. Leeds 10. The Chameleons 11. Wonderland 12. Kirsty MacColl 13. Robyn Hitchcock 14. Island 15. Wanted Man.

HISTORY

1. In which country's army did Guy Fawkes enlist in 1593?

2. Who was consecrated the first black African Methodist Bishop of Rhodesia in 1968?

3. In which year did the first shipment of British convicts sail to Australia?

4. Who was commander of the R.A.F. during the Battle of Britain?

5. Who was the father of Charles the Bold, the last Duke of Burgundy?

6. In which year did spy Guy Burgess die?

7. Which pope crowned Otto I of Germany Holy Roman Emperor in 962?

8. What governmental post did Geoffrey Howe hold from 1970-72?

9. In which year was the Achille Lauro cruise ship hijacked by the PLF?

10. Where is William Ewart Gladstone buried?

11. Which American naval commander defeated the British at the Battle of Lake Erie in 1813?

12. Who was Solicitor-General from 1964-67?

13. In which year was the Secret Treaty of Dover signed?

14. What was the real name of Papa Doc, dictator of Haiti from 1957-71?

15. What was the name of the 1917 declaration by Great Britain in favour of a Jewish national home in Palestine?

ANSWERS 1. Spain's 2. Abel Muzorewa 3. 1787 4. Sir Hugh Dowding 5. Philip the Good 6. 1963 7. Pope John XII 8. Solicitor-General 9. 1985 10. Westminster Abbey 11. Oliver Hazard Perry 12. Sir Dingle Foot 13. 1670 14. François Duvalier 15. The Balfour Declaration.

GENERAL KNOWLEDGE

1. Who directed the 1977 film Eraserhead?

2. Which singer-actress played Evita in the 1996 film of that name?

3. In which year did country singer Jim Reeves die in a plane crash?

4. Who was producer and director of the 1960 film The Fall of the House of Usher?

5. Which pair of aviators made the first non-stop flight across the Atlantic?

6. Who wrote the 1931 stage production Cavalcade?

7. Who penned the 1881 children's book Heidi?

8. Which actress starred in the films The Railway Children and Walkabout?

9. Which river in Africa forms part of the border between the Democratic Republic of the Congo and Angola?

10. The constellation Volans lies between which two other constellations?

11. What was the name of the songwriting brother of George Gershwin?

12. What was the standard monetary unit of Finland until 2002?

13. Which comedian wrote the novel Stark?

14. What is another name for the mountain K2?

15. What canine mammal is also called a prairie wolf?

ANSWERS 1. David Lynch 2. Madonna 3. 1964 4. Roger Corman 5. John W. Alcock and A.W. Brown 6. Noël Coward 7. Johanna Spyri 8. Jenny Agutter 9. Kasai 10. Carina and Hydrus 11. Ira Gershwin 12. Markka 13. Ben Elton 14. Godwin Austen (or Dapsang) 15. Coyote.

ENTERTAINMENT

1. Who plays Daffy in the film The Beach, based on the novel by Alex Garland?

2. Which comedy actor played Uriah Heep in a 1999 BBC adaptation of David Copperfield?

3. Who directed the 1999 film Wonderland?

4. Who plays Jim in the comedy series The Royle Family?

5. Who played Mrs. Nick Leeson in the film Rogue Trader?

6. Which historical figure is played by Christopher Plummer in the 1977 film The Day That Shook the World?

7. In which Mozart opera is the aria Dalla sua pace?

8. Who directed and starred in the 1988 film A New Life with Ann-Margret?

9. Which comedian died during the making of the 1994 film Wagon's East?

10. Who created the 1970s sitcom ...And Mother Makes Three?

11. Who directed the 1997 film Face/Off?

12. Who wrote the sitcom In Sickness and in Health?

13. Who plays Rachel in the ITV comedy drama Cold Feet?

14. Which television show won Best Drama Series at the 1999 Emmy Awards?

15. Who plays the wife of the President of the U.S. in the 1993 comedy film Dave?

ANSWERS 1. Robert Carlyle 2. Nicholas Lyndhurst 3. Michael Winterbottom 4. Ricky Tomlinson 5. Anna Friel 6. Archduke Ferdinand 7. Don Giovanni 8. Alan Alda 9. John Candy 10. Richard Waring 11. John Woo 12. Johnny Speight 13. Helen Baxendale 14. The Practice 15. Sigourney Weaver.

SPORT

1. Which Frenchman won the 1971 U.S. Grand Prix in F1?

2. In which year did tennis star Jean Borotra die?

3. In which year did Cumbria win their first English County Championship in rugby union?

4. In which sport might one make a dry pass or a knuckle shot?

5. In which year did Terry Marsh become IBF super-lightweight world champion?

6. Which athlete was the 1966 Sports Illustrated Sportsman of the Year?

7. In which year was the Royal Montreal Curling Club formed?

8. In which year did cricketer Nathan Batson make his county debut for Warwickshire?

9. SC Magdeburg were the winners of the European Cup in 1981. In which sport?

10. In which year was runner Donovan Bailey born?

11. Which sport does the UIPM govern?

12. Who broke his right tibia in a collision with Steve Waugh on the second day of Australia's first Test against Sri Lanka, in September 1999?

13. Who beat Newport County 13-0 in football's Division Two in October 1946?

14. In cricket, who scored 108 for Gloucestershire versus Northants in the first innings of their 1999 county championship game?

15. Who set a world record of 8.95m for the long jump on 30th August 1991?

POP MUSIC

1. Who had a 1983 hit single with Big Log?

2. Which band did Randy Rhoads play in before joining Ozzy Osborne?

3. Singer Mimi Farina is the sister of which other singer?

4. What age was Clyde McPhatter when he died?

5. Who had a 1984 Top 10 single with I'm Gonna Tear Your Playhouse Down?

6. Which group backed Graham Parker on the 1996 album Live From New York?

7. In which country did Robert Palmer spend much of his childhood?

8. Masters, Naismith, Cooper – which 1980s band?

9. Stewart, Sager, Underwood, Smith – which post-punk group?

10. Who had a hit single in 1980 with DK 50-80?

11. Which was the only album by The International Submarine Band?

12. What was the title of Salaryman's 1999 album?

13. How old was Gram Parsons when he died?

14. Which Welsh folk singer's albums include 1970's Outlander?

15. Which studio album by Pavement features the single Rattled by the Rush?

ANSWERS 1. Robert Plant 2. Quiet Riot 3. Joan Baez 4. 39 5. Paul Young 6. The Episodes 7. Malta 8. Pale Saints 9. The Pop Group 10. John Otway and Wild Willy Barrett 11. Safe at Home 12. Karoshi 13. 26 14. Meic Stevens 15. Wowee Zowee.

WORDS

1. What is a diastema - a space between the teeth or a two-act verse drama?

2. What in World War II was a kriegie?

3. What was a catchpole in medieval England?

4. On which part of the body might you wear your rammies, according to Australian slang?

5. If something is falcate, what is it shaped like?

6. Which musical instrument is known as a woodpile?

7. What is batiste - a type of boat or a type of fabric?

8. To which bird does the Australian term jacko apply?

9. What is eyeservice?

10. What job would you do in the U.S. if you were known as a stew?

11. If you have cafard, are you happy or sad?

12. What in cricket is known as a peg?

13. If you possessed barognosis, what would you have the ability to judge?

14. To which former denomination of British currency does the slang term Bradbury refer?

15. What part of the body is affected by blepharism?

GENERAL KNOWLEDGE

1. In which year was fashion designer Katharine Hamnett born?

2. Which order of insects includes bees and wasps?

3. Which blackish mineral is the principal source of radium and uranium?

4. In which year was Will Carling, former England rugby union captain, born?

5. In which novel by Charles Dickens does the character Smike appear?

6. Which lawyer chaired the commission that investigated the murder of President Kennedy?

7. The River Douro in S.W. Europe forms part of the border between which two countries?

8. Which England cricketer became the first bowler to take 300 Test wickets?

9. Which fruit in Greek mythology induced forgetfulness in those who ate it?

10. Who wrote the 1867 poem Dover Beach?

11. Who was a Best Supporting Actor Oscar nominee for the film Anne of the Thousand Days?

12. In which year did Sonja Henie, Norwegian figure-skater and Hollywood star, die?

13. Which unpleasant character in the novel Great Expectations marries Estella?

14. Which town in Umbria, Italy, was the birthplace of St. Francis?

15. In which African country is the port of Agadir, which was virtually destroyed by an earthquake in 1960?

ENTERTAINMENT

1. The 1999 film drama RKO 281 was about the making of which film?

2. Who played vet Nick in the sitcom Beast?

3. Who directed the 1993 film Dazed and Confused?

4. Who played Mr. Digby in the sitcom The Grimleys?

5. Who played Joseph K in the 1962 film The Trial?

6. Who was the star of the 1965 comedy show ... And So to Ted?

7. What is Gene Kelly's character's name in the film Singin' in the Rain?

8. Friends actress Lisa Kudrow has a degree in what subject?

9. Who played the poet Pablo Neruda in the film Il Postino?

10. Which comedian is behind Channel Four's Trigger Happy TV?

11. Who hosts the comedy quiz show They Think It's All Over?

12. In which opera do Manrico and Leonora appear?

13. Who scored the 1951 film The Day the Earth Stood Still?

14. What is comedian Roy Chubby Brown's real name?

15. In which year did the comedy show Who Do You Do? first appear on television?a

SPORT

1. Which rider won the 1992 King George V Gold Cup on Midnight Madness at the Royal International Horse Show?

2. What nationality is boxer Lou Savarese?

3. Who was the 1968 Olympic men's 100m backstroke swimming champion?

4. In which month is the Sam Maguire Cup played for in Gaelic Football?

5. What nationality is motor-racing driver Pedro Diniz?

6. Who did Brazil play in the quarter-finals of the 2000 Davis Cup?

7. Which horse won the 1960 Hennessy Gold Cup?

8. Which woman won the 1971 WTA Tour Championships singles tennis title?

9. Who was the 1972 Olympic men's 800m champion?

10. Who was the 1952 Wimbledon men's singles tennis champion?

11. In which year did the Mexican Grand Prix gain world championship status in F1?

12. Which athlete was the 1982 BBC Sports Personality of the Year?

13. How many rugby union international caps did Michel Crauste win for France from 1957-66?

14. In which year was the Central Council of Physical Recreation founded?

15. Who was world heavyweight boxing champion from 1926-30?

ANSWERS 1. Michael Whitaker 2. American 3. Roland Matthes 4. September 5. Brazilian 6. Slovakia 7. Knucklecracker 8. Billie Jean King 9. David Wottle 10. Frank Sedgman 11. 1963 12. Daley Thompson 13. 63 14. 1935 15. Gene Tunney.

POP MUSIC

1. Which member of the Kinks wrote the autobiographical book X-Ray?

2. Who produced the 1976 album Howlin' Wind by Graham Parker and the Rumour?

3. Which group recorded the 1975 album Chocolate City?

4. In which year did the Style Council have a Top 10 single with Shout to the Top?

5. What animal features on the cover of the Gallon Drunk single The Last Gasp (Safety)?

6. Which jazz artist recorded the album Sketches of Spain?

7. Which guitarist wrote the soundtrack to the film Death Wish 2?

8. What was the title of the 1999 album by Rage Against The Machine?

9. The string section of which orchestra played on the single Thank You by the Pale Fountains?

10. Who recorded the 1990 album Cowboys From Hell?

11. In which state of the U.S. was singer Joan Osborne born?

12. Which member of the Foo Fighters left the band in 1999?

13. Who recorded the 1982 live album Talk of the Devil?

14. Which U.S. group recorded the 1992 album Happy Hour?

15. In which year did the group Ozric Tentacles form?

ANSWERS 1. Ray Davies 2. Nick Lowe 3. Parliament 4. 1984 5. A cat 6. Miles Davis 7. Jimmy Page 8. The Battle of Los Angeles 9. Geoff Love Orchestra 10. Pantera 11. Kentucky 12. Franz Stahl 13. Ozzy Osbourne 14. King Missile 15. 1983.

SCIENCE

1. To what did the particle to be known as a mesotron have its name changed following an intervention by Werner Heisenberg?

2. Who won the 1992 Nobel prize in chemistry?

3. In which year did the chemist Otto Wallach die?

4. What was the specialist field of the Nobel prize in physics winner Albert Abraham Michelson?

5. Of what is phytopathology the scientific study?

6. Which Briton invented the mass spectrograph?

7. Who won the 1992 Nobel prize in physics?

8. Lu is the symbol of which chemical element?

9. Which has the higher melting point - calcium or lead?

10. In the term NMR spectroscopy, for what do the initials NMR stand?

11. What is the cube root of the number 8?

12. Which Dutch physicist became associated with the phrase "Knowledge through measurement"?

13. Who won the 1999 Nobel prize in medicine?

14. In which country was the Nobel prize-winning scientist Daniel Bovet born?

15. At what temperature in degrees centigrade does sodium boil?

ANSWERS 1. Meson 2. Rudolph A. Marcus 3. 1931 4. Optics 5. Plant diseases and parasites 6. Francis William Aston 7. Georges Charpak 8. Lutetium 9. Calcium 10. Nuclear magnetic resonance 11. 2 12. Heike Kamerlingh Onnes 13. Günter Blobel 14. Switzerland 15. 890.

GENERAL KNOWLEDGE

1. Which golfer captained the 1957 British P.G.A. Ryder Cup-winning team?

2. Which British comedian starred in the 1937 film Oh, Mr. Porter!?

3. Gap is the capital of which department of S.E. France?

4. Christiania is the former name of which European capital city?

5. Who wrote the 1978 novel The Bad Sister?

6. In which year did British aviator Amy Johnson die?

7. Who was the author of the play She Stoops to Conquer?

8. Which actor directed and starred in the 1983 film Sudden Impact?

9. Who was Roman goddess of the hunt and the moon?

10. Which pop singer was born Reginald Dwight in 1947?

11. Which husband and wife team created the television puppet series Thunderbirds?

12. Who was the Tanzanian president from 1964 to 1985?

13. Who wrote the 1930 novel Rogue Herries?

14. On which sea is the port of Odessa in the Ukraine?

15. Who played the female lead in the 1990 film White Palace?

ANSWERS 1. Dai Rees 2. Will Hay 3. Hautes-Alpes 4. Oslo 5. Emma Tennant 6. 1941 7. Oliver Goldsmith 8. Clint Eastwood 9. Diana 10. Elton John 11. Sylvia and Gerry Anderson 12. Julius Nyerere 13. Hugh Walpole 14. Black Sea 15. Susan Sarandon.

ENTERTAINMENT

1. Who starred as a private detective in the 2000 BBC drama series Dirty Work?

2. What was the name of comedian Leslie Crowther's actor father?

3. Who played Beth Jordache in Brookside on television?

4. What was Jodie Foster's character's name in the film Bugsy Malone?

5. Which Biblical character did Orson Welles play in the 1960 film David and Goliath?

6. Who played Brian Quigley in television's Ballykissangel?

7. Who plays Dr. Jekyll in the 1996 film Mary Reilly?

8. Who plays Mr. Murdstone in the 1935 film David Copperfield?

9. Who directed the 1997 film Career Girls?

10. Who directed the 1994 film I'll Do Anything?

11. Who played Mr. Salt in the 1971 film Willy Wonka and the Chocolate Factory?

12. Which comedy duo starred in the 1951 film Sailor Beware?

13. Who directed the 1994 film Disclosure?

14. What was the occupation of the Cowboys in a 1980s sitcom?

15. Who played Mick Travis in the 1968 film If...?

ANSWERS 1. Neil Pearson 2. Leslie Crowther 3. Anna Friel 4. Tallulah 5. King Saul 6. Tony Doyle 7. John Malkovich 8. Basil Rathbone 9. Mike Leigh 10. James L. Brooks 11. Roy Kinnear 12. Jerry Lewis and Dean Martin 13. Barry Levinson 14. Builders 15. Malcolm McDowell.

SPORT

1. Which chess player won the FIDE world championship in August 1999?

2. Which South African cricket competition was superseded by the Castle Cup in 1990?

3. Who took five for twelve for Leicestershire against Sussex at Leicester in 1996?

4. Jos Lux was the 1907 parallel bars champion at the world championships in gymnastics. Which country did he represent?

5. In which sport might one find a "flying mare"?

6. Which country were the 1997 winners of the women's World Cup in judo?

7. Which golfer won the 2000 Buick International golf tournament at Torrey Pines, California?

8. Which Italian club won the 1969 World Club Championship in football?

9. Which male squash player won the U.S. Open in November 1999?

10. Who was men's high jump champion at the 1994 European Championships?

11. By what score did France beat Wales in the 2000 Six Nations tournament in rugby union?

12. Who rode the horse St. Jovite to victory in the 1992 King George VI & Queen Elizabeth Diamond Stakes?

13. Which medal did England win at the 1999 women's European Cup in hockey?

14. In what weight division was Göran Henrysson world champion at powerlifting from 1983-5?

15. How many gold medals did Ukraine win at the 1999 World Athletics Championships?

POP MUSIC

1. In which year did Shakespears Sister have a Top 10 single with You're History?

2. In which year was blues singer Elmore James born?

3. Who did David Bowie marry in 1970?

4. Which group recorded the 1999 single New York City Boy?

5. On what label was Kevin Rowland's solo album The Wanderer released?

6. Martin Duffy played keyboards for the Charlatans at Knebworth in 1996. With which group did he normally play at the time?

7. Who had a 2000 Top 10 hit with Won't Take it Lying Down?

8. In which city were the group Alice in Chains formed?

9. Who had a 1999 Top 10 single with Don't Stop?

10. Eddie Cochran died whilst being driven to which airport?

11. What is Eithne Ni Bhraonain's more familiar name?

12. Who recorded the 1999 album Nexus ...?

13. Which group recorded the 1979 single Tell That Girl to Shut Up?

14. Which group recorded the 1967 album The 5000 Spirits or the Layers of the Onion?

15. In which year was the album Blank Generation by Richard Hell and the Volvoids first released?

ANSWERS 1. 1989 2. 1918 3. Angie Barnett 4. Pet Shop Boys 5. Fontana 6. Primal Scream 7. Honeyz 8. Seattle 9. ATB 10. Heathrow 11. Enya 12. Another Level 13. Holly and the Italians 14. The Incredible String Band 15. 1977.

PEOPLE

1. With which instrument is the performer Hephzibah Menuhin associated?

2. In which year was the television presenter Kirsty Wark born?

3. Which author was born Lula Carson Smith?

4. Who was chairman of Oxford United F.C. from 1982-7?

5. Who composed the theme music for the television series Twin Peaks?

6. What is Prince Henry's second name of four?

7. Who married Graca Machel in 1998?

8. In which year did the U.S. politician Joseph McCarthy die?

9. As what is Birgitte Eva van Deurs better known?

10. What is former British prime minister John Major's middle name?

11. Which ballet dancer authored the 1960 book Giselle and I?

12. In which country was the former New Zealand prime minister William Massey born?

13. Who starred as Billy Fox in the 1980s television drama series Fox?

14. In which year did the artist Sarah Raphael die?

15. Which queen did Lord Guildford Dudley marry?

? GENERAL KNOWLEDGE ?

1. Which Indian Test cricketer took five for 75 against Pakistan at Nagpur in the 1983-84 season?

2. Dundalk is the county town of which county of the Republic of Ireland?

3. Which Biblical herd ran into the sea and drowned after being driven mad?

4. Which 18th century poet and playwright authored the 1750 tragedy The Roman Father?

5. Of which state of North India is Lucknow the capital?

6. Which chart-topping group's hits included the perennial Merry Xmas Everybody?

7. In which year did Italian fascist dictator Benito Mussolini die?

8. Who did actor Jack Lord play in the cop series Hawaii Five-O?

9. Which French composer's works include the three-act opera Pénélope?

10. Which actor played the hero in a 1959 film version of The 39 Steps?

11. Who is the central character in the novel The History Man by Malcolm Bradbury?

12. In which county is the port and resort of Felixstowe?

13. In which year was Canadian ice hockey player Bobby Orr born?

14. Which journalist and broadcaster presented the TV show Question Time from 1979-89?

15. Which comedy duo starred in the 1932 film Scram?

ANSWERS 1. R. J. Shastri 2. Louth 3. The Gadarene swine 4. William Whitehead 5. Uttar Pradesh 6. Slade 7. 1945 8. Steve McGarrett 9. Gabriel Fauré 10. Kenneth More 11. Howard Kirk 12. Suffolk 13. 1948 14. Sir Robin Day 15. Laurel and Hardy.

ENTERTAINMENT

1. Who directed, wrote and stars in the 2001 film The Curse of the Jade Scorpion?

2. Who is the female lead in the 2001 film Riding in Cars with Boys?

3. Who plays Patrick Trueman in the television soap EastEnders?

4. When did the sitcom Whack-O! starring Jimmy Edwards first appear on television?

5. Who produced the Channel 4 series Whose Line Is It Anyway??

6. At which football ground were segments of the 1960s drama series United filmed?

7. Who played Miranda in Bernardo Bertolucci's 1996 film Stealing Beauty?

8. Who directed the 1972 film Fat City?

9. Who composed the original music for the 1955 film Rififi?

10. Which three broadcasters have hosted the radio show Desert Island Discs?

11. Who wrote the 1990s sitcom The Thin Blue Line?

12. Who presented the BBC television current affairs programme Tonight which ran from 1957-65?

13. What is Liz Smith's character's name in the sitcom The Vicar of Dibley?

14. Which quiz show features the 'walk of shame'?

15. Who directed the 1960 film The Thousand Eyes of Dr. Mabuse?

ANSWERS 1. Woody Allen 2. Drew Barrymore 3. Rudolph Walker 4. 1956 5. Dan Patterson 6. Stoke City's Victoria Ground 7. Rachel Weisz 8. John Huston 9. Georges Auric 10. Roy Plomley, Michael Parkinson and Sue Lawley 11. Ben Elton 12. Cliff Michelmore 13. Letitia Cropley 14. The Weakest Link 15. Fritz Lang.

SPORT

1. How many gold medals did North Korea win at the 1999 World Athletics Championships?

2. In cricket, who scored 206 for Warwickshire versus Oxfordshire in their July 1984 NatWest Bank Trophy game?

3. In which sport were Cai Zhenhua and Cao Yanhua world champions in 1985?

4. Who was the 1997 British women's Open Amateur Champion in golf?

5. By what score did Ireland beat Argentina at rugby union in August 1999?

6. At what sport have Sofiya Kondakova and Inga Artamonova been world champions?

7. Who finished second in the 1999 German Grand Prix in Formula 1?

8. What was the full name of the European football competition known as the Fairs Cup?

9. Which golfer won the $1m N.E.C. Invitational in August 1999?

10. Who was the men's triple jump gold medallist at the I.A.A.F. World Cup from 1977-81?

11. From which Irish county does rugby league player Brian Carney come?

12. How many times did jockey Lester Piggott win the Oaks?

13. Which four teams played in Pool 4 of rugby union's 1999/00 Heineken Cup?

14. Which country were the 1997 men's relay world champions at orienteering?

15. What nationality is swimmer Inge de Bruijn?

POP MUSIC

1. In which year did Sonia have a Top 10 single with You'll Never Stop Me Loving You?

2. Which singer and actress did Gregg Allman marry in 1975?

3. Who had a 2000 Top 10 hit with Sitting Down Here?

4. Which studio album by Leonard Cohen features the song Hallelujah?

5. Who recorded the 1999 album The Writing's on the Wall?

6. Which group had a 1984 hit single with Pearly-Dewdrops Drop?

7. Which group recorded the 1979 single Life in Tokyo?

8. Which female singer had a No. 1 hit with Mi Chico Latino?

9. What was Bernard Butler's second solo album called?

10. Who composed the soundtrack for the film Titanic?

11. Which female singer had Top 10 hits with Fine Time and Stand Up For Your Love Rites?

12. On which label is Belle and Sebastian's album Tigermilk?

13. Which group's B-sides include Astral Conversations with Toulouse-Lautrec?

14. Who had a 1999 Top 10 single with (Much Mambo) Sway?

15. From which country do the group Sigur Ros come?

ART & LITERATURE

1. Who wrote the 1959 play A Raisin in the Sun?

2. Which 19th century artist's works include 1864's La Gloria: A Spanish Wake?

3. Which 18th century painter's works include The Ladies Waldegrave?

4. Who wrote the 2001 children's book The Road to Somewhere?

5. In which year were the playwrights Marlowe and Shakespeare born?

6. Which French modern artist's works include the painting Montaigne Sainte-Victoire?

7. Which Mexican painter's works include the 1940 oil painting The Hands of Dr. Moore?

8. Which comedienne authored the 1999 work Life Isn't All Ha Ha Hee Hee?

9. Which American painter's works include the 1931 oil Americana?

10. Who wrote the 1978 novel Young Adolf?

11. In which novel by Charles Dickens does the character Sampson Brass appear?

12. In which play by Shakespeare does the character Autolycus appear?

13. Which French painter's works include the 1937 oil The Mountain?

14. Who wrote the 2001 novel How to be Good?

15. Which sculptor did Isabel Dutaud Nagle marry in 1917?

ANSWERS 1. Lorraine Hansberry 2. John Phillip 3. Sir Joshua Reynolds 4. Helen Armstrong 5. 1564 6. Paul Cézanne 7. Diego Rivera 8. Meera Syal 9. Charles Sheeler 10. Beryl Bainbridge 11. The Old Curiosity Shop 12. The Winter's Tale 13. Balthus 14. Nick Hornby 15. Gaston Lachaise.

GENERAL KNOWLEDGE

1. Which estuary in France is formed by the confluence of the Rivers Dordogne and Garonne?

2. Who was the Austrian author of the novel The Man Without Qualities?

3. Who was a Best Actress Oscar nominee for the film Leaving Las Vegas?

4. What was the name of the character played by Antonio Fargas in the TV cop show Starsky and Hutch?

5. What is the fourth letter in the Greek alphabet?

6. In which year did German idealist philosopher Immanuel Kant die?

7. Which comic servant is the lover of Columbine in the Commedia dell'Arte?

8. Who authored the play Loot?

9. In which year did playwright and actor Noël Coward die?

10. What is the name of the range of mountains in Antarctica on the coast of Victoria Land, northwest of the Ross Sea?

11. Who was second son of Adam and Eve in the Old Testament?

12. On which river is the Texas city of Laredo?

13. In which year was British fashion designer Mary Quant born?

14. For which 1960 film was Spencer Tracy a Best Actor Oscar nominee?

15. Which city in South Africa is the capital of the former Transkei Bantu homeland?

ENTERTAINMENT

1. Who starred as Jason Starbuck in the 1954 film Yankee Pasha?

2. Which female impressionist accompanied Bobby Davro in the 1987 series Bobby Davro's TV Weekly?

3. Who starred as A Yank in the R.A.F. in the 1941 film?

4. Which actor starred as Peter Loew in the 1989 film Vampire's Kiss?

5. Who directed the 1992 action film Year of the Comet?

6. In which year was the comedy series The Darling Buds of May first shown on TV?

7. Who created the computer games Quake and Doom?

8. Which comedian played Lenny on the London stage in 1999?

9. Who did Bernard Wenton win Stars in Their Eyes as in the 1991 final?

10. In which European capital is the 1953 film Act of Love set?

11. Which American football team has its mascot kidnapped in the 1994 film Ace Ventura, Pet Detective?

12. What was Sgt. Wilson's forename in Dad's Army?

13. Who plays Nicolas Cage's bodyguard in the film Gone in 60 Seconds?

14. Who voiced the Ant Hill Mob in the cartoon Wacky Races?

15. Who directed the 1942 film Across the Pacific?

ANSWERS 1. Jeff Chandler 2. Jessica Martin 3. Tyrone Power 4. Nicolas Cage 5. Peter Yates 6. 1991 7. John Romero 8. Eddie Izzard 9. Nat King Cole 10. Paris 11. Miami Dolphins 12. Arthur 13. Vinnie Jones 14. Mel Blanc 15. John Huston

SPORT

1. Which athlete was 1978 BBC Sports Personality of the Year?

2. Which horse won the 1989 Cheltenham Gold Cup?

3. Who was the first Australian to be bowled out for 99 twice in Test cricket?

4. Who was the 1976 Olympic women's 100m champion?

5. Which country won the 1939 Davis Cup in tennis?

6. Who won the 1952 and 1953 Dutch Grand Prix in Formula 1?

7. In which city in southwest England was cricketer P. D. Bowler born in 1963?

8. How many tries did George West score for Hull K. R. against Brookland Rovers in the rugby league Challenge Cup in 1905?

9. In which county is the National Federation of Anglers based?

10. Which country were the 1979 men's ten-pin bowling doubles world champions?

11. Who did Harlequins play in the fifth round of rugby union's Tetley's Bitter Cup in 2000?

12. Which wicket-keeper made seven dismissals for Derbyshire against Lancashire in their 1975 John Player League game?

13. In which city was footballer Paolo di Canio born?

14. In which year was the Amateur Gymnastics Association formed in Britain?

15. With which sport is Vladimir Samsonov associated?

ANSWERS 1. Steve Ovett 2. Desert Orchid 3. Greg Blewett 4. Annegret Richter 5. Australia 6. Alberto Ascari 7. Plymouth 8. Eleven 9. Derbyshire 10. Australia 11. Darlington Mowden Park 12. Bob Taylor 13. Rome 14. 1888 15. Table tennis.

POP MUSIC

1. Of which group are Brian Dougans and Gary Cobain members?

2. Who recorded the 1978 album Darkness on the Edge of Town?

3. In which city did David Bowie record the 1977 single Heroes?

4. In which year did DJ and producer Norman Cook assume the name Fatboy Slim?

5. Which Beatles studio album includes the song While My Guitar Gently Weeps?

6. Which group recorded the 2000 album Seventeen Stars?

7. Which group recorded the 1991 album Green Mind?

8. Abba had two No. 1 singles in 1977. What were they?

9. Which group had a 1995 No. 1 single with the song Some Might Say?

10. In which year did Donna Summer have a No. 1 hit single with the song I Feel Love?

11. Which band recorded the 2000 album Lit Up From the Inside?

12. Who recorded the 1993 album The Greatest Living Englishman?

13. What was the first U.K. Top 20 single by the singer Aaliyah?

14. Which actor recorded the 2001 album When?

15. In which year did the Human League chart with the single Love Action?

ANSWERS 1. Future Sound of London 2. Bruce Springsteen 3. Berlin 4. 1995 5. The White Album 6. The Montgolfier Brothers 7. Dinosaur Jr. 8. Knowing Me, Knowing You and The Name of the Game 9. Oasis 10. 1977 11. Nadine 12. Martin Newell 13. Back and Forth 14. Vincent Gallo 15. 1981.

GEOGRAPHY

1. Which U.S. state is larger in area - Oklahoma or North Dakota?

2. In which European country are the provinces of Pila and Plock?

3. Which country administers the Aleutian Islands?

4. Alderney, Guernsey, Jersey and Sark are part of which island group?

5. Which island is larger - Newfoundland or Cuba?

6. Into which sea does the Ob River flow?

7. In which U.S. state is Glacier Bay?

8. In which English county is Wimpole Hall?

9. Which English city houses St. Mary De Castro church and The Shires shopping centre?

10. In which county are the Howardian Hills, an area of outstanding natural beauty?

11. To which island group do Yap and Truk belong?

12. In which ocean are the Mascarene Islands?

13. In which U.S. state is the Yosemite National Park?

14. What is the capital of Ille-et-Vilaine department in France?

15. In which South American country is the seaport of Florianopolis?

ANSWERS 1. Oklahoma 2. Poland 3. U.S.A. 4. Channel Islands 5. Cuba 6. Kara Sea 7. Alaska 8. Cambridgeshire 9. Leicester 10. North Yorkshire 11. Caroline Islands 12. Indian 13. California 14. Rennes 15. Brazil.

GENERAL KNOWLEDGE

1. What nationality is the jazz pianist Satoko Fujii?

2. Which car manufacturer makes the Impian model?

3. In which year was the ballet The Nutcracker first performed?

4. How many sesame seeds on average are there on a McDonalds Big Mac bun?

5. In which year was the first Rose of Tralee beauty contest?

6. What foodstuff did Kenneth Daigneau famously give a name to in 1937?

7. In which English county is the Eden Project?

8. In which year did Cranks restaurant first open in London?

9. Which comedian was born Harry Illingsworth in 1917?

10. Which two politicians are the subject of James Naughtie's 2001 book The Rivals?

11. Who wrote the serialised internet novel The Plant?

12. Of which D.H. Lawrence book were 1,011 copies seized by the police in a raid on a London publishers in 1911?

13. Which children's television entertainer started out in the chart act the Vipers Skiffle Group?

14. In which year did Edwin Land market his first instant camera?

15. In which year was the Marmite Food Company founded?

ENTERTAINMENT

1. Which poet does Linus Roache portray in the 2000 film Pandaemonium?

2. Which television show did the song Yellow Pearl introduce in the 1980s?

3. Who directed the 1999 film Any Given Sunday?

4. In which 1970s television science fiction show did the character Gay Ellis appear?

5. Who directed the James Bond film Tomorrow Never Dies?

6. Who wrote the sitcom Waiting For God?

7. Which actor played Bart Tare in the 1950 film Gun Crazy?

8. What was the name of the submarine in the television series Voyage to the Bottom of the Sea?

9. Who directed the film Duets, which starred Gwyneth Paltrow?

10. Which ITV television company served the south-west of England from 1961-81?

11. Who directed the 2000 film Memento?

12. Who played M.P. Ivan Cooper in the 2002 film Bloody Sunday?

13. Which actor starred in the 1982 film The Grey Fox?

14. Who played Adam in the television sitcom The Savages?

15. Who plays Sir William Gull in the 2001 film From Hell?

ANSWERS 1. Samuel Taylor Coleridge 2. Top of the Pops 3. Oliver Stone 4. UFO 5. Roger Spottiswoode 6. Michael Aitkens 7. John Dall 8. Seaview 9. Bruce Paltrow 10. Westward Television 11. Christopher Nolan 12. James Nesbitt 13. Richard Farnsworth 14. Marcus Brigstocke 15. Ian Holm.

SPORT

1. On which horse did show jumper Marion Coakes win the 1965 individual world championship title?

2. In what position does rugby league's Sean Long play?

3. Who was 1924 Olympic men's 400m freestyle swimming champion?

4. Who was the Football Writers' Player of the Year in England in 1993?

5. What nationality is runner Paul Kergat?

6. Who did Cédric Pioline beat in the quarter-finals of the 1999 U.S. Open singles tennis tournament?

7. Which horse won the 1916 Grand National?

8. What nationality is swimmer Therese Alshammar?

9. Which team won the 1964 Olympic women's 4 x 100m relay?

10. Who partnered Kathy Jordan to victory in the 1981 Australian Open women's doubles tennis championship?

11. In which car did Jochen Rindt win the 1970 British Grand Prix in Formula 1?

12. What is the name of Gloucester rugby union team's home ground?

13. Which rugby league club have won the Yorkshire Cup most times?

14. In which year did British tennis player Dorothea Chambers die?

15. With which winter sport would you associate Susi Erdmann and Gerda Weissensteiner?

ANSWERS 1. Stroller 2. Scrum half 3. Johnny Weissmuller 4. Chris Waddle 5. Kenyan 6. Gustavo Kuerten 7. Vermouth 8. Swedish 9. Poland 10. Anne Smith 11. Lotus 12. Kingsholm 13. Leeds 14. 1960 15. Luge tobogganing.

POP MUSIC

1. Which glam rock pop star is the father of acclaimed hip-hop producer Adam F?

2. Which group's debut album was 1983's The Crossing?

3. Which group had a 1998 U.S. No. 1 single with the song I Don't Want to Miss a Thing?

4. Which group's first Top 20 single in 1967 was Gin House Blues?

5. With which boyband did the singer Stephen Gateley achieve fame?

6. Which female singer recorded the 2000 album Angels & Cigarettes?

7. What is the real name of the singer Shakin' Stevens?

8. Which vocal group had a 1999 Top 10 single with the song Bomb Diggy?

9. Which member of the group The Blue Aeroplanes recorded the 2001 solo album Record Player?

10. Who was the original drummer in the rock group New York Dolls?

11. Which female singer had a 1998 Top 10 single with the song Real Good Time?

12. Which actor recorded the 2001 album Private Radio?

13. On which record label was Elvis Costello's single (I Don't Want to Go to) Chelsea a hit in 1978?

14. Which Leeds band recorded the 2000 album Two?

15. Which Tom Petty song does Johnny Cash cover on the 2000 album Solitary Man?

ANSWERS 1. Alvin Stardust 2. Big Country 3. Aerosmith 4. Amen Corner 5. Boyzone 6. Eliza Carthy 7. Michael Barratt 8. Another Level 9. Gerard Langley 10. Billy Murcia 11. Aida 12. Billy Bob Thornton 13. Radar 14. Utah Saints 15. I Won't Back Down.